D0929992

DOES EDUCATION REALLY HELP?

DOES EDUCATION REALLY HELP?

Skill, Work, and Inequality

Edward N. Wolff

A Century Foundation Book

OXFORD
UNIVERSITY PRESS

2006

OXFORD
UNIVERSITY PRESS

Oxford University Press, Inc., publishes works that further
Oxford University's objective of excellence
in research, scholarship, and education.

Oxford New York
Auckland   Cape Town   Dar es Salaam   Hong Kong   Karachi
Kuala Lumpur   Madrid   Melbourne   Mexico City   Nairobi
New Delhi   Shanghai   Taipei   Toronto

With offices in
Argentina   Austria   Brazil   Chile   Czech Republic   France   Greece
Guatemala   Hungary   Italy   Japan   Poland   Portugal   Singapore
South Korea   Switzerland   Thailand   Turkey   Ukraine   Vietnam

Copyright © 2006 by The Century Foundation, Inc.

Published by Oxford University Press, Inc.
198 Madison Avenue, New York, New York 10016

www.oup.com

Oxford is a registered trademark of Oxford University Press

Library of Congress Cataloging-in-Publication Data
Wolff, Edward N.
    Does education really help? : skill, work, and inequality / Edward N.
Wolff.
       p. cm.
    Includes bibliographical references and index.
    ISBN-13 978-0-19-518996-4
    ISBN 0-19-518996-5
    1. Labor supply—Effect of education on—United States.
2. Occupational training—United States.   3. Income distribution—United
States.   I. Title.
    HD5724.W6254 2006
    331.11'423—dc22   2005024161

9 8 7 6 5 4 3 2 1

Printed in the United States of America
on acid-free paper

Foreword

Although the U.S. economy is 150 percent larger today than it was some thirty years ago, the lion's share of income and wealth increases have gone to a relatively small fraction of the population. The Economic Policy Institute finds that, a quarter century ago, the top 1 percent of earners had average incomes 33 times that of the bottom 20 percent; today, the top 1 percent have average incomes 88 times that of the bottom 20 percent. Moreover, since 1973, the median family income has increased only slightly, and the real minimum wage has decreased by nearly a fifth. In fact, today the gap between rich and poor in this country is likely greater than that of any other developed nation and among the widest in U.S. history.

Some commentators, while acknowledging our high and growing levels of economic inequality, have argued that the problem is not cause for concern because people can readily climb the economic ladder from the bottom to the middle and then to the top. However, recent studies have shown that actually achieving the American dream is in reality less common in the United States than in other developed countries, including Germany, Canada, Norway, and Sweden. In the United States, only a small share of the children of the poor end up earning high incomes—most remain in or near poverty. Of those born in the bottom fifth of the income distribution, 42 percent remain in the bottom fifth as adults. Thus, economic mobility in and of itself is no answer to the concerns posed by rising inequality.

Arguing that education is the answer, some people point to the correlation between the number of school years completed and income. Among full-time, year-round workers, those without a high school degree earn on average just $23,400. The average high school graduate earns $30,400, a full 30 percent more. Those with a college degree do even better, earning on average

$52,200 a year, and even those with some college earn on average $36,800. But while the correlation is unquestionable, real questions arise about how best to understand the connections between inequality and skills, wages and skills, and productivity and skills.

The issue is complicated by many factors, including the decrease in the number of workers who are unionized, trade imbalances, the increase in the number of companies and jobs moving overseas, a decline in the real minimum wage, changes in the types of jobs available, and changes in the structure of the labor market itself. All of these strands make it difficult to get at the root of the problem in order to find solutions to it. Thus, for several decades, the Century Foundation has been supporting the work of numerous fellows and authors determined to explore inequality in the United States and its causes. Among our many publications in this area are, in addition to Edward Wolff's *Top Heavy: A Study of Increasing Inequality of Wealth* (first published in 1995 and now in its third edition), *Created Unequal* by James Galbraith; *The New Ruthless Economy* by Simon Head; *Growing Prosperity* by Barry Bluestone and Bennett Harrison; *The Missing Middle* by Theda Skocpol; and *Building a Real "Ownership" Society,* by J. Larry Brown, Robert Kuttner, and Thomas M. Shapiro, as well as forthcoming publications such as Joan Fitzgerald's *Moving Up in the New Economy* and Jonas Pontusson's *Inequality and Prosperity.*

In this volume, Wolff, professor of economics at New York University, specifically addresses the role of education in inequality. He assembles a great deal of information that expands our understanding of this difficult issue, presenting data that raise serious questions about the assumption that improving access to a good education will reduce economic inequality. He explores the way the labor market works and the extent to which the demand for people with relatively limited skills leads to downward pressure on incomes. In developing his analysis, Wolff focuses on four apparent paradoxes: (1) in recent decades, educational attainment in the United States has risen faster than the skill requirements that employers seek; (2) even as skill levels and educational attainment have increased, wages have fallen after taking inflation into account; (3) changes in productivity do not appear to be strongly correlated to changes in skills or education, either for particular industries or for the economy as a whole; and (4) as educational opportunities have improved for a broader swath of the U.S. population, economic inequality has not fallen but rather increased.

Wolff does not believe that improving educational and training opportunities should cease to be a priority for policy makers; a strong system of education and training is vital to the United States because better schooling enables people to climb the economic ladder while helping to promote overall economic growth. However, ameliorating economic inequality, Wolff argues, requires different policy instruments such as direct subsidies and tax breaks directed toward low- and middle-income households. He also believes that efforts to enable more workers to join labor unions would help to offset the economic forces widening the gap between the rich and everyone else.

More important, Wolff's work raises questions about some of our most basic assumptions concerning the impact of additional education and skills. He notes especially that the large increment in educational levels after 1973 is not reflected in an upward movement of average wages (inflation adjusted) over the same period. The paradox of increased skills but stagnant wages ought to have a prominent place on policy makers' agendas. The data Wolff offers suggesting that the increasing supply of educated workers is not matched by an increasing demand for their services constitute perhaps the starkest manifestation of this disconnect.

We are far from having a consensus about what caused the persistent slump in wages among hourly workers and others. As Wolff makes clear, we even need to be cautious about how we discuss the roles that education and skills play in the process. We need a better understanding, not only to make more effective use of the limited financial and political resources devoted to these questions but also to prepare for the day—that may yet come—when we see a resumption of aggressive public sector activities and programs designed to address poverty, inequality, and wage growth. Given the importance of these matters, Wolff's continued work to expand our understanding is welcome indeed. On behalf of the trustees of the Century Foundation, I thank him for his efforts.

Richard C. Leone, President
The Century Foundation

Preface

This book represents the culmination of almost 25 years of research on the role of skills and education in the determination of labor earnings. Work on this topic was motivated by two seeming paradoxes—first, since the early 1970s, while educational levels and skills were rising in the United States, average real earnings remained flat, and, second, over the same period, while schooling and skills became more equally distributed, earnings inequality was increasing. Much of the early work in this project was conducted jointly with David Howell of the New School for Social Research. This includes the construction of conformable employment matrices by occupation and industry for the period from 1950 to 1985, the development of skill measures by occupation, and some of the early analysis of the results, particularly on trends in worker skill levels and the role of technology in explaining skill changes. In later work, I extended the period under investigation to both 1990 and 2000 and added considerably more analysis of the effects of both skill and education on labor earnings, earnings inequality, productivity growth, and trade patterns.

Earlier results of this research were presented at many conferences and seminars, including the Eighth International Conference on Input-output Techniques, Sapporo, Japan, 1986; Conference on the National Information Infrastructure, Croydon, England, 1986; American Economics Association, Chicago, 1987; Jerome Levy Economics Institute Workshop on Technology, Information, and Productivity, 1989; FREF Workshop on Productivity and Performance in the Insurance Industry, Paris, France, 1990; Conference Explaining Economic Growth, in Honour of Angus Maddison, Groningen, the Netherlands, 1992; the Wharton Financial Institutions Center Conference,

Philadelphia, 1993; the International Conference on Human Capital Investments and Economic Performance, Santa Barbara, 1993; OECD Expert Workshop on Technology, Productivity, and Employment: Macroeconomic and Sectoral Evidence, Paris, 1995; OECD Workshop on the Information Society, Porvoo, Finland, 1996; NBER Summer Workshop, Cambridge, Massachusetts, 1996; CSLS Conference on Service Sector Productivity and the Productivity Paradox, Ottawa, 1997; AEA meetings, Chicago, 1998; the Twelfth International Conference on Input-output Techniques, New York, 1998; Workshop on Earnings Inequality, Technology, and Institutions, Jerome Levy Economics Institute of Bard College, Annandale-on-Hudson, New York, 1999; International Conference on the Economics and Socioeconomics of Services, Lille, France, 2000; NBER Productivity Summer Institute, Cambridge, Massachusetts, 2000; the Thirteenth International Conference on Input-output Techniques, Macerata, Italy, 2000; Conference on "Should Differences in Income and Wealth Matter?" Palo Alto, 2000; Conference Honoring Richard R. Nelson, Columbia University, New York, 2000; ASSA meetings, New Orleans, 2001; UNU/WIDER Project Meeting on Production, Employment, and Income Distribution in the Global Digital Economy, Helsinki, 2001; Conference on "What Has Happened to the Quality of Life in America and Other Advanced Industrialized Nations?" Jerome Levy Economics Institute of Bard College, Annandale-on-Hudson, New York, 2001; Conference on Rethinking the Wealth of Nations: Interdisciplinary Essays in the Catholic Social Tradition on Wealth Creation and Destruction, St. John's University, Rome, 2001; Conference on Technology, Growth, and the Labor Market, Federal Reserve Board, Atlanta, 2002; U.S. Basic Income Group (USBIG) Conference, New York, 2002; Eastern Economics Association, Boston, 2002; Workshop on Alternative Measures of TFP Growth, Tilburg University, Tilburg, the Netherlands, 2002; Workshop on Growth, Capital Stock, and New Technologies, University of Valencia, Valencia, Spain, 2002; and Workshop on "The Economics of Services and Intangible Goods Revisited: Models and Empirical Evidence," University of Rome "La Sapienza," Italy, 2005. I would like to thank the conference organizers for inviting me and the participants for their helpful comments.

I would also like to express my appreciation to The Century Foundation for its assistance in every phase of this project and to the following sources of financial support for this research: C. V. Starr Center at New York University, the National Science Foundation, the Fishman-Davidson Center for the Study of the Service Sector, the Sloan Foundation, the Ford Foundation, and the Russell Sage Foundation. The project also benefited from the able research assistance of Wayne Farel, Maury Gittleman, Graham Hunter, and Eric Parrado.

Contents

DOES EDUCATION REALLY HELP?

1

Postwar Trends in Income, Earnings, and Schooling

1.1 Introduction

The last three decades have witnessed some disturbing changes in both the standard of living and inequality in the United Sates. Perhaps the grimmest news is that the real wage (average hourly wages and salaries of production and nonsupervisory workers in the total private sector, adjusted for inflation) has been falling since 1973. Between 1973 and 1993, the real wage declined by 14 percent, though it then rose by 10 percent from 1993 to 2003, for a net change of −5 percent.[1] Changes in living standards have followed a somewhat different course. Median family income, after increasing by 13 percent in real terms between 1973 and 1989, fell back to its 1979 level in 1993, though it later grew by 13 percent between 1993 and 2003 and by 6 percent from 1973 to 2003.[2] Despite falling real wages, living standards were maintained for a while by the growing labor force participation of wives, which increased from 41 percent in 1970 to 57 percent in 1988.[3] However, since 1989, married women have entered the labor force more slowly, and by 2003 their labor force participation rate had increased to only 63 percent, which precipitated a slowdown in the growth of real living standards.

Another troubling change is the turnaround in inequality. Inequality in the distribution of family income, which had remained virtually unchanged from the end of World War II to the late 1960s, then increased sharply. What makes the rise in inequality particularly worrisome is that not only has the *relative* share of income fallen among the bottom half of the income distribution but so has their *absolute* income. The poverty rate, which had fallen by half between a postwar peak in 1959 (the first year the poverty rate was computed) and 1973, has since risen.

A major source of the rising inequality of family income stems from changes in the structure of the labor market. Among male workers alone, wage disparities widened between highly paid workers and low-paid ones. Another indication of the dramatic changes taking place in the labor market is the sharp rise in the returns to education (particularly to college) that occurred during the 1980s and 1990s. That trend appears to be continuing during the first decade of the twenty-first century.

Current policy discussions in the United States and other Organization for Economic Cooperation and Development (OECD) countries have emphasized the need for better education of the labor force and the importance of the school-to-work transition. The underlying theme is that more education, more training, apprenticeship programs, and, in general, more skill creation will lead to a more productive labor force and hence higher wages and faster economic growth. Moreover, a more equal distribution of income will presumably ensue from a more equal distribution of human capital.

There is abundant evidence that individual workers benefit in the job market when they receive additional training and education. However, it is much less clear that, in the aggregate, U.S. economic growth will increase and economic inequality will decline if the government enhances opportunities for U.S. citizens to improve their job skills. This book explores the reasons for this apparent paradox by investigating four other underlying paradoxes:

1. In recent decades, educational attainment in the United States has risen faster than the skill requirements that employers seek.
2. Even as skill levels and educational attainment have increased, wages have fallen after taking inflation into account.
3. Changes in productivity do not appear to be strongly correlated to changes in skills or education, either for particular industries or for the economy as a whole.
4. As educational opportunities have improved for a broader segment of the U.S. population, economic inequality has not decreased but rather has increased.

Other analysts have explored these perplexing questions. However, to further unravel these anomalies, this book focuses on the poorly understood issue of job skills: the skills various employers seek, the skills that the U.S. workforce is endowed with, and the interrelationships between the supply and demand for job skills. The goal of the book is to consider whether government investment in education and training would be more or less effective at alleviating economic inequality and strengthening the U.S. economy than direct subsidies to workers who are falling behind. Improved educational and training opportunities are essential for society for several reasons: (1) Education provides benefits that transcend the job market, particularly in creating a more knowledgeable citizenry for a democratic society (this was the original rationale for public education in the United States); (2) greater schooling and skills lead to more satisfying work opportunities; and (3) employer investment in training lowers worker turnover.

However, the evidence the book explores shows that such initiatives will not substantially alleviate inequality or bolster economic growth or labor earnings. Confronting the inequality challenge may require direct subsidies to those at the bottom and tax relief for those workers in the middle, who have also been falling behind. Labor law reform aimed at promoting unionization may also prove necessary to improve living standards for most workers.

Another major focus of the book is on the effects of the much-hyped information technology (IT) revolution on worker earnings and skills. Christopher Freeman has called this transformation a new "techno-economic paradigm," based on microprocessor-driven information technology. According to Freeman, information technology has "emerged in the last couple of decades as a result of the convergence of a number of inter-related radical advances in the field of microelectronics, fibre optics, software engineering, communications and computer technology." He defines it "both as a new range of products and services, and as a technology which is capable of revolutionizing the processes of production and delivery of all other industries and services" (1987, 51). Paul David, writing in 1991, refers to "the paradigmatic shift" from electromechanical automation to information technologies.

Many have argued that the IT revolution will act as a "savior" for workers in terms of both reigniting wage growth and reducing wage inequality. However, this book casts doubt on this premise. Indeed, the analysis suggests, if anything, that the "New Economy" has been a washout for most workers and has actually served to lower average earnings and to increase inequality.

1.2 Recent Trends in Income, Wealth, Poverty, and Inequality

Before discussing trends in schooling and skills, it is helpful to review what has happened to income, poverty, and inequality in the United States since the end of World War II. However, even before doing this, it is useful to say a few words about the price deflator to use. The standard price deflator is the so-called CPI-U (Consumer Price Index for All Urban Consumers), which the U.S. Bureau of Labor Statistics (BLS) has been computing since 1947. The CPI-U has recently been criticized for overstating the rate of inflation. As a result, the BLS has been providing a new consumer price research series, called the CPI-U-RS. The CPI-U-RS makes quality adjustments for housing units and consumer durables such as automobiles and personal computers and employs a geometric mean formula to account for consumer substitution within CPI item categories. As a result, the CPI-U-RS deflator is not subject to the same criticisms as the CPI-U series. Indeed, the Current Population Survey (CPS) data are now normally deflated to constant dollars using the new CPI-U-RS price index.

While the CPI-U-RS deflator incorporates quality and other adjustments, the modifications are made only from 1978 to the present. The CPI-U index is used for the years prior to 1978. The CPI-U-RS shows a much slower rate of inflation after 1973 than the CPI-U: 288 versus 238 percent. If we use the CPI-U-RS deflator, then "real" median family income grew by 22 percent between 1973 and 2000, in comparison to the 6 percent growth rate on the basis of the CPI-U deflator.

While the use of the CPI-U-RS shows a higher growth in real incomes and wages since 1973, it is not clear that the degree of bias in the CPI has risen in recent years. If similar adjustments were made on the pre-1978 price data, it is possible that the inflation rate over the 1947–1973 period would be adjusted downward by an amount similar to the post-1973 inflation rate. As a result, the sharp break in the wage and income series before and after 1973 would likely remain even if the bias in the CPI is corrected for the whole 1947–2003 period. Since my main interest is to compare income and wage trends before and after 1973, I have elected to use the CPI-U series to convert nominal values to real dollars since the CPI-U series is the only consumer price series that runs from 1947 to the present.[4]

Figure 1.1 shows that median family income (the income of the average family, found in the middle of the distribution when families are ranked from lowest to highest in terms of income) grew by 6 percent in real terms between 1973 and 2003.[5] In contrast, between 1947 and 1973, median family income almost exactly doubled. *Mean* family income likewise doubled between 1947 and 1973 but then increased by 21 percent in the succeeding thirty years. This is less than the increase over the preceding quarter century but greater than the rise in median family income. The disparity between the two series is due to differences in time trends between the mean and median. While

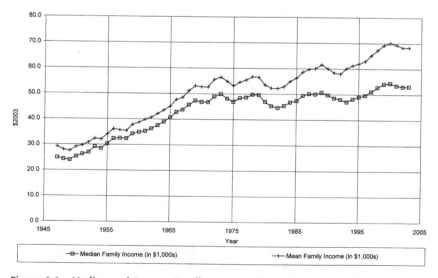

Figure 1.1   Median and Average Family Income, 1947–2003 (2003 dollars, CPI-U adjusted)

mean and median income rose at about the same pace before 1973, mean income grew at a much faster rate than median income after 1973. The discrepancy reflects rising inequality since the early 1970s.

Another troubling change has to do with poverty. Between 1959 and 1973, there was great success in reducing poverty in the United States, with the overall rate declining by more than half, from 22.4 to 11.1 percent (figure 1.2). After that, the poverty rate generally trended upward, climbing to 15.1 percent in 1993, but in 2003 it fell back to 12.5 percent, still above its low point in 1973.[6] Another indicator of the well-being of lower-income families is the share of total income received by the bottom quintile (20 percent) of families. At first, their share fell, from 5.0 percent in 1947 to 4.7 percent in 1961, but then rose rather steadily and reached 5.7 percent in 1974. Since then it has fallen off rather sharply, to 4.1 percent in 2003, its *lowest* level in the postwar period.

A related statistic is the mean income of the poorest 20 percent of families in constant dollars, which shows the *absolute* level of well-being of this group (the share of income shows the *relative* level of well-being). Their average income more than doubled between 1947 and 1974, from $6,800 to $13,800 (both in 2003 dollars), but then rose by only 1.6 percent, to $14,000 in 2003. The difference in post-1974 trends between this series and the share of income of the bottom quintile, which fell sharply, is that mean income was rising in the general population after 1974.

The main reason for this turnaround is that the real hourly wage (average wages and salaries of production and nonsupervisory workers in the total private sector adjusted for inflation) has been falling since 1973. Between 1973 and 2003, the BLS real hourly wages fell by 5 percent (figure 1.3).[7] This contrasts with the preceding years, 1947 to 1973, when real wages grew by

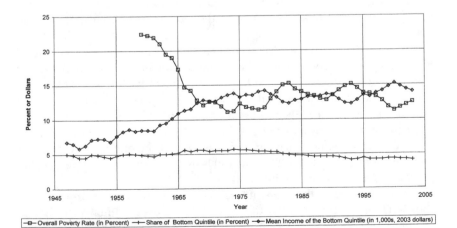

Figure 1.2   The Poverty Rate and the Share and Mean Income of the Bottom Quintile, 1947–2003

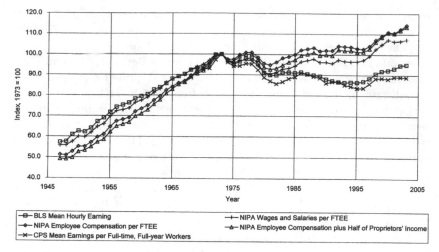

Figure 1.3   Labor Earning Indices, 1947–2003 (Index, 1973 = 100)

75 percent. Indeed, in 2003, the hourly wage was $15.77 per hour, about the same level as in 1971 (in real terms).

Figure 1.3 shows other measures of worker pay. The results are quite consistent among these alternative series. Average wages and salaries per full-time equivalent employee (FTEE) grew by 2.3 percent per year from 1947 to 1973 and then 0.2 percent per year from 1973 through 2003; average employee compensation per FTEE increased by 2.6 percent per year during the first of these two periods and then by 0.4 percent per year in the second; and the sum of employee compensation and half of proprietors' income had an annual gain of 2.7 percent in the first period and 0.4 percent in the second.[8]

CPS mean earnings for year-round, full-time workers grew at an annual rate of 2.7 percent from 1960 to 1973 and by -0.4 percent from 1973 through 2003.

The United States has also seen rising inequality in the last three decades. Figure 1.4 shows three different indices measuring income inequality in the United States. The first series is the Gini coefficient for family income. The Gini coefficient ranges from a value of zero to one, with a low value indicating less inequality and a high value more inequality. Between 1947 and 1968 it generally trended downward, reaching its lowest value in 1968, at 0.348. Since then it has experienced an upward inclination, gradually at first and then more steeply in the 1980s and 1990s, reaching its peak value of 0.432 in 2001 before dropping slightly to 0.430 in 2003.[9]

The second index, the share of total income received by the top five percent of families, has a similar time trend. It declined gradually, from 17.5 percent in 1947 to 14.8 percent in 1974 and then rose after this point, especially in the 1990s, reaching its highest value in 2000, 20.8 percent, before falling somewhat to 19.7 percent in 2003. The third index is the ratio of the

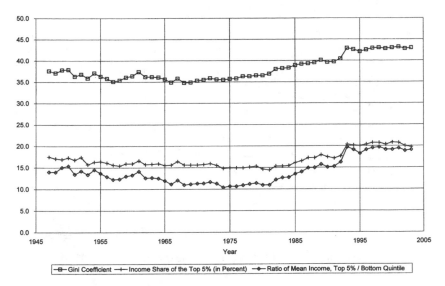

Figure 1.4   Income Inequality Trends, 1947–2003

average income of the richest 5 percent of families to that of the poorest 20 percent. It measures the spread in income between these two groups. This index generally dipped between 1947 and 1974, from 14.0 to 10.4, and then trended steadily upward, reaching 19.7 in 1998, and then declined slightly to 19.1 in 2003.[10]

Figure 1.5 shows another cut on family income inequality, based on "equivalent income." Equivalent income is based on the official U.S. poverty line, which, in turn, adjusts family income for size and composition (the number of people of at least age 65, the number of adults, and the number of children in the family unit). A figure of 3.0, for example, indicates that the income of a family is three times the poverty line that would apply to their family size and composition. The series begins only in 1967 and ends in 2001.[11]

It is first of interest to compare the trend in the equivalent income index of the middle quintile with that of median family income. The former rose by 18.0 percent from 1967 to 1973 and by 15.6 percent from 1973 to 2001. In comparison, median family income increased by 14.3 percent in the first period and by 7.0 percent in the second. The greater increase in equivalent income is consistent with the fact that the average family size fell between 1967 and 2001, particularly after 1973. Moreover, the annual growth of equivalent income slowed for each of the five income quintiles between the two periods. In the case of the middle quintile, the annual growth rate was 1.20 percent from 1967 to 1973 and 0.52 percent from 1973 to 2001.

From the standpoint of inequality, the most telling result is that, between 1973 and 2001, the higher the income level, the greater the equivalent income grew. The differences are marked. Equivalent income increased by 53 percent

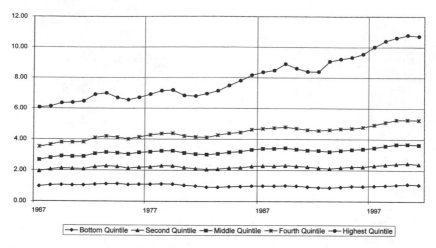

Figure 1.5   Trends in Equivalent Income by Income Quintile, 1967–2001

among families in the highest quintile, 25 percent in the fourth quintile, 16 percent in the middle quintile, 5 percent in the second quintile, and a *negative* 5 percent in the bottom quintile.

To complete the background information, I also show trends in marginal tax rates of the personal income tax since this also affects the well-being of families (figure 1.6).[12] The first series is the top marginal tax rate (i.e., the marginal tax rate paid by the richest tax filers). In 1944, the top marginal tax rate was 94 percent. After World War II, the top rate was reduced to 86.5 percent (in 1946), but during the Korean War it was soon back to 92 percent (in 1953). Even in 1960, it was still at 91 percent. This generally declined over time as Congress implemented various tax laws. It was first lowered to 70 percent in 1966, then raised to 77 percent in 1969 to finance the Vietnam War, then lowered again to 70 percent in 1975, then to 50 percent in 1983 (Reagan's first major tax act), and then to 28 percent in 1986 (through the famous Tax Reform Act of 1986). After that, it trended upward to 31 percent in 1991 (under the first President Bush) and then to 39.6 percent in 1993 (under President Clinton), but by 2003 it was back down at 35.0 percent (under President George W. Bush).

The second series shows the marginal tax rate paid by filers with an income of $135,000 in 1995 dollars. This income level typically includes families in the ninety-fifth percentile (the top five percent). This series generally has the same trajectory as the first, declining in 1966, rising in 1975, falling in 1983 and 1986, increasing in 1991 and again in 1993, and then trending downward from 2000 through 2003.

The last two series show the marginal tax rates at $67,000 and $33,000, respectively, both in 1995 dollars. The time patterns for these differ quite a bit from those for the first two. The marginal tax rate at $67,000 (about

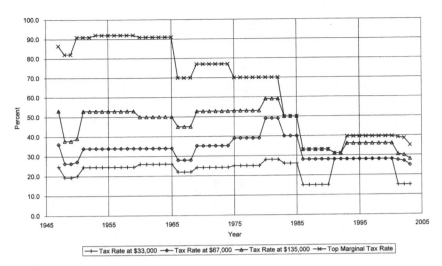

Figure 1.6   Marginal Tax Rates, Selected Income Levels in 2000 Dollars, 1946–2003

the sixtieth percentile) was relatively low in 1946 (36 percent), generally trended upward, reaching 49 percent in 1980 before declining to 28 percent in 1986, where it remained until 2000 before falling to 25.0 percent by 2003. The marginal tax rate at $33,000 (about the thirtieth percentile) was also relatively low in 1946 (25 percent), but it actually increased somewhat over time, reaching 28 percent in 1991, where it also remained through 2000 before dropping to 15 percent from 2001 onward.

All in all, tax cuts over the postwar period have generally been more generous for the rich, particularly the superrich. Since 1946, the top marginal tax rate has fallen by 60 percent, the marginal rate at $135,000 by 47 percent, and the marginal rate at $67,000 by 31 percent, while the rate at $33,000 dropped by 39 percent.

In sum, the last three decades or so have seen both stagnating earnings and income, rising inequality, and no diminution in poverty. In contrast, the early postwar period witnessed rapid gains in both wages and family income, a sharp decline in poverty, and a moderate drop in inequality. Personal tax rates have generally declined over time but by much more for the rich than the middle class or the poor.

1.3 Trends in Schooling and Earnings

One of the great success stories of the postwar era is the tremendous growth in schooling attainment in the U.S. population (figure 1.7).[13] Median years of schooling for adults (25 years old and over) grew from 9.0 years in 1947 to 13.6 in 2003. Most of the gain occurred before 1973. Between 1947 and

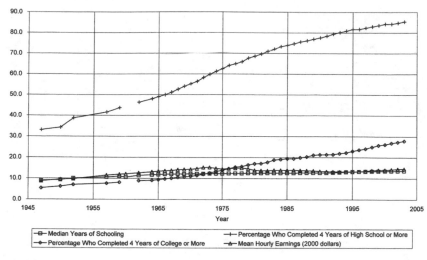

Figure 1.7   Years of Schooling Completed by People 25 Years Old and Over, 1947–2003

1973, median education increased by 3.3 years and from 1973 to 2003 by only another 1.3 years.

Trends are even more dramatic for the percentage of adults who completed high school and college. The former grew from 33 percent of all adults in 1947 to 85 percent in 2003. Progress in high school completion rates was almost as strong after 1973 as before—by 27 percentage points from 1947 to 1973 and by another 25 percentage points after 1973. The percentage of college graduates in the adult population soared from 5.4 percent in 1947 to 27.9 percent in 2003. In this dimension, progress was actually greater after 1973 than before. Between 1947 and 1973, the percentage of adults who had graduated from college rose by 7.2 percentage points, while between 1973 and 2003 it grew by 15.3 percentage points.

Figure 1.7 also shows the trend in real hourly wages between 1947 and 2003. As noted earlier, it rose by 75 percent between 1947 and 1973 and then declined by 5 percent in the ensuing 30 years. However, educational attainment continued to rise after 1973 and, indeed, in terms of college graduation rates even accelerated. This constitutes the second paradox that this book explores—the growing discordance between wages and schooling.

Rising inequality of family income stems in large measure from changes in the structure of the labor market. One indication of the dramatic changes taking place is the sharp rise in the returns to education, particularly resulting in a college degree, that occurred both during and after the 1980s (figure 1.8).[14] Among males, the ratio in annual earnings between a college graduate and a high school graduate increased slightly between 1975 and 1980, from 1.50 to 1.56, and then surged to 1.95 in 2000, though it retreated to 1.88 by

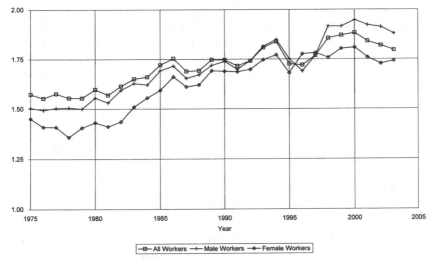

Figure 1.8   Ratio of Mean Annual Earnings between College Graduates and High School Graduates by Gender, 1975–2003 (Includes all workers age 18 and over with earnings)

2003. For females, the ratio actually dipped slightly between 1975 and 1980, from 1.45 to 1.43, before climbing to 1.81 in 2000, though it also came down to 1.74 by 2003.

Among men, the increase in the return to a college degree relative to a high school diploma was due, in part, to the stagnating earnings of high school graduates (figure 1.9). Between 1975 and 2003, their annual earnings

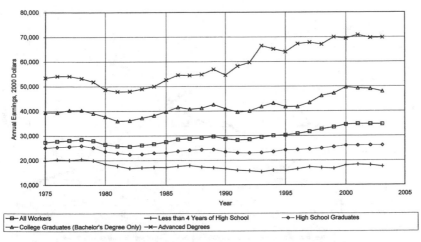

Figure 1.9   Mean Annual Earnings in 2000 Dollars by Educational Attainment Level, 1975–2003

in constant dollars grew only 4 percent, while the earnings of men with a bachelor's degree (but not further schooling) increased by 22 percent. The biggest increase in earnings occurred among males with an advanced degree (master's or higher), who saw their annual incomes grow by 31 percent. Among males who did not graduate from high school, earnings plummeted by *12 percent.*[15]

1.3.1 Schooling Inequality

Another indicator of the country's success in education is the dramatic decline in the inequality of schooling in this country. According to the human capital model, there is a direct and proportional relationship between earnings inequality and the variance of schooling. If the dispersion of schooling declines, so should earnings inequality.[16]

Yet, while income inequality has risen since the late 1960s, the variance of schooling (of adults 25 years of age and older, computed from CPS data) has trended sharply downward since 1950 (figure 1.10). In fact, the variance of schooling fell by 48 percent from 1950 to 2000 (from 12.5 to 6.9).[17] The simple correlation between the two series is, in fact, −0.78. This finding leads to the fourth paradox of the book—namely, the growing discord between the inequality of income and the inequality of human capital.

These descriptive statistics hint at a growing disconnect between earnings and schooling in two dimensions. First, despite the substantial progress in educational achievement in the last three decades, real earnings have generally been stagnant (or declining in the case of average hourly earnings).

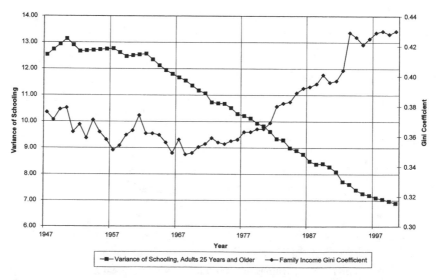

Figure 1.10   Family Income Inequality and the Variance of Schooling, 1947–2003

Second, as the dispersion of schooling has declined, the inequality of earnings has risen. The first of these themes is explored further in chapter 3 of this book, and the second in chapter 6.

1.4 Trends in Productivity and Profitability

Another anomaly is evident when we consider the relationship between productivity and earnings. In particular, the historical connection between labor productivity growth and real wage growth also appears to have broken down after 1973. In an economy characterized by competitive input markets and constant returns to scale, wages and labor productivity should grow at exactly the same rate.[18]

From 1947 to 1973, real wages grew almost in tandem with the overall labor productivity growth (figure 1.11).[19] While the latter averaged 2.4 percent per year, the former ran at 2.6 percent per year. Labor productivity growth plummeted after 1973. Between 1947 and 1973, it averaged 2.0 percent per year, while from 1973 to 2003 it averaged only 1.0 percent per year. The period from 1973 to 1979, in particular, witnessed the slowest growth in labor productivity during the postwar era, 0.5 percent per year, and the growth in real employee compensation per FTEE actually turned negative during this time. Since 1979, the U.S. economy has experienced a modest reversal in labor productivity growth, which averaged 1.2 percent per year from 1979 to 2003, while real wage growth has been 0.6 percent per year.

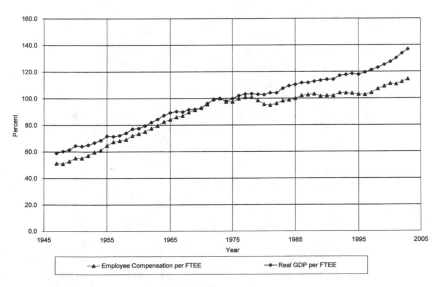

Figure 1.11   Real Labor Earnings and Labor Productivity, 1947–2003

If productivity rose faster than earnings after 1973, where did the excess go? The answer is increased profitability in the United States. The basic data are from the National Income and Product Accounts published by the U.S. Bureau of Economic Analysis (BEA), as well as the bureau's series on net capital stock. For the definition of net profits, I use the BEA's definition of total gross property-type income, including corporate profits, interest, rent, and half of proprietors' income. The definition excludes the capital consumption allowance (CCA). The net rate of profit is defined as the ratio of total net property income to total private net fixed capital. The net profit rate declined by 7.5 percentage points between 1947 and its nadir, 13.1 percent, in 1982 (figure 1.12). It then climbed by 6.0 percentage points from 1982 to 1997 but fell off by 1.1 percentage points between 1997 and 2001. However, after 2001, it surged upward, reaching 20.5 percent in 2003, fairly close to its postwar high of 22.7 percent in 1948.

Figure 1.12 also shows trends in the net profit share in national income. It rose by 2.4 percentage points between 1947 and its peak value of 32.0 percent in 1950 and then fell by 7.2 percentage points between 1950 and its low point of 24.8 percent in 1970. It then generally drifted upward, rising by 4.2 percentage points between 1970 and its next high point of 29.1 percent in 1997. It then declined by 1.7 percentage points between 1997 and 2000 but once again climbed upward to reach 29.4 percent. The results clearly show that the stagnation of earnings in the United States since the early 1970s has translated into rising profits in the economy.[20]

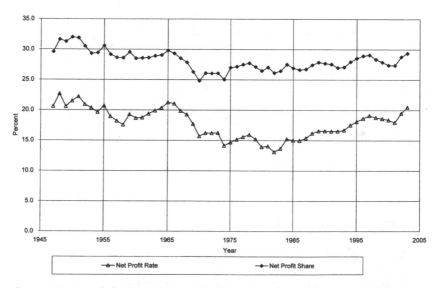

Figure 1.12   Trends in the Net Rate of Profit and the Net Profit Share, 1947–2003

1.5 Some Preliminary Conclusions

The last quarter of the twentieth century and first few years of the twenty-first century saw slow-growing earnings and income for the middle class, as well as a stagnating poverty rate and rising inequality. In contrast, the early postwar period witnessed rapid gains in wages and family income for the middle class, in addition to a sharp decline in poverty and a moderate fall in inequality. The "booming 1990s" did not bring much relief to the middle class, with median family income growing by less than 5 percent between 1989 and 2003. Personal tax rates have generally fallen over time but by much more for the rich than for the middle class. In sum, the middle class has gotten squeezed in terms of income, earnings, and wealth since the early 1970s.

The stagnation of living standards among the middle class in the last 30 years is attributable to the slow growth in labor earnings during this period. While average earnings (employee compensation per FTEE) almost doubled between 1947 and 1973, they advanced by only 14 percent from 1973 to 2003, in spite of substantial progress in educational attainment made since the early 1970s. Moreover, despite incredible success in reducing disparities in schooling within the U.S. population, the inequality of income has not failed to decline but has actually risen sharply in the last three decades. These results suggest a growing disconnect between earnings and schooling.

The main reason for the stagnation of labor earnings derives from a clear shift in national income away from labor and toward capital, particularly since the early 1980s. During this period, both overall and corporate profitability have risen substantially, almost back to postwar highs. The stock market has, in part, been fueled by rising profitability. While the capitalist class has gained from rising profits, workers have not experienced much progress in terms of wages. On the surface at least, there appears to be a trade-off between the advances in income and wealth made by the rich and the stagnation of income and wealth among the working class.

1.6 Plan of the Book

The second chapter confronts the first of the four paradoxes raised here—namely, that educational attainment has exceeded skill requirements in the last few decades. This chapter starts by documenting trends in workplace skills from 1950 to 2000. Results indicate that cognitive and interpersonal skills continued to grow from 1950 to 2000 but that their rate of growth has slowed between the 1960s and the 1990s, while motor skills have declined in absolute terms since the 1960s. In contrast, educational achievement, as measured by the proportion of both high school and college graduates in the workforce, has continued to rise since the 1960s at an accelerating pace.

Chapter 2 also investigates the forces that drive the demand for skills and explains why the growth in that requirement has slowed down since 1970, even though educational attainment has escalated. Moreover, the chapter explores the anomaly that the growth in cognitive and interactive skills has decelerated during a period characterized by a tremendous growth in the use of computers in production and the development of computer-driven information technology.

One possible reason is that demand has shifted toward products that require less in the way of skilled labor to produce. This hypothesis can be analyzed by decomposing the change in overall skill levels into two prox-imate causes: changes in output composition and changes in technology at the industry level. Between 1950 and 2000, a little more than half the growth in cognitive skills among workers was due to skill-augmenting technologi-cal changes at the industry level and the remainder to shifts of employment toward more skill-intensive industries.

A second reason is that technological change has led to the substitution of more-skilled for less-skilled workers at the industry level, but the degree of substitution ("elasticity") has declined in the last few decades. With regard to the role of technological change on skill requirements, economic historians emphasize that, when new technology or products reach the market, they typically are relatively difficult to use, unreliable, in need of frequent atten-tion, and limited in their range of application. Introduction is followed by a relatively long period of improvement that increases reliability, expands uses, and makes them user friendly. The initial period clearly seems to be advantageous to specialized and educated workers, who are needed both to improve and operate the new product. It is therefore relatively disadvan-tageous to unskilled workers. The second stage, user friendliness, appears to reverse the process, making it easier for the unskilled to work with the new items. The simplification of technology facilitates its use by unskilled workers, increasing their demand, while the need for skilled and specialized workers is reduced.

Other factors such as investment in equipment and computers, in partic-ular, expenditures on research and development (R&D), international com-petitiveness, the shift of employment toward services, and the rate of union-ization may also play a role in the demand for skills. Chapter 2 demonstrates that, while the growth in total factor productivity (TFP) generally has little ef-fect on skill change, R&D expenditures have a positive relation to the change in cognitive and "people" skills, while investment in computers has a strong negative relation.

Chapter 3 focuses on the growing bifurcation between wages and skills, as well as a related anomaly, which is the breakdown that has occurred in the historical connection between productivity and wages in the last three decades. With regard to the former, the data indicate that differences in schooling attainment or labor quality do not appear to contribute much to the explanation of differences in wage growth among industries or in the aggregate. With regard to the latter, evidence shows that, at least from 1947 to the early 1970s, real wages have grown almost in tandem with the overall rate of labor productivity growth in the economy. However, since then, while labor productivity has continued to rise (albeit at a slower pace than before), real wages have stagnated or fallen, depending on the measure used.

Chapter 3 begins with a summary of some of the recent literature on wage changes in the U.S. economy. It then presents statistics on trends in the real wage and employee compensation and examines wage trends at the industry level. Wages have clearly changed more in some industries than in others. Variations in overall wage levels result from both changes in wages at the industry level and shifts in employment across industries. The former is normally interpreted as deriving from modifications in technology and the latter from shifting patterns of demand. This chapter also provides a decomposition of changes in overall wages into these two components. The results indicate that, from 1950 to 2000, only a small part of the variation in average wages was attributable to the shift in the composition of employment by industry and almost all to changes in wages at the industry level.

Chapter 3 also investigates the role of technological advances and other factors in explaining changing employee compensation. The appendix of chapter 3 presents econometric results of the effect of changes in average skill levels, schooling, productivity growth, computer intensity, and R&D intensity on the growth of earnings. Other factors are international trade, the shift of employment to services, and variations in the minimum wage and union density. Regressions are performed at both the aggregate and the industry level. I find no evidence that the growth of skills or educational attainment has had any statistically significant relation to earnings growth, which is found to be positively related to overall TFP growth at the aggregate level but negatively related to TFP growth at the industry level. The results also indicate that the growth in earnings is positively associated with the level of unionization and the growth of capital (excluding computing equipment per worker) but negatively related to computerization.

While wages have not risen commensurately with skills, neither has productivity at either the industry level or in the aggregate. Chapter 4 focuses on the third of our four paradoxes. What is the connection between skills and productivity? Standard economic theory predicts that improved skills will lead to increased productivity. Yet, between the 1970s and 1990s, when skill growth fell, productivity growth picked up. Likewise, while educational achievement grew faster in the 1970s, 1980s, and 1990s, overall productivity growth was higher in the 1950s and the 1960s. Moreover, at the industry level, the sectors with the highest skills—namely services—have had the lowest productivity growth.

Chapter 4 concentrates primarily on the relationship of skill and educational growth to productivity growth at the aggregate and industry levels. Other factors that usually affect productivity growth are also included in the analysis, including R&D intensity, capital intensity, degree of computerization, import competition, and export orientation.

In addition, chapter 4 reviews some of the pertinent literature on the role of skill change and computerization in productivity changes. It presents descriptive statistics on postwar productivity trends and tendencies in key variables that shaped the pattern of productivity growth in the postwar period. The appendix to chapter 4 provides regression results. These offer no evidence that the growth of skills or educational attainment has any statistically significant association with industry productivity growth, which is significantly related to R&D intensity, but the degree of computerization is not significant. However, computerization has had a considerable effect on the degree of occupational change.

Fritz Machlup's classic 1962 book, *The Production and Distribution of Knowledge in the United States,* found that, with the growth of clerical occupations at the turn of the century, "the ascendancy of knowledge-producing occupations has been an uninterrupted process . . . a movement from manual to mental, and from less to more highly trained labor" (396–397).

In chapter 5 I document the increase in the number of information workers in the U.S. economy in the postwar period and analyze the sources of their expansion. The growth in the information economy is important for two reasons: First, it may shed additional light on why workplace skills have not kept up with educational attainment and why wages have not increased along with skills and education. Second, it has a direct bearing on the educational and training needs of the labor force. Particular interest is focused on the post-1970 period, which has seen a tremendous growth in the use of computers in production that some have termed a new "technoeconomic paradigm," which is based on computer-driven information technology.

The data in chapter 5 indicate that information workers increased from 37 percent of the workforce in 1950 to 59 percent in 2000. The rate of increase, particularly for knowledge-producing workers, accelerated during the 1970s, coincident with the change in technological regime. Yet, most of the growth in information employment did not take place among highly skilled, highly paid professionals and managers but rather among moderately skilled, relatively low-paid clerical and sales workers.

What are the sources of growth in information employment? One possible explanation is that it is attributable to an increase in the economy's demand for products with a high information content. A second possibility is that technology has favored information jobs over blue-collar ones and caused a substitution of information workers for goods and service workers within the structure of industrial production. Chapter 5 analyzes the respective contributions of these two components to the overall employment growth of information workers. The results show that the growth in the number of information workers was driven not by a shift in tastes toward information-intensive goods and services (as measured by the composition of final demand) but rather by a roughly equal combination of the substitution of information workers for goods and service workers within the structure of industrial production and relative productivity movements (the "unbalanced growth" effect) among industries.

The appendix of chapter 5 explores the role of technological change, capital investment, R&D intensity, the rate of computerization, and international competition in the change in information employment. The data show that R&D expenditures and computers have the strongest effects on the growth of information employment. However, while their effects are positive for knowledge workers (mainly professionals and managers), they are negative for data workers (primarily clerical and sales workers).

Chapter 6 confronts the fourth paradox of the book, namely, that while the dispersion in educational achievement and skills has lessened since the early 1970s, inequality of earnings has jumped dramatically. This chapter reconciles trends in wage inequality with those in skill and schooling disparity.

The chapter begins with a summary of pertinent literature, presents descriptive statistics on trends in the variance of schooling, and looks at the inequality of workplace skills. Results indicate that the decline in overall skill inequality is predominantly due to changes in technology at the industry level rather than to the shift of employment toward those industries with low skill inequality (primarily, services) and away from those with high skill inequality (mainly goods producers).

Chapter 6 also discusses income inequality at the aggregate level and skill inequality at the industry level. The appendix of chapter 6 presents a formal econometric analysis of the factors that might have caused income inequality to rise since the early 1970s. These include the following: (1) skill-biased technological change, favoring highly educated over less-educated workers; (2) declining unionization, which may have widened wage differentials among different types of jobs within an industry; (3) growing international trade, which may have caused the wages of low-skilled workers to fall; and (4) a declining minimum wage in real terms, which may also have put downward pressure on the wages for low-skilled jobs. This analysis is conducted on the aggregate level. Regression analysis is also employed to analyze the factors accounting for changes in skill inequality at the industry level.

There is strong time-series evidence that the acceleration in computer investment has played a significant role in explaining rising income inequality in the United States. The decline in unionization has also been associated with growing inequality. Industry analysis also shows a strong positive association between computer investment and changes in the dispersion of cognitive skills. The decline in the unionization rate has led to an increase in the variance of skills, but rising export intensity has led to a lowering of skill inequality. R&D intensity has also been positively associated with the dispersion of cognitive skills.

Chapter 7 focuses on the skills of workers in both export and import industries to assess the degree to which economic globalization may underlie some of the central paradoxes examined in the book. In particular, it considers the relation between the changing skill base of the U.S. labor force and the country's shifting comparative advantage in the international arena. Standard trade theory predicts that a country will export those products that intensively use resources that are abundant in a country and import products that are intensive in resources that are relatively scarce in that country.

In chapter 7 I investigate the skill composition of exports and imports. Does the United States tend to export products that utilize highly skilled labor and import those that utilize low-skilled labor? How have these trade patterns changed over time? Do they reflect the varying skill composition of the U.S. labor force, which has shifted in favor of cognitive and interactive skills and away from motor skills? How do they relate to the rising number of college graduates at work? Moreover, with the growth of the information economy (assuming that we are also in the forefront of the world in that dimension), is our comparative advantage shifting in that direction as well?

Chapter 7 first reviews the previous literature on the skill composition of trade and then gives descriptive statistics on the composition of U.S. trade from 1947 to 1996. It presents statistics on the skill and educational content (on the basis of input-output data) of U.S. exports and imports for the period and analyzes the factor content of trade.

The results show that the comparative advantage of the United States lies in highly cognitive industries and that the skill gap between exports and imports has widened over time. The data also show that imports are more capital and equipment intensive than exports, but in this case the difference has decreased over time. Moreover, by 1987 exports were more computer intensive than imports. In contrast, while in 1958 the R&D intensity of U.S. exports was much greater than that of imports, by 1996 it was slightly lower.

In the last chapter, I first summarize the empirical results contained in the earlier chapters and then consider some of the policy implications of this research. Current policy discussions in Washington have emphasized better education of the labor force and improved training. Education and training are seen to be the key remedies for four major problems that ail the economy: (1) They will lead to higher skills and thus high-paying jobs and hence to an increase in the real wage; (2) they will generate a more equitable distribution of skills in the labor force and thus reduce wage inequality; (3) they will help promote productivity growth in the economy and thus indirectly boost labor earnings; and (4) they will help increase competitiveness and thus expand exports, reduce imports, and improve our balance of trade. The evidence I discuss in the book seems to cast doubt on each of these presumed remedies.

What else should Washington do? I contend that the most effective way to reverse the decline of the real wage and to reduce income disparities is through incomes policy. Among the remedies that I propose are the following:

1. Restore the minimum wage to its 1968 level. The minimum wage in 2003 was down 34 percent from its peak level in 1968 (when

the unemployment rate was only 3.6 percent). Raising the minimum wage will help increase the earnings of low-wage earners. A more powerful idea is to extend the coverage of "living wage" ordinances, which mandate a minimum wage, usually around $10.00 per hour, for city workers and those employed under city contracts. These programs are now in effect in a few dozen municipalities around the country but could be vastly extended.

2. Extend the earned income tax credit (EITC). The EITC provides supplemental pay to low-wage workers in the form of a tax credit on their federal income tax return. In fiscal year 1999, the EITC provided $31 billion in supplemental aid. An expansion of this credit will further raise the posttax income of low-income families.

3. Make the tax and transfer policy more redistributional. A more potent weapon to meet these objectives would be a redesign of our tax and income support systems so that they transfer more income from the rich to the poor. Tax policies in the last two decades have clearly benefited the rich at the expense of the poor (and capital over labor). Comparisons between the United States and other advanced industrial countries (including Canada), which face similar labor market conditions, indicate that tax and transfer policies can be effective in reducing inequality and increasing posttax income (see, for example, Atkinson, Rainwater, and Smeeding 1995)

4. Reempower labor. The findings presented here and the cross-national evidence compiled elsewhere suggest that one of the principal reasons for the greater level of inequality in this country and its relatively rapid rise in recent years in comparison to other advanced economies is the low level of unionization in the United States (see, for example, Blau and Kahn 1996). This is also a principal factor in explaining declining real wages in this country. Steps should be taken to help promote unionization in the workplace and expand the power of labor generally. This can start with a reform of existing labor laws. Other work has documented the way in which existing labor law is biased against the establishment of new unions and the notorious difficulty of the certification process (see, for example, Gordon 1996).

1.7 Summary of Key Findings

1.7.1 Schooling, Skills, and Earnings

Chapters 1 and 2 document that one of the great success stories of the postwar era is the tremendous growth in schooling attainment in the U.S. population. Median years of schooling among adults (those who are 25 years old and over) grew from 9.0 years in 1947 to 13.6 in 2003, with most of the gain occurring before 1973. Mean years of schooling among employed workers increased from 9.4 in 1948 to 13.7 in 2000, with 40 percent of the change after 1973. The percentage of adults who completed high school grew from

33 percent in 1947 to 85 percent in 2003, with about half of the gain occurring before 1973 and half afterward. The percentage of college graduates in the adult population surged from 5 percent in 1947 to 28 percent in 2003, with almost two-thirds of the progress made after 1973.

Results from chapter 2 also indicate that cognitive skill levels among workers continued to increase after 1970. Moreover, rates of skill growth were about the same after 1970 as before: Cognitive skills grew at an annual rate of 0.42 percent from 1950 to 1970 and by exactly the same amount from 1970 to 2000. Moreover, from chapter 6 we find that there was a pronounced rightward shift of the distribution of cognitive skills in the postwar period, with a big decline of the lowest-skilled jobs and a correspondingly large increase of the most-skilled jobs. In addition, the fraction of adults with fewer than four years of high school fell from 66 percent in 1950 to 15 percent in 2000, and the proportion with four or more years of college increased from 6 to 26 percent.

Human capital theory argues that rising schooling and skills will cause, or at least be associated with, rising wages. However, according to all of the measures of employee compensation, the growth in average wages came to a near standstill by 1973.

These four sets of results constitute the basis of one of the main paradoxes explored in the book—namely, that while educational attainment and worker skill levels have continued to increase since the early 1970s, wages adjusted for inflation have stagnated. Moreover, annual time-series regressions of earnings growth on the change in educational achievement, after controlling for a host of other factors such as unionization and international trade, fail to produce a significant (or even a positive) coefficient on the change in average schooling levels. Cross-industry regressions establish a small but positive effect of changes in the average educational attainment among workers within the industry on the change in average industry earnings, but the coefficient is again not statistically significant. Likewise, both time-series and cross-industry regressions, after controlling for the same set of factors, show no significant effect of skill changes on earnings growth.

While both worker skills and educational achievement rose from 1950 to 2000, the latter far outpaced the former. Cognitive skills grew at an annual rate of 0.4 percent in this period, while median years of schooling of adults age 25 and over increased by 0.8 percent per year, the share of adults with a high school diploma by 1.8 percent per year, and the share of adults with a college degree by 2.9 percent per year.

These results form the basis of another paradox explored here—namely, that educational achievement has risen faster than skill requirements in the last three decades. These findings, moreover, emphasize the lack of correspondence between the growth in the demand for cognitive skills (as suggested by the direct skill measures) and the supply of such skills, as reflected in the educational attainment of the population. Indeed, they suggest that, since the 1960s, the U.S. educational system has been producing far more educated workers than the workplace can effectively absorb.

Chapter 5 also documents the rapid growth of information workers in the U.S. economy. Information workers as a group grew from 37 percent of total employment in 1950 to 59 percent in 2000. Most of that growth did not take place among highly skilled, highly paid professionals and managers (knowledge workers) but rather among moderately skilled, relatively low-paid clerical and sales workers (data workers). Moreover, the time patterns are quite different for knowledge-producing and data workers, with the increase in the share of the former accelerating from 0.5 percentage points in the 1950s to 2.3 percentage points in the 1990s and that of the latter slowing down from 5.0 to 1.7 percentage points.

1.7.2 Productivity and Wages

Another anomaly arises when we compare gains in average earnings with labor productivity growth in the economy. According to conventional economic theory (with a standard constant returns-to-scale production function and under the assumption of competitive input markets), real wages should rise at the same rate as average labor productivity. From 1947 to 1973, U.S. labor productivity grew by 2.4 percent per year, and real employee compensation per full-time equivalent employee by 2.6 percent. After 1973, productivity slowed, but wages slowed even more. From 1973 to 1979, the former averaged 0.5 percent per year, while wages actually declined in real terms. From 1979 to 2003, productivity recovered to 1.2 percent per year, but wages recovered to only 0.6 percent per year.

1.7.3 Productivity and Skills

While wages have not risen commensurately with skills, neither has productivity either at the industry level or in the aggregate. The lack of correspondence between productivity growth and skill change constitutes the third of the four paradoxes explored here.

What is the connection between skills and productivity? Human capital theory predicts that improved skills will lead to increased productivity. Yet, in the 1970s and 1980s, when skill growth fell somewhat, productivity growth picked up. Likewise, while educational attainment grew faster in the 1970s and 1980s, overall productivity growth was higher in the 1950s and 1960s. Moreover, at the industry level, the sectors with the highest skills—namely, services—have shown the lowest productivity growth.

Cross-industry regressions provide no evidence that gains of industry productivity are significantly associated with the increase of workers' skills or educational achievement. There is also no clear relation between high levels of skill within an industry and high rates of productivity growth. Indeed, paradoxically, the evidence points to just the opposite—namely, that high-skill industries (e.g., finance, business services, medical services) have historically had low productivity growth. Productivity growth has been much higher in low-skill industries (e.g., mainly goods industries), where automation can displace labor due to the substitutability of fixed capital for low-skill labor.

1.7.4 Inequality and Skill Differences

Chapter 6 documents three striking trends. First, the dispersion of schooling within the adult population has declined dramatically since the early 1970s. Second, among employed workers, the dispersion of cognitive skills has also diminished since 1970. Third, a pronounced rightward shift also occurred in the distribution of schooling and cognitive skills, with a very large decline in low-skill jobs and a corresponding increase in high-skill positions. Yet, despite these three trends, inequality in family income and labor earnings has risen sharply in the United States since the early 1970s.

Results of time-series regressions of income inequality on the variance of schooling, as well as on other factors such as the unemployment rate and the unionization rate, indicate that the dispersion of schooling is *negatively*— though not significantly—associated with income inequality. In the growth-accounting analysis, the change in the dispersion of schooling is found not to contribute to the rise in inequality after 1970. Indeed, because schooling dispersion declined in value after 1970, its contribution is actually slightly negative.

1.7.5 What about the "New Economy"?

Many have pinned their hopes for a revival of earnings growth (and perhaps a decline in earnings inequality) on the IT revolution. However, I do not perceive any special magic associated with computerization or information technology in general. Computer investment has a decidedly *negative* (and significant) association with the growth of average earnings in both the time-series and the pooled cross-industry time-series regressions. Moreover, in the growth-accounting analysis of both the time-series and the pooled cross-industry regression results, the net effect of computer investment is to *reduce* earnings growth. Moreover, there is no evidence that computer investment provided a large productivity boost, though it did have a pronounced effect on employment restructuring.

Computer investment is also found to be associated with greater earnings inequality, particularly in the 1980s and the 1990s. These results hold up in the time-series regressions. In the growth-accounting analysis, computerization is the principal source of rising earnings inequality since 1970 (at least among the factors considered in the analysis)—accounting for about half of its increase.

Pooled cross-industry regression results also indicate a negative association between computer investment per worker and the growth in both cognitive and interactive skills. The computerization variable is significant at the

1 percent level. Moreover, computerization is found to be positively related to the growth in knowledge workers but negatively related to the growth in data workers. Even though knowledge workers are highly skilled and data workers medium skilled, the negative effect on data workers outweighs the positive effect on knowledge workers, leading to a net reduction in skill levels. Moreover, the results of the pooled cross-industry regressions indicate a strong positive association between computer investment per worker and the variance of skill levels at least as measured by substantive complexity. Taken together with the results of chapter 5, it appears that computerization tends to hollow out the middle of the skill distribution by eliminating medium-skill jobs.

1.7.6 The Role of Other Factors

There is strong evidence that the decline in unionization has played a significant role in the rising wage inequality in the United States. In explaining this inequity, it is the second most important factor after computerization. The time-series regressions also indicate that the reduction in union membership contributed to the stagnation of average pay after 1973. In this case, it is the most important factor of those considered in the study.

The decline in the minimum wage has also played a role in the stagnation of average earnings since the early 1970s. There is also some evidence (though mixed) that the decline in the minimum wage is a factor accounting for the rising earnings inequality in the same period.

Expanding international trade has had a modest effect on both labor earnings and earnings inequality. The growth in exports is found to be negatively and significantly related to the growth of labor earnings in the time-series analysis, but the export variable is not significant in the pooled cross-industry regressions. On the other hand, the growth in import intensity does not appear to have a significant effect on the level of earnings. Moreover, in the growth-accounting exercises, neither imports nor exports apparently play much of a role in accounting for the stagnation of earnings after 1973.

Changes in both import intensity and export intensity do not appear to have an effect on earnings inequality in the time-series analysis. In the growth-accounting analysis, rising imports play only a very small role in accounting for the rise of earnings inequality after 1973, and exports play virtually no role.

The rise in exports appears to account, in part, for the growth of interactive skills and the drop in motor skills but does not play a significant role in explaining gains in cognitive skills. A significant relation is also found between increases in export intensity and the rise in the share of knowledge workers in total employment. Moreover, rising exports appear to lead to a reduction in the variance of cognitive skills. The change in import intensity, on the other hand, does not materialize as a significant factor in these regressions.

1.7.7 Overall Assessment

Unfortunately, the book is mainly negative in its conclusions. First, education, even skill enhancement, does not lead to higher wages. Second, there is no evidence that rising levels of schooling or skill are associated with increased productivity. Third, the pronounced decline in the dispersion of educational attainment and the more moderate declines in the variance of worker skills have not culminated in a reduced level of earnings inequality. Fourth, computerization has not led to a spurt in earnings growth—just the opposite. Moreover, it is a principal culprit in the rise in earnings inequality in the last three decades.

On net, the major factor contributing to the stagnation of labor earnings after 1973, based on the time-series and cross-industry regressions, is the falling unionization rate, which explains almost 30 percent of the slowdown in earnings growth. The second most important factor is the slowdown in overall TFP growth, which accounts for almost 20 percent of the earnings slowdown. The third factor is the slowdown in the growth of noncomputer capital per worker, which explains about 17 percent of the decline in wage growth. The decline in the real value of the minimum wage and the waning of R&D intensity also made modest contributions.

In contrast, the biggest contributor by far to rising inequality is computerization, which accounts for about half of its acceleration between the 1947–1973 and the 1973–2000 periods and even more during the 1980s and the 1990s. The second largest contributor is the sharp fall in the unionization rate, which explains about a third of the rise in inequality. The decline in the hourly minimum wage also makes a modest contribution.

These results support my argument that market forces alone or government intervention in the educational sphere will not revive earnings growth or reduce inequality. Solutions will have to be found in the arena of political economy and a revival of the labor movement.

Notes

1. These figures are based on the Bureau of Labor Statistics (BLS) hourly wage series. The source is the U.S. Council of Economic Advisers (1981, 2005). The BLS converts nominal wage figures to constant dollars on the basis of the consumer price index (CPI-U). See section 1.2 in this chapter for a discussion of the choice of price deflator.
2. The data source is the U.S. Bureau of the Census, "Detailed Historical Income and Poverty Tables from the March Current Population Survey 1947–1998," available on the Internet at http://www.census.gov/hhes/income/histinc/. The CPI-U deflator is used to convert to constant dollars (section 1.2).
3. The source for these data is the U.S. Bureau of the Census (2003).
4. Another price series that has been used by the U.S. Census Bureau in its Current Population Reports is the CPI-U-X1. This series is another

experimental one devised by the BLS and corrects for some technical problems in the CPI-U, especially the treatment of housing prices. Like the CPI-U-RS, it too shows a somewhat lower rate of price inflation after 1973 and thus a somewhat higher growth in real incomes. However, this new price series starts only in 1967.

5. The data source is the U.S. Bureau of the Census, "Detailed Historical Income and Poverty Tables from the March Current Population Survey 1947–1998," available on the Internet at http://www.census.gov/hhes/income/histinc/. Figures are in 2000 dollars unless otherwise indicated. It would actually be preferable to use *household* income rather than *family* income. Unfortunately, the official U.S. Bureau of the Census series on household income begins only in 1967, whereas family income data are available from 1947 onward.

6. The data source for this section is the U.S. Bureau of the Census, "Detailed Historical Income and Poverty Tables from the March Current Population Survey 1947–1998," available on the Internet (footnote 5).

7. The first series is based on the Bureau of Labor Statistics' hourly wage series and refers to the wages and salaries of production and nonsupervisory workers in the total private sector. The next three wage series are the National Income and Product Accounts wages and salaries per FTEE, employee compensation (the sum of wages and salaries and employee benefits) per FTEE, and employee compensation plus half of proprietors' income per person engaged in production (PEP). The fifth series comes from the Current Population Survey (CPS). All series are deflated to constant dollars using the CPI-U price index. Also, see chapter 3 for details.

8. The reason for including only a portion of proprietors' income is that part of the income of self-employed workers is a return on the capital invested in unincorporated businesses. Alternative calculations show that the resulting time series is quite insensitive to the fraction used in the calculation.

9. The data source for the three series in figure 1.4 is the U.S. Bureau of the Census, "Detailed Historical Income and Poverty Tables from the March Current Population Survey 1947–1998," available on the Internet (footnote 5). These figures are based on unadjusted data.

10. It would have been preferable to compare the average income of the top 5 percent with that of the bottom 5 percent, but figures for the latter are not available.

11. The data are from the U.S. Bureau of the Census, "Detailed Historical Income and Poverty Tables from the March Current Population Survey," available on the Internet (footnote 5). The average income-to-poverty ratios are computed by dividing the mean income of families in each quintile (as ranked by family income) by the mean poverty threshold of the families in that quintile. It would have been preferable to compute equivalent income for each family in the sample and then rerank the sample by equivalent income to obtain new "equivalent income" quintiles, but the underlying data are not available.

12. The rates quoted here are for married couples, filing jointly.

13. The data are from the U.S. Bureau of the Census, "Detailed Historical Income and Poverty Tables from the March Current Population Survey,"

available on the Internet (footnote 5). "Adults" refers to people 25 years of age and older in the noninstitutional population (excluding members of the armed forces living in barracks).

14. The figures are for annual earnings, which are not adjusted for hours worked or the experience level of the workers. The source for the data in figure 1.8, as well as for the next three figures, is the U.S. Bureau of the Census, "Detailed Historical Income and Poverty Tables from the March Current Population Survey," available on the Internet (footnote 5).

15. Two other anomalies concern racial and gender differences. The percentage of black males 25 years of age and older with a high school diploma increased from a mere 12.7 percent in 1947 to 74.3 percent in 1996 (the last date of data availability). As a result, the difference in the percentage of white males and black males with a high school diploma narrowed from 20 percentage points in 1947 to 8 percentage points in 1996. The fraction of black males 25 years and older who completed four or more years of college also grew in the postwar period, from 2.4 percent in 1947 to 12.4 percent in 1996. However, the gap in college completion rates between black and white males actually widened over these years, from 4.2 percentage points in 1947 to 14.5 percentage points in 1996. However, despite the apparent success in educational attainment among African Americans, there has been little progress in closing the income gap. Overall, average annual earnings among all black male workers rose from 66 percent of the level of white males in 1975 to 70 percent in 2000 (with much year-to-year variation). All told, the ratio in median family income between African American and white families was only slightly higher in 2000 than in 1975–64 percent compared to 62 percent. Indeed, median family income among black families, after climbing from 51 percent of the corresponding level among white families in 1947 to 61 percent in 1969, has failed to advance much further since then.

   With regard to gender differences, one of the most important changes in the labor market has been the increasing participation rate of women. The percentage of women in the labor force climbed from 33 percent in 1948 to 60 percent in 2000. The participation rates have increased not only for single women but also for married women and, in particular, married women with young children. Despite the large increase in female employment, the gender gap in wages has been narrowing since 1975, with the ratio of annual average earnings between female and male workers advancing from 45 to 58 percent. What makes these relative gains even more notable is that, while real earnings among male workers have been relatively stagnant over these two and a half decades, they have been rising for women. Among females, real annual earnings grew by 52 percent in this period, while among men they advanced by only 13 percent. However, there is no evidence that these large gains in earnings made by women relative to men are due to significant gains in education. Indeed, in 2000, the percentage of women who graduated from high school was exactly the same as the percentage of men, and the percentage of women who attended four or more years of college was actually about 3.8 percentage points lower than the corresponding figure for men.

16. From the standard human capital earnings function,

$$\text{Log } E_i = b_0 + b_1 S_i,$$

where E_i is the earnings of individual i, Log is the natural logarithm, S_i is i's level of schooling, and b_0 and b_1 are coefficients (see, for example, Mincer 1974). This equation states that labor earnings should rise with years of schooling. It then follows that

$$\text{Var(Log } E) = b_1^2 \text{ Var(S)},$$

where Var is the variance. The variance of the logarithm of earnings is a standard inequality index used in the economics literature, and this equation indicates that earnings inequality rises at the same rate as that of the variance (or dispersion) of schooling levels among workers.

17. Because of a change in the educational attainment categories used by the U.S. Bureau of the Census, it is not possible to update the variance of schooling series beyond 2000.

18. In this case,

$$w = \partial X / \partial L = \epsilon_L X / L,$$

where w is the wage rate, X is total output, L is total employment, and ϵ_L is output elasticity of labor, which equals the wage share in this special case (see chapter 3 for details).

19. Results are shown for employee compensation per FTEE. Results are almost identical for employee compensation plus half of proprietors' income per PEP. The data source is the U.S. Bureau of Economic Analysis, National Income and Product Accounts, at http://www.bea.gov/bea/dn/nipaweb/SelectTable.asp.

20. I show the results on profitability just to complete the background information. However, this topic is not pursued in the remainder of the book.

2

Technology and the Demand for Skills

2.1 Introduction

The U.S. economy has undergone major structural changes since 1950. First, there has been a gradual shift of employment from goods-producing to service-providing industries. Second, since the 1970s at least, the availability of new information-based technologies has made possible substantial adjustments in operations and organizational restructuring of firms. Third, this process has been accelerated, in part, by sharply increasing competition from imports and the greater export orientation of U.S. industry. Evidence from industry-level case studies indicates that this restructuring is likely to have important consequences for the level and composition of skills required in the U.S. workplace (Adler 1986; Zuboff 1988).

The direction and extent of changes in skill levels over the longer run have, however, been more indeterminate. Some have argued that "deskilling" has occurred—that is, the composition of jobs has shifted toward lower-skill occupations. Much of this argument is based on analyses of production workers in manufacturing. Others have argued that, although blue-collar work may have been deskilled, the skills of white-collar workers have been upgraded. Case studies often find a deskilling of the content of production jobs, and aggregate studies find little change or at most a gradual upgrading in overall occupation mix (see Spenner 1988 for a survey of the earlier literature on this subject). These trends have considerable policy significance since they help determine education and training needs. One important finding of this chapter is that a growing mismatch has been occurring between the skill requirements of the workplace and the educational achievements of the workforce, with the latter increasing more rapidly than the former. There also appears to be a growing discordance between educational attainment and the educational demands of the workplace and perhaps a growing overeducation of the workforce.

The next section of this chapter documents changes in aggregate skill levels of the workplace from 1950 to 2000. I rely mainly on the *Dictionary of Occupational Titles (DOT)*, which offers direct measures of the skill requirements of detailed jobs (see Rumberger 1981, for example). Cognitive, interactive, and motor skill indices from the fourth edition of the *DOT* are linked to consistent employment matrices for census years 1950, 1960, 1970, 1980, 1990, and 2000 (267 occupations by 64 industries).[1] I also use standard measures of workforce skills based on educational achievement. This section highlights comparisons of the trends of the two types of measures.

The results presented here indicate that the first two dimensions of skill—cognitive and interpersonal—have continued to grow between 1950 and 2000 but that their rate of growth slowed after the 1960s. In addition, motor skills (MS) have declined in absolute terms since the 1960s. In contrast, educational attainment, particularly as measured by the proportion of college graduates in the workforce, has continued to rise since the 1960s at an accelerated pace.

The third part of the chapter investigates skill trends at the industry level. Here it is clear that some industries have been more dynamic than others in both upgrading and downgrading skill requirements. Differences in skill change between goods and service industries receive special attention. Changes in aggregate skill levels result from both changes in skill requirements at the industry level and structural shifts in employment patterns across industries. The former is normally interpreted as deriving from changes in technology, and the latter from shifting patterns of demand. If demand patterns switch toward industries that are intensive in their use of skilled labor (such as medicine and law), then, ceteris paribus, average skill levels will rise. Likewise, if technological change favors more skilled workers, then average skills will also increase. The chapter provides a decomposition of changes into these two components of aggregate skill levels. The results indicate, for example, that a little less than half the growth of cognitive skills is attributable to the shift in the composition of employment toward industries with higher skill levels and somewhat more than half to changes in technology at the industry level (the substitution of highly skilled for low-skilled workers).

What are the factors that lead to the substitution of more-skilled for less-skilled workers? In the appendix of chapter 2 I analyze the role of technological change and other factors in the changing demand for skills. Regression analysis is employed to relate the change in skill indices to various measures of technological activity, including traditional measures of total factor productivity growth, computer intensity, R&D intensity, and capital investment. Other factors are employment shifts between goods producers and services, institutional changes such as union density, and adjustments in the minimum wage. The regressions are performed using industry-level data pooled across five time periods.[2]

2.2 Aggregate Skill Trends, 1950–2000

2.2.1 Measures of Labor Skills

Labor skills appear in a wide variety of dimensions. Jobs are defined by a set of tasks requiring some combination of motor skills (physical strength, manual dexterity, motor coordination), perceptive and interpersonal skills, organizational and managerial skills, autonomy and responsibility, verbal and language skills, diagnostic skills (synthetic reasoning abilities), and analytical skills (mathematical and logical reasoning abilities). Perhaps the best source of detailed economy-wide measures of skill requirements since 1950 is the fourth (1977) edition of the *DOT*. For some twelve thousand job titles, it provides a variety of alternative measures of job-skill requirements based upon data collected between 1966 and 1974.[3] On the basis of this source, three measures of *workplace skills* are developed for each of 267 occupations as follows:

1. Substantive complexity (SC). SC is a composite measure of skills derived from a factor analytic test of *DOT* variables by Roos and Treiman (Miller et al. 1980, appendix F). The results provide strong support for the existence of such a factor: It is highly correlated with general educational development (GED), specific vocational preparation (training time requirements), data (synthesizing, coordinating, analyzing), and three worker aptitudes—intelligence (general learning and reasoning ability), verbal, and numerical.
2. Interactive skills (IS). IS can be measured, at least roughly, by the *DOT* "people" variable, which, on a scale of 0–8, identifies whether a job requires mentoring (0); negotiating (1); instructing (2); supervising (3); diverting (4); persuading (5); speaking and signaling (6); serving (7); or taking instructions (8). For comparability with the other measures, I have rescaled this variable so that its values range from 0 to 10 and reversed the scoring so that mentoring, the highest form of interactive skill, is now scored 10 and taking instructions is scored 0.
3. Motor skills (MS). MS is measured by another factor-based variable from the Miller study (1980, 339). Also scaled from 0 to 10, this measure reflects occupational scores on motor coordination, manual dexterity, and "things"—job requirements that range from setting up machines and precision working to feeding machines and handling materials. These traditional shop-floor skills have been the focus of much of the deskilling debate.
4. Median years of schooling. This measure of workplace skills is derived from the 1970 census of population data (EDUC-1970). It is

computed for each occupation in 1970 on the basis of actual schooling attainment reported by respondents. In a sense, this measure gives us a "constant educational requirements" measure by occupation, in contrast to the actual educational achievement of workers in each occupation on a year-by-year, or "current," basis. This is analogous to constant-dollar-versus-current-dollar output series. If the actual skill requirements of each occupation remain constant, then EDUC-1970 serves as an indicator of the changes in the educational *requirements* of the workplace.

5. Composite skills. I also introduce a measure of composite skill (CP), which is based on a regression of hourly wages in 1970 on SC, MS, and IS scores across the 267 occupations. The resulting formula is

$$CP = 0.454 \ SC + 0.093 \ MS + 0.028 \ IS,$$

where SC is the dominant factor in determining relative wages in 1970, followed by MS and then IS.[4]

Table 2.1 shows the occupations ranked highest and lowest in terms of the various skill dimensions. Not surprisingly, at the top in terms of cognitive skills (CG) are professionals such as lawyers, natural scientists, engineers, and members of the clergy, while at the bottom are unskilled operatives, laborers, and service workers. Judges, lawyers, clergy persons, and doctors also rank at the top in terms of interactive skills, but also included are counselors, social workers, and teachers. The lowest ranked are different types of craftspeople, operatives, and manual laborers.

The ranking is rather different in terms of motor skills. Those ranking highest are surgeons, dentists, chiropractors, hairdressers, decorators, technicians, and machinists. The lowest ranked are clerical workers, lawyers, and members of the clergy. According to the composite skill index, those at the top are doctors, lawyers, natural scientists, engineers, and clergy persons, while those at the bottom are unskilled operatives, laborers, and service workers. The occupational ordering is similar to that based on SC. This is not unexpected since the dominant factor in computing the composite score index is the substantive complexity of the task. Indeed, the correlation coefficient between CP and SC is 0.96.

As might seem evident from table 2.1, the three dimensions of skills represented by SC, MS, and IS are relatively independent. The correlation coefficient between SC and IS, computed for the 267 occupations, is 0.64, that between SC and MS is 0.04, and that between MS and IS is −0.28.

Average industry skill scores are computed as a weighted average of the skill scores of each occupation, with the occupational employment mix of the industry as weights. Computations are performed for 1950, 1960, 1970, 1980, 1990, and 2000 on the basis of occupation by industry employment matrices for each of these years constructed from decennial census data. There are 267 occupations and 64 industries (see the appendix for a listing of occupations

Table 2.1. The Ten Highest- and Lowest-Ranking Occupations by Skill Type

Occup. No.	Occupational Title	1970 Skill Score
A. Substantive Complexity (SC) Score		
17	Lawyers	10.00
16	Judges	9.60
20	Mathematicians	9.50
24	Geologists, physicists, astronomers	9.50
38	Clergypersons	9.30
23	Chemists	9.20
25	Life and physical scientists, nec	9.15
12	Metal, material, mining and petrochemical engineers	9.02
7	Chemical engineers	9.00
31	Physicians, medical and osteopathic	8.90
238	Warehouse workers	1.10
188	Produce graders and packers, nec	1.00
175	Bottling and canning operatives	1.00
256	Child care workers, except private household	1.00
267	Private household workers	0.90
196	Oilers and greasers, except automotive	0.80
85	Newspaper sellers	0.70
178	Clothing ironers and pressers	0.50
231	Garbage collectors	0.30
255	Bootblacks	0.00
B. Interactive Skills (IS) Score		
16	Judges	10.00
38	Clergypersons	10.00
33	Podiatrists and health practitioners, nec	9.94
28	Dentists	9.63
17	Lawyers	9.50
31	Physicians, medical and osteopathic	9.38
57	Vocational and educational counselors	8.75
41	Social workers	8.25
39	Religious workers, nec	8.13
80	School admin., college, elementary, secondary	7.83
45	Elementary and secondary teachers	7.50
44	Adult education teachers	7.38
43	Teachers, college and university	7.26
47	Teachers, except college and university, nec	7.25
117	Blacksmiths	0.00
121	Cabinetmakers	0.00
136	Jewelers and watchmakers	0.00
150	Millwrights	0.00
154	Pattern and model makers, except paper	0.00
161	Roofers and slaters	0.00

Table 2.1. (*continued*)

Occup. No.	Occupational Title	1970 Skill Score
163	Shipfitters	0.00
170	Upholsterers	0.00
175	Bottling and canning operatives	0.00
178	Clothing ironers and pressers	0.00
187	Graders and sorters, manufacturing	0.00
192	Packers and wrappers, except produce	0.00
200	Lathe and milling machine operatives	0.00
203	Riveters and fasteners	0.00
208	Solderers	0.00
236	Teamsters	0.00

C. Motor Skills (MS) Score

31	Physicians, medical and osteopathic	9.90
32	Veterinarians	9.70
27	Chiropractors	9.40
258	Hairdressers and cosmetologists	9.10
33	Podiatrists and health practitioners, nec	8.80
126	Decorators and window dressers	8.70
50	Electrical engineering technicians	8.30
49	Draftspersons	8.30
139	Machinists and apprentices	8.20
132	Painters	8.17
169	Tool and die makers and apprentices	8.00
28	Dentists	7.90
41	Social workers	2.30
96	Insurance adjusters and examiners	2.30
79	Sales managers, except retail trade	2.30
93	Collectors, bills and accounts	2.30
64	Credit persons	2.30
85	Newspaper sellers	2.30
17	Lawyers	2.20
74	Postmasters and mail superintendents	2.20
38	Clergypersons	2.20
104	Real estate appraisers	2.20
16	Judges	0.00

D. Composite Skills (CS) Score

31	Physicians, medical and osteopathic	5.22
24	Geologists, physicists, and astronomers	5.05
2	Architects	5.03
17	Lawyers	5.01
28	Dentists	5.00
23	Chemists	4.95

(*continued*)

Table 2.1.   (*continued*)

Occup. No.	Occupational Title	1970 Skill Score
D. Composite Skills (CS) Score (continued)		
7	Chemical engineers	4.78
12	Metal, material, mining and petrochemical engineers	4.74
32	Veterinarians	4.74
25	Life and physical scientists, nec	4.74
38	Clergypersons	4.71
20	Mathematicians	4.68
22	Biological scientists	4.68
16	Judges	4.64
6	Aero- and aeronautical engineers	4.62
244	Food service workers, except private household	0.92
190	Laundry and dry cleaning operatives, nec	0.91
232	Gardeners and groundskeepers, except farm	0.90
99	Messengers and office workers	0.87
237	Vehicle washers and equipment cleaners	0.84
238	Warehouse workers, nec	0.84
196	Oilers and greasers, except automotive	0.81
267	Private household workers	0.81
256	Child care workers, except private household	0.77
178	Clothing ironers and pressers	0.69
85	Newspaper sellers	0.63
231	Garbage collectors	0.48
255	Bootblacks	0.37

Note: "Nec" indicates not elsewhere classified.

and industries). Since occupation and industry classifications have changed substantially with each census, U.S. Commerce Department compatibility tables for 1950–1960, 1960–1970, and 1970–1980 were used to produce consistent matrices for 1950, 1960, 1970, and 1980. Fortunately, there were only very minor changes in classification between 1980 and 1990. The 2000 occupational classifications reflect a major revamping of the occupational codes. The new system was developed in accordance with the 1997 North American Industrial Classification System (NAICS). Again, the U.S. Bureau of the Census fortunately provided a mapping of the new 2000 occupational (and industrial) classification codes into the 1990 codes.

Computing weighted averages for the IS and MS skill score measures is somewhat problematic since the scoring system is based on discrete rather than continuous values. (SC, on the other hand, is a continuous variable.) I have made no attempt to account for changes in the skill content of specific occupations. Moreover, if the skill requirements of a job change substantially, then the U.S. Bureau of the Census classifies the job as a new occupation. The number of occupations contained in the census data has grown considerably over time—particularly between 1960 and 1980, when the number increased from 277 to 505.

There is evidence that the skill content of some jobs does change over time, though the direction is not unambiguous. Hirschhorn (1986) has noted the increasing importance of diagnostic skills and synthetic reasoning abilities with the use of programmable automation. Similarly, Zuboff (1988, 75–76) has written that operators increasingly require a new kind of thinking that "combines abstraction, explicit inference, and procedural reasoning."

Cappelli (1993), in an interesting study of production jobs in 98 manufacturing establishments between 1978 and 1986 and clerical jobs in 211 firms between 1978 and 1988, investigated changes in the actual skill requirements of particular job titles over time. He found that most production jobs were upgraded in these periods, particularly by requiring more responsibility on the part of the worker. In contrast, changes in clerical jobs were more complex, and there was an almost even split between those that were upskilled and those that were deskilled. Deskilling was found to be associated with the introduction of new office equipment. Head (2003), in a very detailed study of call centers in the United States, documents the deskilling of workers involved in this line of work, from fairly autonomous agents who engage customers in conversation to sell their product to mere "robots" following a scripted scenario on a computer monitor.

Evidence from Horowitz and Hernstadt (1966) and Spenner (1983, 830–831) that looked across all occupations suggests that changes in skill content occur in both directions, and the net effect is small. Autor, Levy, and Murnane (2003) have examined changes in the skill content of individual occupations between 1977 and 1991 using the revised fourth edition of the *Dictionary of Occupational Titles*. They note that only a subset of occupations was reevaluated by *DOT* examiners, and these occupations were chosen partly on the expectation that the job content had changed since the previous examination. As a result, this sample may overstate the actual degree of job change among the full set of occupations. Their analysis of skill change in the United States estimates that 30–40 percent of the growth in cognitive skills between 1960 and 1998 was due to both occupational change within industry and skill upgrading within occupation and the remainder to shifts in industry composition.[5] Moreover, the "within occupation and industry" effect increased in importance over time.

My results for cognitive skills are similar even though I do not consider within-occupation skill upgrading or downgrading. I find that slightly more than half of the overall cognitive skill change between 1950 and 2000 was due to intra-industry changes and that this factor increased in importance over time. Moreover, using GED-MATH as the index for nonroutine cognitive and analytic skills, Autor, Levy, and Murnane (2001) calculated a 10 percent increase in the average value of this skill score (from 3.61 to 3.97) between

1960 and 1998. My figures show an 11 percent increase in GED from 1960 to 2000.[6] I find an even greater increase (21 percent) in the substantive complexity index in this period, where SC is a factor analytic composite of individual indicators of cognitive skill including GED.

However, all in all, one must exercise caution in the interpretation and use of these skill measures. They are, at best, imperfect measures of actual skill requirements by job. Moreover, the fact that I use measures for 1977 to span five decades, 1950–2000, may make the measures even more fragile, particularly in light of the occupational restructuring that has occurred over this long period of time. Still, the main reason for using these skill measures is to apply them as an alternative to the conventional educational attainment measure, which is almost universally employed as a measure of job skill. As imperfect as my skill measures are, they may be better than educational achievement. One positive piece of evidence is that these 1977-based workplace skill measures remain as important as determinants of occupational wages in 2000 as they were in 1970 (appendix table 2.2). Indeed, the goodness of fit in the 2000 regression (the R^2 statistic) is almost identical to that of the 1970 regression.

Educational achievement has typically been employed to measure the skills supplied in the workplace. The usefulness of schooling measures is limited by problems such as variations in the quality of schooling both over time and among areas, the use of credentials as a screening mechanism, and inflationary trends in credential and certification requirements.

Here I include three measures of actual educational attainment: (1) percentage of the adult population (age 25 and over) with a high school diploma; (2) percentage of the adult population with a college (B.A.) degree; and (3) mean schooling of the workforce. (See the data appendix for details on sources and methods.)

2.2.2 Broad Occupational Trends

Some of the changes in occupational composition have been quite dramatic (table 2.2). The proportion of professional and technical workers in total employment increased by a factor of 2.5, from 8.6 percent in 1950 to 21.5 percent in 2003. Managers and administrators also increased substantially, from 8.7 to 12.5 percent. Clerical workers grew from 12.3 percent of total employment in 1950 to 17.7 percent in 1977 but then shrank to 14.2 percent in 2003, a level still higher than in 1950. A much higher proportion of the labor force was also engaged as sales workers by 2003, with most of the increase apparently occurring in the 1980s.[7] The other major increase occurred for service workers (excluding private household workers), whose share more than doubled from 7.8 to 16.0 percent.

The other occupational categories all declined as a share of employment. The proportion of the labor force employed as craftspeople fell from 14.2 to 10.5 percent and as operatives (that is, machine and transportation operators) from 20.4 to 12.2 percent. Nonfarm laborers (that is, unskilled workers)

Table 2.2.   Percentage Distribution of Employment by Occupational Group, 1950–2003

Occupational Group	1950	1960	1970	1977	1988	1995	2003[a]
Professional, technical, and related	8.6	10.8	13.8	14.6	16.1	17.6	21.5
Administrators and managers except farm	8.7	10.2	10.2	10.3	12.4	13.8	12.5
Clerical	12.3	14.5	17.4	17.7	15.9	14.7	14.2
Sales	7.0	6.5	6.1	6.2	12.0	12.1	11.6
Craft and related	14.2	12.9	12.8	13.1	11.9	10.8	10.5
Operatives	20.4	18.6	18.2	15.7	11.3	10.5	12.2
Laborers, nonfarm	6.6	6.0	5.0	5.3	4.2	4.1	—
Private household	2.6	3.3	2.0	1.3	0.8	0.7	—
Service except private household	7.8	9.3	10.5	12.7	12.5	12.9	16.0
Farmers and farm managers	7.4	4.0	2.1	1.5			
					3.0	2.8	1.5
Farm laborers	4.4	3.9	1.8	1.5			
Total	100.0	100.0	100.0	100.0	100.0	100.0	100.0
Total blue-collar	53.0	45.4	39.9	37.1	30.4	28.2	24.1
Total white-collar	47.0	54.6	60.1	62.9	69.6	71.8	75.9

Sources: U.S. Bureau of the Census, *Historical Statistics of the U.S.: Colonial Times to 1970*, bicentennial ed., part 2 (Washington, D.C., 1978); U.S. Bureau of Labor Statistics, *Handbook of Labor Statistics 1978* (1979); U.S. Bureau of Labor Statistics, *Handbook of Labor Statistics 1989* (1990), and U.S. Bureau of the Census, *Statistical Abstract of the United States, 1997, 2004–2005*.

a. In 2003, laborers and private household workers were eliminated as separate categories.

declined from 6.6 percent of employment in 1950 to 4.1 percent in 1995, while domestic servants and other household workers fell from 2.6 to 0.7 percent of total employment in the same period.[8] Farmers, farm managers, and farm laborers collectively plummeted from 11.8 to 1.5 percent.

In sum, the postwar period witnessed a sizable relative reduction in blue-collar work, from 53 to 24 percent of employment, and a corresponding increase in white-collar jobs, particularly professional, technical, and managerial positions, from 47 to 76 percent. Indeed, it is of note that, while blue-collar workers composed the majority of workers in 1950, by 2003 they were a distinct minority. Most employment today is in either white-collar or service jobs.

In terms of skill composition, the trend in employment has generally favored greater cognitive skills, though it is not fully unambiguous. The two highest cognitive-skill occupational groups, professionals and administrators, both showed sizable gains, but so did clerical and sales workers, who generally work in medium-skill occupations, and service workers, who are low-skilled laborers. Large employment losses were sustained by craft workers, who rank among the highest in terms of motor skills, and operatives and farmers, who generally have medium-level motor skills.

Table 2.3 provides greater detail on particular occupations that have grown most rapidly and those that have suffered the greatest declines from 1950 to 1995. In the first group are health administrators, real estate appraisers, computer programmers and analysts, welfare workers, office mangers, teacher aides, child care workers, bank officials, social scientists, and stock and bond brokers. With the exception of child care workers, real estate appraisers, teacher aides, and technicians nec, these occupations are characterized by high cognitive skill levels. Occupations that have lost substantial employment include operatives, typesetters, bootblacks, boarding house keepers, telegraph operators, longshoremen, blacksmiths, judges, and elevator operators. With the exception of judges, these occupations generally have medium or low cognitive skills.

What will the future hold? The U.S. Bureau of Labor Statistics (BLS) periodically produces employment projections for the future decade in order to provide guidance to students. Table 2.4 shows the top 30 occupations in the bureau's 2006 projections. What is at once apparent is that these jobs are all over the board in terms of skill levels. In terms of the bureau's own assessment of educational and training requirements, none of these 30 occupations requires a Ph.D., and only one, speech-language pathologist, requires a master's degree. Ten more require a bachelor's degree, and another four an associate's degree. The other half require only a high school diploma plus some on-the-job training or vocational school. In terms of substantive complexity, only one of the 30 fastest-growing occupations has an SC score above 8.0, only five an SC score of 7.0 or better, 12 with an SC score of 6.0 or higher, and 19 with an SC score of 5.0 or better.

2.2.3 Trends in Average Skill Levels

On the basis of these data, we can now systematically examine several pertinent issues. Are the new jobs that are created more or less skilled (in net terms) than the ones that have disappeared? Are there important differences between decades in the degree of upgrading or downgrading of skills? In particular, have the 1980s and 1990s witnessed a greater net replacement of higher-skilled jobs with lower-skilled jobs than the decades of the 1950s, 1960s, and 1970s?

Figure 2.1 shows that, with the exception of motor skills, changing employment patterns have had the effect of raising the skill requirements of jobs between 1950 and 2000. Of the five indicators of workplace skills, the average SC level in the economy as a whole had the highest growth: 23 percent over the five decades. The composite skill index, CP, rose by 18 percent, while EDUC-1970 grew by 10 percent and IS increased by 11 percent. MS, on the other hand, showed a 5 percent decline over the half century.

Table 2.3. Occupations with the Biggest Growth and Greatest Declines in Employment, 1950–1995, and Their Substantive Complexity (SC) Score in 1970

Occup. No.	Occupational Title	Annual Employment Growth, 1950–1995 (%)	1970 SC Score
66	Health administrators	13.1	7.00
104	Real estate appraisers	12.4	4.10
4	Computer systems analysts	12.0	7.60
5	Computer specialists, nec	11.6	7.50
261	Welfare service aides	11.5	5.20
70	Office managers, nec	9.6	6.30
111	Teacher aides, except school monitors	9.3	4.50
256	Child care workers, except private household	8.9	1.00
3	Computer programmers	8.8	7.40
62	Bank officers and financial managers	7.9	7.47
50	Electrical engineering technicians	7.5	6.20
57	Vocational and educational counselors	7.5	7.50
36	Therapists	7.3	6.30
56	Technicians, nec, including radio operators	7.1	4.80
40	Social scientists	7.1	7.59
87	Stock and bond salespeople	6.9	7.00
213	Weavers	−3.0	2.50
124	Compositors, typesetters and apprentices	−3.1	4.50
255	Bootblacks	−3.2	0.00
254	Boarding and lodging house keepers	−3.2	5.20
211	Knitters, loopers, and toppers	−3.4	1.20
199	Drill press operatives	−3.4	1.90
214	Textile operatives, nec	−3.5	1.70
151	Molders, metal and apprentices	−3.5	3.30
160	Rollers and finishers, metal	−3.6	1.90
194	Mine operatives, nec	−3.7	2.37
112	Telegraph operators	−3.8	3.60
210	Carding, lapping, and combing operatives	−3.8	1.50
233	Longshoremen and stevedores	−4.1	1.40
117	Blacksmiths	−4.8	3.70
181	Drillers, earth	−5.0	2.70
16	Judges	−5.1	9.60
257	Elevator operators	−5.4	1.70
154	Pattern and model makers, except paper	−5.8	4.70
179	Cutting operatives, nec	−10.2	1.90
	All Occupations	1.6	4.07

Note: "Nec" indicates not elsewhere classified.

43

Table 2.4. Bureau of Labor Statistics' Employment Projections of the Fastest-Growing Occupations, 1996–2006

Occupation	Projected Percentage Change in Employment	Educational and Training Requirements	Substantive Complexity (SC) Score
1. Database administrators, computer support specialists, and other computer scientists	118	Bachelor's degree	7.5
2. Computer engineers	109	Bachelor's degree	8.2
3. Systems analysts	103	Bachelor's degree	7.6
4. Personal and home care aides	85	Short-term on-the-job training	1.7
5. Physical and corrective therapy assistants and aides	69	Moderate-term on-the-job training	4.3
6. Home health aides	76	Short-term on-the-job training	4.3
7. Medical assistants	74	Moderate-term on-the-job training	4.3
8. Desktop publishing specialists	74	Long-term on-the-job training	6.0
9. Physical therapists	81	Bachelor's degree	6.3
10. Occupational therapy assistants and aides	69	Moderate-term on-the-job training	4.3
11. Paralegals	68	Associate's degree	4.8
12. Occupational therapists	66	Bachelor's degree	6.3
13. Teachers, special education	59	Bachelor's degree	6.3
14. Human services workers	55	Moderate-term on-the-job training	4.5
15. Data-processing equipment repairers	52	Postsecondary vocational training	5.6
16. Medical records technicians	51	Associate's degree	5.5
17. Speech-language pathologists and audiologists	51	Master's degree	6.3
18. Dental hygienists	48	Associate's degree	5.5
19. Amusement and recreation attendants	48	Short-term on-the-job training	2.7
20. Physician assistants	47	Bachelor's degree	5.5
21. Respiratory therapists	46	Associate's degree	6.3
22. Adjustment clerks	46	Short-term on-the-job training	3.6

Table 2.4. *(continued)*

Occupation	Projected Percentage Change in Employment	Educational and Training Requirements	Substantive Complexity (SC) Score
23. Engineering, science, and computer systems managers	45	Work experience plus bachelor's degree or higher	7.0
24. Emergency medical technicians	45	Postsecondary vocational training	5.5
25. Manicurists	45	Postsecondary vocational training	5.2
26. Bill and account collectors	42	Short-term on-the-job training	4.1
27. Residential counselors	41	Bachelor's degree	5.5
28. Instructors and coaches, sports and physical training	41	Moderate-term on-the-job training	6.8
29. Dental assistants	38	Moderate-term on-the-job training	4.3
30. Securities and financial services sales workers	38	Bachelor's degree	7.0

Source: "Occupational Employment Projections to 2006," *Monthly Labor Review*, November 1997, pp. 58–83.

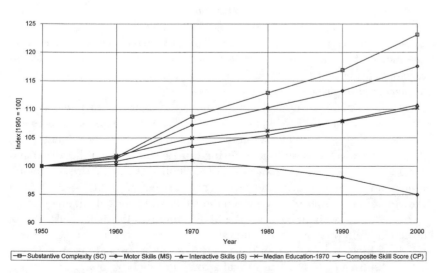

Figure 2.1   Mean Skill Score by Type and Year, 1950–2003 (Index, 1950 = 100)

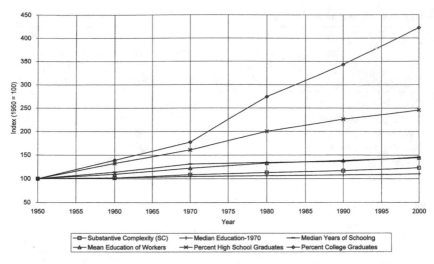

Figure 2.2   Actual Educational Attainment and Workplace Skills, 1950–2000 (Index, 1950 = 100)

Growth in workplace skills was dwarfed by increases in the educational attainment of the workforce and adult population (figure 2.2). The fraction of the adult population (25 years of age and over) with at least a high school diploma more than doubled between 1950 and 2000, from 34 to 84 percent, while the proportion of adults who completed at least four years of college more than quadrupled, from 6.2 to 26.2 percent. Median education among the adult population grew more slowly, by 46 percent, from 9.3 to 13.6 years, and the mean schooling level of employed workers grew by 44 percent. These figures compare to a 23 percent rise in the average SC score and a 10 percent increase in EDUC-1970 (for which it is assumed that educational requirements by occupations remain fixed over time). Thus, in the postwar period, the educational attainment of both the population and the workforce increased considerably faster than the educational requirements of the workplace, at least as measured by these skill scores.

Another striking result is the pronounced slowdown in the rate of growth for all five measures of workplace skills between the 1960s and the 1990s, after a rapid acceleration between the 1950s and 1960s (table 2.5 and figure 2.3). Skill growth was quite low during the 1950s. Between the 1950s and 1960s, it increased more than fourfold for both SC and CP, tripled for IS, more than doubled for MS, and rose by more than half for EDUC-1970. Skill growth peaked in the 1960s. Between the 1960s and 1980s, it fell off by about a third for SC, by about half for CP, and by about two-thirds for EDUC-1970, although it did pick up for the three skill measures in the 1990s. The growth in MS, which was positive in the 1950s and 1960s, turned negative in the 1970s, 1980s, and 1990s. The annual growth in IS fell from 0.27 percent in

Table 2.5. Annual Percentage Rate of Change of Workplace and Workforce Skills, Total Economy, 1950–2000

Skill Dimension	1950– 1960	1960– 1970	1970– 1980	1980– 1990	1990– 2000	1950– 2000
A. Workplace Skills						
Substantive Complexity (SC)	0.16	0.68	0.38	0.35	0.52	0.42
Interactive Skills (IS)	0.09	0.27	0.18	0.24	0.25	0.20
Motor Skills (MS)	0.03	0.07	−0.13	−0.17	−0.32	−0.10
Composite Skills (CP)	0.14	0.56	0.28	0.26	0.37	0.32
Median year of schooling, 1970 (EDUC-1970)	0.19	0.30	0.12	0.16	0.22	0.20
B. Educational Attainment						
Median years of schooling, adult population[a]	1.31	1.41	0.24	0.16	0.66	0.76
Mean years of schooling, employed workers	0.91	1.10	0.83	0.39	0.43	0.73
Percent of adults with 4 years of high school or more[a]	2.81	1.95	2.17	1.23	0.82	1.80
Percent of adults with 4 years of college or more[a]	3.30	2.43	4.35	2.25	2.06	2.88

Source: U.S. Bureau of the Census, *Current Population Reports*, available on the Internet.

a. "Adults" refers to persons 25 of age and over.

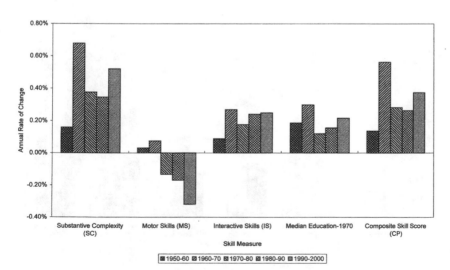

Figure 2.3   Growth in Workplace Skills by Period, 1950–2000

the 1960s to 0.18 percent in the 1970s but then rebounded to 0.25 percent in the 1990s, although it was still somewhat below its pace in the 1960s.

Patterns of skill growth generally correlate with changes in the broad occupational composition of the labor force. The growth in SC, IS, and EDUC-1970 in the five decades reflects the increasing proportion of professionals and managers in the workforce, while the decreasing share of craft workers and operatives in employment appears responsible for the postwar decline in motor skills. The decade-by-decade correspondence is a bit rougher. The peak growth in cognitive skills during the 1960s seems to be due to the particularly rapid increase in the proportion of professionals in the labor force in that period (3 percentage points). The decline in motor skills after 1970 seems to be attributable to the very sharp reduction in the fraction of operatives in the workforce dating from that year. The rebound in IS growth in the 1980s correlates with the large jump in the share of managers and administrators employed in the economy (about 2 percentage points).[9]

Figure 2.4 contrasts the growth in workplace skills with trends in the educational attainment of the population and the workforce on a decade-by-decade basis. As noted earlier, the annual growth rate of SC increased sharply between the 1950s and 1960s, fell off in the 1970s and 1980s, and then picked up in the 1990s. The growth in median years of schooling among the adult population increased slightly between the 1950s and the 1960s, had a sharp decline in the 1970s and 1980s, and then a considerable surge in the 1990s. In the 1950s and 1960s, median education grew more than twice as fast as SC, while in the 1970s and 1980s it grew more slowly. During the 1990s, it grew somewhat faster than SC. Over the full 50-year stretch, median schooling rose almost twice as rapidly as cognitive skills.

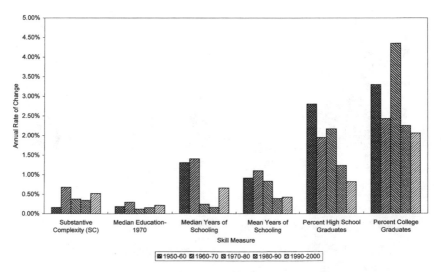

Figure 2.4   Growth in Workplace and Workforce Skills by Period, 1950–2000

Likewise, the growth in the mean education of the workforce increased slightly between the 1950s and the 1960s, declined in the 1970s and again in the 1980s, and then rose somewhat in the 1990s. With the exception of the 1980s and the 1990s, its growth rate was about twice as great as that of SC, and over the whole 1950–2000 period, it averaged a bit less than two times the growth rate of SC.

The time patterns are different for the share of adults with both a high school and a college education. In both cases, the growth rate fell off between the 1950s and the 1960s, picked up in the 1970s, and fell sharply in the 1980s and again in the 1990s. Over the 50-year period, the percentage of adults with a high school education grew at the rate of 1.8 percent per year, and the percentage with a college degree at 2.9 percent per year, while SC increased at 0.4 percent per year and EDUC-1970 at 0.2 percent per year. These results again emphasize the lack of correspondence between the growth in the demand for cognitive skills as reflected in the direct skill measures and the supply of such skills as reflected in the educational achievement of the population.

2.3 Skill Changes at the Industry Level

The differences in skill requirements among different industries in the U.S. economy are striking. Table 2.6 shows nine major industrial groupings in 1970. Mean substantive complexity scores range from a low of 11 percent below average in agriculture to a high of 25 percent above average in finance, insurance, and real estate (FIRE). SC levels were about a fifth higher in services than in goods-producing industries. Median education levels (EDUC-1970) were about 10 percent higher in the service industries than in the goods sectors. The highest median years of schooling are found in the other services sector, which includes a wide range of business and personal services, at 13.2 years, followed by FIRE (13.0 years) and the government sector (12.8 years). The lowest is recorded in agriculture (10.3 years).

Interactive skills were almost twice as great in services as in goods-producing industries. The top three sectors in terms of interactive skills are the same as for median education: the other services sector (49 percent greater than the overall mean), FIRE (28 percent above average), and the government sector (10 percent above average). Manufacturing had the lowest IS level. In contrast, motor skill levels were 14 percent higher in goods industries than in service industries. Not surprisingly, construction had the highest level of motor skills (16 percent above average), followed by manufacturing (8 percent above average), mining (5 percent above average), and transportation, communications and public utilities (5 percent above average). Wholesale and retail trade had the lowest level of motor skills. Composite skills follow roughly the same patterns as SC. FIRE was the leading sector (19 percent above average), followed by other services (12 percent above average), and

Table 2.6. Mean Skill Scores by Major Industry in 1970 and Percentage Change, 1950–2000 (Skill scores normalized so that overall skill score = 100 in 1970)

	Mean Skill Score, 1970					Percentage Change, 1950–2000				
	SC	EDUC-1970	IS	MS	CP	SC	EDUC-1970	IS	MS	CP
Agriculture	89	84	76	98	91	−13.2	7.8	−27.7	−5.5	−11.2
Mining	96	95	69	105	97	34.0	10.3	39.7	−3.7	25.1
Construction	101	93	64	116	103	26.8	7.4	30.9	−3.8	19.6
Manufacturing	88	96	61	108	91	32.3	8.1	23.5	−5.0	23.2
Transportation, communications, public utilities	91	98	85	105	93	18.7	5.5	−4.1	−4.7	13.3
Wholesale and retail trade	94	98	97	90	93	9.8	2.8	−12.9	4.0	8.6
Finance, insurance, real estate	125	106	128	93	119	32.9	7.7	7.6	−9.3	25.6
Other services	114	108	149	97	112	18.3	8.2	−7.8	−5.8	13.7
Government	107	104	110	99	106	16.2	4.5	1.9	−3.3	12.8
Goods industries[a]	90	95	67	107	93	23.4	9.8	10.0	−3.1	17.3
Service industries[b]	107	104	125	94	105	19.2	7.2	−2.4	−1.5	15.4
Total	100	100	100	100	100	23.1	10.3	10.7	−5.0	17.5
Addendum[c]										
Production workers	74	90	48	111	81					
	(38)	(7)	(56)	(23)	(32)					
Nonproduction workers	116	106	133	93	112					
	(50)	(15)	(91)	(35)	(41)					

a. Goods-producing industries are defined as (1) agriculture, (2) mining, (3) construction, (4) manufacturing, and (5) transportation, communications, and public utilities.
b. Service industries are defined as (1) wholesale and retail trade, (2) finance, insurance, and real estate, (3) other services, and (4) government services.
c. Production workers include craft workers, operatives, and laborers. Nonproduction workers include all others. The standard deviation is shown in parentheses.

the government sector (6 percent above average). Agriculture and manufacturing were tied for last (9 percent below average).

Some industries have also been more dynamic than others in upgrading skill requirements. Interestingly, from 1950 to 2000, SC scores grew faster in the goods industries than in the service industries (23 versus 19 percent). Mining led the way with a 34 percent increase, followed closely by FIRE (33 percent) and manufacturing (32 percent). In manufacturing, in particular, the results accord with anecdotal evidence about the "white-collarization" of jobs in this sector (from 24 percent of total manufacturing jobs in 1950 to 38 percent in 2000, by my calculations). The trade sector experienced almost no change in SC levels, while agriculture suffered a 13 percent decline.

A similar pattern holds for EDUC-1970, which grew by 9.8 percent in the goods industries and 7.2 percent in services. Mining, again, was at the top of the list (a 10.3 percent increase), followed by other services (8.2 percent), manufacturing (8.1 percent), agriculture (7.8 percent), and FIRE (7.7 percent). Growth in EDUC-1970 was lowest in the trade sector—2.8 percent over the half century. The upgrading of SC and educational requirements in the goods industries reflects the more rapid growth in white-collar than blue-collar jobs, particularly from the industrial restructuring of the 1980s.

Interactive skills grew in the goods industries but showed a slight decline in services. Growth was strongest in mining (40 percent), construction (31 percent), and manufacturing (24 percent). The trade sector, other services, and transportation, communications, and utilities all showed losses.

Unlike the other measures in this table, motor skills requirements declined after 1950. This was true of every major industry except trade. While case studies have suggested that deskilling has occurred via the decline in the skill content of many blue-collar jobs, these industry results indicate that changes in occupational employment patterns within industry also contributed to a reduction in the demand for manual skills.

Substantive complexity, interactive skills, and motor skills represent three relatively independent dimensions of job skills. Table 2.6 quite clearly shows that industries that are strong in one dimension of skill need not be strong in other dimensions. For example, while FIRE ranked highest in SC in 1970 and second in IS, it ranked second to last in MS. Moreover, industries that grow rapidly in one skill direction did not necessarily grow in others. FIRE, for example again, had the highest growth in SC, ranked about average in IS growth, but recorded the biggest decline in MS. This stresses the importance of considering multiple dimensions of skills rather than a single one, such as educational attainment, that is used in most studies on this subject.

The addendum to table 2.6 provides another bifurcation of jobs—in this case, into production and nonproduction workers on the basis of the BLS definition for the manufacturing sector. Production workers are blue-collar workers with the exception of service workers, while nonproduction workers include white-collar and service workers. This division has been used in many notable productivity and earnings studies, such as Berman, Bound, and Griliches (1994), to distinguish between skilled and unskilled workers.

The results show that production workers score much lower than nonproduction workers in substantive complexity and interactive skills, but, as expected, production workers have substantially higher motor skills. As a result, the difference in the composite skill index between the two groups is less pronounced than that based on SC. The difference between them in schooling attainment in 1970 is only two years, also less marked in percentage terms than the gap in SC.

Another notable result is that the variation in skill levels within each of the two groups of workers is quite high. Indeed, because of the high variance, none of the difference in mean skill values is statistically significant. The standard deviation of skill scores is also considerably higher among nonproduction than production workers, indicating that the former are a more heterogeneous group. These results suggest that it is rather precarious to use production versus nonproduction workers as a demarcation between skilled and unskilled jobs.

2.3.1 Changes in Industry Employment since 1950

Changes in aggregate skill levels result from both changes in skill requirements at the industry level and structural shifts in employment patterns across industries. The former is normally interpreted as deriving from changes in technology, and the latter from shifting patterns of demand.

Before presenting a formal decomposition, let us look at the broad changes in employment composition by industry in the postwar period (table 2.7). One of the most dramatic changes has been in agriculture, which accounted for 14 percent of total employment in 1950 and less than 2 percent in 2003. This percentage has been declining for the last 100 years. In 1929, for example, employment in agriculture amounted to 22 percent of total employment. This proportion fell to 14 percent in 1947, 8 percent in 1960, and 4 percent in 1978, reflecting primarily the exodus of small farm owners and their families.

Another major change occurred in manufacturing, whose share of total employment fell by more than half, from 29 percent in 1950 to 12 percent in 2003. In absolute terms, employment in manufacturing peaked in 1980 at 20.3 million workers and has since fallen to 16.9 million in 2003. Much discussion has recently ensued over this development, which some have labeled the "deindustrialization" of America. However, much of the decline in manufacturing employment is due to the high (labor) productivity growth of this sector. In fact, manufacturing accounted for almost the same share of total output in 2003 as it did in the early 1950s.[10]

The share of employment in mining also declined rather precipitously between 1950 and 2003, from 1.7 to 0.4 percent. The share of employment in transportation, communications, and public utilities fell slightly in this

Table 2.7.   Percentage Distribution of Employment by Major Industry, 1950, 1970, 1995, and 2003

Industry	1950	1970	1995	2003
Agriculture	13.7	4.7	2.9	1.7
Mining	1.7	0.8	0.5	0.4
Construction	4.5	4.8	4.3	7.4
Manufacturing	29.1	26.1	15.3	12.3
Transportation, communications, and public utilities	7.7	6.1	5.1	6.1
Wholesale and retail trade	17.9	20.2	22.9	21.6
Finance, insurance, and real estate	3.6	4.9	5.7	7.1
Other services	10.2	15.5	27.4	27.4
Government	11.5	16.9	16.0	16.2
Total	100.0	100.0	100.0	100.0

Sources: Council of Economic Advisers, *Economic Report of the President, 1999*; U.S. Bureau of the Census, *Statistical Abstract of the United States, 2004–2005*.

period, from 7.7 to 6.1 percent, while the proportion of construction workers rose from 4.5 to 7.4 percent.

If the share of employment fell in agriculture, mining, manufacturing, and transportation, communications, and utilities, where did it increase? The answer is largely the service sectors, which absorbed most of the growth of employment in the postwar period. The proportion of total employment in wholesale and retail trade increased from 18 to 22 percent, the percentage in finance, insurance, and real estate from 3.6 to 7.1, the percentage on government payrolls from 11.5 to 16.2, and the share in other services (personal and business) from 10.2 to 27.4 percent. In sum, two major developments characterize the postwar period. The first is the shrinking share of workers employed in agriculture and manufacturing, and the second is the shift of the workforce out of goods-producing enterprises into services.

2.3.2 Industry Effects on Aggregate Skill Growth

Changes in overall skill levels are a result of changes in the skill levels of individual industries (through changes in occupational mix) and employment shifts among industries. The former is usually interpreted to reflect changes in technology within the industry, and the latter to reflect changes in demand patterns in the economy. Table 2.8 shows the results of this decomposition.[11]

During the 1950s, the entire growth in substantive complexity was due to shifts in the composition of industrial employment. In fact, changes in the occupational composition of the workforce within industry lowered the average SC level. During the 1960s (the period of greatest overall growth in SC), both the occupational composition effect and the industry shift effect were positive and strong. Changes in occupational composition added 0.118

Table 2.8.   Decomposition of the Change in Overall Skill Levels into an Occupational Composition Effect and an Industry Employment Shift Effect, 1950–2000

Period	Actual Change in Overall Skill Level	Decomposition		Percentage Decomposition		
		1st Effect Change in Occupational Composition within Industry	2nd Effect Shifts in Employment among Industries	Total Change	1st Effect Change in Occupational Composition within Industry	2nd Effect Shifts in Employment among Industries
A. Substantive Complexity (SC)						
1950–1960	0.060	-0.008	0.068	100.0	-13.9	113.9
1960–1970	0.267	0.118	0.150	100.0	43.9	56.1
1970–1980	0.156	0.088	0.068	100.0	56.6	43.4
1980–1990	0.149	0.106	0.043	100.0	71.4	28.6
1990–2000	0.234	0.189	0.044	100.0	81.0	19.0
1950–2000	0.866	0.493	0.373	100.0	56.9	43.1
B. Interactive Skills (IS)						
1950–1960	0.019	-0.007	0.027	100.0	-36.6	136.6
1960–1970	0.060	0.007	0.053	100.0	12.1	87.9
1970–1980	0.040	0.016	0.024	100.0	40.2	59.8
1980–1990	0.056	0.040	0.016	100.0	72.2	27.8
1990–2000	0.060	0.007	0.052	100.0	11.8	88.2
1950–2000	0.235	0.064	0.171	100.0	27.1	72.9
C. Motor Skills (MS)						
1950–1960	0.016	0.034	-0.018	100.0	214.0	-114.0
1960–1970	0.038	0.056	-0.017	100.0	145.1	-45.1
1970–1980	-0.068	-0.049	-0.019	100.0	71.5	28.5
1980–1990	-0.085	-0.077	-0.009	100.0	89.8	10.2
1990–2000	-0.157	-0.124	-0.034	100.0	78.6	21.4
1950–2000	-0.256	-0.159	-0.097	100.0	62.0	38.0

Note: The decomposition is based on 64 industries. See footnote 11 for the decomposition formula.

points to the average SC level, and the industry shift effect added 0.150 points. During the 1960s, a bit less than half of the growth in average SC was attributable to changes in occupational composition.

The contribution of the occupational composition effect declined somewhat between the 1960s and the 1970s, from 0.118 to 0.088, but then picked up to 0.106 in the 1980s and 0.189 in the 1990s, while the industry shift effect plummeted between the 1960s and 1970s, from 0.150 to 0.068, and then gradually attenuated in the 1980s and 1990s. As a result, overall SC growth fell sharply between the 1960s and the 1970s, stabilized in the 1980s, and then climbed sharply in the 1990s. The occupational composition effect, which explains 44 percent of overall SC growth in the 1960s, accounts for 57 percent in the 1970s, 71 percent in the 1980s, and 81 percent in the 1990s.

The entire growth in interactive skills during the 1950s is, like the other two skill measures, attributable to employment shifts among industries. The industry shift effect increased between the 1950s and 1960s, declined in the 1970s and again in the 1980s, but then intensified in the 1990s, while the occupational composition effect rose steadily from the 1950s to the 1980s but then collapsed in the 1990s. As a result, the growth in the overall IS level rose sharply between the 1950s and 1960s, decreased in the 1970s, but gained in the 1980s and 1990s.

Changes in motor skills show a very different pattern from the other two skill measures. The industrial shift effect was negative and of very similar magnitude in each of the five decades, reflecting the shift of employment toward services. The occupational composition effect was positive and relatively strong in both the 1960s and 1970s, favoring blue-collar over white-collar jobs and accounting for the overall positive increase in motor skills in these two decades. However, the occupation effect turned negative in the 1970s and then increasingly negative in the 1980s and 1990s, reflecting the dramatic shift of employment toward white-collar jobs and away from blue-collar ones and accounting for the decline in the overall MS level in those two periods.

In sum, from 1950 to 2000, a bit more than half of the growth in the overall SC level of the workforce was attributable to technological change (57 percent) and a bit less than half to shifting demand patterns (43 percent). The former primarily reflects the increasing share of white-collar workers, particularly professionals and managers, within industries, while the latter reflects the continuing shift of employment out of low-skill goods industries toward the higher-skilled services, particularly finance, insurance, and business and professional services. After the 1960s, the effect of changing demand patterns waned in absolute terms. In contrast, after the 1960s, the importance of technological change rose in both absolute terms and in relative importance over the subsequent decades.

Over the five decades, 73 percent of the upgrading in interactive skill levels was attributable to industry shifts, particularly toward high-end services. As with cognitive skills, demand shifts became less important over time, in both absolute and relative terms, except for the 1990s, while changing technology increased in importance. Between 1950 and 2000, 62 percent of the downgrading in motor skills was accounted for by technological changes within industry, and the remaining 38 percent by shifts in industry demand. After the 1960s, the occupational change effect grew more negative, while demand shifts remained negative throughout the 50-year period and very similar in magnitude over the five decades.

2.4 Technology and Skill Growth

2.4.1 The Two Faces of Technology

How does technological change affect skill demand? The role of the characteristic stages of the innovation process is somewhat complicated. Economic historians emphasize that, when new technology or products reach the market, they are typically relatively difficult to use, unreliable, in need of frequent attention, and limited in their range of application. Introduction is followed by a relatively long period of improvement that increases reliability, expands uses, and makes them user friendly. This is the period in which standard measures of technical change (such as total factor productivity, or TFP) show steady growth. Obvious examples range from Watt's improved steam engine to the electronic computer.

The introduction of new technology thus appears to have two phases. In the first, the development and implementation of new inventions calls forth the need for highly skilled and educated workers. This period seems clearly to be advantageous to specialized and educated workers, who are needed both to improve and operate the new product, and *relatively* disadvantageous to the unskilled and, on net, leads to skill upgrading in the workplace.

The second stage, user friendliness, appears to reverse the process, making it easier for the unskilled to work with the new items. The simplification of technology and its routinization reduces the need for highly skilled and educated workers and makes its use by unskilled workers easier, increasing their demand, while the need for skilled and specialized workers is reduced. The second period thus tends to downgrade the skill levels of workers.

This argument is also consistent with product life cycle models. As Vernon (1966, 1979) originally argued, the creation of a new industry or product line usually entails high startup costs, the development of specialized processes, the training of labor for new skills, and so on. However, once this technology is in place, there is constant pressure to routinize the technology so that it becomes cheaper to use. If it becomes routinized, then it may have to rely neither on expensive, highly trained labor nor on special production processes to supply its inputs.

It then appears to be the case that incremental improvements in technology should be associated with a reduction in the skill content of jobs, while radical changes in technology should be accompanied by increased skill demand, though it is hard to operationalize fully the distinction between these two types of technological progress. As an example, one might consider the automobile. When first introduced, it was difficult to operate and required considerable skill on the part of the driver (such as shifting gears and even starting the car). As the technology advanced, it became easier to operate the vehicle, especially with the later introduction of automatic transmission and cruise control.

Moreover, in the early days of motoring, limited repair services were available, so drivers had to be familiar with the mechanical details of the car's engine. Today, with the wide availability of repair operations, drivers need know no details of the inner workings of their vehicles. Also, earlier in this century, with unpaved roads and numerous potholes (and, indeed, no traffic signals), considerable skill was required even to maneuver the car on the road (this is still true of many third-world countries). As the road system improved, particularly with the introduction of expressways, the ease of driving increased. Today in the United States and Western Europe, almost any adult can operate a car.

A similar pattern holds for a wide range of tasks, as the following examples illustrate. Cashiers were once required to add and subtract and then to punch numbers into a machine; now they simply scan products through an optical reader. Telephone operators once had to operate complicated mechanical equipment. Stenographers were once required to master a complex symbolic language but today need only to operate a keyboard. Typists once needed to master spelling and grammar but today can rely on spellcheckers and grammar checkers. Indeed, many of these skill changes are associated with changes in occupational title—from typist to word processor, for example.

Indeed, one might argue that one of the primary goals for the introduction of new technology is to dumb down the job. For example, when Henry Ford introduced the assembly line, one of his specific objectives was the replacement of the highly skilled machinists from automotive manufacturing by low-skilled, easily trainable assembly line workers. The machinists exercised considerable control over the production process and were highly paid workers in the early part of the twentieth century. (An ulterior motive for the elimination of machinists is that they were also represented by a strong union.) Fordism might be viewed as a mechanism to replace highly skilled workers in the workplace with low-skilled assemblers.

A few words should be said about computerization, which also fits into the two-phase scenario. Its introduction can radically alter the workplace, requiring highly skilled computer experts, technicians, and engineers to implement the new technology. However, once in place, the tasks tend to simplify. In telecommunications, for example, new computer software has gradually replaced operators with canned answering programs and menu options. In medicine, new computer programs now read EKGs and diagnose heart ailments more effectively than cardiologists (statistical diagnosis turns out to be a better predictor of heart problems than a doctor's intuition and experience). New software in the insurance industry has displaced the relatively highly skilled work of the underwriter, who was once needed to calculate risks for different insurance policies.

2.4.2 Review of Literature

Most of the literature on the subject has emphasized the first of the two phases, the need for more highly skilled workers to implement new technology. One of the first arguments (i.e., that technological change may stimulate the demand for more skilled or better-educated labor) emanates from the work of Arrow (1962). Arrow introduced the notion of learning by doing, which implies that experience in the application of a given technology or a new technology in the production process leads to increased efficiencies over time. One implication of this is that an educated labor force should learn faster than a less educated group. Industries with more rapid rates of technological progress may thus favor workers with greater potential for learning.

A second rationale comes from the Nelson and Phelps (1966) model, which maintains that a more educated workforce may make it easier for a firm to adopt and implement new technologies. Firms value educated workers because they are more able to evaluate and adapt innovations and to learn new functions and routines than less educated ones. In this model, too, technological change may stimulate the demand for skilled workers. Some supporting evidence is provided by Wozniak (1987), who found that higher levels of education were significantly and positively correlated with early adoption of new technology among a sample of Iowa farms in 1976.

Several studies provide both direct and indirect evidence of a positive relation between the pace of technological activity and the demand for educated labor. Welch (1970) analyzed the returns to education in U.S. farming in 1959 and concluded that a portion of them resulted from the greater ability of more educated workers to adapt to new production technologies. Denny and Fuss (1983), using data from Bell Canada from 1952 to 1972, estimated a negative relation between the rate of technical change in the company and the employment of the least skilled occupations.

Bartel and Lichtenberg (1987), using industry-level data for 61 U.S. manufacturing industries in the 1960–1980 period, found that the relative demand for educated workers was greater in sectors with newer vintages of capital. They have inferred from this that highly educated workers have a comparative advantage with regard to the implementation of new technologies. This result is particularly pertinent to my argument since it supports the hypothesis that it is the introduction of new technologies, rather than incremental improvements in existing technology, that increases the demand for skilled workers.

A related finding by Mincer and Higuchi (1988), using U.S. and Japanese employment data, indicates that returns to education are higher in sectors undergoing more rapid technical change. One from Gill (1989), who used data from the U.S. Current Population Survey for 1969–1984, indicates that returns to education for highly schooled employees are greater in industries with higher rates of technological change.

Berman, Bound, and Griliches (1994), using data from the Annual Survey of Manufactures from 1979 to 1987 for 450 manufacturing industries, found that increased use of nonproduction workers (relative to production workers) within manufacturing industries strongly correlated with both R&D expenditures and investment in computers. Berndt, Morrison, and Rosenblum (1992), using two-digit Bureau of Economic Analysis industry data, also found complementarity between high-tech capital and the share of nonproduction workers in total employment.

Autor, Katz, and Krueger (1998) estimated greater shifts toward college-educated workers in industries in which computer usage and computer stock per worker were growing faster—indeed, explaining as much as 30–50 percent of the increase in the growth rate of the relative demand for college-educated workers after 1970. They also found that industries that had the largest growth in computers also tended to shift their employee composition from administrative support workers toward managers and professionals.

Falk and Seim (1999), using firm-level panel data on German service industries in the period 1994–1996, also found a positive and significant relation between the share of skilled labor (primarily university graduates) and the use of information technology (IT). However, the IT effect is not very large and varied across sectors, explaining from 6 percent of skill upgrading in business services to 25 percent in banking and insurance. Bresnahan, Brynjolfsson, and Hitt (2002), using firm-level data for the United States, have found that the greater use of information technology was associated with a higher employment share of highly educated workers. They have also found that IT is complementary with new workplace organization, including more decentralized decision making and more self-managing teams, and that new workplace organization is complementary with worker skill levels.

More recently, Autor, Levy, and Murnane (2003) claim that computer capital substitutes for a limited and well-defined set of tasks. Using census of population data for 1970, 1980, and 1990, as well as *DOT* skill scores, they conclude that computer intensity on the industry level is associated with a declining relative demand for routine manual and information-processing skills and increasing relative demand for nonroutine information-processing skills.

Murphy and Welch (1993b), in contrast, dispute the importance of the diffusion of information technology in skill growth. After examining decennial census of population data on employment by occupation from 1940 to 1980 and CPS data for the period from 1989 to 1991, they found that there was a steady increase in the demand for skilled labor between 1940 and 1990 but no particular acceleration during the 1970s and 1980s.

A related set of arguments comes from the sociology literature. Bell (1973) and Hirschhorn (1986) have argued that automated-process technologies replace physically repetitive tasks with more conceptual work. They suggest that new technologies, on net, eliminate unskilled jobs and therefore raise worker skills on average. On the other side of the debate are Braverman (1974), Noble (1984), and Shaiken (1984), who view new technologies as essentially skill displacing. They argue that, by transferring skills from labor to machines, management is able to gain greater control over the production process with a less skilled and less well-paid workforce. Much of their work focuses on production workers on the shop floor. However, Keefe (1991) has found that the spread of numerically controlled machine tools in 57 machining jobs from 1975 to 1983 had a minimal effect on worker skills—neither deskilling nor upgrading.

Leontief (1982, 1983) also argues that, during a period of industrialization, technological change essentially involves machines taking over many of the physical tasks that workers had previously performed. Moreover, machines are now assuming many of the mental functions that white-collar workers have traditionally performed. As a result, technological change has become even more deskilling than in the past. However, there is little direct evidence of this effect.

A related view that has received widespread support is the capital-skills complementarity hypothesis. The argument is that greater investment in equipment is associated with greater demand for skilled labor since new equipment normally embodies the latest and presumably more complex technology, which requires greater skills for operationalization (Griliches 1969). Measures of investment are used to allow for the possibility that new technology may normally be embodied in new capital, particularly new equipment and machinery. The average annual growth of the ratio of capital stock to employment may be interpreted as an indicator of the rate at which new vintages of capital are introduced into industry. Standard measures of TFP growth do not adequately capture this effect.

Evidence of complementarity between total capital and the share of nonproduction workers was reported by Berndt, Morrison, and Rosenblum (1992). Doms, Dunne, and Troske (1997) have found in a cross-section of establishments that U.S. manufacturing plants that used more advanced technology also employed more educated workers. However, the results are not very robust when firm-level effects are introduced. Moreover, over time there was little correlation between skills upgrading and the adoption of new technologies. Indeed, Goldin and Katz (1998) trace the origins of capital-skill complementarity in the United States back to the early 1900s, with more capital-intensive industries hiring more educated blue-collar workers and employing a higher share of nonproduction workers. Using a panel of manufacturing plants owned by chemical firms from 1974 to 1988, Adams (1999) estimates that both equipment capital and product R&D increased the relative demand for skilled labor within the plant. He also found a secondary contribution of R&D, which, by favoring equipment purchases over structures, also augmented the relative demand for skilled labor.

Several articles have established a complementarity between employer training and capital investment. Lynch and Black (1998), using 1994 establishment data, have found that the proportion of workers receiving training was highest in establishments that had made large investments in physical capital or adopted new forms of work organization. Bartel (1998), using COMPUSTAT line-of-business data, has also reported a positive relation between capital investment and the probability of worker training, while Osterman (1994, 1995) has found that the incidence of formal training programs was higher in establishments that adopted high-performance workplace systems such as Total Quality Management.

2.4.3 Description of Technology Indicators and Other Variables

In this study I use two indices of technological activity: (1) the rate of TFP growth and (2) the ratio of R&D expenditures to gross domestic product (GDP).[12] These are relatively standard measures of technological activity. Investment activity may also influence the change in skill levels, as the capital-skills complementarity hypothesis suggests. The variables used here are (1) the growth in the ratio of the office, computing, and accounting equipment (OCA) to total employment[13] and (2) the growth in the ratio of equipment and machinery, excluding OCA, to total employment. OCA is singled out because, as noted earlier, many economists have argued that computerization may play a particularly important role as a transmitter of new technologies.

According to the "two phases of technology" hypothesis, TFP growth should have a negative effect on skill growth since it largely reflects incremental technological advances, which are associated with declining skill requirements. In contrast, R&D intensity and new equipment investment are indicators of the development of new technology and should have a positive effect on the growth in worker skills. The capital-skills complementarity hypothesis offers a similar prediction about the effect of new equipment investment on skill growth. Predictions regarding computerization, on the other hand, may be ambiguous, depending on whether it is associated with the first or second phase of technology.

Another factor that may affect the rate of skill change is international competitiveness, as measured by changes both in the ratio of exports to GDP and in the ratio of imports to GDP. There are two possibilities. One is that industries competing in international product markets or directly against imports might be forced to upgrade skills faster than domestic industries in order to remain competitive (the high-road hypothesis). A second likelihood is that such industries might be forced to compete on the basis of cost and thus have an incentive to replace highly paid workers with low-paid ones and downgrade skill levels (the low-road hypothesis).

Structural and organizational dimensions of production may also affect the demand for skills. Here I investigate three factors: (1) the share of employees belonging to unions, (2) employment in services as a share of total employment, and (3) the minimum wage in constant dollars.[14] Unionization may reduce the growth in skills by restricting the flexibility of employers to restructure the workplace with the advent of new technology. The shift of employment to services may accelerate aggregate changes in skill levels since services are generally more skill intensive than goods producers (at least in terms of cognitive and people skills). Average skill levels may be sensitive to the minimum wage since a falling minimum wage may induce employers to hire a greater number of low-skilled workers.

Figure 2.5 shows decade changes in cognitive skills, as well as TFP growth and R&D intensity. As discussed earlier, the growth in cognitive skills accelerated between the 1950s and the 1960s, declined in the 1970s, and fell slightly in the 1980s before picking up in the 1990s. In contrast, TFP growth was strongest in the 1950s (1.4 percent per year), fell a bit in the 1960s (to 1.0 percent per year), then plummeted by almost two-thirds in the 1970s (to 0.4 percent per year), and recovered in the 1980s and 1990s (to 1.1 and 0.9 percent per year, respectively). As a result, there appears to be no clear correspondence between the change in cognitive skills and the growth in TFP. Between the 1960s and 1970s the intensity of R&D, like the growth in SC, fell but then picked up in the 1980s and remained unchanged in the 1990s. The time trend for R&D intensity is a bit closer to that of SC growth than is the time trend for TFP growth.

Investment in machinery and equipment per worker rose rather steadily from $1,400 in the 1950s to $2,600 in the 1980s and then jumped to $5,300 in the 1990s (figure 2.6). A similar pattern is evident for investment in OCA per worker, which rose from virtually zero in the 1950s, 1960s, and 1970s

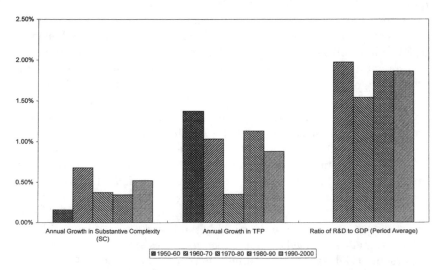

Figure 2.5   Annual Growth in Substantive Complexity, Annual TFP Growth, and R&D Intensity by Decade, 1950–2000

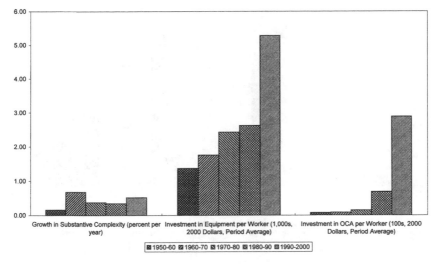

Figure 2.6   Annual Growth in Substantive Complexity, Investment in Equipment per Worker, and Investment in OCA per Worker by Decade, 1950–2000

to $69 in the 1980s and then accelerated tremendously to $289 in the 1990s. Neither pattern directly resembles that of the growth in cognitive skills. In fact, though the growth in SC picked up in the 1990s relative to the 1980s, the relative change was substantially less than that of either equipment or OCA investment per worker.

Trade intensity was quite low in the early postwar years and then exploded after 1970. Exports as a share of GDP averaged 4.5 percent in the 1950s and 4.9 percent in the 1960s, climbed to 7.3 percent in the 1970s and then to 8.5 percent in the 1980s and 10.7 percent in the 1990s. Likewise, imports as a percentage of GDP soared from 4.2 in the 1950s and 4.5 in the 1960s to 7.6 in the 1970s, 10.3 in the 1980s, and 11.9 in the 1990s. The biggest surges in both export and import intensity occurred in the 1970s and 1990s (figure 2.7). During the 1970s, SC growth was relatively low, while during the 1990s SC growth was robust. As a result, the change in cognitive skills weakly correlates with the change in both exports and imports as a share of GDP. Figure 2.7 also shows trends in the unionization rate, which shrank almost monotonically over the half century, from an average rate of 24.5 percent in the 1950s to 15.0 percent in the 1990s. This pattern does not seem to correspond either positively or negatively with the trend in SC growth.[15]

2.5 Conclusion

Between 1950 and 2000, both cognitive and interactive skills showed positive growth. Motor skills, on the other hand, experienced an absolute decline. The rate of growth in all five workplace skill indices (SC, IS, MS, CP, and

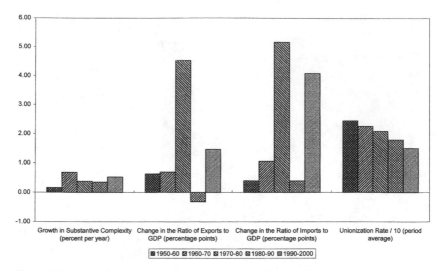

Figure 2.7   Annual Growth in Substantive Complexity, the Change in the Ratio of Exports to GDP and of Imports to GDP, and the Unionization Rate by Decade, 1950–2000

EDUC-1970) peaked in the 1960s. In the case of cognitive skills, this was due to strong effects from both demand shifts and technological change at the industry level. In the case of interactive skills, this was primarily a result of changing demand patterns that favored industries high in interactive skills. For motor skills, however, technological change played the predominant role (in fact, demand shifts had a negative effect).

The growth of cognitive skills fell between the 1960s and 1970s and again between the 1970s and 1980s, almost entirely as a consequence of the lessening effect of demand shifts on skill growth. On the other hand, the effect of technological changes climbed between the 1970s and 1990s, with the result that, by the 1990s, that effect was at its highest point and the rate of growth of cognitive skills picked up again, though it was still below its peak in the 1960s.

The growth in interactive skills fell sharply between the 1960s and 1970s but then recovered in the 1980s (because of a high technological change effect) and again in the 1990s because of strong demand effects. The growth in motor skills turned negative in the 1970s and even more negative in the 1980s and 1990s, due mainly to a rapid restructuring of jobs within industry.

Overall, there is no evidence of deskilling in the 1980s or the 1990s, except for motor skills. Moreover, in the case of all three skill measures (particularly SC), technological change became increasingly dominant as a determinant of skill change, while industrial shifts fell in importance.

Changes in educational attainment appear to have outstripped changes in workplace skills (especially cognitive skills). If we can loosely interpret the direct skill indices as indicators of the demand for skills, then these results suggest a lack of correspondence between the growth in the demand for cognitive skills and the supply of such skills, as reflected in the educational achievement of the population. Indeed, the results suggest that, since the 1960s, the U.S. educational system has been producing more educated workers than the workplace can effectively absorb.

An examination of the factors that affect changes in skill levels provides some support for the two-phase model of innovation. Technological activity as reflected in R&D investment has a positive bearing on the change in both substantive complexity and interactive skills, though the coefficient of R&D intensity is only marginally significant. These results are consistent with the first phase of innovation, when the development and implementation of new inventions call for highly skilled workers to improve and operate the new product.

TFP growth has a negative association with the growth of cognitive, interactive, and motor skills (although the coefficients are not statistically significant). These results are roughly consistent with the second phase of the introduction of new technology, which emphasizes the constant pressure to routinize new technology so that it becomes less reliant on skilled mental labor. Equipment (excluding OCA) investment per worker has a positive bearing on the growth in both cognitive and interactive skills and a negative relation to the growth in motor skills, though here, too, the coefficients are not significant. These results are roughly consistent with the capital-skills complementarity hypothesis.

Perhaps the most striking finding is that investment in OCA per worker has a very strong and significant *negative* association with the growth of both cognitive and interactive skills. Computerization has a positive, though marginally significant, effect on gains in the employment of what I call "knowledge workers" and a negative and highly significant effect on the growth in what I call "data workers" (see chapter 5). The negative effect of computer investment on the growth of data workers apparently outweighs its positive effect on the employment of knowledge workers; on net, therefore, computerization is deskilling. In fact, the introduction of information technology appears to "hollow out" the skill distribution by decreasing the employment of middle-skill data workers. Moreover, computerization has a significant positive effect on changes in earnings inequality (see chapter 6). These results also suggest that computerization falls mainly into the second phase of technological change—namely, that on net it helps to routinize new technology so that it becomes less reliant on skilled labor.

The regression results also provide evidence that export-oriented industries upgrade interactive skills (the coefficient is marginally significant) and downgrade motor skills (its coefficient is highly significant) more rapidly than domestically oriented ones. These findings suggest that export industries remain competitive by providing greater sales effort and substituting low-skill manual workers for more highly skilled ones in order to cut costs

(the low-road hypothesis). These results are also consistent with those discussed in chapter 7, which finds that the cognitive skill content of exports
both in absolute terms and relative to imports has been rising since 1950,
while the motor skill content of exports has been falling both absolutely and
relative to imports.

Regression results on the occupational level indicate that the return to
cognitive abilities, after rising steeply between 1950 and 1970, fell off in 1980
but then surged in 2000 to its highest point in the half century. This finding
is consistent with the general evidence that the returns to a college degree
relative to a high school diploma have been intensifying since around the
mid-1970s (see, for example, Katz and Murphy 1992). In contrast, the returns
to motor skills have been declining since 1960, while interactive skills have
been growing in importance since 1950 and by 1990 had overtaken motor
skills as a factor in explaining occupational earnings. These results suggest
that the rising return to schooling observed since the mid-1970s might be
partly a consequence of the increasing importance of communication and
other interactive skills transmitted in the educational process.

Appendix

Pooled Industry-Level Regressions of Skill Change

Regression analysis is used to formally analyze the relation between skill
change on the one hand and technological advance and investment, trade,
and structural and institutional factors on the other. The analysis is conducted through the use of pooled cross-section time-series data, covering 44
industries in three ten-year periods—the 1960s, the 1970s, and the 1980s—
and 32 industries in the 1990s.[16] The dependent variable in the regressions
is the change in skill level over the ten-year period.[17] Results are shown in
appendix table 2.1.[18]

As predicted, TFP growth has a negative effect on the change in substantive complexity, but its coefficient is not statistically significant. The coefficient of R&D intensity is positive and significant (though at only the 10
percent level), whereas the coefficient of the growth of investment in equipment (less OCA per worker) is also positive but not significant. However, the
coefficient of investment in OCA per worker is negative and highly significant (at the 1 percent level). This result provides powerful evidence of the
deskilling effects of OCA.[19]

The coefficients of the two trade variables are positive but not significant.
The coefficient of the unionization rate is negative but very insignificant. Regression results for the change in the composite skills and the interactive skills
indices are very similar to those for the change in cognitive skills. The only
notable difference is that, in the IS regression, the coefficient of the change in
export intensity is now marginally significant (at the 10 percent level).

Appendix 2.1.   Regressions of the Change in Workplace Skill on Technology and Other Variables Using Pooled Cross-Section Industry-Level Data, 1960–2000

Independent Variables	Dependent Variable			
	Change in Substantive Complexity (SC)	Change in Interactive Skills (IS)	Change in Motor Skills (MS)	Change in Composite Skills (CP)
Constant	0.297 **	0.101 #	−0.176 **	0.126 **
	(4.27)	(1.86)	(4.12)	(3.88)
TFP growth	−0.911	−0.617	−0.108	−0.440
	(1.12)	(0.97)	(0.22)	(1.15)
Ratio of R&D expenditures to total output	1.695 #	1.136 #	−0.689	0.764 #
	(1.92)	(1.84)	(1.14)	(1.74)
Investment in equipment less OCA (in 1,000s, $2,000) per worker	0.438	0.479	−0.384	0.178
	(1.03)	(1.44)	(1.46)	(0.89)
Investment in OCA (in 1,000s, $2,000) per worker	−0.327 **	−0.289 **	0.075	−0.152 **
	(3.82)	(4.34)	(1.43)	(3.80)
Change in the ratio of imports to total output	0.278	0.149	0.050	0.135
	(1.13)	(0.77)	(0.33)	(1.17)
Change in the ratio of exports to total output	1.458	1.951 #	−2.224 **	0.518
	(1.14)	(1.96)	(2.82)	(0.86)
Unionization rate	−0.022	−0.020	0.047	−0.006
	(0.17)	(0.20)	(0.58)	(0.09)
R^2	0.143	0.190	0.249	0.141
Adjusted R^2	0.087	0.137	0.200	0.084
Standard error	0.2699	0.2101	0.1663	0.1264
Sample size	164	164	164	164

Note: The sample consists of pooled cross-section time-series data, with observations on each of the 44 industries in 1960–1970, 1970–1980 and 1980–1990 (sector 45, public administration, is excluded because of a lack of appropriate capital stock data) and 32 industries in 1990–2000. Dummy variables are included for time periods 1960–1970, 1970–1980, and 1980–1990 (results not shown). The coefficients are estimated using the White procedure for a heteroschedasticity-consistent covariance matrix. The absolute value of the t-statistic is in parentheses below the coefficient. See the appendix for data sources and methods.

Significance levels: # 10%; * 5% level; ** 1% level.

Results for the change in motor skills are very different from those for the other three skill variables—indeed, almost the opposite. The coefficient of R&D intensity is negative, that of investment in equipment (less OCA per worker) is also negative, and that of investment in OCA per worker is positive, although none of these coefficients is significant. The coefficient of the change in import intensity remains positive and insignificant, while that of the change in export intensity is now negative and highly significant (at the 1 percent level). The coefficient of the unionization rate is positive (as predicted) but not significant.

Wages and Skills on the Occupational Level

The last part of the analysis considers the way in which returns to skills have changed between 1950 and 2000. For this analysis I use measures of skill scores and wages on the occupational level to determine how the relation between wages and skills has developed over time. Appendix table 2.2 shows the results for the different components of workplace skill. In 1970, substantive complexity was the most important factor in determining relative wages, both in terms of coefficient value and significance level (at the 1 percent level), followed by motor skills, significant at the 5 percent level, and interactive skills, which are not significant.

Appendix 2.2.   Regressions of Hourly Wages in 1970 Dollars (HOURWAGE) on Workplace Skills across Occupations, 1950–2000

Independent Variables	Year					
	1950	1960	1970	1980	1990	2000
Constant	0.836 **	0.742 **	1.145 **	1.452 **	1.363 **	1.173 **
	(4.63)	(2.78)	(4.78)	(5.99)	(4.84)	(3.30)
SC	0.292 **	0.414 **	0.454 **	0.315 **	0.370 **	0.509 **
	(10.52)	(10.28)	(12.14)	(8.36)	(8.44)	(9.40)
MS	0.054 #	0.123 **	0.093 *	0.098 *	0.084 #	0.057
	(1.87)	(2.86)	(2.37)	(2.49)	(1.84)	(0.99)
IS	−0.017	−0.006	0.028	0.085 *	0.150 **	0.143 *
	(0.60)	(0.13)	(0.70)	(2.14)	(3.21)	(2.48)
R^2	0.503	0.487	0.535	0.418	0.457	0.531
Adjusted R^2	0.495	0.480	0.530	0.411	0.451	0.524
Standard error	0.652	1.016	1.037	1.039	1.208	1.342
Sample size	196	215	267	262	262	208

Note: The unit of observation is the occupation. The absolute value of the t-statistic is shown in parentheses below the coefficient estimate. The 1950 hourly wage is estimated as median income by occupation in 1950 divided by average hours worked per year for all workers in 1970 (1,961 hours). The 1960 hourly wage by occupation is estimated as median labor earnings by occupation in 1960 divided by average hours worked per year for all workers in 1970 (1,961 hours). For 1970, 1980, 1990, and 2000, hourly wage by occupation is computed as mean annual earnings for that occupation divided by average hours worked per year in the occupation.

Significance levels: # 10%; * 5% level; ** 1% level.

Some notable changes have occurred over time. The return to substantive complexity, both in terms of its coefficient value and its significance level, rose markedly between 1950 and 1970, fell off sharply in 1980, recovered somewhat in 1990, and then grew enormously in 2000. In fact, in 2000, the coefficient value was at its highest point in the half century. The returns to motor skills also show a sharp increase between 1950 and 1960, with the coefficient value more than doubling and its significance level rising from 10 percent to 1 percent. After 1960, the returns to motor skills tumbled, with the coefficient declining by more than half by 2000. By 2000, the coefficient of MS was no longer significant. In contrast, the returns to interactive skills have gradually risen. In 1950 and 1960, its coefficient was actually negative, although not significant. By 1980 its coefficient reached 0.085 and was significant at the 5 percent level. By 2000 its coefficient had jumped to 0.14 and was significant at the 1 percent level. Indeed, in 2000, interactive skills were second in importance to substantive complexity as a determinant of occupational wages.

Notes

1. This part extends the analysis contained in Howell and Wolff (1991a), which was based on actual census employment matrices for 1960, 1970, and 1980 and a statistically imputed matrix for 1985, and Wolff (1996b), which updates the analysis to 1990.
2. This section updates previous econometric analysis (Howell and Wolff 1992), which was conducted on skill changes from 1970 to 1985.
3. For a discussion of some of the limitations of these data, see Miller et al. (1980) and Spenner (1983).
4. See section C of the appendix to chapter 2 for more discussion, analysis, and corresponding regression results for other years.
5. Their analysis is unclear on the relative importance of skill change within occupation versus changes in occupational composition within industry.
6. I do not present results on GED in this chapter.
7. The data show an increase in the share of sales workers from 6 percent in 1977 to 12 percent in 1988. However, these numbers should be interpreted with some caution because the Census Bureau changed its classification of sales jobs during the 1980s.
8. In 2003, these two occupational groups were eliminated as separate categories by the U.S. Bureau of the Census.
9. Apparent anomalies are that interactive skills grew faster in the 1960s than in the 1950s, whereas the share of managers in total employment grew faster in the earlier decade, and that motor skills had positive growth in the 1950s while the share of both craft workers and operatives in the labor force declined.
10. If a sector's output share remains constant and its labor productivity growth is greater than average, then its share of total employment must, of consequence, fall. This mechanism is often referred to as the "unbalanced

growth" effect. See Baumol, Blackman, and Wolff (1989), chapter 6, for more discussion.

11. The formal decomposition is as follows. Let

N = the occupation-by-industry employment matrix, where N_{ij} shows the total employment of occupation i in industry j

H = row vector showing total employment by industry, where $H_j = \Sigma_i N_{ij}$

h = row vector showing the distribution of employment among industries, where $h_j = H_j/\Sigma H_j$

S = row vector showing the average skill level by industry

$s = hS'$ = a scalar showing the overall average skill level of employed workers

where an apostrophe (') indicates the transpose of the vector. Since our data are for discrete time periods, the change in the average skill level is given by

(2.1) $$\Delta s = h\Delta S' + (\Delta h)S',$$

where $\Delta S = S^2 - S^1$, $\Delta h = h^2 - h^1$, and superscripts refer to time period. The results are based on average period weights, which provides an exact decomposition. The first term on the right-hand side of equation 2.1 measures the effect of changes in the occupational composition within industry, while the second term measures the effect of shifts in industry employment.

12. An alternative measure of R&D activity is the number of scientists and engineers engaged in R&D as a share of total employment. However, almost by construction, this variable will be correlated with the overall skill level of the workforce because of the high cognitive skills of scientists and engineers.

13. Two alternative indicators of information technology used here are (1) the sum of OCA and communications equipment (or OCACM) and (2) the sum of computers and peripheral equipment. The statistical results reported below are very similar for the three alternative measures, and I report only those for OCA. Furthermore, in the 1997 revision to the national accounts, the Bureau of Economic Analysis added software as a form of investment. As of May 2005, the software series has been extended backward in time to only 1987; as a result, my measure of OCA excludes software for consistency with the earlier data.

14. In previous work, I investigated the role of several other factors as well: (1) the share of employees working in large establishments, (2) the average size of establishments in an industry, (3) the concentration ratio of the industry, and (4) the ratio of the minimum wage to the average hourly wage. I found these factors not to be statistically significant. See Howell and Wolff (1992) for details.

15. I also considered two other institutional variables here. The first of these, the minimum wage in real terms, spiked upward from the 1950s to 1960s, where it peaked, came down slightly in the 1970s, and then dropped sharply in both the 1980s and the 1990s. The second, service employment

as a share of total employment, grew rather continuously over the period, from 48 percent in 1950 to 72 percent in 2000.

16. The period from 1950 to 1960 cannot be included in the regression analysis because information on R&D spending and unionization rates at the industry level are generally not available before 1960. Moreover, because of differences in the industry classification schemes of the underlying data sources, the original 64 industries are first aggregated to 45 industries. The government sector is then excluded because of a lack of data on OCA investment, resulting in 44 industries. Also, because of a major change in industrial classification in 1997 with the adoption of the NAICS in the United States, the 1990–2000 sample consists of only 32 industries (excluding the government sector).

17. The error terms are assumed to be independently distributed but may not be identically distributed. I use the White procedure for a heteroschedasticity-consistent covariance matrix in the estimation (see White 1980).

18. The industry-level regression results are broadly consistent with those reported in Wolff (1996b) for the all-industry sample, despite the use of some slightly different variables, as well as an extension of the time period covered back to 1960.

19. A similar regression in which the dependent variable is the change in mean years of schooling by industry also yields a negative coefficient on investment in OCA per worker, though the coefficient is significant at only the 10 percent level.

3

Wages and Skills

3.1 Introduction

In chapter 2, I discuss the ways in which major structural changes in the U.S. economy since 1950 have affected skill levels in the U.S. workplace. Four sources of structural change received special attention. First, employment has shifted from goods-producing industries to services. Second, since at least the 1970s, a rapid increase has occurred in investment in new information-based technologies. Third, this has been accompanied by substantial adjustments in operations and the organizational restructuring of firms. Fourth, concomitant with these changes, the country has witnessed increased competition from imports and greater orientation toward exports.

In this chapter, I examine the way in which these sources of structural change have affected wage movements in the U.S. economy. In so doing, I discuss the second major paradox of the book—namely, that while skill levels and educational achievements of the labor force have continued to rise since 1973, real wages have fallen. The trend is slightly different when we consider both direct wages and salaries and the fringe benefits provided by employers, which have increased slightly since 1973. However, even in this case, employee compensation exhibits a substantially smaller rise than the increase in skills and schooling levels after the early 1970s.

Generally following the same procedure as in chapter 2, I begin with a summary of some of the recent literature on wage changes in the U.S. economy (section 3.2). Section 3.3 then presents statistics on trends in the real wage and employee compensation. Alternative wage series are used, including average hourly earnings of nonsupervisory employees and the employment cost index. I compare trends in earnings with those of skills, schooling, and productivity.

Section 3.4 examines wage trends at the industry level, where wages have changed more in some industries than in others (particularly in the goods and service industries). Changes in overall wage levels result from both variations in wages at the industry level and shifts in employment across industries. The former is normally interpreted as deriving from advances in technology and the latter from shifting patterns of demand. If demand patterns switch toward higher-wage industries, then, ceteris paribus, average wage levels will rise. Likewise, if technological change is biased toward better-paid workers, then average wages will also increase. Section 3.4 provides a decomposition of changes in overall wages into these two components. The results indicate that, from 1950 to 2000, only a small part of the change in average wages was attributable to the shift in the composition of employment by industry, and almost all of the change was a result of variation in wages at the industry level.

What factors lead to changes in real wages? Section 3.5 investigates the role of technological advances and other issues in explaining changing employee compensation. Section 3.6 considers the relation (indeed, confusion) between high-tech and high-wage industries. Conclusions and a summary are presented in section 3.7.

The formal model is developed in section A.1 of the appendix to this chapter. In section A.2 of the appendix, multivariate regression analysis is employed to relate the change in wages to variations in average skill levels and human capital (as measured by educational attainment and mean years of experience) and to various measures of technological activity, including traditional measures of total factor productivity (TFP) growth, changes in computer intensity, and R&D intensity. Other factors are international trade, the shift of employment to services, and modifications in the minimum wage and union density. The regressions are performed at both the aggregate and the industry levels.

3.2 Review of Literature

In contrast to the literature on rising earnings inequality (see chapter 6), relatively little work has been done to explain the growth of average wages in the United States, particularly its slowdown since 1973. Levy and Murnane (1996a) point to skills as an important determinant of changes in earnings. One of their major findings is that employers are now screening employees more on actual skills already possessed rather than simply years of schooling or a college degree. Using two large sets of panel data (the first of high school graduates in 1972 and the second of high school graduates in 1980), they determined the relation between math and reading scores on standardized tests and the earnings of the high school graduates six years after graduating. Levy and Murnane found that the correlation between earnings and test scores was higher for the later panel than the earlier one and that, for the later graduates, high math test scores were, in particular, more highly correlated with wages. They identified several basic skills that were then more highly valued by employers: (1) the ability to read and perform mathematics at a ninth-grade level, (2) effective oral and written communication skills, (3) the ability to work effectively with workers from different social, racial, and ethnic backgrounds, and (4) computer skills. The policy message emanating from this study is that the content of education (that is, what the student actually learns)—not the number of years of schooling—is crucial to success in the labor market.

Some have identified technology as the main determinant of wage changes. Johnson and Stafford (1993) argue that the erosion of large returns from U.S. technological leadership has been the principal factor in explaining the stagnation of wages in the United States since 1973. Acs and Danziger (1993), using Current Population Survey (CPS) data from 1979 to 1989, report that average earnings declined among male workers. They attribute the decline mainly to increases in the returns to education and experience, which they interpret as deriving mainly from technological changes. They do not find any significant effect from shifts in industrial employment patterns on the basis of 13 broad industry groupings.

Another view is that the expansion of international trade after 1973 is a principal factor in wage stagnation. The prevailing argument derives from the Heckscher-Ohlin model of international trade (see chapter 7 for detailed discussion). As Leamer (1992) argues, increased capital formation among U.S. trading partners abroad has led toward factor price equalization—in particular, wage equalization across countries. Wage convergence can come about either through an increase in wages among the United States' trading partners or through a decline in U.S. wages. It is likely that the latter trend has dominated in the last three decades. Wood (1994) makes a similar argument.

However, Lawrence and Slaughter (1993) conclude that international trade has played almost no role in the slow growth of worker compensation since the 1970s, especially in relation to labor productivity growth. Instead, using aggregate time-series data for the U.S. business sector, they find that the stagnation of real wages in the United States (and its convergence with that of trading partners) was mainly a result of slow productivity growth in the non-traded goods sectors of the U.S. economy between 1979 and 1991. Indeed, worker compensation deflated by production prices (instead of the CPI) grew just as rapidly as worker productivity in this period.

Others have looked to institutional factors, such as unionization and the minimum wage. Freeman (1993) contends that the decline of unions in the U.S. economy and/or the decline in the real value of the minimum wage since the late 1960s removed the "safety net" supporting the wage level of unskilled workers, thereby allowing it to fall. Ferguson (1996), using three-digit industry-level data on unionization and aggregate time-series data on wages from 1978 to 1986, estimates that 18 percent of the increase in the gap between real wage growth and aggregate labor productivity growth can be ascribed to the decline in unionization and perhaps another 25 percent to the declining ability of unions to raise wages.

Gordon (1996) maintains that the change in these two factors was part of a broader range of institutional changes in the 1980s in which corporate mangers in the United States exerted increasing pressure on workers, partly in reaction to mounting international competition. Gordon further documents the declining real wages of U.S. workers and claims that the growing power of management and the concomitant decline in worker power were largely responsible for this trend. Reich (1998) takes issue with Gordon and reports that most of the increase in managerial labor occurred in the early part of the postwar period, when labor power was increasing.

3.2.1 Industry-Level Wages

A few articles have discussed the connection between technological change and wages in industry. Using CPS data for 1979 and 1989 segmented into 39 industries, Allen (2001) finds that returns to schooling are greater in industries that are intensive in R&D and high-tech capital and that wage differentials between industries are positively related to R&D intensity, intensity of usage of high-tech capital, capital vintage, the growth in TFP, and the growth of the capital-labor ratio. However, Bartel and Sicherman (1999), matching industry-level measures of technological activity to the National Longitudinal Survey of Youth between 1979 and 1993 and controlling for individual fixed effects, have found no evidence of a correlation between the industry wage premium and the industry rate of technology change.

Autor, Levy, and Murnane (2003), using representative data on job task requirements from 1960 to 1998, have found that computerization was associated with the declining relative industry demand for routine manual and cognitive tasks and increased relative demand for nonroutine cognitive tasks. They have determined that the sum of within-industry and within-occupation task changes emanating from computer usage explains 30–40 percent of the observed shift in relative demand favoring college over noncollege labor between 1970 and 1998.

Several researchers have looked at the effects of trade on industry-level wages. Freeman and Katz (1991) have found from regressing industry-level wages in industry imports and exports that the former had a depressing effect on wages while the latter had a positive impact. Davis (1992), using industry-level wage data from nine advanced countries and four middle-income countries, have found that the growth of the import share induced a large and statistically significant convergence toward the average structure of relative industry wages, while the growth in export share caused a smaller but statistically significant divergence. Gaston and Treffler (1994), using 1984 CPS data with worker characteristics matched with trade data, report that exports had a positive wage effect and imports a smaller negative wage effect, even after controlling for worker characteristics.

In their survey of sources of earnings inequality, Levy and Murnane (1992) have concluded that firm- and plant-specific effects are important sources of earnings differences among workers. Davis and Haltiwanger (1991), using data on U.S. manufacturing plants from 1963 to 1986, provide some evidence of this, particularly that one-half of the total wage variation among manufacturing workers is accounted for by differences in average wages among plants. Moreover, these plant-specific effects on wages are associated with factors such as plant size and age, industry, and capital intensity. Groshen (1991a) provides similar evidence—namely, that occupation and establishment alone explain more than 90 percent of the variation in the wages of blue-collar workers.

Dunne and Schmitz (1992), also using manufacturing plant data, estimate that workers at establishments classified as the most technology intensive earned 16 percent more than those at the least technology-intensive plants. Dunne, Foster, Haltiwanger, and Troske (2004), using more recent establishment data, have concluded that a substantial portion of the rising dispersion in wages is due to increases in wage differentials among establishments. The latter, in turn, are attributable to plant-level productivity differences and are correlated with both computer intensity and overall capital intensity.

Another factor considered in the literature is profitability. Using panel data for the manufacturing sector derived from the CPS from 1964 to 1985 and controlling for workers' characteristics, unionization, and fixed effects in industry, Blanchflower, Oswald, and Sanfey (1996) have concluded that an increase in an industry's profitability leads (after a lag) to increased average wages within the industry. They estimate that rent sharing alone may account for as much as one-quarter of earnings inequality among full-time workers.

3.3 Overall Earnings Trends

Figure 3.1 and table 3.1 display trends in both average wages and salaries and average employee compensation, defined as wages and salaries plus the fringe benefits provided by employers, from 1947 to 2003. I have used as wide an assortment of measures of labor compensation as possible from available data sources. Fortunately, the results are quite consistent among these alternative series. These include the Bureau of Labor Statistics (BLS) series on hourly wages and salaries of production and nonsupervisory workers in the total private sector and the employment cost index (ECI) for all workers in private industry; National Income and Product Account (NIPA) data on employee compensation for all workers, including those in the government; and Current Population Survey data on median and mean earnings for year-round, full-time workers. With regard to the NIPA data, I also include a portion of proprietors' income in my measure of total labor earnings and divide this total by the sum of employed and self-employed workers (persons engaged in production [PEP]). The reason for including only a portion of proprietors' income is that part of the income of self-employed workers

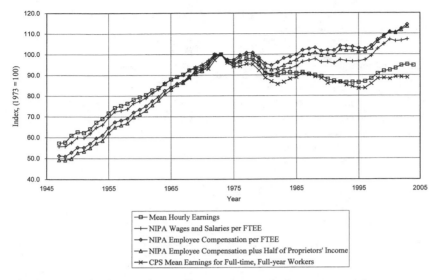

Figure 3.1   Real Labor Earnings Indices, 1947–2003 (Index, 1973 = 100)

is a return on the capital invested in unincorporated businesses. The results show that the resulting time series is quite insensitive to the fraction used in the calculation. Conversion of the wage series to constant dollars is based on the standard CPI-U deflator.[1]

The data show a very rapid growth in wages and salaries from 1947 to 1973 and then very slow growth or a moderate decline between 1973 and 2003. Before 1973, annual growth rates for wages and salaries range from 1.8 to 2.7 percent. Between 1973 and 2003, four of the seven series show a decline in real earnings, ranging from −0.2 to −0.6 percent per year, while the other three show either no change or a very modest increase (at most, 0.3 percent per year). All of the wage series show some pickup in wage growth (or at least a smaller decline) after 1989, compared to the 1973–1989 period.

The results are somewhat different for total employee compensation, which is the sum of wages and salaries and fringe benefits. As with real wages and salaries, all of the series show robust growth before 1973 (2.6–2.7 percent per year). Between 1973 and 2003, the data show a slight increase, from 0.3 to 0.4 percent per year. Here, too, the growth in compensation accelerated after 1989. A comparison of lines 3 and 12 in table 3.1 indicates the reason for the difference in time trends between wages and salaries and total employee compensation. While the former remained relatively flat after 1973, employee benefits grew very rapidly, at 1.4 percent per year.

3.3.1 Wages and Skills at the Aggregate Level

I now confront one of the most perplexing issues of recent years. According to standard human capital theory, wages should grow in tandem with

Table 3.1.   Annual Percentage Growth Rate of Real Labor Earnings per Worker, Selected Measures, 1947–2003

Earnings Measure	1947– 1973	1973– 1989	1989– 2003	1973– 2003
A. Wages and Salaries				
1. BLS mean hourly earnings	2.1	−0.7	0.4	−0.2
2. BLS mean weekly earnings	2.0	−1.3	0.3	−0.6
3. BLS ECI Wage and Salary Index		0.1[b]	0.5	0.3[a]
4. NIPA wages and salaries per FTEE	2.3	−0.2	0.8	0.2
5. NIPA wages and salaries plus half of proprietors' income per PEP	2.4	−0.4	1.1	0.3
6. CPS median earnings for year-round, full-time workers	2.4[c]	−0.4	0.0	−0.2
7. CPS mean earnings for year-round, full-time workers	2.5[d]	−0.8	0.0	−0.4
B. Total Employee Compensation				
8. NIPA employee compensation per FTEE	2.6	0.1	0.8	0.4
9. NIPA employee compensation plus half of proprietors' income per PEP	2.7	0.0	0.9	0.4
10. NIPA employee compensation plus three-fourths of proprietors' income per PEP	2.6	−0.1	1.0	0.4
11. BLS employment cost index (ECI)		−0.1[f]	0.8	0.3[e]
12. BLS ECI fringe benefit index		1.5[b]	1.4	1.5[a]
C. Labor Productivity				
13. GDP (2000 dollars) per FTEE	2.0	0.8	1.3	1.0
14. GDP (2000 dollars) per PEP	2.4	0.8	1.4	1.1

Note: See the data appendix for sources and methods.

Key:
  FTEE: Full-time equivalent employees
  PEP: Persons engaged in production

a. 1980–2003

b. 1980–1989

c. 1960–1973

d. 1967–1973

e. 1976–2003

f. 1976–1989

schooling and skills (see, for example, Mincer 1974). However, despite the continued growth in educational attainment and even the continued growth in workplace skills, real wages have fallen or generally stagnated since the early 1970s.

Figure 3.2 shows time trends for selected measures of schooling, skills, and employee compensation from 1947 to 2003. Median years of schooling among all those who were 25 years old and over grew from 9.0 years in 1947

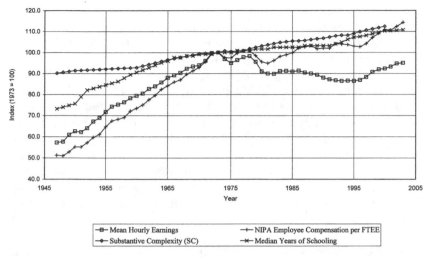

Figure 3.2   Real Labor Earnings, Skills, and Schooling, 1947–2003 (Index, 1973 = 100)

to 13.6 in 2003. Most of the gain occurred before 1973. Between 1947 and 1973, median education increased by 3.3 years and from 1973 to 2003 by another 1.3 years.

Trends are even more dramatic for the percentage of adults who completed high school and college (results not shown). The former grew from 33 percent of all adults in 1947 to 85 percent in 2003. Progress in high school completion rates was just as strong before and after 1973 (from 33 percent in 1947 to 60 percent in 1973 and then to 85 percent in 2003). The percentage of college graduates in the adult population soared from 5.4 percent in 1947 to 27.9 percent in 2003. In this dimension, progress was actually greater after 1973 than before. Between 1947 and 1973, the percentage of adults who had graduated from college rose by 7.2 percentage points, while between 1973 and 2003 it grew by 15.3 percentage points.

I next compare skill changes to earnings. The indices I used indicate no evidence of a slowdown in the growth of substantive complexity (SC) or interactive skills (IS) after 1973. The former index increased by 0.41 points between 1947 and 1973 and by 0.51 from 1973 to 2000, and the latter index by 0.22 and 0.25, respectively. On the other hand, the motor skills (MS) index rose by 0.03 in the earlier period and fell by 0.30 in the later one. The composite skill index gained 0.20 from 1947 to 1973 and 0.22 from 1973 to 2000.

Figure 3.2 illustrates that average earnings tracked both schooling and cognitive skills very closely from 1947 to 1973, but after 1973 the time paths deviated from each other. Between 1947 and 1973, BLS mean hourly earnings correlate almost perfectly with trends in both substantive complexity and the composite skill index (CP); median years of schooling; the percentage of high school graduates and the percentage of college graduates among those age 25 and over; and the mean years of schooling of the labor force. However, from 1973 to 1997, the reverse is true: Mean wages show an almost direct inverse correlation with both skill levels and educational levels, with correlation coefficients ranging from −0.84 to −0.94.

Like BLS hourly earnings, NIPA mean wages and salaries and NIPA mean employee compensation are almost perfectly correlated with skill levels and schooling levels from 1947 to 1973. Between 1973 and 2000, NIPA mean earnings have virtually zero correlation with both skill and schooling levels. Results for the post-1973 period are better for NIPA mean employee compensation. In this case, the correlation coefficients are positive, ranging from 0.57 to 0.61, though still smaller than the correlation coefficients for the pre-1973 period. In sum, for all three earnings measures, a significant break in the association of wages to both skills and schooling occurs in the early 1970s. These results suggest a growing bifurcation between wages and skills at least since the early 1970s.

Another apparent anomaly is the apparent breakdown in the historical connection between labor productivity growth and real wage growth after 1973. As I demonstrate in section A.1 of the appendix, under the assumptions of competitive input markets and constant returns to scale, wages and labor productivity should be perfectly correlated. From 1947 to 1973, real wages grew almost in tandem with the overall growth in labor productivity. The correlation coefficient between labor productivity and the three indices of real wages ranges from 0.99 to 1.00 for this period.

Labor productivity growth plummeted after 1973 (figure 3.3). Between 1947 and 1973, it averaged 2.0 or 2.4 percent per year, depending on the measure, while from 1973 to 2003 it averaged about 1.0 or 1.1 percent per year (section C of table 3.1). The years 1973 to 1979, in particular, witnessed the

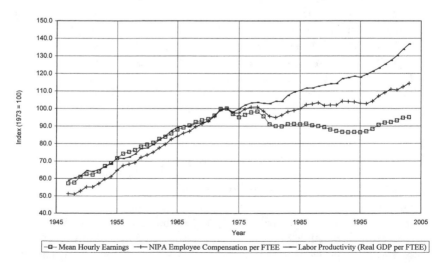

Figure 3.3   Real Labor Earnings and Productivity, 1947–2003 (Index, 1973 = 100)

slowest growth in labor productivity during the postwar period, 0.5 percent per year, and the growth in real wages actually turned negative during this time by all measures. After 1979, the U.S. economy experienced a modest reversal in labor productivity growth, which averaged 1.2 percent per year by both measures from 1979 to 2003, while real wage growth ranged from −0.2 to 0.6 percent per year, depending on the index. Consequently, from 1973 to 1997, the correlation coefficients between labor productivity and real earnings are substantially lower than in the early postwar period—highly negative in the case of hourly earnings, slightly positive in the case of NIPA mean wages and salaries, and a value of 0.76 in the case of average employee compensation. In appendix section A.2 of this chapter I return to the issue of how well wages have tracked labor productivity movements.

3.4 Industry Effects and Overall Wage Growth

Changes in average earnings are due to changes in both wages at the industry level and shifts of employment between low-wage and high-wage industries. In this section I discuss whether the stagnation of real wages that has occurred in the last two and a half decades is primarily attributable to across-the-board wage stagnation at the industry level or to the shift of workers from high-wage industries (such as durables manufacturing) to low-wage ones (such as retailing).

Table 3.2 shows average earnings by major sector in 1970 relative to the overall mean. By all three measures, agriculture had by far the lowest earnings (about half of the overall level), followed by retail trade (about three-fourths of the overall level), and other services (about 80 percent of the overall figure). The highest-paying sector by all three measures is utilities (30–43 percent above average), followed by mining, construction, durable manufacturing, transportation, and communications (the rank order of the five sectors varies a bit depending on the measure). Goods-producing industries pay about 10 percent above average, while services pay 7–8 percent below average.

The spread is even more extreme on the basis of data for individual industries. The ratio of average employee compensation to the overall average in 1970 ranged from lows of 0.25 in private households, 0.44 on farms, 0.62 in hotels, 0.66 in personal services, and 0.68 in retail trade to highs of 1.57 in transportation equipment (including automobiles), 1.63 among security and commodity brokers, 1.67 in air transportation, and 1.81 in petroleum and coal products.

Table 3.2 also shows the percentage increase of average earnings by major sector from 1950 to 2000. Here also is considerable variation. Employee compensation per full-time equivalent employee (FTEE) ranges from a paltry 20 percent in retail trade to 173 percent in communications. Between 1950 and 2000, earnings grew faster in goods industries overall than in services (about a 10 percentage point difference).[2]

Table 3.2. Mean Earnings by Major Industry in 1970 and the Percentage Change in Mean Earnings from 1950 to 2000

	Mean Earnings, 1970			Percentage Change, 1950–2000		
	NIPA Wages per FTEE	NIPA Comp per FTEE	NIPA Comp + Half PI per PEP	NIPA Wages per FTEE	NIPA Comp per FTEE	NIPA Comp + Half PI per PEP
Agriculture, forestry, and fishing	54	52	55	98	126	87
Mining	122	126	132	124	145	164
Construction	127	124	118	49	68	81
Durable manufacturing	115	117	120	80	104	105
Nondurable manufacturing	99	101	103	77	101	103
Transportation	121	122	122	44	67	66
Communications	113	125	129	153	173	187
Electric, gas, and sanitary services	130	135	143	126	154	187
Wholesale trade	119	116	118	65	85	80
Retail trade	76	74	74	9	20	27
Finance, insurance, and real estate	101	102	107	125	148	136
Other services	83	80	82	114	140	135
Government	103	104	107	81	124	125
Goods industries	110	112	110	78	120	113
Service industries	93	92	93	70	112	97
Total	100	100	100	68	91	98

Note: Earnings levels are normalized so that the overall wage level = 100 in 1970. See the data appendix for data sources and methods.

Key:

Wages: NIPA wages and salaries
Comp: NIPA total employee compensation
PI: Proprietors' income
FTEE: Full-time equivalent employees
PEP: Persons engaged in production

Goods-producing industries include (1) agriculture, (2) mining, (3) construction, (4) manufacturing, and (5) transportation, communications, and public utilities.

Service industries include (1) wholesale and retail trade, (2) finance, insurance, and real estate, (3) other services, and (4) government services.

Changes in the overall earnings level are a result of variations in both the wage levels of individual industries and employment shifts among industries. The former is usually interpreted to reflect advances in technology within the industry, as well as other industry-specific factors such as the presence of unions and exposure to competition from imports. The latter depend mainly on modifications in demand patterns among consumers.[3]

Table 3.3 shows the results of this decomposition.[4] For both the 1950s and the 1960s, more than 90 percent of the change in average earnings was due to changes in mean earnings within industry according to all three earnings measures. The employment shift effect, on the other hand, was minimal.

This is not to say that employment was not shifting among industries during these years. Three major changes occurred. First, employment shifted out of low-wage agriculture (a 1.4 percentage point decline in farm employment in the 1950s and a 1.6 percentage point decline in the 1960s). Second, there was an offsetting decline in employment share in high-paying manufacturing (a 2.35 percentage point drop for the entire sector in both the 1950s and the 1960s). Third, there were substantial gains in employment in the government sector, particularly state and local government, which paid close to average wages (a 2.8 percentage point increase in the 1950s for the entire government sector and a 1.9 percentage point increase in the 1960s). However, the employment shifts were, on net, offsetting (actually slightly positive with regard to the change in average earnings).

Four major changes took place after 1970. First, compensation gains at the industry level fell off sharply compared to the preceding two decades. Second, by 1970 employment in agriculture had fallen to 2.0 percent of total employment, so further declines in the agricultural share had a minimal effect on average earnings. Third, the decline in the share of total employment in high-wage manufacturing continued unabated after 1970 and indeed accelerated (the share dropped by 3.6 percentage points in the 1970s, 4.5 points in the 1980s, and 3.5 points in the 1990s). Fourth, government employment as a proportion of total employment actually peaked in 1970 and fell off thereafter.

As a result, the employment released from manufacturing was absorbed primarily in relatively low-paying service industries, and the employment shift effect turned negative in the 1970s, 1980s, and 1990s. Coupled with the smallest growth of earnings at the industry level of any of the five decades, this development led to the lowest increase in earnings—during the 1970s—of any of the five decades.

During the 1980s, earnings at the industry level grew considerably faster than in the 1970s, while the employment shift effect became even more negative. However, on net, average earnings increased faster during this decade than in the 1970s. During the 1990s, earnings growth at the industry level picked up substantially, and overall earnings growth strengthened despite the negative effect of intensified employment shifts.

Over the whole half century, the predominant effect on overall earnings growth came from the growth of earnings at the industry level. This was due

Table 3.3. Decomposition of the Change in Overall Employee Compensation per FTEE into an Industry Effect and an Employment Shift Effect, 1950–2000 (Earnings are in 2000 dollars)

	Decomposition			Percentage Decomposition		
Period	Actual Change in Average Overall Earnings	1st Effect Change in Earnings within Industry	2nd Effect Shifts in Employment among Industries	Total Change	1st Effect Change in Earnings within Industry	2nd Effect Shifts in Employment among Industries
1950–1960	6,695	6,504	190	100	97	3
1960–1970	7,135	6,978	157	100	98	2
1970–1980	981	1,353	−372	100	138	−38
1980–1990	2,365	3,266	−901	100	138	−38
1990–2000	3,647	6,710	−3,063	100	184	−84
1950–2000	20,823	22,697	−1,874	100	109	−9
1970–2000	6,993	11,329	−4,336	100	162	−62

Note: The decomposition is based on 65 industries (see endnote 3). See the data appendix for data sources and methods.

Key:

FTEE: Full-time equivalent employees

to the very large increases in industry earnings during the 1950s, 1960s, and 1990s. On net, the industry shift effect was negative but relatively small—resulting in a 9 percent decline in average employee compensation. These results accord with those of Bound and Johnson (1992) and Katz and Murphy (1992), who also found that the change in earnings at the industry level was the main determinant of overall earnings growth over similar periods. However, from 1970 to 2000, because there were no further gains in average wages from the release of labor from agriculture, employment shifts offset increases in industry earnings by a substantial 62 percent.

It is also instructive to contrast the pattern of earnings growth with that of substantive complexity (SC). Over the five decades from 1950 to 2000, the industry effect accounted for 57 percent and the employment shift effect for 43 percent of the overall growth of SC (table 2.8). In contrast, all (actually, more than 100 percent) of the growth in overall mean earnings was due to the industry effect (the increase in earnings within industry). The major reason for this difference is that, while the employment shift effect became negative after 1970, in the case of average earnings (employment shifted toward low-paying industries), it remained positive for the change in substantive complexity (employment continued to shift toward industries with high skills) and, in fact, generally increased in intensity between the 1950s and 1990s. These results again illustrate the growing disparities between earnings and skills.

3.5 Determinants of Wage Changes

I next investigate the factors that affect wage growth on both the aggregate and the industry level. The primary variables of interest are changes in average skill levels and human capital. What other factors, besides skills and human capital, affect the growth of real wages? I again turn to the same set of factors I used to analyze skill change in chapter 2. These include (1) technological change such as productivity growth and computerization, (2) international trade, (3) structural dimensions such as the split of employment between goods and service industries, and (4) institutional characteristics such as union density.

As I argued in chapter 2, the introduction of new technology appears to have two distinct stages. In the first, with the development of new technologies, the demand for skilled and educated workers is high, and, as a result, wages during this period should rise. In the second, the new technology becomes "routinized," and the demand for skilled workers lessens while the demand for unskilled and semi-skilled workers rises. Therefore, during the second period, average wages should fall (or their rate of increase diminish).[5]

If we accept this argument, then R&D activity, which is an indicator of the development of new technology, should be positively correlated with the growth in earnings. In this regard, the evidence is mixed. Industry R&D

Figure 3.4   Earnings and R&D Investment, 1947–2003 (Index, 1973 = 100)

expenditures as a share of GDP rose between the 1950s and the 1960s, fell off in the 1970s, increased once again in the 1980s, and then stabilized in the 1990s (figure 3.4). As a result, it is positively correlated with wage changes over time. However, the number of scientists and engineers engaged in R&D per employee rose almost continuously between the late 1950s and the 1990s, and this variable is negatively correlated with earnings changes.

With regard to investment, the prevailing view is the capital-skills complementarity hypothesis. This states that greater investment may lead to a greater demand for skilled and therefore highly paid labor since new capital normally embodies the latest and presumably more complex technology, which requires greater skills to put into operation (see, for example, Griliches 1969). Measures of investment are used to allow for the possibility that innovative technology will normally be embodied in new capital, particularly new equipment and machinery. The growth in the ratio of capital stock to employment may also reflect the rate at which new vintages of capital are introduced into the industry.

With regard to computerization investment, we can say that computers are like a two-edged sword. Their introduction can radically alter the workplace, requiring highly skilled computer technicians and engineers to implement the new technology and therefore be positively associated with earnings. However, once in place, computers tend to simplify tasks and thus increase the demand for low-skilled and lower-paid workers.

Here, again, the descriptive statistics yield mixed results. From the late 1940s to 2003, the net stock of total equipment per worker gradually trended upward (figure 3.5), and this variable is slightly negatively correlated with

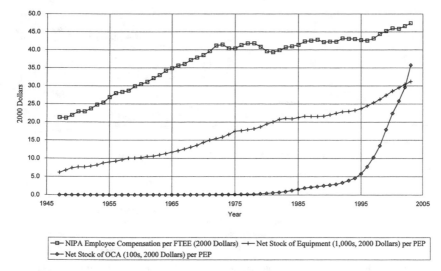

Figure 3.5   Earnings, Equipment Investment, and OCA Investment, 1947–2003

earnings changes.[6] In contrast, the net stock of office, computing, and accounting machinery (OCA) per worker, after rising slowly from the late 1940s
to the late 1970s, accelerated in the ensuing 30 years (figure 3.5). As a result,
this variable is highly negatively correlated with earnings growth.

As Leamer (1992), among others, argues, international competitiveness
may also affect earnings growth in two possible ways. One is that industries
competing in international product markets or directly against imports might
be forced to upgrade skills faster than domestic industries in order to remain
competitive (the high-road hypothesis). A second possibility is that such
industries might be forced to compete on the basis of cost and thus have an
incentive to replace highly paid workers with low-paid ones and downgrade
skill levels (the low-road hypothesis). As figure 3.6 shows, both export and
import intensity (the ratio of exports and imports to GDP), after rising very
slowly from 1947 to 1973, more than doubled between 1973 and 2003, at the
same time that earnings stagnated. As a result, the two series have a strong
negative correlation.

Structural and organizational dimensions of production may also affect
wage growth. As Freeman (1993), among others, argues, unionization may be
associated with earnings growth since unionized trades, firms, and industries
typically pay more than nonunionized ones. The unionization rate, after
peaking in 1953, has fallen steadily over time (figure 3.6) and has a strong
positive correlation with wage gains. The minimum wage should have a
positive effect on earnings growth since it raises wages at the bottom and
may, through an "accordion effect," increase wages through the bottom of
the occupational ladder (see, for example, Lee 1999 or Neumark, Schweitzer,

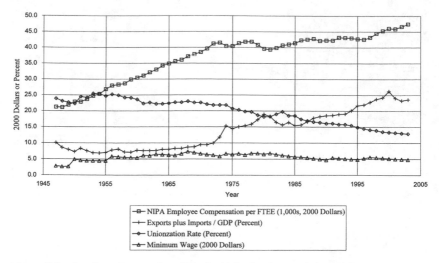

Figure 3.6   Earnings, International Trade, Unionization, and the Minimum Wage, 1947–2003

and Wascher 2004). As figure 3.6 illustrates, the minimum wage in constant dollars reached its peak value in 1968 and generally fell over time until the early 1990s before again rising slightly through 1997 and then once again diminishing. As a result, the minimum wage valued in constant dollars has a small negative correlation with earnings growth.

Since services generally pay less than goods producers, another factor that may affect average earnings is the shift of employment to services. This process has been in evidence almost continually since the 1940s. As a result, this variable has a relatively strong negative correlation with the growth in earnings.

3.6 High-Tech and High-Wage Industries

Another interesting question is whether high-tech industries are necessarily high skill or high wage. These terms often cause confusion, but the popular view is that they are synonymous. Thus, people often believe that, to increase wages, all that is necessary is to promote and expand the high-tech industries of a country.

I use several criteria to define high-tech industries: (1) the ratio of R&D expenditures to sales, (2) scientists and engineers engaged in R&D per employee, (3) total capital per worker, (4) the stock of equipment per worker, and (5) the stock of OCA equipment per worker. However, these criteria lead to different rankings of industries. According to the R&D investment measure, the primary high-tech industries in 1990 were industrial machinery (including computers), scientific instruments and related products, electrical and electronic equipment, chemicals, and motor vehicles and equipment.[7] If we use the stock of total equipment and machinery per employee as the indicator, then the most technologically advanced industries are utilities, telephone and telegraph (communications), petroleum and coal products, oil and gas extraction, and primary metal products. In contrast, banking, insurance, petroleum and coal products, auto services and repairs, and oil and gas extraction rank highest in OCA investment per employee.

In 1990, the most highly paid workers (in terms of average employee compensation) were employed in petroleum and coal products, followed by tobacco products, motor vehicles, chemicals, coal mining, and utilities. If we now rank sectors by educational attainment, the five highest, in order, are all service sectors—educational services, legal and professional services, banking, real estate, and broadcasting. Ranked in terms of the average level of substantive complexity, the top sectors are legal and professional services, insurance, radio and TV broadcasting, banking, and educational services.

Table 3.4 shows the correlation coefficients between the various indicators of the degree of technological sophistication of a sector in 1990 and its corresponding level of earnings, education, and skills. All three measures of mean earnings are positively correlated with all five indicators of technological sophistication. The correlation coefficients range from 0.29 to 0.65. Earnings are most strongly correlated with total equipment per worker, followed by total capital per worker, the number of scientists and engineers engaged in R&D per employee, OCA per worker, and the ratio of R&D expenditures to sales. In contrast, average years of schooling and average skill levels

Table 3.4.   Correlation Coefficients between the Technological Sophistication of a Sector and Its Mean Earnings, Educational Attainment, and Skill Level, 1990

Indicator	R&D/ Sales	SCIENG	Capital/ PEP	Equipment/ PEP	OCA/ PEP
1. Mean employee compensation per FTEE	0.31	0.42	0.54	0.65	0.37
2. Mean years of schooling	−0.01	−0.01	0.19	0.18	0.37
3. Mean Substantive Complexity (SC)	0.02	0.04	0.19	0.20	0.56
4. Mean Composite Skills (CP)	0.02	0.05	0.19	0.21	0.54

Note: Correlation coefficients are computed from 45 industries. Earnings data are from NIPA.

Key:
1. R&D/Sales: ratio of R&D expenditures to total industry net sales
2. SCIENG: scientists and engineers engaged in R&D per full-time equivalent employee
3. Capital/PEP: total capital stock per person engaged in production (PEP)
4. Equipment/PEP: stock of machinery and equipment per PEP
5. OCA/PEP: stock of office, computing, and accounting equipment per PEP

are only weakly correlated with R&D intensity, the number of scientists and engineers engaged in R&D per employee, total capital per worker, and total equipment per worker. However, schooling and skills, especially the latter, show a relatively strong correlation with OCA per worker.[8] Autor, Levy, and Murnane (2003) also report a positive correlation between cognitive skills and computerization.

These results provide some support for the argument that high-tech industries also pay quite well. However, this is true primarily if we define "high tech" in terms of the amount of equipment per worker (or total capital per worker). Correlations of earnings are weaker with OCA per worker and indicators of R&D intensity. Educational achievement and skills are virtually uncorrelated with these technological indicators, with the exception of OCA per workers. However, even the positive correlation of skills and wages with OCA is mainly due to the high values of these variables in the banking and insurance industries—industries that we do not normally consider high tech. Indeed, if we eliminate these two industries from the calculation, then the correlation of OCA per worker with mean years of schooling falls from 0.37 to 0.26 and from 0.56 to 0.41 with average cognitive skills.

3.7 Conclusion

One of the basic tenets of human capital theory is that increased schooling will cause, or at least be associated with, rising wages. However, this chapter begins by raising the seeming paradox that, while earnings and education did grow in tandem from the end of World War II to the early 1970s, this association appears to have ended after this point. After 1973, in fact, while earnings stagnated (or declined, in the case of BLS average hourly and weekly earnings), educational attainment continued to grow.

Annual time-series regressions of earnings growth on the change in (or growth rate of) educational achievement fail to produce a significant (or even a positive) coefficient. Pooled time-series, cross-industry regressions establish a small but positive effect of changes and growth in average educational attainment among workers within the industry on the change in average industry earnings, but the coefficients are still insignificant. A growth-accounting analysis indicates that changes in educational achievement are not quantitatively important in accounting for earnings changes.

Evidence that establishes a positive and significant connection between earnings growth and changes in worker skill levels is similar. As with educational attainment, cognitive and people skills continued to grow after 1973 at about the same pace as before 1973, while earnings either flattened or declined. As a result, both annual time-series regressions and pooled time-series, cross-industry regressions fail to establish any significant relation between gains in earnings and changes in skill levels. Moreover, as with schooling, skill changes did not prove quantitatively important in accounting for wage changes in the growth-accounting analysis.[9]

I have also shown theoretically that, in a competitive economy characterized by competitive input markets and constant returns to scale, earnings should rise at exactly the same rate as overall labor productivity. This was generally the case from 1947 to 1973, with correlations between earnings growth and labor productivity growth close to unity, but after 1973 correlations between the two are much lower (and, in some cases, negative). In annual time-series regressions over the full period from 1947 to 2000, TFP growth is a positive and highly significant (at the 1 percent level) determinant of earnings growth. In contrast, in the pooled time-series, cross-industry regressions, the coefficient of TFP growth is negative and significant at the 5 percent level. The latter result is not too surprising since low-productivity growth sectors (e.g., finance, insurance, real estate, and business services) enjoyed greater wage increases than high-productivity growth manufacturing industries in the postwar period. The result is also not inconsistent with the finding of Bartel and Sicherman (1999) that industry wage premia were not correlated with industry rates of technological change, though this result may conflict with the finding of Allen (2001) that industry wage differentials correlated with industry TFP growth.[10] Results of the growth-accounting exercise indicate that the slowdown of TFP growth after 1973 accounts for about 20 percent of the decline in wage growth between the two periods.

These results imply first of all that earnings in an industry are influenced primarily by economy-wide productivity growth, not that of the particular industry. A similar result was reported by Leslie (1985) on the basis of regression analysis of labor productivity growth in 20 two-digit manufacturing industries from 1948 to 1976. This makes sense since labor market forces tend to equalize wages across industries unless there are barriers, such as those imposed by unions, to cross-industry labor mobility.[11]

R&D investment is positively associated with earnings growth in both the time-series and pooled cross-industry regression analysis, but in neither case are the coefficients on R&D investment statistically significant.[12] In the growth-accounting exercise, R&D investment does not play an important role in the slowdown of wage growth beginning in the early 1970s because R&D intensity has remained relatively constant over time.

Another factor that might affect wage growth is investment activity. The prevailing view is the capital-skills complementarity hypothesis. This states that investment leads to greater demand for skilled labor since new capital embodies the latest technology, which requires greater skills to put into operation and thus highly paid workers. Results from both the annual time-series and the cross-industry regressions indicate that investment in total capital (excluding OCA) creates positive effects on wage growth. Its coefficient is not significant in the time-series regressions but is highly significant in the pooled cross-industry regressions. These results are also roughly

consistent with the regression results reported in chapter 2 (i.e., that investment in equipment, excluding OCA per worker, has a positive but insignificant association with the growth in both cognitive skills and the composite
skill index). Davis and Haltiwanger (1991) also found that plant-level wages
were positively associated with capital intensity. In the growth-accounting
exercise, the slowdown in growth of total capital less OCA per worker after
1973 accounts for about 20 percent of the decline in wage growth.

An additional factor is computerization, which, I maintain, may have two
contradictory effects. The first is that the introduction of computers can radically alter the workplace, requiring highly skilled computer experts and engineers to implement the new technology. The second is that, once in place,
computers tend to simplify tasks and thus increase the demand for low-
skilled and lower-paid workers. The regression results on both the annual
time-series data and the pooled cross-industry data provide strong support
for the second hypothesis, that computerization depresses wage growth. This
finding is consistent with the regression results reported in chapter 2 (i.e.,
that the growth in OCA per worker has a negative and significant effect on the
growth in cognitive and composite skills). These results appear to contrast
with the findings of Allen (2001), who states that industry wage premia correlate with the use of high-tech capital, and with those of Dunne and Schmitz
(1992), who report that workers earned more at more technology-intensive
plants. The same results also contrast with those of Dunne et al. (2000), who
observe that plant-level wages are positively associated with computer intensity. However, these latter studies investigated the relationship between
wage *levels* and IT. In the growth-accounting analysis, the speed-up in the
growth of OCA per worker after 1973 accounted for about 15 percent of the
slowdown in earnings growth.

I also contend that international trade may have two opposing effects. One
is the high-road hypothesis that industries competing in international product markets or directly against imports might be forced to upgrade skills in
order to remain competitive. The other is the low-road hypothesis that such
industries might have to compete on the basis of cost and thus have an incentive to replace highly paid workers with low-paid ones. The time-series
regression results indicate that the growth in exports has a decidedly negative and significant association with earnings growth, while the results of
the pooled cross-industry regressions find a negative but insignificant relation between export growth and earnings growth. In contrast, in chapter 2
I report that the change in export intensity has a positive association with
the change in cognitive skills as well as the composite skill index, although
the effect is not statistically significant. My results appear to conflict with
the findings of Freeman and Katz (1991) and Gaston and Treffler (1994), who
state that exports had a positive effect on industry wages. In their time-series
analysis, Lawrence and Slaughter (1993), on the other hand, found no effect
of international trade on worker compensation after 1970.

With regard to the change in import intensity, the time-series regressions indicate a negative association with earnings growth, while the pooled cross-industry analysis shows a positive association, but in neither case are the coefficients significant. In comparison, in chapter 2 the change in the ratio of imports to sales was found to have a positive but not statistically significant effect on changes in cognitive skills and in the composite skill index. Both Freeman and Katz (1991) and Gaston and Treffler (1994) find that imports have a negative (but small, in the case of the latter) effect on industry wages.

The decline in unionization also plays a major role in explaining wage stagnation in the United States. In the time-series regressions, the coefficient of unionization is positive and generally significant, whereas in the pooled cross-industry regressions, its coefficient is again positive but not significant. In the growth-accounting analysis, unionization is found to have the largest effect on earnings growth, and the decline in unionization explains about one-third of the decline in wage growth after 1973. This result is as strong as those reported by Freeman (1993), Ferguson (1996), and Gordon (1996).

The aggregate time-series results provide some, though relatively weak, evidence to support the view that the falling minimum wage in the United States has contributed to wage stagnation. Quantitatively, the shrinking minimum wage plays only a small role in the decline in wage growth after 1973.

The final factor is interindustry employment shifts. Over the entire postwar period, employment has generally shifted out of high-paying, goods-producing industries into low-paying services. During the 1950s and 1960s, this negative effect of employment shifts on average earnings was offset by the reduction of jobs in low-paying agriculture, resulting in a minimal net effect. However, between 1970 and 2000, further reduction of employment in agriculture was limited, so the net effect of employment shifts was substantially negative, offsetting increases in industry earnings. Over the full five decades from 1950 to 2000, the "industry effect" is virtually zero.

What, then, is responsible for the stagnation of labor earnings after 1973? The major factor appears to be the decline in unionization. The second most important is the decline in the growth of total capital less OCA per worker between the two periods; the third is the slowdown in TFP growth, which fell by about two-thirds between the studied periods: 1947–1973 and 1973–2000. Fourth in importance is the acceleration in the growth of OCA per employee, which almost doubled from one period to the other.

A final word should be said about IT and other forms of high-tech investment. As the results of section 3.6 indicate, while the correlation between various forms of high-tech investment and earnings is positive, it tends to be rather small. Moreover, as the econometric results demonstrate, computerization has had a largely negative effect on earnings. Thus, like investment in education, high-tech investment is unlikely to be a panacea for earnings stagnation.

Appendix

A.1   Modeling Framework

Following Stiroh (2002), I begin with a standard neoclassical production function f_j for sector j:

(3.1) $$X_j = Z_j f_j(KC_j, KO_j, LAB_j, RD_j),$$

where X_j is the gross output of sector j, KC_j is the input of IT-related capital, KO_j is the input of other capital goods, LAB_j is the total labor input, RD_j is the stock of R&D capital, and Z_j is a Hicks-neutral TFP index that shifts the production function of sector j over time.[13] For convenience, I have suppressed the time subscript. Moreover, capacity utilization and adjustment costs are ignored. It then follows that

(3.2) $$d \ln X_j = d \ln Z_j + \epsilon_{Cj} d \ln KC_j + \epsilon_{Oj} d \ln KO_j + \epsilon_{Lj} d \ln LAB_j$$
$$+ \epsilon_{Rj} d \ln RD_j,$$

where ϵ represents the output elasticity of each input and $d \ln Z_j$ is the rate of Hicks-neutral TFP growth. If we now impose the assumption of competitive input markets and constant returns to scale, it follows that an input's factor share (α_j) will equal its output elasticity. Let us now employ the standard measure of TFP growth π_j for sector j:

(3.3) $$\pi_j \equiv d \ln X_j/dt - \alpha_{Cj} d \ln KC_j/dt - \alpha_{Oj} d \ln KO_j/dt$$
$$- \alpha_{Lj} d \ln LAB_j/dt - \alpha_{Lj} d \ln L_j/dt.$$

It then follows that

(3.4) $$\pi_j = d \ln Z_j/dt + \alpha_{Rj} d \ln RD_j/dt.$$

Let us now define labor productivity growth as

(3.5) $$LP_j \equiv d \ln X_j/dt - d \ln L_j/dt.$$

If we again impose the assumption of competitive input markets and constant returns to scale, it follows that

(3.6) $$LP_j = d \ln Z_j/dt + \alpha_{Cj} d \ln kc_j/dt + \alpha_{Oj} d \ln ko_j/dt + \alpha_{Rj} d \ln RD_j/dt,$$

where lowercase symbols indicate the amount of input per worker. I next include the change in average worker skills in the production function. There are two possible approaches. First, let the effective or quality-adjusted labor input in sector j be given by $Q_j = LAB_j\ S_j$, where S measures average worker skills in sector j. Then equation 3.1 can be rewritten as

(3.7) $$X_j = Z_j\ f_j^*(KC_j, KO_j, Q_j, RD_j).$$

Again assuming competitive input markets and constant returns to scale (to the traditional factors of production) and still using equation 3.6 to define labor productivity growth, we obtain

(3.8) $LP_j = d \ln Z_j/dt + \alpha_{Cj}\ d \ln kc_j/dt + \alpha_{Oj}\ d \ln ko_j/dt + \alpha_{Lj}\ d \ln S_j/dt$
$\qquad + \alpha_{Rj}\ d \ln RD_j/dt.$

In this formulation, the rate of labor productivity growth should increase directly with the *rate of growth* of average worker quality or skills.

The second approach derives from the standard human capital earnings function. From Mincer (1974),

$$\ln w = a_0 + a_1 S,$$

where w is the wage, S is the worker's level of schooling (or skills), and a_0 and a_1 are constants. It follows that

$$(d \ln w)/dt = a_1(dS/dt).$$

By definition, the wage share in sector j is $\alpha_{Lj} = w_j\ LAB_j/X_j$. Under the assumptions of competitive input markets and constant returns to scale, $\alpha_{Lj} = \epsilon_{Lj}$, a constant. Therefore, $X_j/LAB_j = w_j/\epsilon_{Lj}$. In this case, effective labor input Q is given by the equation $Ln\ Q = S + \ln LAB$. It follows from equation 3.6 that

(3.9) $LP_j = d \ln Z_j/dt + \alpha_{Cj}\ d \ln kc_j/dt + \alpha_{Oj}\ d \ln ko_j/dt + \alpha_{Lj}\ dS_j/dt$
$\qquad + \alpha_{Rj}\ d \ln RD_j/dt.$

In other words, the rate of labor productivity growth should be proportional to the *change in the level* of average worker quality or skills over the period.

Finally, under the assumptions of competitive input markets and constant returns to scale,

$$w_j = \partial X_j/\partial LAB_j = \alpha_{Lj}\ X_j/LAB_j,$$

where w_j is the average wage in sector j. As a result, from equations 3.8 and 3.9, there are two alternative forms for estimating the wage growth equations:

(3.8′) $d \ln w_j/dt = d \ln Z_j/dt + \alpha_{Cj}\ d \ln kc_j/dt + \alpha_{Oj}\ d \ln ko_j/dt$
$\qquad + \alpha_{Lj}\ d \ln S_j/dt + \alpha_{Rj}\ d \ln RD_j/dt$

and

(3.9′) $d \ln w_j/dt = d \ln Z_j/dt + \alpha_{Cj} \, d \ln k_{Cj}/dt + \alpha_{Oj} \, d \ln ko_j/dt$
$$+ \alpha_{Lj} \, dS_j/dt + \alpha_{Rj} \, d \ln RD_j/dt.$$

A.2 Regression Analysis

A.2.1 Aggregate Time-Series Regression Analysis

I next turn to regression analysis, which is conducted in two ways. The first uses annual time-series data for wage changes and other variables of interest. The second employs pooled cross-section, time-series data covering 44 industries in three time periods (1960–1970, 1970–1980, and 1980–1990) and 32 industries from 1990 to 2000 (see the data appendix). The dependent variable in the first set of regressions is the annual growth in real compensation per employee (FTEE).[14] On the basis of equations 3.8′ and 3.9′, the estimation form is given by

(3.10) $\text{EARNGRT}_t = \beta_0 + \beta_1 \, \text{TFPGRT}_t + \beta_2 \, \text{RDGDP}_t + \beta_3 \, \text{CAPXOCAGRT}_t$
$$+ \beta_4 \, \text{OCAGRT}_t + \beta_5 \, \text{CHEXPGDP}_t + \beta_6 \, \text{CHIMPGDP}_t$$
$$+ \beta_7 \, \text{UNION}_t + \beta_8 \, \text{CHMINWAGE}_t + \beta_9 \, \text{CHSERVTOT}_t$$
$$+ \beta_{10} \, \text{SKILLCHG}_t + u_t,$$

where EARNGRT_t is the annual growth of real labor earnings in year t, TFPGRT_t is TFP growth in year t, RDGDP_t is the ratio of R&D expenditures to GDP in year t, CAPXOCAGRT_t is the growth in total net capital less OCA in year t, OCAGRT_t is the growth of the net stock of OCA, CHEXPGDP_t is the change in the ratio of exports to GDP in year t, CHIMPGDP_t is the change in the ratio of imports to GDP in year t, UNION_t is the unionization rate in year t, CHMINWAGE_t is the change in the minimum wage (in constant dollars) in year t, CHSERVTOT_t is the change in the ratio of service to total employment in year t, SKILLCHG_t is a measure of skill change, and u_t is a stochastic error term.

Several modifications to 3.8′ and 3.9′ have been made. First, I have included RDGDP, the ratio of R&D expenditures to GDP, instead of the growth rate of the stock of R&D capital, since the former is directly measurable.[15] Second, I have added the change in both export and import intensity. The argument is that, if export or import competition raises or depresses wages, then the growth of wages should correlate with the change in export or import intensity. Third, I have added UNION, the unionization rate. Since unions typically negotiate contracts involving wage increases, the argument here is that the growth of wages should be positively associated with the degree of unionization (not its change over time).[16]

Fourth, I have included CHMINWAGE, the change in the minimum wage. If the level of the minimum wage affects the wages of the lowest-paid workers and hence average earnings, then the change in average wages should be positively associated with the change in the minimum wage (in constant dollars). This can be seen by a modification of equation 3.10:

$$\Delta \bar{e} = p_{low} \Delta w_{low} + \Delta(1 - p_{low}) w_{high},$$

where the subscript "low" refers to low-wage workers and the subscript "high" refers to other workers. Insofar as the wages of low-wage workers rise with an increase in the minimum wage, either by raising the wages of workers at or near the minimum wage or by increasing the wages of all low-wage workers through an accordion effect, the average wage will likewise rise.

Finally, I have also included CHSERVTOT, the change in service employment as a share of total employment. As I suggested earlier, since services generally pay less than goods producers, the average wage should depend on the share of service employment, and wage growth should be negatively associated with the change in the share of service workers. This can also be seen by a modification of equation 3.10:

$$\Delta \bar{e} = p_{serv} \Delta w_{serv} + \Delta(1 - p_{serv}) w_{goods},$$

where the subscript "serv" refers to service workers and the subscript "goods" refers to workers employed in goods-producing industries. The change in the average wage should be negatively correlated with the change in the share of service workers in total employment.[17]

From 3.8' and 3.9' I use six different specifications to measure the change in worker skills. The first is the annual growth in the three direct indices of worker skills: SC, IS, and MS; the second is the annual growth of the composite skill score, CP; the third is the annual *change* in SC, IS, and MS; and the fourth is the annual change of CP. For the schooling equation, I rely on the extended human capital earnings function, which includes both years of schooling and years of experience (see Mincer 1974).[18] The fifth estimation form includes terms for both the annual growth of mean years of schooling and the growth in mean years of experience. The sixth includes terms for the annual *changes* in mean schooling, mean experience, and the square of mean experience.

Appendix table 3.1 shows results from 1953 to 2000. The series begins in 1953 because that is the first year for which R&D data are available. The coefficient of TFP growth has the predicted positive sign and is highly significant (at the 1 percent level) in all five specifications. The coefficient of R&D intensity is positive, as predicted, but not significant.[19] The growth in total capital less OCA also has the predicted positive coefficient but is not significant. On the other hand, the coefficient of the growth in OCA per worker is *negative* and significant at the 5 percent level in three of the five specifications.[20]

Appendix 3.1. Time-Series Regressions of the Annual Growth in Real Employee Compensation per FTEE on Technology and Other Variables, 1953–2000

Independent Variables	Specification				
	(1)	(2)	(3)	(4)	(5)
Constant	−0.020	−0.023	−0.026	−0.022	−0.017
	(0.99)	(0.81)	(1.21)	(1.13)	(0.83)
Annual TFP growth	0.555 **	0.540 **	0.551 **	0.523 **	0.497 **
	(3.91)	(3.53)	(3.87)	(3.68)	(3.37)
Ratio of R&D expenditures to GDP	0.309	0.675	0.701	0.422	0.463
	(0.47)	(0.77)	(0.87)	(0.64)	(0.70)
Growth in total capital less OCA per worker	0.188	0.264	0.265	0.257	0.307
	(1.08)	(1.30)	(1.35)	(1.43)	(1.60)
Growth in OCA per worker	−0.051 *	−0.037	−0.037	−0.049 *	−0.053 *
	(2.37)	(1.30)	(1.40)	(2.28)	(2.38)
Change in the ratio of exports to GDP	−0.748 *	−0.687 #	−0.689 #	−0.822 *	−0.889 *
	(2.01)	(1.75)	(1.81)	(2.21)	(2.31)
Change in the ratio of imports to GDP	−0.185	−0.256	−0.254	−0.067	−0.036
	(0.40)	(0.53)	(0.54)	(0.14)	(0.08)
Unionization rate	0.157 *	0.150	0.159 *	0.175 *	0.151 #
	(2.37)	(1.61)	(2.39)	(2.62)	(2.01)
Change in minimum wage in constant dollars	0.0064	0.0078	0.0078 #	0.0072 #	0.0077 #
	(1.47)	(1.58)	(1.68)	(1.66)	(1.74)

	(1)	(2)	(3)	(4)	(5)
Change in the ratio of service to total employment	−0.498 (0.82)	−0.848 (1.13)	−0.816 (1.15)	−0.764 (1.21)	−0.880 (1.34)
Annual change in Substantive Complexity (SC)		−0.194 (0.67)			
Annual change in Interactive Skills (IS)		0.029 (0.08)			
Annual change in Motor Skills (MS)		0.053 (0.05)			
Annual change in Composite Skill index (CP)			−0.353 (0.86)		
Annual change in mean years of schooling				−0.032 (1.34)	−0.034 (1.39)
Annual change in mean years of experience					−0.009 (0.76)
R^2	0.78	0.79	0.79	0.79	0.80
Adjusted R^2	0.73	0.71	0.72	0.73	0.73
Standard error	0.0098	0.0102	0.0099	0.0097	0.0098
Durbin-Watson	1.67	1.77	1.73	1.66	1.65
Sample size	48	48	48	48	48

Note: The sample is based on time-series data from 1953 to 2000. The t-value is shown below the coefficient. See the data appendix for sources and methods. TFP growth is measured using net capital stock and Persons Engaged in Production (PEP).

Significance levels: # 10% level; * 5% level; ** 1% level.

99

The coefficients of the change in both export and import intensity are negative. They are significant in the case of the change in export intensity (at the 5 or 10 percent level) but are not statistically significant in the case of the change in import intensity. The coefficient of the unionization rate has the predicted positive sign and is significant in four of the five cases (at the 5 or 10 percent level). The coefficient of the change in the minimum wage in constant dollars has the predicted positive sign and is significant at the 10 percent level in three of the five cases. The coefficient of the change in the share of service employment in total employment has the predicted negative sign but is not significant.

The adjusted R^2 statistic ranges from 0.71 to 0.73, indicating a good fit for a growth equation. The Durbin-Watson statistic falls within the acceptable range.[21] Other time-series variables were also included in the regressions, including female workers as a share of total employment, black and Hispanic workers as a share of total workers, and part-time workers as a share of total employment. None of these variables proved significant.

When I add the skill-change variables to the regression (specifications 2 and 3), the most salient result is that none of them is statistically significant. In fact, the coefficients of both the change in and the growth of substantive complexity and the composite skill score are negative. The coefficient of the change in SC remains negative even when the change in the two other skill measures are omitted from the equation and when TFP growth, capital growth, and OCA growth are omitted from the regression equation.

When the standard human capital variables are included (specifications 4 and 5), the most salient result is that the coefficients of the change in both mean education and mean experience are not statistically significant and are, in fact, negative. This result also holds up when TFP growth, capital growth, and OCA growth are omitted from the regression equation.[22]

When either the skill or human capital variable is included, the coefficients of the other variables and their significance levels remain generally unchanged. The major exception is that the coefficient of the growth of OCA per worker, while remaining negative, becomes insignificant when the skill variables are added, although it remains significant when the human capital variables are included.

Because of the sharp break that occurs after 1973 in all of the wage series, I have also replicated the regressions in appendix tables 1 through 3, with the inclusion of a dummy variable for the years 1973 to 2000. When this is done, the coefficient on the dummy variable is found to be negative in every case but not significant (results not shown). The coefficient estimates and significance levels of the other variables remain largely unchanged. One implication of the results of these new regressions is that the factors that account for wage changes in the "peculiar" 1973–2000 period are by and large very much the same as those that explain wage changes during the whole postwar period.

To gauge the quantitative importance of the various factors in explaining earnings growth, I next develop a decomposition of earnings growth by component (results not shown). By far the largest positive contribution to earnings growth is made by the unionization rate (about 3.1 percentage points), followed by R&D intensity (between 0.8 and 1.3 percentage points),[23] TFP growth (about 0.5 percentage points), and the growth in the total stock of capital less OCA (about 0.4 percentage points). The growth in OCA per worker produces the highest negative effect of earnings growth (between 0.6 and 0.8 percentage points), followed by the change in the share of service workers in total employment (0.4 percentage points). The change in average SC and the change in mean years of schooling both have fairly strong negative effects on earnings growth as well (0.4 and 0.3 percentage points, respectively). The other variables—the change in both export and import intensity, the change in the minimum wage, and the change in mean years of experience—all have minor effects on wage growth.

Between the 1953–1973 and the 1974–2000 periods, the annual growth of mean employee compensation fell from 2.7 percent to 0.4 percent. The most important factor is the decline in the unionization rate, which fell from an average of 23.3 percent between 1953 and 1973 to 17.6 percent between 1974 and 2000 and explains about one-third of the slowdown in wage growth. The second most important factor is the decline in the growth rate of the stock of total capital less OCA per worker, which plummeted from 2.2 percent per year in the first period to 0.5 percent per year in the second and explains about 20 percent of the slowdown. The third is the steep drop in TFP growth, from 1.5 to 0.6 percent per year, which accounts for 18–20 percent of the falloff in real wage growth. Fourth in importance is the acceleration in the growth of OCA per worker, from 11.1 to 19.9 percent per year, which explains 12–19 percent of the earnings slowdown. The contributions of the other factors, including the unexplained residual, are quite small.

A.2.2 Pooled-Industry Time-Series Regressions

I next turn to multivariate regressions at the industry level, covering 44 industries in the three time periods (1960–1970, 1970–1980, and 1980–1990) and 32 industries from 1990 to 2000.[24]

With regard to interpreting the regression results, part of the growth in earnings is due to earnings changes at the industry level, and the remaining part to intersectoral shifts in employment. Some factors (e.g., import competition) exercise their influence by causing some industries to grow and others to shrink. The effect of such a factor may therefore be seen in the aggregate time-series data regressions but not in the industry-level analysis. The results of other factors are seen only at the industry level since they are associated with industry wage differentials. Still, for other variables, we find that the coefficient signs may actually "flip," if cross-industry effects differ from time-trend effects. The interpretation of the regression results will thus depend on the findings at the two levels of analysis. However, with the exception of only one variable (TFP growth), the results are remarkably consistent between the two sets of regressions.

It is also the case that wage changes at the industry level in a given period reflect changes in both overall wages and industry-specific effects. In principle, with labor mobility across sectors, labor market forces should make wage levels that are conditional on human capital or skills equal across industries at a given time and should equalize wage changes across sectors in a given time period. However, because of efficiency wage factors or other industry-specific effects, wage levels, in general, differ across industries even after controlling for human capital or skill differences, as do wage changes.[25]

I generally use the same set of independent variables for the industry-level regressions as for the aggregate ones (see equation 3.10). The exceptions are CHMINWAGE and CHSERVTOT, which are aggregate-level variables. Moreover, I do not include time-period dummy variables since-time period effects are already captured, in part, by differences in TFP growth over time.

Appendix table 3.2 shows the results for employee compensation per FTEE.[26] Here, the results are quite similar to the aggregate wage regressions shown in appendix table 3.1 with a couple of exceptions. The coefficient of TFP growth is now negative and significant at the 5 percent level. In contrast, its coefficient is positive and significant at the 1 percent level in the aggregate regressions. The difference is understandable since aggregate wages tend to rise with aggregate productivity, whereas wages at the industry level tend to equalize across industries. The equalization of wages across industries with different rates of productivity growth can also be directly derived from the "unbalanced growth model" (see Baumol, Blackman, and Wolff 1989, chapter 6, for more discussion). In fact, here the coefficient on industry TFP growth is negative, which reflects the fact that the slowest wage growth has occurred in high-productivity growth industries (e.g., manufacturing), and the highest wage growth has been found in high-end services (e.g., finance and business services) that have experienced very low productivity growth.

The coefficient of R&D intensity remains positive and insignificant. The coefficient of the growth in total capital less OCA per worker remains positive but is now highly significant (at the 1 percent level). Likewise, the coefficient of the growth of OCA per worker stays negative and significant (at the 5 percent level). The coefficient of the change in the ratio of exports to total sales remains negative but is no longer significant. The coefficient of the change in the ratio of imports to total sales is now positive but, as before, not significant. The coefficient of the unionization rate remains positive but is no longer insignificant. The coefficients of the change in both substantive complexity and mean education are now positive but still insignificant.[27]

Appendix 3.2. Regressions of the Annual Growth of Mean Compensation per FTEE Using Pooled-Industry, Time-Series Data for 1960–2000

Independent	Specification		
Variables	(1)	(2)	(3)
Constant	0.011	0.011	0.011
	(5.93)	(5.74)	(4.88)
Annual TFP growth	−0.078 *	−0.078 *	−0.077 *
	(2.48)	(2.46)	(2.44)
Ratio of R&D expenditures	0.012	0.012	0.017
to sales	(0.33)	(0.33)	(0.45)
Growth in total capital less	0.170 **	0.169 **	0.169 **
OCA per worker	(4.34)	(4.23)	(4.30)
Growth in OCA per worker	−0.021 *	−0.021 *	−0.022 *
	(2.17)	(2.13)	(2.22)
Change in the ratio of exports	−0.009	−0.009	−0.016
to sales	(0.19)	(0.19)	(0.33)
Change in the ratio of imports	0.007	0.007	0.007
to sales	(0.69)	(0.66)	(0.72)
Unionization rate	0.394	0.396	0.338
	(0.84)	(0.85)	(0.71)
Change in substantive		0.068	
Complexity (SC)		(0.22)	
Change in mean years			0.160
of schooling			(0.73)
R^2	0.17	0.17	0.17
Adjusted R^2	0.13	0.13	0.13
Standard error	0.0107	0.0107	0.0107
Sample size	164	164	164

Note: The sample consists of pooled cross-section, time-series data, with observations on each of the 44 industries in 1960–1970, 1970–1980 and 1980–1990 (sector 45, public administration, is excluded because of a lack of appropriate capital stock data) and 32 industries in 1990–2000. The coefficients are estimated using the White procedure for a heteroschedasticity-consistent covariance matrix. The absolute value of the t-statistic is shown in parentheses below the coefficient estimate. See the data appendix for sources and methods. The dependent variable is the annual growth of sectoral real employee compensation per FTEE. TFP growth is measured using net capital and FTEE. Mean schooling and skills are computed for the employees in each sector.

Significance levels: * significant at the 5% level; ** significant at the 1% level.

Notes

1. The CPI has recently been criticized for overstating the rate of inflation. While this may be true, it is not clear that the degree of bias in the CPI has risen in recent years. As a result, the sharp break in the wage series before and after 1973 would likely still remain even if the bias in the CPI were corrected. The CPS data are deflated to constant dollars using the new CPI-U-RS price index. The CPI-U-RS series makes quality adjustments for housing units and consumer durables such as automobiles and personal computers and employs a geometric mean formula to account for consumer substitution within CPI item categories. However, the adjustments in the CPI-U-RS deflator are made only from 1978 to the present, and the CPI-U index is used for the years prior to 1978.

2. It might seem paradoxical that average employee compensation increased faster in both the goods-producing sector (120 percent) and services (112 percent) than overall (91 percent). The reason is that the change in overall earnings depends on both changes in earnings in each sector and the shift of employment among sectors. In this case, employment shifted out of high-wage goods producers to the low-wage services, which had a negative effect on the variation in the overall wage level.

3. The formal decomposition is as follows. Let

   u_j = share of workers in industry j
   w_j = average earnings in industry j
   $\bar{e} = \Sigma u_j w_j$ = overall average earnings of employees.

   Since our data are for discrete time periods, then

   $$\Delta \bar{e} = \Sigma u_j \Delta w_j + \Sigma (\Delta u_j) w_j,$$

   where $\Delta w = w^2 - w^1$, $\Delta u = u^2 - u^1$, and superscripts refer to time period. The results are based on average period weights, providing an exact decomposition. The first term on the right-hand side of equation 1 measures the effect of changes in the wage levels within industry, while the second term measures the effect of shifts in industry employment.

4. Results are very similar for the three earnings measures; thus I show results here only for employee compensation per FTEE.

5. This argument is also consistent with product life cycle models. See Vernon (1966, 1979), for example.

6. In November 1999, the U.S. Bureau of Economic Analysis (BEA) released a major revision of the U.S. national accounts. One major element of the revision is the treatment of software expenses as a capital good rather than as an intermediate purchase. However, as of June 2005, the revised capital stock data are available only back to 1987. For consistency with the earlier data, the figures on total equipment and OCA exclude software.

7. At the individual industry level, the most R&D-intensive industry in 1990 was aircraft (its R&D amounted to 15.3 percent of net sales in the 1980s). On the 43-sector aggregation, aircraft is absorbed into the other transportation equipment sectors.

8. Correlations were also calculated for 1950, 1960, 1970, and 1980 with similar results.

9. One possibility is that increases in human capital or skill levels affect wages indirectly by promoting productivity growth. However, the skill and human capital variables remain insignificant even when the labor productivity growth variable is eliminated from the aggregate regression equation.

10. However, neither Allen nor Bartel and Sicherman investigated factors that affected *changes* in industry wages.

11. Industries with low labor productivity growth adjust to this by raising relative prices. See Baumol, Blackman, and Wolff (1989, chapter 6) for more discussion of the unbalanced growth effect.

12. Allen (2001) has found that industry wage differentials were positively associated with industry R&D intensity.

13. This is a modified form of the production function used by Stiroh (2002).

14. Regressions were also run on the annual growth of BLS hourly wages, NIPA wages and salaries per FTEE, and NIPA employee compensation plus half of proprietors' income per PEP, as well as two CPS earnings series: median and mean wages and salaries of workers. The results are very similar and are not shown here.

15. The two forms are equivalent. The proof is that RDGDP = dR/X. From equations 2 and 4 it follows that

$$\pi = \epsilon_R \ (dR/R) = \epsilon_R \ (dR/X)(X/R) = (\epsilon_R \ X/R)(dR/X).$$

Therefore,

$$\beta_2 = (\epsilon_R \ X/R) = (dX/X)(X/R)/(dR/R) = dX/dR.$$

16. In fact, when the change in the unionization rate was tried as an independent variable, its coefficient was uniformly insignificant.

17. Another variable that was tried but did not prove significant is the change in the share of women in the labor force. The argument is that, because of the increasing labor force participation of women in the last two decades, my estimate of mean experience, based on the difference between age and years of schooling, may be biased upward. Moreover, because of the historically lower wages of women, the increased share of women in the labor force may depress average wages. However, after controlling for age and schooling, this variable did not prove significant.

18. Unfortunately, data are not available that would allow me to include a term for the mean value of the square of years of experience.

19. The result is similar for the alternative measure of R&D intensity, that is, the number of scientists and engineers engaged in R&D per 1,000 full-time equivalent employees.

20. Alternative measures were also used for the computerization variable. The coefficients of the growth of information processing and related equipment per employee, as well as those of the growth in OCA plus communication equipment per employee, are all negative as well and usually significant, although the coefficients of the growth of computers and peripheral equipment per employee are generally not significant. However, the strongest effect comes from the OCA variable.

21. Because the dependent variables in these regressions are annual rates of growth, there is unlikely to be a problem with nonstationarity. However,

to be sure, I use the Dickey-Fuller (DF) unit root test statistic to test for nonstationarity in the four dependent variables. Each of the regressions includes a time trend and the lagged value of the dependent variable. The results are as follows:

	Z Test Critical Reject	Variable Statistic Value (5%)	Unit Root?
Growth in BLS mean hourly earnings	−33.17	−20.70	Yes
Growth in NIPA mean wages and salaries	−35.02	−20.70	Yes
Growth in NIPA mean employee compensation	−39.12	−20.70	Yes
Growth in NIPA mean employee compensation plus one-half of proprietors' income	−35.77	−20.70	Yes

Similar results are found using the t-statistic test. In each case, we can reject the hypothesis of a unit root at the 5 percent level.

22. Results are similar for the growth in the skill variables and the growth in mean education and mean experience and are not shown here.

23. The R&D effect is much smaller in the human capital regression form (section B) because of the positive correlation between R&D intensity and the change in mean years of schooling.

24. The period from 1950 to 1960 cannot be included in the regression analysis because the R&D series begins fully only in 1958. The government sector is excluded because of a lack of data on OCA investment. Moreover, because of a major change in industrial classification in 1997, with the adoption of the North American Industrial Classification System (NAICS) in the United States, the 1990–2000 sample consists of only 32 industries (excluding the government sector).

25. See, for example, Slichter (1950) and Dunlop (1957) for a discussion of industry wage contours. See Dickens and Katz (1987) and Krueger and Summers (1988) for a discussion of efficiency wage theory.

26. Results are broadly similar for the two other NIPA wage variables. The BLS hourly earnings data and the CPS earnings data are not available at the industry level.

27. Results are similar for the annual growth of SC and mean education.

4

Productivity and Skill Change

4.1 Introduction

In chapter 4 we switch gears and look at the relationship between productivity growth and the growth in worker skills. Productivity growth is important because it is one of the key determinants of both wages and the standard of living. While wages have not risen commensurately with skills, neither has productivity at either the industry level or in the aggregate. Chapter 4 focuses on this third of our four paradoxes.

What is the connection between skills and productivity? Standard economic theory predicts that rising educational achievement and skills will lead to increasing productivity. Considerable policy discussion has also focused on the importance of education and skill upgrading as an ingredient in promoting productivity growth. Yet, while overall productivity growth in the United States slowed down after 1973, the growth of schooling levels and skills continued unabated. Indeed, college completion rates accelerated after 1970. In the time-series data from 1947 to 2000, there is virtually no correlation between the growth of total factor productivity on the one hand and that of skills or educational attainment on the other. Likewise, at the industry level, sectors with the fastest-growing skills have not had appreciably higher productivity growth than sectors with little increase in skills. A growing discordance has thus come to exist between skills and productivity.

A similar anomaly exists between productivity growth and computerization. Robert Solow was perhaps the first to point out the incongruity between productivity growth and computerization. Indeed, he quipped that we see computers everywhere except in the productivity statistics. As we shall see, industries that have experienced the greatest investment in computers (namely, financial services) have ranked among the lowest in terms of conventionally measured productivity growth. Moreover, at least until recently, there has been little evidence of a payoff for computer investment in terms of productivity growth.

Another recent phenomenon of considerable visibility has been the rapid restructuring of U.S. industrial corporations. Standard measures of productivity growth are only one indicator of structural change. There are others such as changes in direct input and capital coefficients. Changes in occupational mix and the composition of inputs were greater in the 1980s than in the preceding two decades. This is coincident with the sharp rise in computerization.

Though most of the attention in the literature has focused on the connection between information technology (IT) and productivity, little work has been conducted on the link between IT and broader indicators of structural change. One purpose of this chapter is to help fill this gap. Indeed, I find evidence from regression analysis that the degree of computerization has had a statistically significant effect on changes in industry input coefficients and other dimensions of structural change.

This chapter concentrates on the relationship of skills, education, and computerization to productivity growth and other indicators of technological change at the industry level. I find no evidence that the growth of cognitive skills or educational attainment has any statistically measurable effect on industry productivity growth. Moreover, the degree of computerization is not significant. In contrast, computerization has had a statistically significant effect on changes in industry input coefficients.

The chapter is organized as follows: Section 4.2 reviews some of the pertinent literature on the role of skill change and computerization with regard to productivity changes in the U.S. economy. Section 4.3 presents descriptive statistics on postwar productivity trends and key variables that shaped the pattern of productivity growth in the postwar period. Section 4.4 presents concluding remarks. Section A.1 of the appendix to this chapter describes the formal accounting framework and model, while section A.2 explains a multivariate analysis at the industry level.[1]

4.2 Review of Literature

Human capital theory views schooling as an investment in skills and hence as a way of augmenting worker productivity (see, for example, Schultz 1960 and Becker 1975). This line of reasoning leads to growth-accounting models in which productivity or output *growth* is derived as a function of the *change* in educational attainment. The early studies on this subject show very powerful effects of educational change on economic growth. Griliches (1970) has estimated that the increased educational achievement of the U.S. labor force accounted for one-third of the aggregate technical change between 1940 and 1967. Denison (1979) has estimated that about one-fifth of the growth in U.S. national income per person employed (NIPPE) between 1948 and 1973 can be attributed to increases in the educational levels of the labor force. Jorgenson and Fraumeni (1993) have calculated that improvements in labor quality account for one-fourth of U.S. economic growth between 1948 and 1986.

Yet, some anomalies have appeared in this line of inquiry. In his analysis of the productivity slowdown in the United States between 1973 and 1981, Denison (1983) reports that the growth in NIPPE fell by 0.2 percentage points, whereas increases in educational attainment contributed a *positive* 0.6 percentage points to the growth in NIPPE. Maddison (1982) reports similar results for other OECD countries for the 1970–1979 period. Using various series on educational attainment among OECD countries, Wolff (2001) has found no statistically significant effect of the growth in mean years of schooling on the growth in GDP per capita among OECD countries from 1950 to 1990.

Numerous studies, perhaps inspired by Solow's quip, have now examined the link between computerization (or IT) in general and productivity gains. The evidence is mixed. Most of the earlier studies failed to find any excess returns to IT, over and above the fact that these investments are normally in the form of equipment. These studies include Franke (1989), who found that the installation of automatic teller machines (ATMs) was associated with a lowered real return on equity; Bailey and Gordon (1988), who examined aggregate productivity growth in the United States and found no significant contribution of computerization; Loveman (1988), who reported no productivity gains from IT investment; Parsons, Gotlieb, and Denny (1993), who estimated very low returns on computer investments in Canadian banks; and Berndt and Morrison (1995), who found negative correlations between labor productivity growth and high-tech capital investment in U.S. manufacturing industries. Wolff (1991) found that the insurance industry had a negative rate of total factor productivity growth over the 1948–1986 period in the United States even though it ranked fourth among 64 industries in terms of computer investment.

The later studies generally tend to be more positive. Both Siegel and Griliches (1992) and Steindel (1992) have estimated a positive and significant relationship between computer investment and industry-level productivity growth. Oliner and Sichel (1994) report a significant contribution of computers to aggregate U.S. output growth. Lichtenberg (1995) estimates firm-level production functions and finds an excess return to IT equipment and labor. Using detailed industry-level manufacturing data for the United States, Siegel (1997) has found that computers are an important source of quality change and that, once output measures were corrected for quality change, computerization has a significant positive effect on productivity growth.

Brynjolfsson and Hitt (1996, 1998) have found a positive correlation between firm-level productivity growth and IT investment over the 1987–1994 time period when accompanied by organizational changes. Lehr and Lichtenberg (1998) used data for U.S. federal government agencies over the 1987–1992 period and found a significant positive relation between productivity growth and computer intensity. Lehr and Lichtenberg (1999) have investigated firm-level data among service industries over the 1977–1993 period and also reported evidence that computers, particularly personal computers, contributed positively and significantly to productivity growth. Developing a new measure of direct and indirect productivity gains, ten Raa and Wolff (2000) have found that the computer sector was the leading area in the U.S. economy during the 1980s as a source of economy-wide productivity growth. They have also found very high productivity spillovers between the computer-producing sector and sectors using computers. In their imputation procedure, these large spillovers were attributable to the high rate of productivity growth within the computer industry.

Stiroh (1998) and Jorgenson and Stiroh (1999, 2000) used a growth-accounting framework to assess the impact of computers on output growth. Jorgenson and Stiroh (1999) calculated that one-sixth of the 2.4 percent annual growth in output can be attributed to computer outputs, compared to about 0 percent over the 1948–1973 period. The effect came from capital deepening rather than from enhanced productivity growth. A study by Oliner and Sichel (2000) provides strong evidence for a substantial role of IT in the spurt of productivity growth during the second half of the 1990s. Using aggregate time-series data for the United States, they found that both the use of IT in sectors purchasing computers and other forms of information technology, as well as the production of computers, appear to have made an important contribution to the speedup of productivity growth in the latter part of the 1990s. Hubbard (2001) investigated the way in which onboard computer adoption affected capacity utilization in the U.S. trucking industry between 1992 and 1997. He has found that their use improved communications and resource allocation decisions and led to a 3 percent increase in capacity utilization within the industry.

One other factor that is used in the data analysis is research and development. A large body of literature, beginning with Mansfield (1965), has now almost universally established a positive and significant effect of R&D expenditures on productivity growth (see Griliches 1979 and 1992 and Mohnen 1992 for reviews of the literature).

4.3 Descriptive Statistics

4.3.1 Technological and Structural Change

Table 4.1 shows the annual rate of TFP growth for 12 major sectors between 1950 and 2003. The five decadal periods are chosen to correspond to the employment by occupation and industry matrices. Factor shares are based

Table 4.1. Total Factor Productivity (TFP) Growth by Major Sector, 1950–2003 (Average annual growth in percentage points)

Sector	1950–1960	1960–1970	1970–1980	1980–1990	1990–2000	1950–2000	1995–2003
A. Goods-producing Industries							
Agriculture, forestry, and fisheries	0.41	-0.59	-1.62	3.76	2.44	0.88	5.68
Mining	0.42	2.19	-3.51	-1.32	0.70	-0.30	-2.87
Construction	3.99	-2.40	-3.86	0.90	-2.07	-0.69	-2.58
Manufacturing, durables	0.54	1.61	1.44	4.74	3.10	2.28	5.14
Manufacturing, nondurables	2.35	1.63	1.39	2.69	2.13	2.04	2.44
Transportation	1.20	2.99	0.24	2.30	2.38	1.82	1.87
Communications	2.76	2.50	2.63	1.78	2.68	2.47	2.16
Electric, gas, and sanitary services	4.39	2.86	2.07	1.91	1.44	2.53	2.48
B. Service Industries							
Wholesale and retail trade	0.82	0.68	-0.84	1.31	2.60	0.91	3.58
Finance, insurance, and real estate	1.06	-0.52	-0.06	-2.19	1.12	-0.12	1.06
General services	0.01	0.38	0.48	-0.07	-0.44	0.07	-0.53
Government and government enterprises	-0.19	0.14	0.04	-0.17	-0.10	-0.06	-0.11
Total goods	2.22	1.47	0.26	2.58	1.80	1.66	2.27
Total services	0.67	0.80	0.55	0.35	0.53	0.58	0.84
Total economy (GDP)	1.37	1.03	0.35	1.13	0.88	0.95	1.18

Note: The TFP estimates are based on Persons Employed in Production (PEP) and net capital stock.

See the data appendix for sources and methods.

111

on period averages (the Tornqvist-Divisia index). The labor input is based on persons engaged in production (PEP)—the number of full-time and part-time employees plus the number of self-employed people; the capital input is measured by fixed nonresidential net capital stock (2000 dollars).[2] See the appendix to chapter 4 for the definition of TFP growth and the data appendix for details on sources and methods and a listing of the 45 industries.

As table 4.1 shows, the annual rate of TFP growth for the entire economy dipped slightly between the 1950s and 1960s, from 1.4 to 1.0 percent per annum, plummeted in the 1970s to 0.4 percent per year (the productivity slowdown period), and then recovered to 1.1 percent per year and then 0.9 percent per year in the 1980s and 1990s, respectively. Over the entire half century, overall TFP growth averaged 0.95 percent per year. The years 1995–2003 are also shown since this period was heralded as the era of the "new economy."[3] However, in terms of conventional TFP growth, it was unremarkable, with an average annual TFP growth of 1.18 percent, slightly higher than its long-term trend.

In the goods-producing industries (including communications, transportation, and utilities[4]), there was generally a modest decline in TFP productivity growth between the 1950s and 1960s, followed by a sharp slowdown in the 1970s (with agriculture, mining, and construction recording negative productivity growth) and then a substantial recovery in the 1980s, followed by a modest downswing in the 1990s. TFP growth in the goods-producing industries as a whole averaged 2.2 percent per year from 1950 to 1960, fell to 1.5 percent per year in the 1960s, and then collapsed to 0.3 percent in the 1980s, before climbing back to 2.6 percent per year in the 1980s and then dipping to 1.7 percent per year in the 1990s. There was no noticeable acceleration in TFP growth between 1995 and 2003, although it was greater than during the 1990s as a whole.

TFP growth has been much lower in the service sector than among goods-producing industries—0.88 percent per year over the five decades for the former, compared to 1.66 percent per year for the latter. The pattern over time is also generally different for the service industries. TFP growth in wholesale and retail trade has a pattern similar to that in the goods industries—relatively strong in the 1950–1960 period (0.8 percent per year) before falling slightly to 0.7 percent in the 1960s, turning negative in the next decade, and then rebounding to 1.3 percent per year in the 1980s and 2.6 percent per year in the 1990s. Indeed, there was a big jump in TFP growth in this sector in the 1995–2003 period, to 3.6 percent per year. In finance, insurance, and real estate (FIRE), TFP growth remained very low or negative between the 1950s and 1980s but showed some gains in the 1990s and the 1995–2003 period (to 1.1 percent per year). TFP growth in general services and the government sector stayed low or negative throughout the five decades, with no pickup in the 1990s. Overall, annual TFP growth among all services was low for the entire 53-year period, with perhaps a very modest uptick in the 1995–2003 period.

Table 4.2.   Dissimilarity Index (DIOCCUP) of the Distribution of Occupational Employment by Major Sector, 1950–1990

Sector	1950–1960	1960–1970	1970–1980	1980–1990	Average 1950–1990
A. Goods Industries					
Agriculture, forestry, and fisheries	0.000	0.001	0.001	0.017	0.005
Mining	0.022	0.025	0.020	0.045	0.028
Construction	0.040	0.025	0.005	0.053	0.031
Manufacturing, durables	0.100	0.039	0.014	0.096	0.062
Manufacturing, nondurables	0.077	0.050	0.023	0.088	0.060
Transportation	0.030	0.024	0.014	0.048	0.029
Communications	0.032	0.061	0.043	0.128	0.066
Electric, gas, and sanitary services	0.078	0.169	0.053	0.105	0.101
B. Service Industries					
Wholesale and retail trade	0.026	0.019	0.029	0.078	0.038
Finance, insurance, and real estate	0.043	0.117	0.033	0.080	0.068
General services	0.061	0.091	0.029	0.047	0.057
Government and government enterprises	0.046	0.054	0.042	0.045	0.047
Total goods	0.063	0.061	0.014	0.110	0.062
Total services	0.022	0.056	0.026	0.077	0.045
All industries	0.050	0.056	0.019	0.095	0.055

Note: Computations are based on employment by occupation aggregated for each of the major sectors.

I also develop three measures of structural change (see the appendix to chapter 4 for technical details). The first index is DIOCCUP, which measures the degree to which the occupational structure shifts over time (table 4.2).[5] The DIOCCUP index for the total economy, after rising slightly from 0.050 in the 1950–1960 period to 0.056 in the 1960s, dropped to 0.019 in the 1970s but then surged to 0.095 in the 1980s, its highest level of the four decades. This pattern is similar to that of TFP growth for the total economy (figure 4.1). These results also confirm anecdotal evidence of the substantial degree of industrial restructuring during the 1980s. Similar patterns are evident for the major sectors as well. In fact, seven of the twelve major sectors experienced their most rapid degree of occupational change during the 1980s. The three sectors that experienced the greatest occupational restructuring over the four decades were utilities (0.101), FIRE (0.068), and communications (0.066). Occupational change was particularly low in agriculture (0.005), mining (0.028), transportation (0.029), and construction (0.031).

The association between the DIOCCUP index and industry TFP growth is quite loose (figure 4.2). Though the degree of occupational restructuring has been somewhat greater in the goods-producing industries than in services (average scores of 0.062 and 0.045, respectively, for the 1950–1990 period),

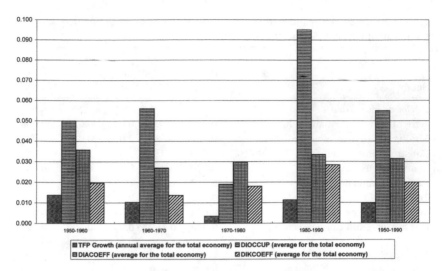

Figure 4.1   Annual TFP Growth, DIOCCUP, DIACOEFF, and DIKCOEFF for the Total Economy by Decade, 1950–1990

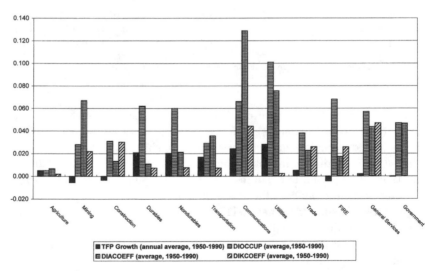

Figure 4.2   Annual TFP Growth, DIOCCUP, DIACOEFF, and DIKCOEFF by Major Sector, 1950–1990

the difference is not nearly as marked as for TFP growth (annual rates of 1.7 percent and 0.6 percent, respectively, over the 1950–2000 period). Moreover, while FIRE ranks second highest in terms of occupational change, it is the third lowest in TFP growth. In contrast, while agriculture ranks seventh highest in terms of TFP growth, it ranks lowest in occupational restructuring.

The DIOCCUP index provides a separate and relatively independent dimension of the degree of technological change occurring in an industry.

The second index is DIACOEFF, which reflects changes in the interindustry coefficients.[6] Table 4.3 shows that the DIACOEFF index for the total economy, after falling from 0.036 in the 1950s to 0.027 in the 1960s, rose to 0.030 in the 1970s and again to 0.033 in the 1980s. This contrasts with the pattern of productivity growth over time, where TFP growth fell sharply between the 1960s and 1970s before rising again (figure 4.3). Eight of the twelve major sectors also recorded an increase in the degree of change in their interindustry coefficients between the 1960s and the 1980s. The three sectors with the greatest interindustry coefficient change over the four decades were communications (0.129), utilities (0.075), and mining (0.067), and the two with the least variation were agriculture (0.007) and durable manufacturing (0.013).

The correlation between the DIACOEFF index and industry TFP growth is again quite small (figure 4.2). While TFP growth was much higher in goods-producing industries than in services, DIACOEFF was higher for services than for the goods sector. While agriculture, durable manufacturing, and nondurable manufacturing all ranked high in TFP growth, they were the three lowest in coefficient changes. The DIACOEFF index provides another independent indicator of the degree of technological change in industry.

Table 4.3.   Dissimilarity Index DIACOEFF for Technical Interindustry Coefficients by Major Sector, 1950–1990

Sector	1950–1960	1960–1970	1970–1980	1980–1990	Average 1950 1990
A. Goods Industries					
Agriculture, forestry, and fisheries	0.008	0.006	0.004	0.009	0.007
Mining	0.041	0.065	0.070	0.092	0.067
Construction	0.012	0.004	0.028	0.008	0.013
Manufacturing, durables	0.013	0.007	0.009	0.014	0.011
Manufacturing, nondurables	0.022	0.012	0.027	0.025	0.021
Transportation	0.043	0.067	0.016	0.017	0.036
Communications	0.270	0.024	0.051	0.170	0.129
Electric, gas, and sanitary services	0.048	0.087	0.020	0.147	0.075
B. Service Industries					
Wholesale and retail trade	0.015	0.049	0.017	0.010	0.023
Finance, insurance, and real estate	0.015	0.033	0.010	0.010	0.017
General services	0.034	0.047	0.066	0.027	0.043
Government and government enterprises	0.054	0.046	0.026	0.061	0.047
Total goods	0.020	0.017	0.024	0.029	0.023
Total services	0.057	0.046	0.043	0.045	0.048
All industries	0.036	0.027	0.030	0.033	0.031

Note: Sectoral figures are based on unweighted averages of industries within the sector.

Table 4.4.   Dissimilarity Index DIKCOEFF for Capital Coefficients, 1950–1990

Sector	1950– 1960	1960– 1970	1970– 1980	1980– 1990	Average 1950– 1990
A. Goods Industries					
Agriculture, forestry, and fisheries	0.002	0.000	0.001	0.005	0.002
Mining	0.016	0.008	0.025	0.038	0.022
Construction	0.011	0.016	0.032	0.061	0.030
Manufacturing, durables	0.005	0.007	0.009	0.007	0.007
Manufacturing, nondurables	0.009	0.006	0.006	0.009	0.008
Transportation	0.002	0.009	0.011	0.008	0.007
Communications	0.015	0.028	0.045	0.087	0.044
Electric, gas, and sanitary services	0.003	0.001	0.002	0.003	0.002
B. Service Industries					
Wholesale and retail trade	0.045	0.019	0.014	0.024	0.026
Finance, insurance, and real estate	0.020	0.014	0.027	0.043	0.026
General services	0.057	0.033	0.035	0.062	0.047
Total goods	0.008	0.007	0.011	0.014	0.010
Total services (except government)	0.038	0.024	0.029	0.050	0.035
Total economy (except government)	0.020	0.014	0.018	0.028	0.020

Note: Sectoral figures are based on unweighted averages of industries within the sector. Data on investment by type are not available for the government and government enterprises sectors.

The third index, DIKCOEFF, measures the change in capital coefficients within an industry. Table 4.4 shows that the DIKCOEFF index for the total economy, which declined from 0.020 in the 1950s to 0.014 in the 1960s, increased to 0.018 in the 1970s and to 0.028 in the 1980s. This time trend once again differs from that of TFP growth (figure 4.1). DIKCOEFF rose in nine of the eleven major sectors (capital stock by type is not available for the government sector) between the 1960s and the 1980s. General services and communications showed the greatest change in capital coefficients between 1950 and 1990 period, and agriculture and utilities the least. Here, again, while TFP growth was much higher in goods than in the service industries, DIKCOEFF was higher for the latter (figure 4.2). Moreover, while agriculture, durable manufacturing, and nondurable manufacturing were all among the top industries in TFP growth, they were among the lowest in capital coefficient changes.

4.3.2 Changes in Skills and Educational Attainment

The human capital model predicts a positive relation between changes in average education or average skill levels and productivity growth. Figures on mean years of schooling by industry are derived directly from decennial census of population data for 1950, 1960, 1970, 1980, 1990, and 2000.

Educational achievement has been widely employed to measure the skills used in the workplace. However, the usefulness of schooling measures is limited by problems such as variations in the quality of schooling both over time and among areas, the use of credentials as a screening mechanism, and inflationary trends in credential and certification requirements. Indeed, evidence presented in chapter 2 suggests that years of schooling may not closely correspond to the technical skill requirements of the jobs. As a result, I also make use of the direct skill measures developed in chapter 2 as factors in accounting for productivity movements over time.

Figure 4.3 shows changes (by decade from 1950 to 2000) in substantive complexity (SC), mean education of the workforce, and the percentage of adults with a college degree or more. Substantive complexity does not appear to be closely correlated with TFP growth. The average decadal change in the SC index between 1950 and 1970 was 0.0164 points, while TFP growth averaged 1.20 percent per year and 0.180 points between 1970 and 2000, when TFP grew at only 0.79 percent per year. Indeed, the highest TFP growth was recorded during the 1950s, when SC grew at the slowest rate. Moreover, the growth of college graduates in the adult population was much greater in the later period, averaging 5.1 percentage points per year, than in the earlier period, when it averaged only 2.4 percentage points per decade. In fact, the 1970s saw the greatest change in the share of adults with a college degree (6.0 percentage points) and the lowest growth in TFP. Mean schooling, on the other hand, tracks TFP more closely. The average decade change in mean

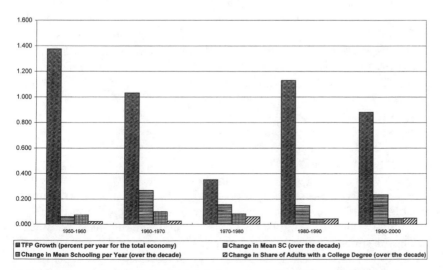

Figure 4.3   Annual TFP Growth and the Change in Substantive Complexity and Schooling by Decade, 1950–2000

education was 1.05 years between 1950 and 1970 and 0.69 years from 1970 to 2000. Nonetheless, the change in mean years of schooling was second highest during the 1970s.

There is also very little cross-industry association between skill levels and productivity growth. Table 4.5 illustrates that cognitive skill levels, as measured by substantive complexity, were, on average, very similar in both the service sector and the goods sector, even though TFP growth was much lower in the latter. In 2000, employees in FIRE had the highest average SC score (5.61), followed by communications (5.29), general services (5.00), and the government sector (4.98). With the exception of communications, these three areas ranked among the bottom five in terms of TFP growth. Moreover, the change in mean SC was somewhat higher in services (1.16 points) than in goods-producing industries (0.97 points) between 1950 and 2000.

The pattern is very similar for the mean education of the workforce. Average schooling levels were quite comparable in both services and the goods sector and in 2000 were led by general services (14.3 years), followed by the government sector (14.2 years), FIRE (14.2 years), and communications (also 14.2 years). The change in mean education over the five decades was also somewhat greater in the goods sector (3.4 years) than in the service sector (3.1 years).

4.3.3 Investment in OCA

My measure of IT capital is the stock of office, computing, and accounting equipment (OCA) in 2000 dollars, which is shown in the capital data provided by the Bureau of Economic Analysis (BEA) (see the data appendix for sources). These figures are based on the BEA's hedonic price deflator for computers and computer-related equipment.[7] Table 4.6 and figure 4.4 show that investment in OCA per PEP grew almost 40-fold between the 1950s and the 1990s, from $8 (in 2000 dollars) per PEP to $289. Indeed, by 2000, it had reached $916 per worker. By the 1990s, the most OCA-intensive sector by far was FIRE, at $2,007 per employee, followed by communications ($1,557), utilities ($598), and mining ($508). On the whole, the overall service sector has been investing more intensively in computer equipment than has the goods sector, but this is largely due to the very heavy investments made by FIRE. The trade and general service sectors were actually below average in OCA investment per PEP. The growth of OCA per worker was also greater in services (a factor of 45) than in the goods sector (a factor of 29). Total investment in OCA was still only 5 percent of total investment in equipment, machinery, software, and instruments (including OCA), even in the 1990s, although by 2000 it accounted for 11 percent of total equipment investment.

On the surface, at least, there does not appear to be much correlation between OCA intensity and TFP growth. While investment in OCA per worker rose very sharply in the postwar period, TFP growth tracked downward from the 1950s to the 1970s, climbed in the 1980s, and then dipped somewhat in

Table 4.5. Average Skill Level by Period and Year, 1950–2000

Sector	1950	1960	1970	1980	1990	2000	Change 1950–2000
1. Mean Years of Education							
A. Goods Industries							
Agriculture, forestry, and fisheries	7.7	8.4	9.7	11.2	11.7	11.7	4.1
Mining	8.6	10.0	11.0	12.2	12.7	12.6	4.0
Construction	9.2	9.9	10.6	11.8	12.3	12.0	2.8
Manufacturing, durables	9.1	10.1	10.9	11.9	12.5	12.7	3.6
Manufacturing, nondurables	10.7	11.4	12.0	12.9	13.3	13.7	2.9
Transportation	9.4	10.2	10.9	12.0	12.6	12.8	3.5
Communications	11.2	11.7	12.3	12.9	13.7	14.2	3.0
Electric, gas, and sanitary services	10.3	11.1	11.3	12.3	13.1	13.6	3.3
B. Service Industries							
Wholesale and retail trade	10.4	11.0	11.5	12.4	12.7	12.9	2.5
Finance, insurance, and real estate	11.4	12.1	12.6	13.3	13.8	14.2	2.7
General services	11.7	12.1	12.4	13.2	13.7	14.3	2.7
Government and government enterprises	11.2	11.8	12.3	13.1	13.6	14.2	3.0
Total goods	9.6	10.6	11.2	12.0	12.7	13.0	3.4
Total services	9.5	10.2	10.9	11.8	12.5	12.7	3.1
Total economy	9.9	10.8	11.6	12.5	13.1	13.4	3.5

(continued)

119

Table 4.5. (continued)

Sector	1950	1960	1970	1980	1990	2000	Change 1950–2000
2. Mean Substantive Complexity							
A. Goods Industries							
Agriculture, forestry, and fisheries	3.68	3.67	3.62	3.59	3.68	2.80	−0.89
Mining	3.19	3.52	3.90	4.05	4.15	4.10	0.92
Construction	3.45	3.90	4.13	4.19	4.23	4.22	0.77
Manufacturing, durables	3.36	3.46	3.68	3.78	3.91	4.10	0.74
Manufacturing, nondurables	4.20	4.15	4.37	4.52	4.62	4.82	0.62
Transportation	3.16	3.17	3.32	3.38	3.26	3.55	0.40
Communications	3.92	4.13	4.39	4.62	4.85	5.29	1.37
Electric, gas, and sanitary services	3.93	3.78	3.97	4.17	4.48	4.92	0.99
B. Service Industries							
Wholesale and retail trade	3.98	3.85	3.82	3.94	4.05	4.15	0.17
Finance, insurance, and real estate	4.43	4.83	5.09	5.17	5.32	5.61	1.17
General services	4.38	4.27	4.66	4.80	4.87	5.00	0.62
Government and government enterprises	4.26	4.22	4.38	4.54	4.70	4.98	0.71
Total goods	3.26	3.41	3.68	3.73	3.90	4.22	0.96
Total services	3.01	3.05	3.35	3.53	3.72	4.17	1.16
Total economy	3.75	3.81	4.07	4.23	4.38	4.61	0.87

Note: Figures are weighted averages of individual industries within each major sector.

Table 4.6. Annual Investment in Office, Computing, and Accounting Equipment (OCA) per Persons Engaged in Production (PEP), 1950–2000 (2000 dollars, period averages)

Sector	1950–1960	1960–1970	1970–1980	1980–1990	1990–2000	Ratio of 1990–2000 to 1950–1960
A. Goods Industries						
Agriculture, forestry, and fisheries	0.0	0.1	0.6	1.5	29.7	1,295.9
Mining	4.5	9.0	16.7	123.1	507.5	113.2
Construction	2.1	2.2	1.8	2.4	55.0	25.8
Manufacturing, durables	12.9	12.9	21.3	74.9	215.7	16.7
Manufacturing, nondurables	8.9	8.6	13.2	52.8	238.2	26.8
Transportation	13.7	11.4	9.3	22.8	268.9	19.6
Communications	15.4	13.7	16.0	89.4	1,556.5	101.3
Electric, gas, and sanitary services	14.8	13.1	17.1	196.9	598.1	40.5
B. Service Industries						
Wholesale and retail trade	4.4	6.4	13.3	87.7	205.2	46.8
Finance, insurance, and real estate	43.9	51.0	106.3	379.4	2,007.2	45.8
General services	7.2	7.3	7.2	46.4	187.6	26.1
Total goods	8.3	8.7	13.2	50.8	242.2	29.2
Total services (except government)	6.8	8.2	15.6	77.7	308.1	45.1
Total economy (except government)	7.5	8.4	14.7	68.8	288.8	38.3

Note: Data on investment in OCA are not available for the government and government enterprises sectors.

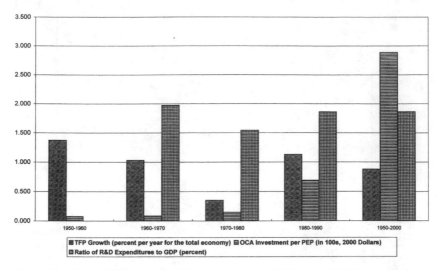

Figure 4.4 Annual TFP Growth, OCA Investment per Worker, and R&D Intensity by Decade, 1950–2000

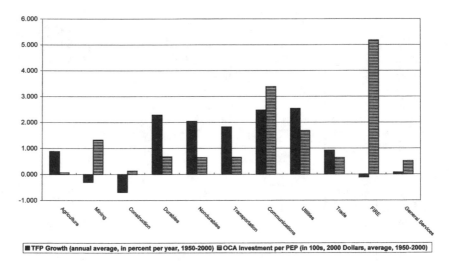

Figure 4.5 Annual TFP Growth and OCA Investment per Worker by Major Sector, 1950–2000

the 1990s (figure 4.3). Moreover, the sector with the highest amount of OCA investment per worker, FIRE, averaged close to zero in TFP growth over the postwar period (figure 4.5).

On the other hand, OCA investment seems to line up well with measures of structural change. Figure 4.6 illustrates that the sectors with the two highest rates of investment in OCA per PEP over the 1950–1990 period are

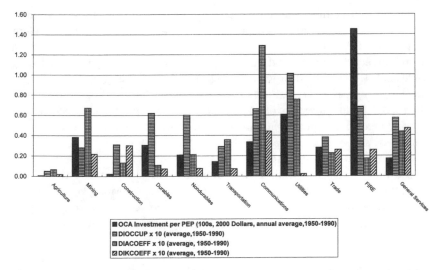

Figure 4.6   OCA Investment per Worker, DIOCCUP, DIACOEFF, and DIKCOEFF by Major Sector, 1950–1990

FIRE and utilities, which also rank in the top two in the average value of DIOCCUP in the same period. The sector with the lowest investment in OCA per worker is agriculture, which also ranks lowest in terms of DIOCCUP. Utilities ranks highest in terms of DIACOEFF between 1950 and 1990 and second highest in OCA investment per employee, while agriculture ranks lowest in both dimensions. The association is not quite as tight between OCA investment and DIKCOEFF. However, here again agriculture ranks lowest in both dimensions.

4.3.4 R&D

Figure 4.4 shows that the ratio of R&D expenditures to total GDP has remained relatively constant over time, at least in comparison to the wide fluctuations in TFP growth. It averaged 2.0 percent in the 1960s, fell to 1.5 percent in the 1970s, recovered to 1.9 percent in the 1980s, and remained at this level during the 1990s. The pattern is very similar for individual industries, with the notable exceptions of industrial machinery (including OCA) and instruments, which show a continuous rise during the three periods. The ratio of R&D to sales was considerably higher in durable manufacturing than in nondurables—by a factor of almost three. In the 1990s, within manufacturing, it ranged from a low of 0.5 percent in food products to a high of 18.3 percent in other transportation equipment (including aircraft). The other major R&D-intensive industries, in rank order, are instruments, electric and electronic equipment, industrial machinery, chemicals, and motor vehicles.

An alternative indicator of R&D activity is the number of full-time equivalent scientists and engineers engaged in R&D per 1,000 full-time equivalent employees. Like the ratio of R&D expenditures to GDP, this series shows a drop between the 1960s and 1970s, from 5.4 to 4.8, and a recovery in the 1980s to 6.4. However, it shows a further increase to 7.3 in the 1990s. This indicator also gives a very similar industry ranking. The leading industries in the 1990s, in rank order, are other transportation equipment, chemicals, electric and electronic equipment, industrial machinery, instruments, and motor vehicles.

R&D expenditures line up with TFP growth much better than either OCA or equipment investment. Both R&D intensity and TFP growth fell between the 1960s and 1970s and then recovered in the 1980s. Moreover, there is a strong cross-industry correlation between TFP growth and R&D intensity—for example, both R&D intensity and TFP growth are higher in durable manufacturing than in nondurable manufacturing.

4.4 Conclusion and Interpretation of Results

Three sets of findings emerge in this chapter. First, the regression results provide no evidence that productivity growth is positively linked to skill growth. The coefficients of the change in (and growth of) both cognitive skills, as measured by substantive complexity, and the composite skill index are insignificant and, indeed, negative. The coefficient of the change in (and growth of) the mean education of the workforce, while positive, is not statistically significant and virtually zero in magnitude. Its estimated elasticity is 0.110. Since mean education grew, on average, by 0.69 percent per year over the 1950–2000 period, its growth would have added only 0.07 percentage points to annual labor productivity growth.

These findings appear to be inconsistent with growth-accounting models, which have attributed a substantial portion of the growth in U.S. productivity to increases in schooling levels (see section 4.2). The conflict stems from methodological differences in the two techniques. Growth accounting simply *assigns* to schooling (or measures of labor quality) a positive role in productivity growth based on the share of labor in total income. In contrast, in regression analysis, an estimation procedure is used to determine whether a variable such as education is a significant factor in productivity growth.

The findings on the role of education in productivity growth also appear to be at variance with the standard human capital model. There are several possible reasons for this. First, the causal relationship between productivity and schooling may be the reverse of what is normally assumed. In particular, as per capita income rises within a country, schooling opportunities increase, and more and more students may seek a college education (see Griliches 1996 for a discussion of the endogeneity of education). Second, the skills acquired in formal education, particularly at the university level, may not be relevant to the workplace. Rather, higher education may perform a screening function, and a university degree may serve employers mainly as a signal of potential productive ability (see Arrow 1973 or Spence 1973). As enrollment rates rise, screening or educational credentials may gain in importance, and a higher proportion of university graduates may become overeducated relative to the actual skills required in the workplace.

A third possibility is that university education may be associated with rent-seeking activities rather than leading directly to productive ones. This may be true for many professional workers, such as lawyers, accountants, advertising personnel, and brokers. A fourth possible explanation is the increasing absorption of university graduates by "cost disease" sectors characterized by low productivity growth, such as health, teaching, law, and business (see Baumol, Blackman, and Wolff 1989). These are essentially labor activities and, as such, are not subject to the types of automation and mechanization that occur in manufacturing and other goods-producing industries. Moreover, these industries may be subject to output measurement problems, particularly in regard to quality change.

Second, there is no evidence that computer investment is positively linked to TFP growth. In other words, there is no residual correlation between computer investment and TFP growth over and above the inclusion of OCA as normal capital equipment in the TFP calculation. This result holds not only for the 1960–2000 period but also for the 1980–2000 and 1990–2000 periods. The result also holds among exclusively goods-producing industries and exclusively manufacturing industries. This finding also seems at variance with more recent work on the subject. Oliner and Sichel (2000), for example, have found a strong effect of computers on productivity growth beginning only in the mid-1990s.

Third, in contrast, computerization is strongly and positively associated with other dimensions of structural change such as occupational restructuring and changes in the composition of intermediate inputs. The evidence is a bit weaker for its effects on changes in the composition of industry capital stock.

The bottom line is that the diffusion of IT appears to have shaken up the U.S. economy, beginning in the 1970s. However, it is a technological revolution that shows up more strongly in measures of structural change rather than in terms of productivity. My results indicate that OCA has had strong effects on changes in occupational composition and input structure dating from the early 1970s.

These results might reflect the high adjustment costs associated with the introduction of new technology. The paradigmatic shift from electromechanical automation to information technologies might require major changes in the organizational structure of companies before the new technology can be realized as measured productivity gains (see David 1991 for greater elaboration of this argument). The results on computerization are also consistent with an alternative interpretation of its role in modern industry. The argument is that a substantial amount of new technology (particularly, information technology) may be used for product differentiation rather than for productivity enhancement. Computers allow for greater diversification of products, which, in turn, also allows for greater price discrimination (e.g., airline pricing systems) and the ability to extract a large portion of consumer surplus. Greater product diversity might increase a firm's profits, though not necessarily its productivity. Chakraborty and Kazarosian (1999) provide some evidence of the production differentiation effects of computers for the U.S. trucking industry (for example, speed of delivery versus average load).

Overall, the results generally support the view that brainpower—whether human or artificial—has not greatly boosted productivity growth as conventionally measured. However, information technology appears to play a positive role in accounting for another indicator of technological dynamism—the degree of occupational change occurring within industries.

On a final note, the lesson here is not that education does not matter for growth. Indeed, among least developed countries (LDCs), inadequate schooling may be the biggest stumbling block to development. Instead, the message is that a certain threshold of schooling is required, but once beyond this level of social capability, additional general education has little marginal return, at least on measured productivity. However, specific types of schooling and training may still have direct relevance to growth among advanced economies. In this regard, efforts to promote additional economic growth in these countries should focus on these specific forms of schooling rather than on general education.

Appendix

A.1 Modeling Framework

I begin with a standard neoclassical production function f_j for sector j:

$$(4.1) \qquad X_j = Z_j f_j(KC_j, KO_j, LAB_j, INT_j, RD_j),$$

where X_j is the gross output of sector j, KC_j is the input of IT-related capital, KO_j is the input of other capital goods, LAB_j is the total labor input, INT_j are total intermediate inputs, RD_j is the stock of R&D capital, and Z_j is a Hicks-neutral TFP index that shifts the production function of sector j over time.[8] For convenience, I have suppressed the time subscript. Moreover, capacity utilization and adjustment costs are ignored. It then follows that

$$(4.2) \qquad d \ln X_j = d \ln Z_j + \epsilon_{Cj} \, d \ln KC_j + \epsilon_{Oj} \, d \ln KO_j + \epsilon_{Lj} \, d \ln LAB_j$$
$$+ \epsilon_{Nj} \, d \ln INT_j + \epsilon_{Rj} \, d \ln RD_j,$$

where ϵ represents the output elasticity of each input and $d \ln Z_j$ is the rate of Hicks-neutral TFP growth. If we now impose the assumption of competitive input markets and constant returns to scale, it follows that an input's factor share (α_j) will equal its output elasticity. Let us now employ the standard measure of TFP growth π_j for sector j:

(4.3) $$\pi_j \equiv d \ln X_j/dt - \alpha_{Cj} \, d \ln KC_j/dt - \alpha_{Oj} \, d \ln KO_j/dt$$
$$- \alpha_{Lj} \, d \ln LAB_j/dt - \alpha_{Nj} \, d \ln INT_j/dt.$$

It then follows that

(4.4) $$\pi_j = d \ln Z_j/dt + \alpha_{Rj} \, d \ln RD_j/dt.$$

In particular, in the standard neoclassical model, there is no special place reserved for IT capital in terms of its effect on TFP growth.

As Stiroh (2002) argues, there are several reasons that we might expect the standard necoclassical model to fail in the case of the introduction of a radically new technology that might be captured by IT investment. These include the presence of productivity spillovers from IT, problems of omitted variables, the presence of embodied technological change, measurement error in variables, and reverse causality. If, for one of these reasons, the output elasticity of IT ϵ_{Cj} exceeds its measured input share α_{Cj}, say, by u_{Cj}, then

(4.5) $$\pi_j = d \ln Z_j/dt + \alpha_{Rj} \, d \ln RD_j/dt + u_{Cj} \, d \ln KC_j/dt.$$

In other words, conventionally measured TFP growth π_j will be positively correlated with the growth in ICT capital.

A similar argument applies to labor productivity growth, LP, defined as

(4.6) $$LP_j \equiv d \ln X_j/dt - d \ln LAB_j/dt.$$

If we again impose the assumption of competitive input markets and constant returns to scale, it follows that

(4.7) $$LP_j = d \ln Z_j/dt + \alpha_{Cj} \, d \ln kc_j/dt + \alpha_{Oj} \, d \ln ko_j/dt$$
$$+ \alpha_{Nj} \, d \ln int_j/dt + \alpha_{Rj} \, d \ln RD_j/dt,$$

where lowercase symbols indicate the amount of the input per worker.[9] If, for the reasons already cited, there is a special productivity "kick" from IT investment, then the estimated coefficient of kc_j/dt should exceed its factor input share.

However, very few studies, with the exception of Siegel and Griliches (1991), have found a direct positive correlation between industry TFP growth and IT investment. As a result, in this study I consider other indicators of the degree of structural change in an industry. These include variations in the occupational composition of employment and changes in the input and capital composition within an industry. Productivity growth and changes in input composition usually go hand in hand. To see this, let

A = a 45-order matrix of technical interindustry input-output coefficients, where A_{ij} is the amount of input i used per constant dollar of output j (the matrices for the technical coefficient A were constructed on the basis of current dollar matrices and sector-specific price deflators; see the data appendix for details)

g = a 45-order matrix of capital coefficients, where g_{ij} is the net stock of capital of type i (in 1992 dollars) used per constant dollar of output j

c = an occupation-by-industry employment coefficient matrix, where c_{ij} shows the employment of occupation i in industry j as a share of total employment in industry j

Then, since for any input I in sector j, $\alpha_{Ij} = p_I I_j / p_j X_j$, where p is the price, I rewrite equation 4.3 as

$$(4.8) \qquad \pi_j = -\left[\Sigma_i \, p_i \, dA_{ij} + \Sigma_i \, p_{ig} \, dg_{ij} + \Sigma_i \, w_{OCCi} \, dn_{ij} \right] / p_j,$$

where p_i is the price of intermediate input i, p_{ig} is the price of capital input i, $n_{ij} = c_{ij} L_j$ is the total employment of occupation i per unit of output in industry j, L_j shows employment per unit of output in sector j, and w_{OCCi} is the wage paid to workers in occupation i. In this formulation, it is clear that measured TFP growth reflects changes in the composition of intermediate inputs, capital inputs, and occupational employment. Using the multiplication rule for derivatives, I rewrite equation 4.8 as

$$(4.9) \qquad \pi_j = -\left[\Sigma_i \, p_i \, dA_{ij} + \Sigma_i \, p_{ig} \, dg_{ij} + \Sigma_i \, w_{OCCi} L_j \, dc_{ij} \right.$$
$$\left. + \, \Sigma_i \, w_{OCCi} c_{ij} \, dL_j \right] / p_j.$$

From 4.5 it follows that in the circumstances just enumerated, there may be a positive correlation between measures of coefficient changes (such as dA_{ij}, dg_{ij}, and dc_{ij}) and IT investment.

Even though productivity growth and changes in input composition are algebraically related, they may deviate for several reasons. First, certain costs of adjustments are associated with radical restructuring of technology, possibly resulting in a considerable time lag between the two (see David 1991, for example). Second, while new technology is generally used to lower costs and hence to increase measured output per unit of input, new technology might serve additional purposes such as product differentiation or differential pricing. Third, in the case of services in particular, output measurement problems might prevent us from correctly assessing growth in industry productivity. This problem could, of course, be partly a consequence of product differentiation and price discrimination. Measures of structural change may therefore provide a more direct and robust test of the effects of computerization on changes in technology than standard measures of productivity growth. This is especially so when a radically new technology is introduced and the consequent adjustment period is lengthy.

I next include the change in average worker skills in the production function. There are two possible approaches. Let the effective or quality-adjusted labor input in sector j be given by $Q_j = LAB_j \, S_j$, where S measures average worker skills in sector j. Then equation 4.1 can be rewritten as

(4.10) $X_j = Z_j \, f_j^*(KC_j, KO_j, Q_j, INT_j, RD_j).$

Again assuming competitive input markets and constant returns to scale (to the traditional factors of production) and still using equation 4.6 to define labor productivity growth, we obtain

(4.11) $LP_j = d \ln Z_j/dt + \alpha_{Cj} \, d \ln kc_j/dt + \alpha_{Oj} \, d \ln ko_j/dt$
$$+ \alpha_{Nj} \, d \ln int_j/dt + \alpha_{Lj} \, d \ln S_j/dt + \alpha_{Rj} \, d \ln RD_j/dt.$$

In this formulation, the rate of labor productivity growth should increase directly with the *rate of growth* of average worker quality or skills.

The second approach derives from the standard human capital earnings function. From Mincer (1974),

$$\ln w = a_0 + a_1 S,$$

where w is the wage, S is the worker's level of skills (or schooling), and a_0 and a_1 are constants. It follows that

$$(d \ln w)/dt = a_1 (dS/dt).$$

By definition, the wage share in sector j is $\alpha_{Lj} = w_j \, LAB_j/X_j$. Under the assumptions of competitive input markets and constant returns to scale, $\alpha_{Lj} = \epsilon_{Lj}$, a constant. Therefore, $X_j/LAB_j = w_j/\epsilon_{Lj}$. In this case, effective labor input Q is given by this equation: Ln Q = S + ln LAB. It follows from 4.6 that

(4.12) $LP_j = d \ln Z_j/dt + \alpha_{Cj} \, d \ln kc_j/dt + \alpha_{Oj} \, d \ln ko_j/dt$
$$+ \alpha_{Nj} \, d \ln int_j/dt + \alpha_{Lj} \, dS_j/dt + \alpha_{Rj} \, d \ln RD_j/dt.$$

In other words, the rate of labor productivity growth should be proportional to the *change in the level* of average worker quality or skills over the period.

Finally, I develop three measures of structural change. The first determines the degree to which the occupational structure shifts over time. For this I employ an index of similarity. The similarity index for industry j between two time periods 1 and 2 is given by

$$(4.13) \qquad SI^{12} = \left(\Sigma_i \ c_{ij}^1 c_{ij}^2 \right) \Big/ \left[\Sigma_i \left(c_{ij}^1 \right)^2 \Sigma_i \left(c_{ij}^2 \right)^2 \right]^{1/2}.$$

The index SI is the cosine between the two vectors s^{t1} and s^{t2} and varies from 0 (the two vectors are orthogonal) to 1 (the two vectors are identical). The index of occupational dissimilarity, DI, is defined as

$$(4.14) \qquad DIOCCUP^{12} = 1 - SI^{12}.$$

A second index reflects changes in the technical interindustry coefficients within an industry:

$$(4.15) \qquad DIACOEFF^{12} = 1 - \left(\Sigma_i \ A_{ij}^1 A_{ij}^2 \right) \Big/ \left[\Sigma_i \left(A_{ij}^1 \right)^2 \Sigma_i \left(A_{ij}^2 \right)^2 \right]^{1/2}.$$

A third index measures the change in capital coefficients within an industry:

$$(4.16) \qquad DIKCOEFF^{12} = 1 - \left(\Sigma_i \ g_{ij}^1 g_{ij}^2 \right) \Big/ \left[\Sigma_i \left(g_{ij}^1 \right)^2 \Sigma_i \left(g_{ij}^2 \right)^2 \right]^{1/2}.$$

A.2 Regression Analysis

In the first regression, the dependent variable is the rate of industry TFP growth. The independent variables are R&D expenditures as a percentage of net sales and the growth in the stock of OCA capital. The statistical technique is based on pooled cross-section time-series regressions on industries for the decades that correspond with the decennial census data. The sample consists of 44 industries in the three time periods (1960–1970, 1970–1980, and 1980–1990) and 32 industries in the 1990–2000 period.[10] The estimating equation is

$$(4.17) \qquad TFPGRTH_j = \beta_0 + \beta_1 \ RDSALES_j + \beta_2 \ OCAGRTH_j + v_j,$$

where $TFPGRTH_j$ is the rate of TFP growth in sector j, $RDSALES_j$ is the ratio of R&D expenditures to net sales in sector j, OCAGRTH is the rate of growth of the stock of OCA capital, and v_j is a stochastic error term. The time subscript has been suppressed for notational convenience. It is assumed that the v_{jt} are independently distributed, but they may not be identically distributed. The regression results use the White procedure for a heteroscedasticity-consistent covariance matrix.

From equation 4.4 it follows that the constant β_0 is the pure rate of Hicks-neutral technological progress. From Griliches (1980) and Mansfield (1980), the coefficient of RDSALES is interpreted as the rate of return of R&D, under the assumption that the average rate of return to R&D is equalized across sectors.[11] Time dummies for the 1970s and 1980s are introduced to allow for period-specific effects on productivity growth attributable to neither R&D nor OCA investment. A dummy variable identifying the 10 service industries is also included to partially control for measurement problems in service sector output.

A.2.1 Basic Regression Results

Regression results for the full sample are shown in columns 1 and 2 of appendix table 4.1. The constant term ranges from 0.014 to 0.017 over the full 1960–2000 period and from 0.022 to 0.026 for the 1980–2000 period. These estimates are comparable to previous estimates of the Hick-neutral rate of technological change (see Griliches 1979, for example). The coefficient of the ratio of R&D expenditures to net sales is significant at the 5 percent level. The estimated rate of return to R&D ranges from 0.13 to 0.16 (across all regressions). These estimates are about average compared to previous work on the subject (see Mohnen 1992, for example, for a review of previous studies).[12]

The coefficient of the growth of OCA is negative but not statistically significant. The same result holds for two alternative measures of IT: (1) the stock of computers and peripherals and (2) the stock of OCACM (i.e., the sum of OCA and communications equipment) (results not shown). As noted earlier, these specifications actually measure the excess returns to computer investment over and above those to capital in general since TFP growth already controls for the growth of total capital stock per worker. The coefficient of the dummy variable for service industries is significant at the 1 percent level; its value is -0.019. The coefficient of the dummy variable for the 1970s is negative but not significant, and those for the 1960s and the 1980s are positive but not significant.

Because of difficulties in measuring output in many service industries, regressions were also performed separately for the 31 goods-producing industries (see the data appendix).[13] The coefficient values and significance levels of the constant term, R&D intensity, the dummy variable for services, and the three time-period dummy variables are strikingly similar to those for the all-industry regressions (see specifications 3 and 4 of appendix table 4.1). The coefficient of the growth in computer stock remains negative but insignificant (specification 4).[14]

In the next two regressions, I focus on the "computer age," the period from 1980 to 2000. Does the effect of computerization on productivity growth now show up for this restricted sample? The answer is still negative, as shown in specifications 5 and 6 of appendix table 4.1. The coefficients of the other two computerization variables—the rate of growth in the stock of computers and the rate of OCACM—are also insignificant (results not shown). R&D intensity remains significant in these regressions, and the estimated return to R&D is higher, at 16 percent. The same results for computerization and R&D investment are found when the sample is further restricted to the period from 1990 to 2000.

Appendix 4.1. Cross-Industry Regressions of Industry TFP Growth on R&D Intensity and OCA Growth

Independent Variables	Specification					
	(1)	(2)	(3)	(4)	(5)	(6)
Constant	0.014 **	0.017 **	0.014 *	0.015 *	0.026 *	0.022 *
	(2.78)	(2.73)	(2.31)	(1.99)	(2.57)	(1.74)
Ratio of R&D expenditures to sales	0.131 #	0.136 #	0.148 #	0.150 #	0.160	0.161
	(1.68)	(1.72)	(1.64)	(1.64)	(1.25)	(1.07)
Annual growth in OCA		−0.025		−0.010	−0.078	−0.062
		(0.91)		(0.28)	(1.36)	(0.82)
Dummy variable for services	−0.019 **	−0.019 **			−0.030 **	
	(4.24)	(4.20)			(3.71)	
Dummy variable for 1960–1970	0.002	−0.001	0.001	0.000	0.005	0.009
	(0.41)	(0.08)	(0.12)	(0.04)	(0.69)	(1.02)
Dummy variable for 1970–1980	−0.008	−0.008	−0.012	−0.012		
	(1.31)	(1.35)	(1.53)	(1.51)		
Dummy variable for 1980–1990	0.005	0.005	0.010	0.010		
	(0.93)	(0.85)	(1.26)	(1.25)		
R^2	0.169	0.170	0.096	0.096	0.199	0.051
Adjusted R^2	0.143	0.139	0.064	0.056	0.154	−0.004
Standard error	0.0253	0.0256	0.0283	0.0284	0.0301	0.0331
Sample size	168	164	118	118	76	56
Sample	All	All	Goods	Goods	All	Goods
Period	1960–2000	1960–2000	1960–2000	1960–2000	1980–2000	1980–2000

Note: The full sample consists of pooled cross-section, time-series data, with observations on each of 44 industries in 1960–1970, 1970–1980, and 1980–1990, and 32 industries in 1990–2000 (sector 45, public administration, is excluded because of a lack of data on OCA). The goods sample consists of 31 industries (industries 1–31 in appendix table 1). The coefficients are estimated using the White procedure for a heteroschedasticity-consistent covariance matrix. The absolute value of the t-statistic is in parentheses below the coefficient. See the data appendix for sources and methods.

Significance levels: # 10% level; * 5% level; ** 1% level.

A.2.2 Regression Results with Worker Skills

Appendix table 4.2 shows the regression results for various measures of worker skills. Following equations 4.11 and 4.12, I use labor productivity growth as the dependent variable. The first specification does not include skill change but splits total capital into OCA and other capital. The coefficient of the growth of OCA per worker is virtually zero, and the t-statistic is close to zero. This provides further corroboration of a lack of a special effect of OCA investment on productivity growth.

In the third specification, I include the change of the three measures of workplace skills: substantive complexity (SC), interactive skills (IS), and motor skills (MS). I also include the growth of total capital per worker. None of the skill variables is statistically significant in this regression. The coefficient of the change in MS is, in fact, negative. When the change in cognitive skills is included by itself, its coefficient becomes negative but remains insignificant (specification 4). The change in the composite skill index CS is also negative and insignificant (specification 5). The coefficient of the change in mean education is virtually zero and not statistically significant (specification 6).[15] This set of results remains robust among alternative samples—goods-producing industries only and for the 1980–2000 period.[16]

In the set of regressions shown in appendix table 4.2, R&D intensity is significant at the 10 percent level, and its estimated value is about the same as in the corresponding TFP regressions (appendix table 4.1). The coefficient of the dummy variable for services is slightly lower (in absolute value) than in the TFP regressions. The coefficient of the growth of total capital per worker is in the range of 0.32 to 0.34, about the same as its income share, and is significant at the 1 percent level in all cases.

As discussed in the introduction, Brynjolfsson and Hitt (1996, 1998) have found a positive correlation between firm-level productivity growth and IT investment when the introduction of IT was accompanied by organizational changes. This finding suggests that interaction effects may exist between OCA investment and changes in occupational composition. This was investigated by adding an interaction term between the growth of OCA per worker and DIOCCUP to the labor productivity regression equation derived from 4.11. The regression was estimated for the full sample of industries as well as for goods industries only over both the 1960–2000 and the 1980–2000 periods. The coefficient of the interaction term is statistically insignificant in all of the cases and actually negative in about half of them.[17]

A.2.3 Other Indicators of Technological Activity

In the last set of regressions (appendix table 4.3), measures of structural change are used as dependent variables. As before, the statistical technique is based on pooled cross-section time-series regressions on industries and on the decades that correspond with the decennial census data. The sample

Appendix 4.2. Cross-Industry Regressions of Industry Labor Productivity Growth on R&D Intensity, Capital Investment, and Skill Change, 1960–2000

Independent Variables	Specification					
	(1)	(2)	(3)	(4)	(5)	(6)
Constant	0.021 **	0.020 **	0.020 **	0.021 **	0.021 **	0.019 **
	(3.31)	(3.68)	(3.00)	(3.82)	(3.80)	(3.40)
Ratio of R&D expenditures to sales	0.164 #	0.182 #	0.174 #	0.184 #	0.164 #	0.170 #
	(1.73)	(1.86)	(1.84)	(1.95)	(1.73)	(1.77)
Growth in OCA per worker	−0.010					
	(0.37)					
Growth in total capital less OCA per worker	0.335 **					
	(3.45)					
Growth in total capital per worker		0.321 **	0.328 **	0.335 **	0.333 **	0.319 **
		(3.39)	(3.39)	(3.50)	(3.48)	(3.35)
Change in Substantive Complexity: DEL(SC)			0.002	−0.007		
			(0.12)	(1.00)		
Change in Interactive Skills: DEL(IS)			0.002			
			(0.10)			
Change in Motor Skills: DEL(MS)			−0.014			
			(0.74)			
Change in Composite Skills: DEL(CP)					−0.014	
					(0.94)	

	(1)	(2)	(3)	(4)	(5)	(6)
Change in mean education						0.001
						(0.23)
Dummy variable for services	−0.017 **	−0.018 **	−0.019 **	−0.018 **	−0.018 **	−0.017 **
	(3.80)	(3.90)	(4.05)	(3.98)	(3.97)	(3.81)
Dummy variable for 1960–1970	−0.003	−0.002	−0.001	−0.002	−0.002	−0.002
	(0.49)	(0.32)	(0.18)	(0.36)	(0.32)	(0.36)
Dummy variable for 1970–1980	−0.012 *	−0.012 *	−0.011	−0.013 *	−0.012 *	−0.013 *
	(2.01)	(1.99)	(1.58)	(2.10)	(2.07)	(1.82)
Dummy variable for 1980–1990	0.002	0.001	0.003	0.001	0.001	0.001
	(0.26)	(0.24)	(0.46)	(0.14)	(0.16)	(0.17)
R^2	0.221	0.218	0.229	0.223	0.222	0.218
Adjusted R^2	0.186	0.188	0.184	0.188	0.187	0.183
Standard error	0.0250	0.0250	0.0251	0.0250	0.0250	0.0251
Sample size	164	164	164	164	164	164

Note: The sample consists of pooled cross-section, time-series data, with observations on each of 44 industries in 1960–1970, 1970–1980 and 1980–1990 and 32 industries in 1990–2000 (public administration is excluded because of a lack of OCA data). The estimation uses the White procedure for a heteroschedasticity-consistent covariance matrix. The absolute value of the t-statistic is in parentheses below the coefficient. See the data appendix for sources and methods.

Significance levels: # 10% level; * 5% level; ** 1% level.

135

consists of 44 industries and two time periods (1970–1980 and 1980–1990).[18] The basic estimating equation is of the same form as equation 4.17, with R&D intensity and the growth of OCA stock as independent variables. Dummy variables are also included for the service sector and the 1970s. Moreover, following 4.11, I also use the growth of OCA per worker and OCA investment per worker as independent variables in place of the growth of total OCA stock.

The first of the dependent variables is the change in occupational composition (DIOCCUP). In contrast to the TFP regressions, the coefficient of investment in OCA per worker is positive and significant at the 1 percent level in the regression without the service and time-period dummy variables and positive and significant at the 5 percent level when the dummy variables are included. The coefficients of the alternative computerization measures, the growth in OCA per employee, investment in OCACM per worker, and the rate of growth in the stock of OCACM per employee are also significant at the 1 or 5 percent level (results not shown). However, the best fit is provided by investment in OCA per worker. The results also show that R&D intensity is not a significant factor in accounting for changes in occupational composition. Nor is the dummy variable for services. However, the time-period dummy variable is significant at the 5 percent level.[19]

The second variable is DIACOEFF, a measure of the degree of change in interindustry technical coefficients. In this case, too, computerization is significant at the 1 percent level with the predicted positive coefficient. The best fit is provided by investment in OCA per worker. The coefficient of R&D intensity is positive but not statistically significant, as is the coefficient of the dummy variable for services. The coefficient of the time dummy variable is virtually zero.

The third index of structural change is DIKCOEFF, a measure of how much the composition of capital has changed over the period. In this case, it is not possible to use investment in OCA as an independent variable since, by construction, it will be correlated with changes in the capital coefficients. Instead, I use the initial level of OCA per worker. The computerization variable has the predicted positive sign and is significant, though only at the 10 percent level. The coefficient of R&D is positive but insignificant. However, the dummy variable for services is positive and significant at the 1 percent level. The coefficient of the dummy variable for 1970–1980 is negative but not significant.

In sum, computerization is found to be strongly linked to occupational restructuring and changes in material usage and weakly linked to changes in the composition of capital. With regard to the first result, it might be appropriate to say a few words about the construction of industry OCA by the Bureau of Economic Analysis. The allocation of investment in OCA is based partly on the occupational composition of an industry. As a result, a spurious correlation may be introduced between industry-level OCA investment and the skill mix of an industry. The cross-industry correlation between OCA

Appendix 4.3. Cross-Industry Regressions of Indicators of Structural Change on Computer Investment

Independent Variables	Dependent Variable					
	DIOCCUP	DIOCCUP	DIACOEFF	DIACOEFF	DIKCOEFF	DIKCOEFF
Constant	0.048 **	0.055 **	0.001	−0.02 *	0.016 **	0.008
	7.29	(8.00)	(0.13)	(2.24)	(2.98)	(1.02)
Ratio of R&D expenditures to sales	0.251	0.214	0.136	0.309	0.206	0.129
	(1.10)	(0.97)	(0.59)	(1.57)	(1.17)	(0.71)
Investment in OCA per worker	0.060 **	0.048 *	0.043 **	0.024 **		
	(3.07)	(2.23)	(5.24)	(2.98)		
Initial level of OCA per worker					0.032 #	0.031 #
					(1.81)	(1.66)
Dummy variable for services		0.008		0.017		0.026 **
		(0.08)		(1.51)		(2.83)
Dummy variable for 1970–1980		−0.021 *		−0.001		−0.007
		(2.30)		(0.12)		(0.89)

(continued)

Appendix 4.3. (continued)

Independent Variables	Dependent Variable					
	DIOCCUP	DIOCCUP	DIACOEFF	DIACOEFF	DIKCOEFF	DIKCOEFF
R^2	0.112	0.145	0.250	0.271	0.135	0.165
Adjusted R^2	0.091	0.104	0.223	0.227	0.104	0.114
Standard error	0.0470	0.0457	0.0429	0.0410	0.0339	0.0341
Sample size	88	88	88	88	88	88
Industries	All	All	All	All	All	All

Note: The sample consists of pooled cross-section, time-series data with observations on each of 44 industries (excluding the government sector) in 1970–1980 and 1980–1990. The coefficients are estimated using the White procedure for a heteroschedasticity-consistent covariance matrix. The absolute value of the t-statistic is shown in parentheses below the coefficient estimate.

Key:
DIOCCUP: dissimilarity index for occupational coefficients
DIACOEFF: dissimilarity index for technical interindustry coefficients
DIKCOEFF: dissimilarity index for capital coefficients

Significance levels: # significant at the 10% level; * significant at the 5% level; ** significant at the 1% level per worker and the mean SC level is 0.48 in 1970, 0.39 in 1980, and 0.56 in 1990, while that between OCA per worker and the mean schooling level of an industry is 0.46 in 1970, 0.29 in 1980, and 0.37 in 1990.

However, there is no indication that this allocation procedure should affect the *change* in occupational composition and hence introduce a spurious correlation between OCA investment and the DIOCCUP variable. Moreover, the time-series evidence shows a marked acceleration in the degree of occupational change between the 1970s and 1980s, when OCA investment rose substantially. Regressions of the change in occupational composition (DIOCCUP) on both the growth of equipment per worker and the growth of total capital per worker fail to yield significant coefficients. As a result, we can surmise that this finding is on solid ground.

Notes

1. The results reported in this chapter update previous work in Wolff (1999a). Because of the use of different data sources, time periods, and regression specifications, the findings reported here differ somewhat from those of my earlier article.
2. A second index of TFP growth was also used, with full-time equivalent (FTE) employees as the measure of labor input, as well as labor productivity growth. Results are very similar on the basis of this measure and are not reported here.
3. In November 1999, the U.S. Bureau of Economic Analysis (BEA) released a major revision of the U.S. national accounts. The new BEA data showed a faster rise in real GDP and hence labor productivity during the 1990s than the older data indicated. One major element of the revision is the treatment of software expenses as a capital good rather than as an intermediate purchase. The results reported here for the 1990s use the new BEA output and capital stock data.
4. These three sectors are classified with the other goods-producing sectors because their productivity patterns are very similar and they do not suffer from the same kinds of output measurement problems experienced by the more traditional service sectors.
5. With the adoption of the North American Industrial Classification System (NAICS) in the United States in 1997, a major change occurred in the occupational classifications used between the 1990 and 2000 decennial censuses. As a result, it was not possible to compute DIOCCUP for the 1990s.
6. Calculations of DIACOEFF and DIKCOEFF could not be updated to the 1990s because, as of May 2005, the new BEA benchmark input-output table for 2002 was still not available (as of May of 2005).
7. In 1997, the BEA revised its capital stock series to include software as a form of equipment investment. As of May 2005, the software series has been backdated to only 1987. For consistency with the earlier years, I exclude software from OCA.
8. This is a modified form of the production function used by Stiroh (2002).

9. Technically, we impose the assumption of constant returns to scale of the traditional factors of production, so that

$$\alpha_{Cj} + \alpha_{Oj} + \alpha_{Nj} + \alpha_{Lj} = 1.$$

10. The 1950–1960 period cannot be included in the regression analysis because the R&D series begins fully only in 1958. The government sector is excluded because of a lack of data on OCA investment. Moreover, because of a major change in industrial classification in 1997 with the adoption of the NAICS in the United States, the 1990–2000 sample consists of only 32 industries (excluding the government sector).

11. The proof is that RDSALES = dR/X. From 4.2 and 4.4 it follows that

$$\pi = \epsilon_R (dR/R) = \epsilon_R (dR/X)(X/R) = (\epsilon_R X/R)(dR/X).$$

Therefore,

$$\beta_1 = (\epsilon_R X/R) = (dX/X)(X/R)/(dR/R) = dX/dR.$$

The term dX/dR is the marginal productivity of R&D capital, which is equivalent to the rate of return to R&D.

12. The coefficient of the number of full-time equivalent scientists and engineers engaged in R&D per employee is also significant in every case, typically at the 1 percent level. In the tables, I present the results using R&D expenditures because it is more conventional.

13. Since output measurement problems are less likely to affect transportation, communications, and utilities, they are classified as goods-producing industries here.

14. Results are again similar when the sample of industries is further restricted to the 20 manufacturing industries (results not shown).

15. Results are similar when the rate of growth of skills and mean education are used instead of their change over the period.

16. Results remain almost unchanged when an alternative measure of labor productivity growth, based on full-time equivalent employees (FTEE) instead of PEP, is used as the dependent variable.

17. Regressions were also estimated with interaction terms between the growth of OCA per worker and the growth or change in SC, CS, and mean education. None of these interaction terms is found to be statistically significant.

18. The 1950s and the 1960s are not included in the regression analysis because OCA investment was very small during these decades. The government sector, moreover, cannot be included because of a lack of data on OCA investment.

19. It is not possible to use changes in skill levels or education as independent variables since, by definition, they would be associated with shifts in occupational composition.

5

The Growth of the Information Economy

5.1 Introduction

Fritz Machlup's classic 1962 book, *The Production and Distribution of Knowledge in the United States,* states that, with the growth of clerical occupations at the turn of the twentieth century, "the ascendancy of knowledge-producing occupations has been an uninterrupted process . . . a movement from manual to mental, and from less to more highly trained labor" (396–397). Since the book's appearance, several studies, including Porat (1977), Beniger (1986), Rubin and Huber (1986), Baumol, Blackman, and Wolff (1989), and Reich (1991) have documented the growth in the relative size of the information economy. Baumol, Blackman, and Wolff (1989, chapter 7), in particular, found that information workers increased from about 42 percent of the workforce in 1960 to 53 percent in 1980.

In this chapter I document the growth of information workers in the U.S. economy during the postwar period and analyze the sources of this expansion. The growth in the information economy is important for two reasons: First, it may shed additional light on the factors that explain why workplace skills have not kept up with educational attainment and wages have not grown along with skills and education. Second, it has a direct bearing on the educational and training needs of the labor force.

The next part of this chapter, section 5.2, updates the statistics on the composition of the workforce between information and noninformation jobs up to 2000. Particular interest is focused on the post-1980 period, which experienced tremendous growth in the use of computers in production and which Christopher Freeman (1987) and others have termed a new "techno-economic paradigm," based on computer-driven information technology. For

this analysis I rely again on matrices of employment by occupation and industry derived from the decennial U.S. censuses of 1950, 1960, 1970, 1980,
1990, and 2000. The occupations are aggregated into four categories: (1)
knowledge producers, (2) data processors, (3) service workers, and (4) goods-
processing workers.

I find that information workers (the sum of the first two categories) increased from 37 percent of the workforce in 1950 to 59 percent in 2000, with
the rate of increase for knowledge-producing workers peaking in the 1960s
and 1970s and then slowing down somewhat, while that of data workers
peaked in the 1960s and then tapered off. Yet, all in all, most of the growth
in information employment did not take place among highly skilled, highly
paid professionals and managers but rather among moderately skilled, relatively low-paid clerical and sales workers. Another interesting finding is that,
while more than half of total employment in 1950 was in blue-collar jobs, this
proportion slipped to less than a quarter by 2000. As Machlup predicted, we
have moved from a society in which we work with our hands to one in which
we work with our minds.

The section 5.3 uses a decomposition analysis to break down the changes
in the information workers' share of the labor force into three parts: (1) the
substitution of information labor for other types of labor within the production process—that is, the change in the proportion of information workers
in each industry's labor force; (2) the change in each industry's share of the
economy's total output; and (3) the change associated with relative variations
in labor productivity of the different industries.

The first of these three components indicates the extent to which the composition of the labor force in a typical industry has become more information
intensive (assuming all other things remain the same). The second element
relates to different industries' shares of the economy's final output and is
pertinent in determining the extent to which the expansion in information-
related employment is attributable to an increase in the economy's demand
for products with a high information content. The third component tests the
role of unbalanced growth in the information explosion—that is, the extent
to which the increase in the number of information workers can be attributed
to relatively lower productivity growth in industries using more information.

I find that the growth in the number of information workers was driven
not by a shift in tastes toward information-intensive goods and services (as
measured by the composition of final demand) but rather by a roughly equal
combination of the substitution of information workers for goods and service
workers within the structure of production of industries and the unbalanced-
growth effect.

The appendix to chapter 5 relies on econometric analysis to analyze the
sources of growth in the number of information workers at the industry level.
The dependent variables are the changes in knowledge as a percentage of total employment and in data workers as a share of employment in the industry
over the period. As in the earlier chapters, independent variables include

(1) total factor productivity (TFP) growth, (2) expenditures on research and development, (3) investment in new equipment, and (4) investment in office, computer, and accounting machinery (OCA). The regressions also control for a number of structural and organizational dimensions of production, such as the unionization rate, as well as the degree of international competitiveness of an industry.

The most significant factor in the increase in the number of knowledge workers is R&D expenditures, but it is negatively associated with the rise in the number of data workers. Investment in OCA exerts a positive effect on the employment of knowledge workers but has a strong negative effect on the employment of data workers.

5.2 Growth of Information Employment

The basic data are from the U.S. decennial censuses of 1950, 1960, 1970, 1980, 1990, and 2000. In the calculations, the figures in the census tables of employment by occupation and industry are first aggregated, in conformity with an internally consistent classification scheme, into 267 occupations and 64 industries (see the data appendix for details). The occupations are aggregated once more into the following six categories:

  knowledge production
  data processing
  supply of services
  goods production
  a hybrid class including both knowledge and data activities
  a hybrid class including both data and service activities

I then (somewhat arbitrarily) classify half of those that fall into the hybrid knowledge/data category as knowledge workers and the other half as data workers. In similar fashion, I split the hybrid data/service category half into data and half into service workers. The resulting groups are referred to as the "total knowledge," "total data," and "total service" categories. Information workers are then defined as the sum of total knowledge and total data workers. The noninformation category is composed of the residual—including total service and goods-processing workers.[1]

In the classification schema, professional and technical workers are generally classified as knowledge or data workers, depending on whether they are producers or users of knowledge (see appendix table 4 for details). The line is somewhat arbitrary at points, and there I have made judgment calls. Moreover, in some cases, professional workers are classified as data-service workers. For example, doctors and nurses are treated in this way since they use information and also perform a personal service. Management personnel are taken to perform both data and knowledge tasks since they produce new information for administrative decisions and also use and transmit this information. Clerical workers are classed as data workers for obvious reasons. I classify all labor that transforms or operates on materials or physical objects as goods-processing workers. These include craftpeople, operatives (including transportation workers who move physical goods), and unskilled labor. The remaining group is made up of the service workers, who perform primarily personal services.

Table 5.1 breaks down total employment by type of worker from 1950 to 2000, the corresponding growth rates in each category, and the percentage of composition.[2] Over the five decades, knowledge workers were the fastest-growing group, increasing 3.1 percent per year. They were followed by data workers and service workers at 2.5 percent per year and 2.4 percent per year, respectively. In contrast, goods producers increased their number by only 0.2 percent per year. Altogether, employment of information workers grew 2.6 percent per year (1 percentage point above average), while noninformation workers increased 0.8 percent per year (about 1 percentage point below average).

The developments differ by decade. Between 1950 and 1960, the fastest-growing group was service workers, whose numbers grew by 3.4 percent per year, followed by data workers (2.7 percent per year) and knowledge workers (1.7 percent). Goods producers declined in absolute number. In the next decade, knowledge workers led the way at 3.5 percent per year, followed by data workers (3.3 percent) and service workers (1.9 percent). The number of goods producers again fell in absolute terms.

The 1970s again saw knowledge workers with the highest growth rate (3.7 percent per year), followed by data and service workers (2.8 percent) and goods-processing workers, whose employment increased in absolute terms by 1.0 percent per year. During the 1980s knowledge workers again led all of the groups, at 3.1 percent per year, followed by data and service workers at 1.9 and 2.0 percent per year, respectively, and goods-processing workers at 1.0 percent per year. The 1990s again saw knowledge workers in the lead, at 3.1 percent per year, followed by data and service workers at 1.8 and 1.7 percent per year, respectively, while goods-producing workers again declined in absolute terms.

The last section of table 5.1 (as well as figure 5.1) provides another way of viewing the growth of the information sector. In 1950, 8 percent of total employment consisted of knowledge workers, and 29 percent consisted of data workers. Altogether, 37 percent of the employed labor force was made up of information workers. Goods workers formed a majority of total employment, at 52 percent, while service workers constituted only 10 percent of total employment. By 2000, the proportion of information workers in total employment had increased to 59 percent of the total. The number of knowledge workers had risen to 15 percent and that of data workers to 44 percent

Table 5.1. Employment Growth and Percentage Composition of Employment by Type of Worker, 1950–2000

Type of Worker	Total Employment (in millions)					
	1950	1960	1970	1980	1990	2000
1. Knowledge	2.2	2.8	4.8	6.8	9.4	13.9
2. Data	14.2	19.0	26.9	34.7	41.1	49.1
3. Knowledge/data	4.5	5.0	5.4	8.2	11.9	14.0
4. Data/services	1.7	2.0	3.0	4.9	5.4	7.2
5. Services	6.0	8.4	10.2	13.5	16.5	19.5
6. Goods	30.4	28.6	28.3	31.2	34.4	33.2
7. Total knowledge	4.4	5.3	7.5	10.9	15.3	20.9
8. Total data	17.2	22.5	31.1	41.2	49.8	59.7
9. Total information	21.7	27.8	38.6	52.1	65.1	80.6
10. Total noninformation	37.2	38.0	40.0	47.2	53.6	56.3
11. Total employment	58.9	65.8	78.7	99.3	118.8	136.9

Type of Worker	Annual Rate of Growth of Employment (in percent)					
	1950–1960	1960–1970	1970–1980	1980–1990	1990–2000	1950–2000
Total knowledge	1.7	3.5	3.7	3.4	3.1	3.1
Total data	2.7	3.3	2.8	1.9	1.8	2.5
Total services	3.4	1.9	2.8	2.0	1.7	2.4
Goods	−0.6	−0.1	1.0	1.0	−0.4	0.2
Total information	2.5	3.3	3.0	2.2	2.1	2.6
Total noninformation	0.2	0.5	1.6	1.3	0.5	0.8
Total	1.1	1.8	2.3	1.8	1.4	1.7

Type of Worker	Percent Distribution of Employment					
	1950	1960	1970	1980	1990	2000
Total knowledge	7.5	8.0	9.6	11.0	12.9	15.2
Total data	29.2	34.2	39.6	41.5	41.9	43.6
Total services	10.2	12.8	13.0	13.6	13.9	14.2
Goods	51.7	43.5	36.0	31.4	29.0	24.3
Total information	36.8	42.2	49.1	52.5	54.8	58.9
Total noninformation	63.2	57.8	50.9	47.5	45.2	41.1
Total	100.0	100.0	100.0	100.0	100.0	100.0

Note: The total for knowledge workers (line 7) is given by the sum of line 1 and half of line 3. The total for data workers (line 8) is given by the sum of line 2, half of line 3, and half of line 4. The total for information workers (line 9) is defined as the sum of line 7 and line 8. The total for noninformation workers (line 10) is the residual.

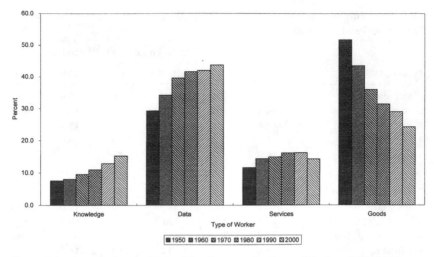

Figure 5.1   Percent Composition of Employment by Type of Worker, 1950–2000

of total employment. Service workers were up to 14 percent, and goods producers had dropped dramatically to 24 percent.

In sum, knowledge workers grew as a share of total employment in each of the five decades and constituted the fastest-growing group in all but the 1950s. However, its biggest increase in relative terms occurred during the 1980s and 1990s, when its share of total employment increased by about 2 percentage points in each decade. Data workers enjoyed their largest growth in relative terms during the 1950s and 1960s. There was a marked slowdown in the increase of their share of total employment in the 1970s, while during the 1980s there was virtually no change in their share. The share of service workers in total employment rose quite rapidly in the 1950s and much more slowly thereafter. The share of goods producers in total employment fell in every decade, and in the 1950s, 1960s, and 1990s its number declined in absolute terms as well.

5.3 Industry Changes in Information Employment

Since our subsequent analysis depends substantially on comparative shifts in the share of information workers among industries, I first examine the relative information intensity of the major sectors of the economy (see appendix table 4 for details on the classification scheme). Table 5.2 and figure 5.2 show that, in 2000, the finance, insurance, and real estate sector had the highest percentage of knowledge workers in their employment (about 22 percent), followed by business and other services and the government sector in a virtual tie (at about 19 percent). Mining (largely geologists and engineers),

Table 5.2.   Knowledge and Data Workers as a Percentage of Total Employment
by Major Industry, 1950–2000

Sector	1950	1960	1970	1980	1990	2000
A. Knowledge Workers						
Agriculture	0.5	0.9	2.3	3.4	3.6	9.7
Mining	4.5	7.6	10.5	12.6	14.8	13.4
Manufacturing	5.9	7.0	9.3	9.8	11.9	17.8
Construction	4.9	7.2	7.7	7.6	10.1	8.4
Transportation, communications, and utilities	5.8	6.7	7.8	9.5	11.3	14.5
Trade	10.6	7.9	7.0	9.3	10.7	6.0
Finance, insurance, and real estate	9.2	10.6	10.6	12.1	15.4	21.7
Business and other services	12.0	11.1	12.5	13.7	15.6	18.7
Government	12.4	11.8	13.9	15.5	16.1	18.6
Total goods	4.4	6.1	8.3	9.0	10.9	14.4
Total services	11.2	9.9	10.5	12.2	14.0	15.6
Total	7.5	8.0	9.6	11.0	12.9	15.2
B. Data Workers						
Agriculture	0.7	1.4	3.9	6.2	7.2	13.7
Mining	11.2	17.3	23.4	26.3	28.5	24.3
Manufacturing	21.8	22.9	25.9	27.3	27.1	28.3
Construction	7.8	12.2	17.5	19.8	19.2	22.6
Transportation, communications, and utilities	32.4	31.9	35.7	37.1	36.1	39.0
Trade	51.9	54.5	52.9	51.6	53.0	60.8
Finance, insurance, and real estate	69.2	79.1	80.3	79.3	75.8	65.5
Business and other services	31.1	35.1	43.5	45.1	45.0	45.3
Government	53.7	54.2	52.9	51.1	48.2	37.5
Total goods	16.0	19.7	24.4	26.1	25.8	28.3
Total services	45.0	48.2	51.0	51.2	50.9	50.2
Total	29.2	34.2	39.6	41.5	41.9	43.6

Note: Calculations are shown for total knowledge workers and total data workers. The goods sector consists of agriculture; mining; manufacturing; construction; and transportation, communications, and utilities. The service sector includes trade; finance, insurance, and real estate; business and other services; and government.

manufacturing, and transportation, communications, and utilities followed in a second group. At the bottom were agriculture, construction, and trade. All told, service industries had a slightly higher share of knowledge workers than goods-producing sectors—15.6 versus 14.4 percent.

The share of data workers among sectors exhibits greater variation. In 2000, the finance, insurance, and real estate sector led the way at 66 percent, and it was also the most information intensive: About 87 percent of its employees were knowledge or data workers. The trade sector was next in line,

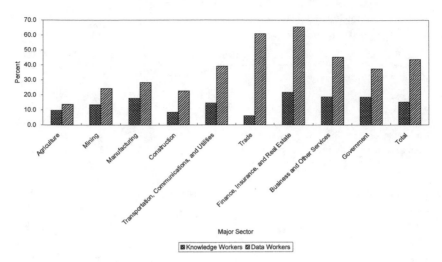

Figure 5.2   Knowledge and Data Workers as Percentage of Employment by Major Sector, 2000

at 61 percent, followed by business and other services at 45 percent; transportation, communications, and utilities at 39 percent; and the government sector at 38 percent. In agriculture, mining, construction, and manufacturing, data workers comprised 14–28 percent of total employment. The share of data workers in total employment was almost twice as high in services as in goods industries.

Marked differences also occur in time trends between goods-producing sectors and services. The former saw an almost steady rise in both knowledge workers and data workers as a share of total industry employment between 1950 and 2000. In manufacturing, in particular, information workers constituted 46 percent of total employment by 2000 (up from 28 percent in 1950), and blue-collar production workers made up 52 percent (down from 70 percent in 1950); service workers constituted the remainder. This result confirms the growing "white-collarization" of manufacturing in the United States that the press often alludes to.

Among service industries, the percentage of knowledge workers in employment fell off between 1950 and 1960 (as well as 1970 in one case), followed generally by a steady rise through 2000 (with the trade sector an exception). In contrast, data workers increased relative to total employment in all four service sectors between 1950 and 1960. In the trade sector, the share of data workers held steady from 1960 to 1990 and then climbed in 2000; in finance, insurance, and real estate, the share remained relatively constant between 1960 and 1980 and then declined from 1980 to 2000; in business and other services, the share increased from 1960 to 1980 and then remained constant from 1980 to 2000; and in the government sector, the share of data workers in total employment from 1960 to 2000 gradually declined. All told, between 1950 and 2000, information workers increased in number relative to noninformation workers in all major sectors except the government.

The growth in the overall share of information workers in total employment is due to two proximate causes. The first is technological change at the industry level, which may favor information workers relative to noninformation workers. This may be attributable to the increasing sophistication and complexity of productive techniques, which require more producers, manipulators, and transmitters of knowledge. The second is shifts in the industrial composition of employment. In particular, industries that are more intensive in their use of information workers may have grown in terms of employment relative to industries that rely more heavily on service and goods-processing workers.

The second can be further decomposed into two additional effects. The first of these is from changes in the composition of final output. In particular, an increasingly educated population may be demanding products with an ever-expanding information content. The second may arise from differential movements in industry labor productivity. In particular, from the unbalanced-growth hypothesis, employment in activities with relatively slower rates of productivity growth must increase relative to employment in high productivity growth activities, even with constant output proportions (see, for example, Baumol 1967 or Baumol, Blackman, and Wolff 1989, chapter 6). The presumption is that information-intensive industries, such as business services and the government, may suffer from relatively stagnant productivity growth.

I can address this issue formally through the use of an input-output model.[3] The resulting equation decomposes the change in the occupational composition of employment into three parts:

1. The first term corresponds to the change in the employment shares of different occupations within industry. In other words, this term reflects the extent to which production processes within industries have changed their techniques so as to substitute information labor for other types of labor. This is referred to as the *substitution effect.*
2. The second term involves the change in the vector of quantities of direct plus indirect labor per unit of output by industry—that is, the change in the reciprocal of each industry's total labor productivity. This term also captures the unbalanced-growth effect—that is, the fact that total labor productivity grows at different rates in different industries. I call this the *productivity effect.*
3. The final term reflects changes in the composition of final output among different industries, which I call the *final output effect.*

If the last term turns out to be significant and substantial in an empirical calculation, this will imply that the growth in information employment is indeed attributable to an information revolution, for a large third term would indicate that buyers are typically turning increasingly to outputs whose production has a large information content. The same may also be true, in part, of a large first term, which would indicate that a typical production process has increased in reliance on information labor. However, if the second term turns out to be substantial and significant, it would suggest that a corresponding portion of the increase in share of information labor is attributable not to an upsurge in information use, but rather to unbalanced growth—the shift of labor out of activities whose productivity growth is atypically large.

The primary data source consists of U.S. standard 87-order (benchmark) Bureau of Economic (BEA) analysis input-output tables for 1947, 1958, 1963, 1967, 1972, 1977, 1982, 1987, and 1992 and the "annual" BEA input-output table for 2000, which I have used to compute both the vector of final demand and the vector that shows the direct and indirect labor requirements (see the data appendix for details on sources and methods for the input-output data). These data are aggregated to 45 sectors to align with the occupation-by-industry matrices already described (see appendix table 3 for details on the alignment).[4] Table 5.3 shows the results of the decomposition.[5]

The substitution effect gained continuing strength over time as a source of growth of employment for knowledge workers (section 1). During the 1950s, in fact, the effect was negative, indicating that industries substituted other types of workers for knowledge workers in their employment. During the 1960s, this effect contributed 0.8 percentage points to the increase in the share of knowledge workers in total employment; in the 1970s, 1.1 percentage points; and in the 1980s and the 1990s, 1.5 percentage points.

In contrast, the productivity effect was a generally diminishing source of growth for knowledge workers between 1950 and 1980, accounting for 0.9 percentage points in the 1950s, 0.7 percentage points in the 1960s, and 0.2 percentage points in the 1970s and then picking up to 0.4 percentage points in the 1980s and 0.8 percentage points in the 1990s. Differences in productivity growth between information-intensive industries and other industries fell considerably between the first two decades of the period and the second two, a reflection mainly of the sharp drop in overall productivity growth between the two 20-year periods (see chapter 4, table 4.1). These differences then widened in the last decade, as overall productivity growth rebounded.

Changes in final output composition played virtually no role at all in the growth of the share of knowledge workers in the labor force. All told, about three-fifths of the growth in this share over the half century was attributable to the substitution of knowledge workers for other types of workers within industry and the other two-fifths or so to the unbalanced-growth effect.

Results for data workers differ from those for knowledge workers. The substitution effect was much stronger in the 1950s and 1960s than in the 1970s and 1980s. In fact, the substitution effect fell from 1.6 percentage points in the 1950s to virtually zero in the 1980s. However, as with knowledge workers, the productivity effect shows a diminishing influence over time, falling from 3.3 percentage points in the 1950s to 0.3 percentage points in the 1980s, though it did rebound to 0.9 percentage points in the 1990s. Changes in the composition of final output played a modest role in the changes in the share of data workers in total employment in the 1960s, although the effect was

Table 5.3. Decomposition of the Change in Employment Composition by Type of Worker into a Substitution, Productivity, and Output Effect, 1950–2000

Type of Worker	Decomposition in Percentage Points				Percent Decomposition			
	Substitution Effect	Productivity Effect	Output Effect	Total Change	Substitution Effect	Productivity Effect	Output Effect	Total Change
1. Knowledge Workers								
1950–1960	−0.40	0.91	−0.03	0.49	−81.6	187.3	−5.7	100.0
1960–1970	0.79	0.71	0.02	1.53	51.8	46.6	1.6	100.0
1970–1980	1.11	0.24	0.08	1.42	77.8	16.6	5.5	100.0
1980–1990	1.49	0.39	0.06	1.94	76.8	19.9	3.3	100.0
1990–2000	1.53	0.77	0.03	2.33	65.7	33.0	1.3	100.0
1950–2000	4.51	3.01	0.17	7.70	58.6	39.2	2.2	100.0
2. Data Workers								
1950–1960	1.57	3.31	0.03	4.91	32.0	67.4	0.6	100.0
1960–1970	1.89	4.07	−0.57	5.40	35.1	75.5	−10.6	100.0
1970–1980	0.63	1.32	0.02	1.97	32.0	67.0	1.0	100.0
1980–1990	−0.02	0.34	0.09	0.40	−5.6	84.5	21.1	100.0
1990–2000	0.93	0.74	0.02	1.69	55.1	43.6	1.3	100.0
1950–2000	5.01	9.78	−0.41	14.38	34.8	68.0	−2.9	100.0

(continued)

Table 5.3. (continued)

Type of Worker	Decomposition in Percentage Points				Percent Decomposition			
	Substitution Effect	Productivity Effect	Output Effect	Total Change	Substitution Effect	Productivity Effect	Output Effect	Total Change
3. Service Workers								
1950–1960	1.14	1.29	0.33	2.76	41.4	46.6	12.1	100.0
1960–1970	-0.54	0.91	0.20	0.57	-94.0	159.1	35.0	100.0
1970–1980	0.13	0.61	0.45	1.18	10.7	51.5	37.8	100.0
1980–1990	-0.69	0.08	0.69	0.08	—	—	—	—
1990–2000	-0.27	0.94	0.03	0.71	-37.5	132.6	4.9	100.0
1950–2000	-0.23	3.83	1.71	5.31	-4.3	72.2	32.1	100.0
4. Goods-Processing Workers								
1950–1960	-2.32	-5.31	-0.54	-8.16	28.4	65.0	6.6	100.0
1960–1970	-2.14	-4.68	-0.67	-7.50	28.6	62.5	8.9	100.0
1970–1980	-1.86	-1.33	-1.38	-4.57	40.7	29.2	30.1	100.0
1980–1990	-0.77	-1.34	-0.31	-2.42	31.9	55.5	12.6	100.0
1990–2000	-2.20	-2.56	0.03	-4.73	46.5	54.2	-0.7	100.0
1950–2000	-9.29	-15.23	-2.86	-27.38	33.9	55.6	10.4	100.0

Note: Calculations are shown for total knowledge workers, total data workers, total service workers, and goods producers. Average period weights are used in all cases. The substitution, productivity, and output effects refer, respectively, to the three terms of equation 5.3.

152

negative (−0.6 percentage points). In the other decades, the effect was very small. Over the entire five decades, output changes had only a very minor bearing on the growth of data workers in total employment. The dominant effect was uneven productivity growth, which accounted for about two-thirds of the increase in its share of total employment, while the substitution effect contributed the other one-third or so.

For service worker employment, the substitution effect was positive and relatively strong in the 1950s, contributing 1.1 percentage points to the growth in their share of total employment. However, the effect was very weak thereafter. During the 1960s, 1980s, and 1990s, the effect was actually negative, indicating that information workers were substituted for service employees. The unbalanced-growth effect was also strong in the 1950s, 1.3 percentage points, then gradually lessened over time, reaching 0.1 percentage points in the 1980s, but then climbed to 0.9 percentage points in the 1990s. Changes in output composition had a positive effect on the employment of service workers. It generally increased over time, from 0.3 percentage points in the 1950s to 0.7 percentage points in the 1980s, reflecting primarily the increased demand for medical, educational, social, and personal services, but then tailed off to virtually zero in the 1990s. Over the entire 1950–2000 period, the principal source of growth in the share of service employment in total employment was the productivity effect, which accounted for more than 70 percent of its growth, followed by changes in output composition, which accounted for 32 percent, and, finally, the substitution effect, which accounted for only about −4 percent.

The story for goods-processing workers is very different from that for the other types of workers. All three effects were strongly negative, and each played a role in the decline in the share of goods-processing workers in total employment. The strongest influence was the differential productivity effect, which accounted for more than half of its total decrease between 1950 and 2000. The effect was extremely strong in the 1950s and 1960s (−5.3 and −4.7 percentage points, respectively) and accounted for more than 60 percent of the relative decline of goods workers in those two decades. In the 1970s and 1980s, the effect fell to −1.3 percentage points, though here, too, it strengthened in the 1990s to −2.6 percentage points. The substitution effect explains another third of the decrease in the share of goods-processing workers in total employment over the entire half century. The effect gradually diminished, from −2.3 percentage points in the 1950s to −0.8 percentage points in the 1980s, though it once again picked up to −2.2 percentage points in the 1990s. Changes in output composition also played a role, accounting for 10 percent of its overall decline as a share of total employment over the entire period. The effect was particularly strong in the 1970s, when it contributed −1.4 percentage points, or 30 percent of the drop in its share.

In sum, on the production side of the economy, a large contribution was made by technological change within each industry that substituted information labor for other types of labor. The substitution component explains almost three-fifths of the growth in the share of knowledge workers and more than a third of the growth in the share of data workers. It also accounts for more than a third of the decline in the share of goods-processing workers but for none of the growth in the percentage of service workers in total employment.

The unbalanced-productivity component was the strongest of the three effects. The absorption of workers from industries whose productivity grew relatively slowly explains almost two-fifths of the increase in the share of knowledge workers in total employment, two-thirds of the increase in the share of data workers, more than 70 percent of the rising share of service workers, and more than half of the decline in the share of goods-processing workers. The output composition effect contributed almost nothing to the growth of information employment but accounted for almost a third of the growth in the share of service workers in total employment and 10 percent of the decline in the share of goods-processing workers.

These results also imply that the so-called information explosion is almost entirely a consequence of unbalanced growth and the substitution of information labor within production. Demand shifts toward intensive information-using products did not play a role in the growth of information workers.

5.4 Conclusion

This chapter documents the rapid growth of information workers in the U.S. economy. Information workers as a group grew from 37 percent of total employment in 1950 to 59 percent in 2000. However, the time patterns are quite different for knowledge-producing and data workers, with the increase in the share of the former accelerating from 0.5 percentage points during the 1950s to 2.3 percentage points in the 1990s and that of the latter slowing down from 5.0 to 1.7 percentage points.

About two-fifths of the growth in the share of knowledge workers in total employment and two-thirds of the increase in the share of data workers between 1950 and 2000 is attributable to differential rates of productivity movements among the industries of the economy. However, the unbalanced-growth effect diminished during the first four decades, a reflection of the general slowdown in overall productivity growth between the 1950s and 1960s and the ensuing two decades, although it picked up in the 1990s as overall productivity growth rebounded.

On the production side of the economy, the substitution component explains almost three-fifths of the growth in the share of knowledge workers during the five decades and about a third of the growth in the share of data workers. The substitution effect increased in importance over time in the case of knowledge workers (from −0.4 percentage points in the 1950s to 1.5 percentage points in the 1990s) but generally diminished for data workers (from 1.6 to 0.0 percentage points in the 1980s but then up to 0.9 percentage points in the 1990s). It also accounted for a third of the decline in the share of goods-processing workers.

In contrast, demand shifts toward intensive information-using products contributed virtually nothing to the growth of information employment. In other words, the relative growth in the number of information workers has resulted from changes in production technology, not from the substitution of information-intensive products for others among final consumers.

The results of the regression analysis reveal that R&D expenditures had the strongest influence on the growth of knowledge workers. OCA investment and the change in export intensity also produced positive effects. On the other hand, investment in OCA exerted a strong depressive effect on the growth in the number of data workers. Investment in equipment other than OCA was not a significant determinant of the growth in either.

The share of knowledge workers has grown steadily from 1950 to 2000. Indeed, if anything, its growth accelerated during the 1990s. Will the rapid growth of knowledge workers continue into the future? The results from the regression analysis indicate that a large proportion of the growth in the number of knowledge workers in the 1990s was spurred by heavy investment in computers. This, in turn, was a result of the high-tech explosion of the late 1990s. I believe that it is unlikely that knowledge workers will continue their very rapid growth in the first decade of the twenty-first century. The foremost reason is that the high-tech explosion has already subsided. A second reason is that, since 2000, there has been a steady trend in outsourcing of knowledge work abroad—most notably, computer programming and systems analysis to India and R&D to Chinese laboratories. This development is partly a response to the much lower salaries of professional workers in these two countries than in the United States and partly a consequence of the availability of worldwide Internet communication facilities that help make outsourcing cost effective. Since these two factors will remain in play over the next decade, it is likely that the outsourcing trend will continue and that the rate of growth in jobs for knowledge workers in the United States will thereby diminish in the near future.

Still, in 2000, only 15 percent of employment in the United States consists of knowledge workers. As a result, it is not clear why we need to send half of our high school graduates to college and beyond, as we are currently doing. The vast majority of jobs in 2000 did not require much beyond a solid high school education (and this is presumably still true today).

Appendix

Technology and the Growth in Information Employment

Though about half of the growth in information employment has resulted from the less rapid productivity growth of the more information-intensive industries in the economy, the other half has arisen from changes in employment patterns within industry. This appendix uses econometric methods to analyze the sources of growth of information workers at the industry level. As in the earlier chapters, I use four sets of independent variables: (1) measures of technological activity, (2) investment, including computerization, (3) indices of international competitiveness, and (4) organizational dimensions of production.

As I maintain in chapter 2, technological change may be characterized by two distinct phases. In the first, the development and implementation of new inventions calls forth the need for highly skilled and educated workers. As a result, the initial period is characterized by a growth in the demand for knowledge workers. In the second stage, the simplification of the new technology and its routinization reduces the need for highly skilled and educated workers and makes its use by unskilled workers easier. This phase therefore sees an increased demand for data workers.

As a result, R&D activity, which is an indicator of the development of new technology, should be positively correlated with the growth in the number of knowledge workers and negatively correlated with the change in the share of data workers. TFP growth, which is an indicator of routinized technological change, should have the opposite effects—a negative correlation with the change in the share of knowledge workers and a positive correlation with the growth in the number of data workers.

With regard to equipment investment, the dominant view is the capital-skills complementarity hypothesis. Greater investment in equipment should be associated with a greater demand for knowledge workers and a reduced demand for other types of workers.

The effects of computerization on the demand for knowledge workers is ambiguous. On the one hand, the introduction of computers can radically alter the workplace, requiring highly skilled computer experts, technicians, and engineers to implement the new technology and therefore be positively associated with the employment of knowledge workers. On the other hand, once in place, computers tend to simplify tasks and thus may increase the demand for data employees.

The case study literature also suggests that, with the introduction of new information technologies, there is a growing demand for various professional, technical, and skilled production occupations, while the shares of lower- and middle-level managers and supervisors, inspectors, semiskilled operatives, and many clerical occupations decline. In their 1991 study on employment restructuring at a GM auto assembly plant, Milkman and Pullman found strong support for this pattern. Freeman (1987) has reported that extensive research conducted by the Science Policy Research Unit at the University of Sussex shows that information technology tends to reduce the requirements for lower management and clerical employees but increases the need for skilled systems designers and engineers. Osterman (1986) has found that a 10 percent increase in a company's computing power led to a 1 percent reduction in managerial employment. In a study of several manufacturing plants, Zuboff (1988) concluded that lower and middle managers were particularly vulnerable to deskilling and displacement by the introduction of information technologies.

International competitiveness may also affect the rate of change in the employment of information workers. One possibility (the high-road hypothesis) is that industries competing in international product markets or directly against imports might be forced to innovate faster and thus increase their hiring of knowledge workers relative to the other types. An alternative possibility (the low-road hypothesis) is that these industries might have to compete on the basis of cost and thus have an incentive to replace knowledge workers with lower grades of labor.

Organizational dimensions of production may also affect the employment of different classes of workers. In particular, unionization may be associated with the growth in both goods-producing and service workers relative to information workers since the former two groups are more heavily unionized than knowledge or data workers.

The regression analysis uses pooled cross-section time-series data covering 44 industries in three 10-year time periods (1960–1970, 1970–1980, and 1980–1990) and 32 industries for the 1990–2000 time period.[6] The dependent variables in the regressions are the change in the percentage share of knowledge and data workers in total industry employment over the 10-year period.[7] The same set of independent variables is used as in the cross-industry regressions reported in chapter 2. The error terms are assumed to be independently distributed but may not be identically distributed, and I use the White procedure for a heteroschedasticity-consistent covariance matrix in the estimation (see White 1980). Results are reported in appendix table 5.1.

The strongest effect on the growth of knowledge workers comes from R&D investment (the ratio of R&D expenditures to industry output). Its coefficient is positive and highly significant at the 1 percent level. Its coefficient is negative for the growth in data workers and also significant, though at the 5 percent level. The regression results of chapter 2 also reveal a positive and significant relation between R&D activity and the growth in cognitive skills. These results are consistent with the hypothesis that new technology increases the need for highly skilled workers relative to less-skilled workers.

Computerization has a positive and marginally significant effect on gains in knowledge employment and a negative and highly significant effect (at the 1 percent level) on the growth in the number of data workers. In contrast, the regression results of chapter 2 reveal a negative and highly significant connection between computerization and the growth in cognitive skills. It appears that the negative effect of computer investment on the employment of data workers outweighs its positive effect on the employment of knowledge workers, resulting in a net decline in cognitive skill levels. These results also suggest that computerization falls mainly into the second phase of

Appendix 5.1.   Regressions of the Share of Information Workers in Total Employment on Technology and Other Variables Using Industry-Level Data, 1960–2000

Independent Variables	Dependent Variable	
	Change in the Employment Share of Knowledge Workers	Change in the Employment Share of Data Workers
Constant	0.028 **	0.053 **
	(3.71)	(4.82)
TFP growth	−0.033	−0.088
	(0.37)	(0.68)
Ratio of R&D expenditures	0.253 **	−0.324 *
to total output	(2.68)	(2.01)
Investment in equipment less OCA	0.072	0.067
(in 1,000s, $2,000) per worker	(1.57)	(0.98)
Investment in OCA	1.692 #	−11.294 **
(in 1,000s, $2,000) per worker	(1.88)	(9.97)
Change in the ratio of	0.033	−0.003
imports to total output	(1.24)	(0.08)
Change in the ratio of	0.313 *	0.320
exports to total output	(2.26)	(1.57)
Unionization	−0.950	−1.491
rate	(0.67)	(0.71)
Time dummies	Yes	Yes
R^2	0.15	0.47
Adjusted R^2	0.09	0.43
Standard error	0.0292	0.0431
Sample size	164	164

Note: The sample consists of pooled cross-section, time-series data with observations on each of the 44 industries in 1960–1970, 1970–1980 and 1980–1990 (sector 45, public administration, is excluded because of a lack of appropriate capital stock data) and 32 industries in 1990–2000. The coefficients are estimated using the White procedure for a heteroschedasticity-consistent covariance matrix. The absolute value of the t-statistic is in parentheses below the coefficient. See the appendix for data sources and methods.

Significance levels: # 10%; * 5% level; ** 1% level.

technological change—namely, the increase in the demand for low-skilled workers relative to highly skilled ones.

On the other hand, investment in total equipment excluding OCA per worker has a positive but statistically insignificant effect on the change in the share of knowledge workers. Its effect on the change in the proportion of data workers is also positive but again not significant. These new regression results are consistent with those of chapter 2, which establish a positive though not significant association between investment in equipment less OCA per worker and the growth in cognitive skills.

The other variables used in the regression analysis, including TFP growth, changes in trade intensity, and unionization, are not statistically significant except for the change in export intensity in the case of the growth in the number of knowledge workers. Its coefficient is positive and significant at the 5 percent level. This result contrasts with that of chapter 2, which reports a negative though insignificant association between the growth in cognitive skills and the change in export intensity. The difference in findings is partly due to the fact that the knowledge worker category includes only those actively engaged in the creation of new knowledge as well as design (such as architects) and therefore excludes intensive cognitive skill professionals (such as doctors). These results suggest that export-oriented industries might require knowledge workers for the development of new products, product design and styling, and process innovation (increasing efficiency in the production of existing products). Three dummy variables for the time periods 1960–1970, 1970–1980, and 1980–1990 are significant for the growth of both knowledge and data workers (results not shown). One other point of interest is that the goodness of fit is much stronger in the case of data workers than knowledge workers. The high R-square for the former is primarily attributable to the extremely significant and negative effects of OCA investment on the employment of data workers (a t-ratio of almost 10.0).

Notes

1. Other ratios were used to split the hybrid groups, with little effect on the results of the data analysis.
2. I have made some minor changes in the classification scheme used in earlier work; thus, the results reported here differ slightly from those reported in Baumol, Blackman, and Wolff (1989, chapter 7).
3. The formal decomposition is as follows: First, define the following matrix and vector components, where all variables are in constant (1992) dollars, unless otherwise indicated:

   X = column vector showing the total output (gross domestic output, or GDO) by sector

   Y = column vector showing the final output by sector

   N = the employment matrix, where N_{ij} shows the total employment of occupation i in industry j

   H = row vector showing total employment by industry, where $H_j = \Sigma_i N_{ij}$

   B = column vector of total employment by occupation, where $B_i = \Sigma_j N_{ij}$

   Let us now define the following coefficients:

A = the square matrix of interindustry input-output coefficients, where A_{ij} indicates the amount of input i (in 1992 dollars) required per unit of output j (in 1992 dollars)

y = column vector showing the percentage distribution of total final output by sector, where $y_i = Y_i / \Sigma Y_i$

n = employment coefficient matrix, showing employment by occupation per unit of output, where $n_{ij} = N_{ij}/X_j$

c = an employment distribution matrix, showing the percentage distribution of employment by occupation within each sector, where $c_{ij} = N_{ij}/H_j$

L = row vector of labor coefficients showing total employment per unit of output, where $L_j = H_j/X_j$

To derive the basic relationship, I start with the basic Leontief identity:

(5.1) $$X = (I - A)^{-1}Y.$$

It then follows that

$$B = nX = n(I - A)^{-1}Y = cL(I - A)^{-1}Y = c\lambda^{\circ}Y,$$

where $\lambda = L(I - A)^{-1}$, which shows the direct plus indirect labor requirements per unit of output, and a superscript ($^{\circ}$) connotes a diagonal matrix whose elements are those of the associated vector. Then, for a given percentage output vector y,

(5.2) $$B(y) = c\lambda^{\circ}y,$$

where B(y) shows employment by occupation generated by the final output vector y. We then have

(5.3) $$\Delta B(y) = (\Delta c)\lambda^{\circ}y + c(\Delta\lambda^{\circ})y + c\lambda^{\circ}(\Delta y),$$

where the symbol Δ indicates change over the period.

4. Since the occupation-by-industry matrices are for years that differ from those for the input-output data, geometric interpolation of industry employment for the input-output data was used to align industry employment in the input-output data with the census years from 1950 to 1990.

5. As in earlier chapters, average period weights are used in the decomposition.

6. The public administration sector is excluded because of a lack of OCA capital stock data. Because of the adoption of the North American Industrial Classification System (NAICS) in 1997, only 33 industries in the 1990–2000 period could be constructed that were compatible with earlier years (the public administration sector is again excluded because of a lack of OCA capital stock data). Moreover, because there are no continuous time-series data available on the share of information workers in total employment, I am not able to perform any time-series regressions.

7. Because of the heterogeneous nature of both service and goods-producing workers, no clear predictions are possible regarding the factors that affect the change in their employment shares.

6

Skill Dispersion and Earnings Inequality

6.1 Introduction

In the last three decades, some disturbing changes in inequality have occurred in the United States. Inequality in the distribution of family income, which remained virtually unchanged from the end of World War II to 1968, has increased sharply since then. This rising inequality appears to stem from changes in the structure of the labor market.

This chapter confronts the third of our paradoxes. Standard human capital theory predicts that, as the variance (dispersion) in educational attainment declines, so should the inequality of earnings. Yet, while the variance in schooling did, in fact, lessen substantially after the early 1970s, the inequality of earnings jumped dramatically. Moreover, the variance of workplace skills has also declined since 1970. This chapter reconciles trends in wage inequality with those in skill and schooling inequality.

Another indication of the dramatic changes in the labor market is the sharp rise in the returns to education, particularly for a college degree, that has occurred since 1975, especially in the 1980s. The ratio in annual earnings between male college graduates and male high school graduates climbed from 1.50 in 1975 to 1.88 in 2003. For females, the ratio grew from 1.45 in 1975 to 1.74 in 2000. Among men, the increase in the return to school for a college degree relative to a high school diploma was due, in part, to the stagnating earnings of high school graduates. Between 1975 and 2003, their annual earnings in constant dollars grew by only 4 percent, while the earnings of men with a bachelor's degree increased by 22 percent. The biggest increase in earnings occurred among males with an advanced degree (master's or higher), who saw their annual incomes surge by 31 percent. Among males who did not graduate from college, earnings plummeted by 12 percent.

Another notable change has been the widespread diffusion of computers in the United States in the past 30 years. I focus particular interest on the post-1980 period, which witnessed a tremendous growth in the use of computers in production and which Christopher Freeman (1987) and others have termed a new "techno-economic paradigm," based on computer-driven information technology. The other principal focus of the chapter is the extent to which the computer revolution is responsible for the upsurge of inequality in the United States.

I begin with a recapitulation of the various explanations that have been proposed to account for rising earnings inequality in the United States and their associated literatures. These include (1) skill-biased technological changes that favor highly educated over less-educated workers; (2) growing international trade, which has caused the relative wages of low-skilled workers to fall; (3) the shift of employment to services, which are characterized by a greater dispersion of earnings than with goods producers; (4) declining unionization, which has widened wage differentials among different types of jobs within an industry; (5) a declining minimum wage in real terms, which has put downward pressure on the wages of low-skilled jobs; (6) corporate restructuring and downsizing in the 1980s and 1990s, which may have widened earnings differentials within firms; and (7) the role of education and ability.

The next section provides descriptive statistics on aggregate trends in the overall inequality of income and earnings and the dispersion of educational attainment in the population from 1947 to 2000. Time trends on technological factors, computerization, international trade, and pertinent institutional factors are also reviewed.

The following section presents statistics on the dispersion of workplace skills from 1950 to 2000. Changes in overall skill inequality result from both variations in skill dispersion at the industry level and shifts in employment across industries. The former is normally interpreted as deriving from modifications in technology and the latter from shifting patterns of demand. This section also develops a decomposition of changes in the overall inequality of skill levels into these two components. Results are shown for the four decades between 1950 and 1990.

The next section presents descriptive statistics of earnings inequality levels by industry, and the final section provides concluding remarks. Section A of the appendix develops the modeling framework. In section B of the appendix, regression analysis is conducted on the aggregate level to determine the effects of technological, structural, and institutional factors, as well as trade openness, on trends in income inequality. In section C of the appendix, I employ regression analysis to relate changes of skill inequality at the industry level to four sets of factors: (1) various indicators of technological change; (2) investment activity, including the change in the stock of computer equipment; (3) international trade; and (4) structural and institutional factors, including the degree of unionization of an industry.

6.2 Review of Literature

Considerable literature has now accumulated on factors that might have caused earnings inequality to rise since the early 1970s. At the outset, it is important to distinguish among three separate but related trends. The first is the actual rise in the dispersion of earnings among all workers (or among all male workers) in the economy. The second is the rising returns to schooling, particularly a college education, over the same period. The third is the large increase in earnings dispersion within education-experience cells—that is, even after controlling for education and experience—during these years as well (see, for example, Levy and Murnane 1992 or Juhn, Murphy, and Pierce 1993). A successful model must be able to account for all three phenomena simultaneously. Several candidates are put forward to explain these changes in earnings patterns.

6.2.1 Skill-Biased Technological Changes

The most prevalent view of the cause of rising wage inequality is biased technological change, due to the introduction of computers and the general diffusion of information technology. The argument is that the last twenty years have witnessed a major technological revolution led by widespread computerization and the consequent diffusion of IT. This change has skewed the income distribution by placing a high premium on college-educated and skilled labor while reducing the demand for semiskilled and unskilled workers. One important piece of evidence is that the rate of return to a college education (the wage premium paid to a college graduate relative to a high school graduate) almost doubled between the 1980s and the 1990s.

This argument has been made by Bound and Johnson (1992) and Berman, Bound, and Griliches (1994), who identify the declining ratio of production to nonproduction workers *within industry* as the major determinant of changes in relative wages between skilled and unskilled workers. The fact that both the employment share and relative wages shifted in favor of nonproduction workers is evidence of biased technological change.

Work on the subject has been limited in three ways. First, most of the studies measure skills by the relative shares of production and nonproduction workers in total employment. However, as we saw in chapter 2 (see table 2.6), this division does not constitute a particularly sharp distinction between skilled and unskilled jobs (Burtless 1995 makes a similar criticism). Second, because of available data, the analysis is generally confined to manufacturing, which accounted for only 15.3 percent of total employment in 1995. It may be precarious to make inferences about other sectors on the basis of the results for manufacturing. Third, the measure of skill bias is indirect—that is, it is inferred from the rising share of nonproduction workers in conjunction with their rising relative earnings. Very few direct tests of skill-biased technological change exist.

Mincer (1991), using aggregate time-series data for the United States over the period 1963 to 1987, and Davis and Haltiwanger (1991), using data on production and nonproduction workers in U.S. manufacturing plants from 1963 to 1986, have provided some of the early evidence to support this hypothesis. Mincer found that R&D expenditures per worker explain a significant part of the year-to-year variation in educational wage differentials, while productivity growth was also a significant factor but had weaker explanatory power. Davis and Haltiwanger found that the employment shift toward nonproduction workers occurred disproportionately in large plants between 1977 and 1986 and that this was accompanied by a sharp upgrading of worker education and occupational skill levels. Lawrence and Slaughter (1993) reached a similar conclusion after eliminating international trade as a culprit in rising earnings inequality.

Katz and Murphy (1992) have developed a model that accounts for changes in both the demand and supply of unskilled and skilled labor. Using Current Population Survey (CPS) data over the period 1963 to 1987, they have concluded that, even though the supply of college graduates fluctuated over time, there was a steady increase in the demand for skilled labor in the United States over the period.

Berman, Bound, and Griliches (1994), using data from the Annual Survey of Manufactures over the period 1979 to 1987 for 450 manufacturing industries, found that more than two-thirds of the increase in the ratio of nonproduction to production workers within manufacturing was due to the increased use of the former within industry and that less than one-third resulted from a reallocation of labor among industries. From this they infer the existence of skill-biased technological change. Berman, Bound, and Machin (1998) have also provided evidence that the increase in the share of skilled (nonproduction) workers in total employment occurred across a wide range of OECD countries. However, they also found that the trend decelerated in almost all of the OECD countries during the 1980s (with the notable exception of the United States). Allen (2001) has concluded that technology variables accounted for 30 percent of the increase in the college wage premium from 1979 to 1989. Juhn, Murphy, and Pierce (1993), using a time-series of CPS data between 1963 and 1987, documented the rising variance of earnings within schooling and experience groups and concluded that it was due to rising employer demand for (and hence premium on) unobservable skills.

In a more direct test of the effects of new technology on earnings, Adams (1997), using world patent and CPS earnings data for 24 manufacturing industries between 1979 and 1993, found that a rise in patenting activity was associated with a widening of the earnings gap between college and high school graduates. Betts (1997) has provided a direct test of skill-biased technological change for Canadian manufacturing industries between 1962 and 1986. Using a translog cost-share equation and treating production and nonproduction workers as separate inputs, he found evidence of bias away from production workers in 10 of the 18 industries used in the analysis.

A counterargument was presented by Howell (1997), who points out an important anomaly—namely, that while employment in low-skill jobs was declining relative to more skilled jobs, the proportion of low-wage workers has actually been rising. He has also found that the entire increase in the ratio of nonproduction to production workers since 1979 took place between 1980 and 1982; between 1983 and the early 1990s, the ratio remained essentially unchanged. Glynn (1997) has found, after dividing U.S. workers into educational quartiles, that the employment position of the less schooled workers sharply deteriorated between 1973 and 1981, when wage inequality grew slowly, but declined very little after 1981, when wage inequality surged.

Mishel, Bernstein, and Schmitt (1997) claim that, in order to explain the sharp rise in earnings inequality after 1979, the rate of bias in technological change must have accelerated during the 1980s. However, there is no evidence to this effect, and, indeed, the rate of conventionally measured productivity growth slowed down after the early 1970s. Murphy and Welch (1993b), after examining decennial census of population data on employment by occupation from 1940 to 1980 and CPS data for 1989–1991, found that there was a steady increase in the demand for skilled labor between 1940 and 1990 but no particular acceleration during the 1970s and 1980s. Juhn (1999), including 1990 census of population data, has reported similar results.

6.2.2 The IT "Revolution"

Two relatively early works have called the rapid introduction and diffusion of computers and associated information technology a "technological revolution." Christopher Freeman, writing in 1987, has termed this transformation a new "techno-economic paradigm," based on microprocessor-driven information technology. According to Freeman, information technology has "emerged in the last couple of decades as a result of the convergence of a number of inter-related radical advances in the field of microelectronics, fibre optics, software engineering, communications and computer technology." He defines it "both as a new range of products and services, and as a technology which is capable of revolutionizing the processes of production and delivery of all other industries and services" (51). Paul David, writing in 1991, has referred to "the paradigmatic shift" from electromechanical automation to information technologies.

One result of this technological revolution is a transformation of the skills required in the labor market. According to Freeman, the results of extensive research conducted by the Science Policy Research Unit (SPRU) of the University of Sussex show that information technology "reduces the requirements for inspection and lower management (and clerical) employees, but increases the requirement for skilled systems designers and engineers and the level of responsibility for skills for maintenance" (1987, 66).

Doeringer (1991, 166) states that "New information technologies may be particularly important for facilitating organizational adjustment" and refers to Osterman's (1986) finding that "a 10% increase in company computing power led to a 1% reduction in managerial employment." And in the plants that she observed, Zuboff (1988) notes that lower and middle managers were particularly vulnerable to deskilling and displacement by information technologies (284, 358–359). David (1991) has argued that the shift to information technologies might entail major changes in the organizational structure of companies.

In chapter 4, I also present evidence on the "disruptive" effects of computerization on the labor market and the structural adjustments that have ensued. The econometric results indicate that the coefficient of computerization as measured by the rate of growth of OCA per worker is statistically significant at the 1 percent level and that computerization is strongly and positively associated with the degree of occupational restructuring within an industry over time.

Several other works have examined the effects of computer usage, or IT, on earnings. Reich (1991) has argued that U.S. workers are divided into two distinct groups: "symbolic analysts," who produce knowledge and new information technology, and ordinary clerical and production workers, who are outside the IT revolution. Globalization has rewarded the first group of workers with increased earnings but depressed the earnings of the second group.

Krueger (1993) has argued that pronounced declines in the cost of personal computers caused their widespread adoption in the workplace and shifted the production function in ways that favored more skilled workers. He has also estimated the rate of return to computer usage at 15–20 percent. This finding was later challenged by DiNardo and Pischke (1997), who, using German household data, estimated a similar return to the use of pencils. They have argued that computer use per se was not causing workers to earn a premium but rather was associated with unmeasured skills that were being rewarded in the workplace. Handel (1998) also showed that the returns to computers decrease by half in cross-sectional estimates when other correlates, such as "reading news or magazine articles," are included as explanatory variables. However, in later work, Autor, Katz, and Krueger (1998) supplied new evidence of a substantial and increasing wage premium associated with computer use, despite a large growth in the number of workers with computer skills. However, Bresnahan (1999) has argued, after a review of the pertinent literature, that there is no direct evidence that the actual use of IT (particularly personal computers) is associated with job enrichment. He has concluded that "There is little complementarity between highly skilled workers and PC use, certainly not enough to affect skill demand" (33).

6.2.3 Growing International Trade

The increasing trade liberalization, beginning in 1973 with the end of the Bretton-Woods agreement and continuing through the 1990s, is perhaps the second leading contender to explain rising inequality. Imports into the U.S. economy grew from 5.4 percent of GDP in 1970 to 14.0 percent in 2003, while the share of exports grew from 5.5 to 9.5 percent. According to standard trade theory, as trade increases, factor prices—particularly wages—tend to equalize across countries (see chapter 7 for more discussion of the standard trade model). This can take the form of rising wages among our trading partners, as well as declining wages in our own labor force. As imports of manufactured products produced in low-income countries such as Indonesia, China, Thailand, Mexico, and Brazil increased, downward pressure was placed on the wages of unskilled and semiskilled workers in U.S. manufacturing industries. This process may explain both the falling average real wage of U.S. workers and the increasing gap between blue-collar workers and professionals who work in industries (e.g., law, medicine, education, and business services) that are well shielded from imports.

Much literature has also accumulated on the effects of international trade on wage differentials. In the main, two different approaches have been used to analyze the link between trade and earnings inequality. The first is the factor content of trade model, advanced mainly by labor economists, which puts primary emphasis on the effective supplies of less skilled and more skilled labor (see, for example, Berman, Bound, and Griliches 1994). Imports embody both unskilled and skilled labor, which, when added to the domestic supply of these two factors, determines their effective supply. Because imports to the United States are generally less skill intensive than domestic production (see chapter 7 for empirical support), the opening of the domestic economy to imports augments the relative effective supply of low-skilled workers and lowers that of highly skilled workers, thereby putting downward pressure on the wages of the former relative to the latter.[1]

The alternative view, advanced primarily by trade economists, derives from the Stolper-Samuelson theorem, an off-shoot of the Heckscher-Ohlin model of international trade (see chapter 7). The principal contention is that exogenous output prices, not endogenous factor quantities, determine relative wages between skilled and unskilled workers (see, for example, Leamer 1996). The Stolper-Samuelson theorem provides a direct link between factor prices and output prices, which are set on the world market. The model shows that, if two countries have the same technology and face the same world output prices, those two countries will have the same relative wage structure, regardless of the level of trade. Therefore, if trade is liberalized with underdeveloped countries that are less skill intensive, the relative output price of the less-skill-intensive products will fall in a country such as the United States, as will the relative wage paid to less-skilled workers. The movement of relative wages in the advanced country is thus linked to changes in relative output prices, not to the volume of trade.

Studies that emanate from the first theoretical approach, the factor content of trade, generally conclude that increased trade had a minimal effect on relative wage movements. The reason is that U.S. international trade is just too small to have much impact on wages or employment. Almost all of these studies estimate that the rising volume of imports in the United States accounted for no more than 20 percent of the shift in demand between low-skilled and highly skilled workers. Borjas, Freeman, and Katz (1992) state that rising trade flows explain at most 15 percent of the increase in the earnings differential between college graduates and high school graduates between 1980 and 1988. Bound and Johnson (1992), Bhagwati and Dehejia (1993), Krugman and Lawrence (1994), Bhagwati and Kosters (1994), Berman, Bound, and Griliches (1994), and Richardson (1995) have also found very little effect of international trade on the divergence in compensation between more-skilled and less-skilled workers. However, Krugman and Lawrence (1994) did find that imports from developing countries significantly reduced employment of unskilled production workers in developed countries (see Freeman 1995, for a review of these studies).

The notable exception is Wood (1991, 1994), who, using this approach, found significant effects, with international trade accounting for as much as half of the decreased demand for low-skilled workers. Wood (1994, 57) concludes that "the main cause of the deteriorating situation of unskilled workers in developed countries has been the expansion of trade with developing countries." However, in later work, Wood and Anderson (1998) conclude that trade expansion during the 1980s had a greater effect on the acceleration in skill upgrading than on skill upgrading itself.

There is a wider range of estimates of the effects of international trade on relative wages in the United States devolving from the second approach. Lawrence and Slaughter (1993) have found little effect of changes in output prices on the earnings structure during the 1980s. Sachs and Shatz (1994) have constructed a special database detailing imports and exports of goods for 131 manufacturing industries and 150 trading partners. They state that the increase in net imports from 1978 to 1990 was associated with a drop of 7.2 percent in production jobs in manufacturing and only a 2.1 percent decrease in nonproduction jobs in manufacturing. They surmise that these trends contributed to the widening wage gap between skilled and unskilled workers, although technology changes also played a role. Leamer (1996) claims that trade effects were responsible for 40 percent of the decline in wages of less-skilled workers, but his model required long lags because he relied on price changes in the 1970s to account for changes of wages in the 1980s (also see Burtless 1995 for reviews of the literature on trade and inequality).

Krugman (1995) has offered a way of reconciling these two approaches. He maintains that the relevant counterfactual to consider is what the prices of tradeable goods and services (and therefore factor prices) would have been if trade had not increased. Using observed changes in commodity prices is inappropriate since such changes reflect a whole host of characteristics besides international trade. He suggests that the change in world prices depends critically on the *volume* of trade. If trade expanded less, then its impact on world prices would be smaller. He then developed a computable general equilibrium (CGE) model of world prices on the basis of commonly accepted supply and demand elasticities with which to infer changes in the prices of tradeables induced by trade expansion.

Krugman concludes that world supply and demand would not have changed very much if trade increases had been small relative to the world totals of such products. With the assumed price elasticities, prices would have had to adjust only slightly to absorb the resulting changes in world demand. Consequently, only a small proportion of actual changes in relative commodity prices and hence of factor prices reflects the expansion of world trade. Moreover, using simulated price changes in tradeables yields similar results even with the Stolper-Samuelson approach.

Several other studies that do not fit neatly into these two categories also investigated the effects of international trade on earnings. Murphy and Welch (1991) found a close correspondence between changes in net imports over the 1967–1986 period among three industry groups—durables, nondurables, and services—and changes in employment patterns of less educated and more highly educated workers. In particular, they concluded that changes in trade patterns were largely responsible for the loss of low-skilled employment in U.S. manufacturing. Using the NBER manufacturing productivity database for the period 1979–1990, Feenstra and Hanson (1995, 1997, 1999) estimated in the first study that rising imports explained 15–33 percent of the increase in the wages of nonproduction workers relative to production workers during the 1980s in manufacturing. In the second study, they found that foreign outsourcing of intermediate inputs and expenditures in high-technology capital, particularly computers, explained a substantial amount (a minimum of 35 percent) of the relative increase in the wages of nonproduction workers in manufacturing during the 1980s.

Borjas and Ramey (1994, 1995) have argued that the impact of imports on wages and employment would be particularly pronounced in highly concentrated industries such as the automobile industry. Using data from the Standard Metropolitan Statistical Areas (SMSA), they have reported a strong negative correlation between the share of employment in high-concentration import industries and the relative wages of less-skilled workers, both over time within cities and in a cross-section of cities. Bernard and Jensen (1997), using plant-level data, claim that rising exports accounted for almost all of the increase in the wage differential between highly skilled and low-skilled workers.

6.2.4 The Shift to Services

One of the notable changes in the composition of the labor force during the postwar period is the shift of jobs from goods-producing industries to services. The share of employment in services grew from 47 percent in 1947 to 74 percent in 2003. Almost all of the employment growth during the 1980s and 1990s occurred in the service sector. Some have argued that the dispersion of earnings is greater in services than in goods-producing industries because of the greater mix of professional and managerial jobs with relatively low-skilled clerical and manual work, so that the employment shift leads to rising inequality.

Bluestone and Harrison (1988a, 1988b), who were among the first to observe rising earnings inequality in the United States beginning in the 1970s, have argued that the proximate cause of both rising inequality and the growth in low-wage employment was the deindustrialization of the U.S. economy, particularly the shift of workers out of high-wage manufacturing and toward low-wage service industries.

Various estimates of the effect of structural shifts in employment have been offered. Grubb and Wilson (1989), using census of population data for 1960 and 1980 and 14 economic sectors, calculated that almost two-thirds of the overall increase in earnings inequality (measured by the Theil coefficient) over this period can be explained by shifts in the sectoral composition of employment. However, Blackburn (1990), using CPS data and 41 industry classifications, has stated that at most 20 percent of the increase in male earnings inequality between 1967 and 1985 can be attributed to the changing industrial composition of the labor force. Blackburn, Bloom, and Freeman (1990), using a 43 industry classification, have also estimated that about 20 percent of the increase in the earnings differential between white male college graduates and high school graduates is accounted for by shifts of employment among these industries.

Katz and Murphy (1992), dividing employment into 50 industries and three broad occupational groups, have found that shifts in employment among both industries and occupations within those industries clearly favored more-educated workers relative to less-educated ones between 1947 and 1987. The demand for more educated (and experienced) workers within industry and/or occupation cell accelerated during the 1980s, especially within manufacturing. Karoly and Klerman (1994), using regional data for the United States, have estimated that between 15–20 percent of the rise in male wage inequality between 1973 and 1988 was due to shifts in the industrial composition of the workforce. Murphy and Welch (1993a) have likewise attributed only 16 percent of the overall change in the demand for college-educated workers to changes in industrial shares. Bernard and Jensen (2000) investigated inequality at the state level within the United States and found that increases in inequality at the state level strongly correlated with changes in industrial mix, particularly the loss of durable manufacturing jobs.

Gittleman (1994) estimates that about one-third of the rising wage premium for a college education in the 1980s was attributable to shifts in occupational demand. Groshen (1991b), using a special panel survey of firms in Cleveland, Cincinnati, and Pittsburgh, also found that during the 1980s the main factor in the rising inequality was the widening of occupational wage differentials.

6.2.5 Institutional Factors

Two institutional trends in particular have achieved prominence in the literature on rising inequality. The first of these is declining unionization. The proportion of the workforce represented by unions peaked in 1954 at 25.4 percent (and at 34.7 percent as a fraction of the nonfarm labor force). After 1954, the trend was downward, and by 2003 only 12.9 percent of workers were union members. Unions have historically negotiated collective bargaining agreements with narrow wage differentials among different types of jobs. This is one reason that the dispersion of earnings in manufacturing has tended to be lower than that in service industries. The argument is that the decline in unions has led to widening differentials in the overall wage structure.

The second factor is the declining minimum wage, which has fallen by 34 percent in real terms between its peak in 1968 and 2003. This has put downward pressure on the wages of unskilled workers and may account, in part, for the growing wage disparities between unskilled and skilled workers and the decline in the average real wage since 1973. Gordon (1996) argues that the change in unionization and the minimum wage was part of a broader range of institutional changes in the 1980s in which U.S. corporate managers exerted increasing pressure on workers, partly in reaction to rising international competition.

Freeman (1993) states that the decline of unions in the U.S. economy and/or the decline in the real value of the minimum wage since the late 1960s removed the "safety net" supporting the wage level of unskilled workers, thereby allowing it to fall. Blackburn, Bloom, and Freeman (1990) contend that as much as 20 percent of the rising differential of earnings between college graduates and other educational groups between 1980 and 1988 might be due to deunionization. He has also found that changes in the minimum wage, on the other hand, had a minimal impact. Both Freeman (1993) and Card (1992) estimate that 10–20 percent of the increased wage inequality among men was due to the decline in unionization.

Horrigon and Mincy (1993) attribute considerably less than a third of the declining share of earnings received by the bottom quintile of wage earners to the fall in the minimum wage. DiNardo, Fortin, and Lemieux (1996), using a semiparametric estimation technique on CPS data from 1979 to 1988, have concluded that the decline in the real value of the minimum wage in this period accounts for up to 25 percent of the increase in male wage inequality and up to 30 percent of the rise in female wage inequality. Fortin and Lemieux (1997) estimate that about 30 percent of rising-wage rate dispersion in the United States was due to the decline in the real value of the minimum wage. Using regional data from the CPS together with regional minimum wage levels in the 1980s, Lee (1999) concludes that the decline in the real minimum wage during the period accounted for as much as 70 percent of the rise in wage dispersion in the lower tail of the wage distribution among men and 70–100 percent among women.

There is also cross-national evidence that points to the importance of unionization and the minimum wage in explaining inequality differences. In a comparison of changes in wage inequality in the United States, Great Britain, Japan, and France, Katz, Loveman, and Blanchflower (1993) found that, in the case of France, sharp rises in the national minimum wage and the strength of French labor unions prevented wage differentials from expanding between 1967 and 1987. Blau and Kahn (1996), using cross-national data for OECD countries, attribute a large part of the intercountry differences in wage inequality among men to differences in unionization patterns. DiNardo and Lemieux (1997) have compared the increase in wage inequality in Canada and the United States and estimated that two-thirds of the faster rise of inequality in the latter between 1981 and 1988 was due to a more severe decline in the rate of unionization.

6.2.6 Downsizing and Outsourcing

Another suspect is the corporate restructuring that occurred during the 1980s and 1990s. This process took two forms. First, permanent employees were replaced by part-time, temporary, and "leased" employees. Second, a number of important corporate functions such as maintenance, cafeteria services, legal services, and data processing, which were traditionally performed by in-house employees, were outsourced (i.e., substituted for) by purchasing these operations from other companies. Both processes reduced the relative number of permanent employees in large corporations. Corporate employees have traditionally enjoyed high wages, good benefits, job security, career-ladder-type jobs, and good working conditions. This set of job characteristics is referred to as an *internal* or *primary labor market* (see Doeringer and Piore 1971). In contrast, wages tend to be low in secondary jobs found in part-time employment and small businesses. The shift of employment out of the primary labor force to the secondary labor market may have been another factor in the rising income inequality.

One work that discusses this issue is Groshen and Levine (1998), who argue that declines in the extent of internal labor markets within U.S. industry might have led to both phenomena since internal labor markets keep pay structures within a firm equitability and help maintain high wages. However, using data from 228 large Midwestern employers over the past four decades, they found no evidence of a weakening of internal labor markets in this period.

6.2.7 Education and Ability

There is much literature dating back to Becker (1964, 1975) and Mincer (1974) that emphasizes the importance of schooling and human capital as determinants of earnings. Another work of the same period is Freeman (1976), who argued that an oversupply of college graduates appeared during the 1970s due to both increased college enrollment resulting from the coming of college age of the baby-boom generation and a slackening of growth in industries that employed college-educated workers. The human capital approach was criticized by Jencks (1972, 1979), who has stressed the importance of family background as a factor influencing both schooling attainment and success in the labor market.

Although their evidence is relatively weak, Hernstein and Murray (1994) have argued that genetic differences, particularly racial ones, are the primary cause of differences in intelligence and earnings. Danziger and Gottschalk (1995) investigated causes of increasing poverty and inequality, particularly the role of economic growth and changes in the racial and ethnic composition of the population and family structure. They concluded that demographic changes played little role in explaining the rising inequality in the 1970s and 1980s. Frank and Cook (1995) maintain that the increasing prevalence of winner-take-all markets was the primary factor in the increasing concentration of income at the very top of the income distribution.

Several other works have pointed to changes in schooling patterns or skill levels as proximate causes of rising inequality. Bishop (1991) has argued that declines in the quality of U.S. education at the primary and secondary level, as evidenced by falling SAT scores, may have lowered the marketability of low-skilled workers and therefore their relative wages. However, Jencks and Phillips (1998) found no evidence of a decline in test scores among 17-year-olds between 1971 and 1986. Using data from the National Assessment of Educational Progress, they report that both reading and math test scores had risen, both overall and among white and black students separately.

Blackburn and Neumark (1993) have found that the rise in the return to education was concentrated among people with both high education and high ability. Murnane, Willet, and Levy (1995) used math ability at the end of high school as a measure of cognitive ability and estimated that 38–100 percent of the increase in the return to education for 24-year-olds from 1978 to 1986 can be attributed to increasing returns to ability.

Grogger and Eide (1996) have determined that as much as one-fourth of the increase in the male college wage premium in the 1980s was due to a shift away from low-skill college subjects such as education toward high-skill subjects such as engineering. For women, the rise in the college premium was largely a result of the increase in the returns to math ability. However, Cawley, Heckman, and Vytlacil (1997), using nonparametric econometric techniques on data from the National Longitudinal Sample of Youths (NLSY), found little evidence that the increase in the return to education was centered among those with the highest ability scores.

Bluestone (1990) has called attention to the apparent inconsistency between rising earnings inequality and declining dispersion of schooling. On the basis of CPS data, he has reported that, while wage inequality (measured by the variance of the logarithm of earnings) among full-time, full-year workers increased from 0.56 in 1963 to 0.63 in 1987, the coefficient of variation of their schooling levels fell from 0.27 to 0.20.

6.3 Time Trends in Inequality and Explanatory Variables on the Aggregate Level

Figure 6.1 shows trends in income inequality in the United States in the postwar period based on the March supplement to the Current Population Survey. The CPS reports family income and is the longest consistent series available, running from 1947 to 2003.[2] Inequality shows a slightly downward trend from 1947 to 1968, with the Gini coefficient falling by 7 percent. The series bottoms out in 1968 and then rises thereafter, with the rate of increase accelerating after 1976. The 2003 Gini coefficient is 0.430, which is 0.082 points above its 1968 value.

As I note in the introduction to this chapter, a leading argument is that skill-biased technological change is the major cause of rising earnings inequality. Figure 6.1 also shows time trends in both labor productivity growth and total factor productivity (TFP) growth.[3] These two technology indicators trend downward from the high growth period of 1947–1973 (annual growth rates of 2.4 and 1.7 percent per year, respectively) to the productivity slowdown of 1973–1979 (annual growth rates of 0.5 and 0.4 percent per year, respectively) before recovering in the 1979–2003 period (annual growth rates of 1.2 and 0.9 percent per year, respectively). Not surprisingly, the productivity growth rates are negatively correlated with income inequality, but the correlations are very low in absolute value: −0.21 and −0.07, respectively.

The second set of technological indicators includes measures of R&D activity—the ratio of total R&D expenditures to GDP and the number of scientists and engineers engaged in R&D per 100 employees. Figure 6.2 shows that

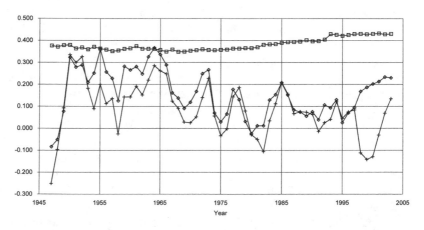

—▣— Gini Coefficient for Family Income   —+— Annual TFP Growth x 10 (Three-year Running Average)
—◆— Annual Labor Productivity Growth x 10 (Three-year Running Average)

Figure 6.1   Family Income Inequality, Labor Productivity Growth, and TFP Growth, 1947–2003

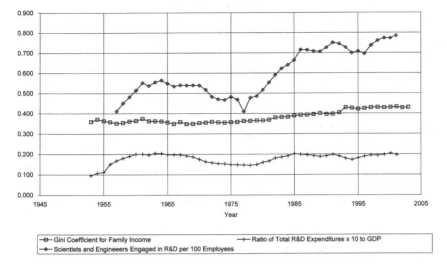

Figure 6.2   Family Income Inequality and R&D Intensity, 1953–2003

these two variables track much better with movements in income inequality than does productivity growth. The ratio of total R&D to GDP rose between the early 1950s and the 1960s and then fell in the 1970s before rising again in the 1980s and 1990s. Its correlation with family income inequality is 0.29. In contrast, the number of scientists and engineers engaged in R&D per 100 employees increased between the late 1950s and the early 1960s, leveled out, and then fell in the early 1970s before rising sharply after 1976. It has a much higher correlation with income inequality (0.87).

Another potential source of bias in technological change might derive from investment in equipment and machinery—particularly computers. Figure 6.3 shows time trends in both investment in equipment per worker and investment in OCA per worker. Equipment investment per PEP remained relatively flat between 1947 and 1961 and then tripled between 1961 and 2003. It is highly correlated (0.78) with family income inequality. Investment in OCA per PEP grew slowly from 1947 to 1977 and then surged at an incredible pace thereafter, increasing by a factor of 221 between 1977 and 2003. It is apparent that the huge growth of OCA investment occurred after the upswing in inequality. Despite this, OCA investment per employee correlates even more strongly with family income inequality than does total equipment investment per worker (a coefficient of 0.81).[4]

A fourth factor, shown in figure 6.4, measures trade intensity. After increasing slightly from 7.3 percent in 1950 to 9.4 percent in 1970, the ratio of the sum of exports plus imports to GDP shot up to 23.5 percent in 2003. There is a sharp break in this series in the early 1970s, almost coincident with the rise in income inequality. The correlation of income inequality with the ratio of the sum of exports plus imports to GDP is 0.75.

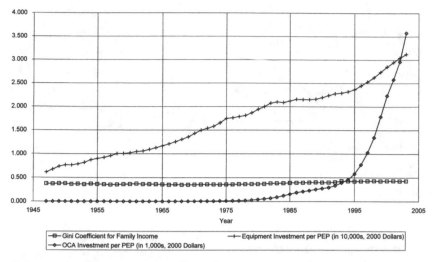

Figure 6.3   Family Income Inequality and Investment in Equipment and OCA per PEP, 1947–2003

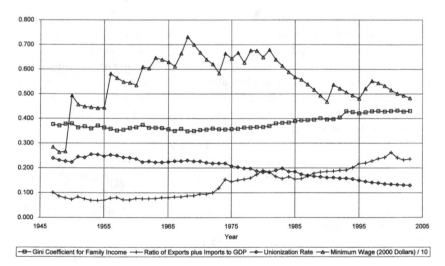

Figure 6.4   Family Income Inequality, International Trade, Unionization, and the Minimum Wage, 1947–2003

A fifth variable, also shown in figure 6.4, is the overall unionization rate. The proportion of the workforce represented by unions peaked in 1954 at 25.4 percent and then diminished almost continually to 12.9 percent in 2003. On the surface, the timing is different from the trend in inequality, which began its upward spiral in the late 1960s. Still, the correlation between the two series (−0.83) is very strong. Another variable is the minimum wage in constant dollars, which peaked in 1968, the same year as income inequality bottomed out. The correlation between the two series is −0.50. A related variable is the ratio of the minimum wage to average hourly earnings. This also peaked in 1968, and its correlation with family income inequality is −0.66.

The next variable, shown in figure 6.5, has to do with the schooling of adults 25 years of age or older, as computed from CPS data. As I discuss in the appendix to this chapter, according to the standard human capital model (see equation 8), the variance of the logarithm of earnings should be proportional to the product of the variance of schooling and the rate of return to schooling squared. The variance of schooling has trended sharply downward since 1947, falling by 48 percent from its peak value of 13.1 in 1950 to 6.9 in 2000. The simple correlation between this series and the Gini coefficient for family income is −0.78.

However, evidence from numerous studies cited earlier indicates that the return to schooling has risen since the early 1970s. Figure 6.5 also shows a series for the rate of return to a college education from 1956 to 2000.[5] The rate of return shows a considerable increase from 1975 to 2000, from 11.9 to 16.9 percent. However, the return to a college education also climbed sharply from 11.2 percent in 1956 to its earlier peak of 14.4 percent in 1970 and then fell to 11.9 percent in 1974 before rising again. Nonetheless, the simple correlation between the rate of return to college and the Gini coefficient for family income is 0.64.[6] On net, the correlation between the Gini coefficient for family income and the more critical variable, the square of the rate of return to college *multiplied* by the variance of schooling, is negative, −0.23.

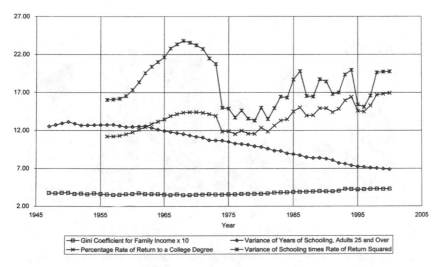

Figure 6.5   Family Income Inequality and Educational Trends, 1947–2000

6.4 Postwar Trends in the Dispersion of Skills

I next investigate changes in the distribution of skills among employed workers from 1950 to 2000. Figure 6.6 displays the coefficient of variation (the ratio of the standard deviation to the mean) of skill levels, computed for the full set of 267 occupations. The first notable result is that substantive complexity (SC) inequality fell between 1950 and 2000. The coefficient of variation of SC declined by 6 percent between 1950 and 1970 and by another 9 percent from 1970 to 2000. In contrast, the dispersion of both motor skills (MS) and interactive skills (IS) rose during the period—MS by 9 percent between 1950 and 1970 and another 13 percent between 1970 and 2000 and IS by 14 percent and 14 percent, respectively. However, inequality in the overall composite skill (CP) score diminished over the four decades—by 4 percent between 1950 and 1970 and 8 percent from 1970 to 2000.

These results again suggest the potential importance of distinguishing among types of job skills. While employment shifts have led to an increasing gap between workers with high job control, autonomy, and responsibility requirements and those who simply receive instructions, as well as between workers whose jobs require high and low levels of motor skills, differences among workers in the cognitive skill requirements of their jobs have declined over time.

The dispersion in years of schooling among the adult population (age 25 and over) shows an even more dramatic decline between 1950 and 1990. The coefficient of variation plummeted by 19 percent from 1950 to 1970 and by another 32 percent from 1970 to 2000. Figure 6.7 shows the size distribution

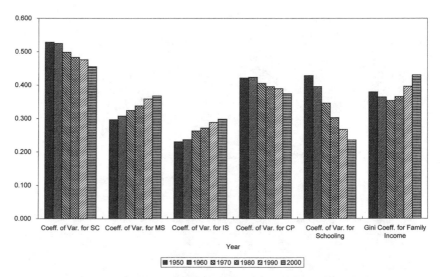

Figure 6.6   Dispersion in Workplace Skills, Educational Attainment, and Income, 1950–2000

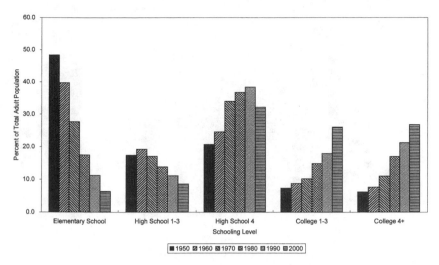

Figure 6.7   Size and Distribution of Schooling for Adults Age 25 and Over, 1950–2000

of schooling from 1950 to 2000. The dispersion of schooling evidently fell during the postwar period, but its mean level rose. The fraction of adults with less than four years of high school plunged from 66 percent in 1950 to 15 percent in 2000, and the proportion with four years or more of college skyrocketed from 6 to 27 percent. In this period, moreover, the schooling distribution shifted from a rightward skew to a leftward skew.

While both schooling and cognitive skills grew steadily less unequal over these years, income inequality took a different course. The Gini coefficient for family income inequality, after declining by 7 percent between 1950 and 1970, increased by 22 percent from 1970 to 2000 (figure 6.6). Over the entire 1950–2000 period, the Gini coefficient for income inequality rose by 13 percent, while the coefficient of variation in education dropped by 45 percent (and the variance of schooling by 48 percent), while the coefficient of variation in cognitive skills declined by 14 percent.

Another perspective on changes in skill inequality is provided by figure 6.8, which shows changes in the distribution of employment by quintile for the 1950–2000 period. I first rank occupations by their 1970 substantive complexity (SC) score; then I compute the cumulative distribution of 1970 employment over the ranked occupations and divide the distribution into quintiles (or as close as possible to quintile shares since I am using a discrete variable). Thus, based on 1970 employment by occupation, occupations with SC scores of 0–2.00 accounted for approximately the bottom 20 percent of total employment (as ranked), and occupations with SC scores of 6.07–10.0 for approximately the top 20 percent. Figure 6.8 shows the percentage of total employment found in the same set of occupations in 1950, 1960, 1970, 1980, 1990, and 2000.

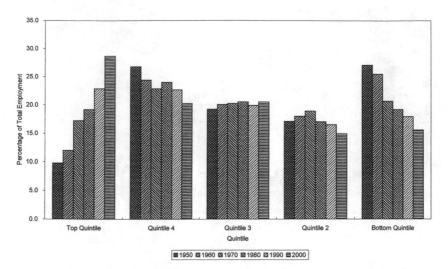

Figure 6.8   Employment Quintile Shares, 1950–2000 (Occupations ranked by 1970 SC score)

The results show that the share of total employment in the bottom skill quintile based on SC scores declined from 27 to 16 percent between 1950 and 2000, while the employment share of the top quintile increased from 10 to 29 percent. The former fell, and the latter increased in each of the individual decades as well. The share of total employment in the fourth quintile fell steadily over time, from 27 percent in 1950 to 20 percent in 2000. The share in the middle quintile rose slightly from 1950 to 1970 and then dropped somewhat from 1970 to 2000, with very little net change over the four decades. The employment share in the second quintile also increased slightly from 1950 to 1970 and then fell sharply, for a net change of −2.2 percentage points over the half century. The results are very similar for the composite score index CP (not shown).

Both the substantive complexity index and the composite skill score show a pronounced rightward shift of the distribution of skills over the postwar period, with a big decline in the least skilled jobs and a correspondingly large increase in the most skilled jobs. The distribution of schooling shows a similar and an even more marked shift over this period toward more highly educated workers. All three variables likewise show a decline in the overall dispersion of skills during the four decades. Yet, paradoxically, the dispersion of labor earnings has risen over this period as well.

6.4.1 Employment Shifts and Skill Inequality

I next consider the connection between skill inequality and employment growth by industry. The evidence is that industries with lower skill inequality (particularly, services) grew faster than the high skill inequality sectors (mainly goods producers). The correlation coefficient between the 1970 coefficient of variation of substantive complexity (SC) within industry and the percentage of change in industry employment over the 1950–1990 period is −0.39.

The change in the overall inequality of skill levels is due to both changes of skill inequality within industry and shifts in employment among industries. Unfortunately, unlike changes in the overall mean, there is no simple decomposition of the change in the overall inequality into an industry employment shift effect and an occupation mix effect (see chapters 2 and 3 for decompositions of changes in mean skill levels and mean earnings, respectively). However, we can simulate the change in overall skill inequality that would result from a shift in the industry composition of employment, while holding constant the mix of skill levels within each industry.

Results of the simulation are shown in table 6.1 for substantive complexity (SC), the composite skill score (CP), and hourly wage in 1970 (where occupations are scored on the basis of their 1970 hourly wage) between 1950 and 1990.[7] For substantive complexity (SC), about two-thirds of the decrease in the overall coefficient of variation in skill between 1950 and 1990 is due to changes in the occupational distribution of employment within industry (that is, from changes in technology), and about one-third is due to shifts in the employment mix among industries (toward industries with lower skill inequality). Changes in technology reduced the dispersion of cognitive skills in each decade as well, and the changes were fairly uniform throughout the four decades. In contrast, employment shifts among industries (with technology fixed) were strongest in reducing inequality during the 1960s and 1970s.[8]

Results are similar for the composite skill index, CP. About three-quarters of the overall decline in skill inequality for this measure were from shifts in the occupational distributions within industry, and the other one-fourth resulted from changes in industry employment. Here, again, the technology effects were quite stable throughout the four decades.

The overall coefficient of variation of the 1970 hourly wage measure declined from 0.412 in 1950 to 0.388 in 1990. However, for this measure, all of the decline in dispersion occurred between 1950 and 1970, while dispersion actually showed a modest increase between 1970 and 1990. Like cognitive skill and composite skill inequality, about three-quarters of the decline was due to changes in occupational composition within industry, and the remainder to industry employment shifts over the four decades. However, between 1970 and 1990, the industry shift effect was either neutral or disequalizing, depending on the occupational distribution used in the simulation, and changes in the occupational distribution of employment within industry had a less pronounced effect on the dispersion of this measure than over the preceding two decades.

To summarize, the results of the analysis of skill inequality consist of two major findings. First, as economy-wide skill requirements have increased

Table 6.1.   Skill Inequality under Alternative Assumptions regarding Industry Employment Weights and Industry Occupational Distributions, 1950–1990

Fixed Industry Employment Weights	Fixed Occupational Distributions by Industry					Change 1950– 1990
	1950	1960	1970	1980	1990	
A. Substantive Complexity (SC)						
1950	0.528	0.522	0.509	0.501	0.495	−0.034
1960	0.531	0.525	0.509	0.498	0.490	−0.041
1970	0.527	0.513	0.498	0.488	0.479	−0.048
1980	0.522	0.508	0.493	0.483	0.474	−0.048
1990	0.519	0.503	0.491	0.482	0.476	−0.043
Change, 1950–1990	−0.009	−0.019	−0.018	−0.019	−0.019	
B. Composite Skill (CP)						
1950	0.421	0.419	0.409	0.404	0.398	−0.023
1960	0.426	0.423	0.411	0.403	0.396	−0.030
1970	0.426	0.418	0.405	0.397	0.389	−0.037
1980	0.424	0.417	0.404	0.395	0.387	−0.037
1990	0.422	0.412	0.401	0.394	0.389	−0.032
Change, 1950–1990	0.000	−0.007	−0.008	−0.010	−0.009	
C. Hourly Wage 1970						
1950	0.412	0.406	0.398	0.388	0.386	−0.026
1960	0.408	0.398	0.389	0.379	0.378	−0.030
1970	0.415	0.395	0.386	0.376	0.375	−0.039
1980	0.420	0.403	0.393	0.383	0.380	−0.040
1990	0.418	0.393	0.385	0.377	0.388	−0.030
Change, 1950–1990	0.006	−0.013	−0.013	−0.011	0.002	

Note: The coefficient of variation is defined as the ratio of the standard deviation to the mean. Employment weights for 267 occupations and 64 industries are used in the calculation. In each row, total employment by industry is assumed fixed at the indicated year. In each column, the occupational composition of employment in each industry is assumed fixed at the indicated year.

since 1950, skill inequality among occupations has narrowed, particularly as measured by cognitive skills and the composite skill index. The change in overall skill inequality has taken the form of an increase in the share of the high-skill occupations and a corresponding decline in the low-skill ones. There appears to be no declining middle of the skill distribution, at least according to the direct skill measures and educational attainment. However, the middle of the skill distribution has declined modestly, as measured by 1970 hourly wages since 1970. Second, the decline in overall skill inequality was mainly due to changes in the occupational distribution of employment within industry (technology) and to a lesser extent to the shift of employment toward those industries with low skill inequality (primarily, services) and away from industries with high skill inequality (mainly goods producers).

6.5 Skill Inequality at the Industry Level

The last set of descriptive statistics, shown in table 6.2, is a ranking of industries by the coefficient of variation of substantive complexity.[9] Among the most unequal sectors in skill dispersion are both services and goods-producing sectors. In 1970, business and personal services topped the list, followed by textile products, apparel, leather products, and hotels and motels. Business and personal services, apparel, leather products, and hotels and motels remained in the top five in 1980; textiles fell out, while the category of meat and dairy products was added to the list. In 1990 apparel, leather products, meat and dairy products, and textiles were in the top five, while rubber and plastic products were a new addition.

There was even more stability at the bottom of the list. Barber and beauty shops, radio and TV broadcasting, and insurance ranked as the three most equal sectors in terms of SC in that order in all three years. Postal services were in the bottom five in all three years as well, while advertising appeared in two of the three years, and auto services and repair show up in one of the three years. Services generally rank among the most equal of industries in terms of skill inequality and, on average, are considerably more equal than goods-producing industries. The correlation coefficients for the coefficient of variation of SC are 0.93 between 1970 and 1980, 0.94 between 1980 and 1990, and 0.91 between 1970 and 1990.

6.6 Concluding Remarks

This chapter documents four striking trends. First, inequality in the distribution of family income, which remained virtually unchanged from the end of World War II to 1968, increased sharply after that period. Second, in contrast, the dispersion (variance) of schooling within the adult population has declined dramatically since the early 1970s. Third, among employed workers, the dispersion of skill levels, as measured by both substantive complexity and the composite skill index, has also diminished since 1970. Fourth, a pronounced rightward shift also occurred in the distribution of schooling, cognitive skills, and the composite skill index, with a very large decline in low-skill jobs and a corresponding increase in highly skilled positions. There appears to be no declining middle of the skill distribution, at least according to these direct skill measures, or of the distribution of educational attainment. This chapter confronts the third of the paradoxes raised in chapter 1, namely, whereas schooling and skill inequality declined after the early 1970s, family income inequality and labor earnings inequality in the United States have risen sharply.

The chapter also documents that most (between two-thirds and three-fourths, depending on the measure used) of the decline in overall skill

Table 6.2. The Coefficient of Variation of Substantive Complexity (SC): Five Highest and Lowest by Year, 1970–1990

Industry	Coefficient of Variation of SC
1970	
Business and personal services	0.729
Textile mills and textile products	0.634
Apparel	0.620
Leather and leather products	0.617
Hotels, motels, and lodging	0.604
Postal service	0.297
Advertising	0.294
Insurance	0.291
Radio and TV broadcasting	0.245
Barber and beauty shops	0.127
Overall	0.498
Goods producers (average)	0.529
Services (average)	0.405
1980	
Hotel, motels, and lodging	0.632
Apparel	0.613
Meat and dairy products	0.613
Leather and leather products	0.609
Business and personal services	0.604
Auto services and repair	0.305
Postal service	0.305
Insurance	0.282
Radio and TV broadcasting	0.245
Barber and beauty shops	0.137
Overall	0.483
Goods producers (average)	0.528
Services (average)	0.396
1990	
Apparel	0.634
Leather and leather products	0.623
Meat and dairy products	0.609
Textile mills and textile products	0.602
Rubber and misc. plastic products	0.593
Postal service	0.295
Advertising	0.286
Insurance	0.275
Radio and TV broadcasting	0.267
Barber and beauty shops	0.131
Overall	0.476
Goods producers (average)	0.521
Services (average)	0.391

Note: The industries shown here are based on the original 64-sector classification scheme.

inequality was due to changes in skill inequality within industry. The remainder was due to the shift of employment toward those industries with low skill inequality (primarily, services) and away from industries with high skill inequality (mainly goods producers).

When we consider the aggregate time-series regression and growth-accounting results, we find that the largest effects on income inequality come from OCA investment. In the time-series analysis, the coefficient of lagged investment in OCA per worker is positive and highly significant, and the variable accounts for 44–52 percent of the rise in income inequality between 1968 and 2000. Non-OCA equipment investment per worker, on the other hand, is found to have a positive but not significant relation to income inequality. According to the growth-accounting decomposition, it has a very weak effect on changes in income inequality over time, and OCA investment, as the dominant element, heavily outweighs non-OCA investment in accounting for the increase in income inequality.

In the pooled cross-industry analysis, the coefficient of investment in OCA per worker is positive and highly significant in explaining industry differences in the degree of cognitive skill change over time. Moreover, these findings are consistent with the pooled industry regression results in chapter 4, which also show a very strong connection between investment in OCA per worker and changes in occupational composition. These results suggest that computerization leads to a hollowing out of the middle of the skill distribution. Once again, investment in equipment less OCA per worker does not play a significant role in explaining industry skill changes.

Unionization is also an important explanatory variable. The unionization rate has a decidedly negative relation to income inequality. The effect is consistently strong in the time-series data. The decline in unionization is found to account for 36–44 percent of the rise in family income inequality between 1968 and 2000. Changes in the unionization rate are also negatively and significantly related to changes in industry skill dispersion. These results are consistent with the pooled cross-industry regression results in chapter 4, which indicate that unions tend to inhibit changes in occupational composition. Unions thus appear to retard the restructuring of jobs in the workplace and thereby help mitigate increases in both earnings and skill inequality. These results are also consistent with some of the findings in the earlier literature, including Blackburn, Bloom, and Freeman (1990); Freeman (1993); Gordon (1996); and DiNardo and Lemieux (1997).

The change in export intensity has a negative and significant association with changes in skill inequality at the industry level. It is also negatively though not significantly related to income inequality. Changes in import intensity, on the other hand, do not play a substantial role in either case. The results on export intensity are roughly consistent with those in chapter 2, which indicate that export-oriented industries upgrade cognitive skills (the coefficient is positive but not significant) and interactive skills (the coefficient is marginally significant) and downgrade motor skills (its coefficient is highly significant) more rapidly than domestically oriented ones. These findings suggest that export industries remain competitive by substituting white-collar for blue-collar workers, thereby reducing both earnings and skill dispersion.

In the time-series regressions, the dispersion of schooling is negatively associated with income inequality although its coefficient is not significant. On the other hand, the coefficient of the variance in schooling multiplied by the rate of return to schooling squared has the positive sign predicted by the human capital model but is not statistically significant. The variable also played almost no role in accounting for the rise in income inequality between 1968 and 2000 because the value of the variable changed little over the period.

In the time-series regressions, the unemployment rate is a highly significant determinant of income inequality. However, this variable played little role in accounting for the rise of inequality after 1968 because its value was almost the same in 2000 as in 1968. Even though the minimum wage in real terms peaked in 1968, its coefficient has the predicted negative sign in the time-series regressions on income inequality but is generally not significant. The decline in the minimum wage after 1968 also played a fairly minor role in explaining the increase in inequality after 1968.

TFP and labor productivity growth at the aggregate level, as well as at the industry level, have no statistical effect on either income or skill inequality. On the other hand, R&D investment (and the number of scientists and engineers engaged in R&D per employee) is positively associated with skill inequality at the industry level, although it does not play a role with regard to income inequality. It is likely that R&D—induced innovations (e.g., OCA investment) tend to eliminate middle-skill jobs, thus increasing skill variance. My results are consistent with those of Mincer (1991) and Adams (1997), who both report a positive association between R&D expenditures and educational wage differentials.

Appendix

A.1 Modeling Framework

Following Stiroh (2002), I begin with a standard neoclassical production function f_j for sector j:

$$(6.1) \qquad X_j = Z_j f_j(KC_j, KE_j, KS_j, LAB_j, RD_j),$$

where X_j is the gross output of sector j, KC_j is the input of IT-related capital, KE_j is the input of other machinery and equipment capital goods, KS_j is the input of plant and other structures, LAB_j is the total labor input, RD_j is the stock of R&D capital, and Z_j is a Hicks-neutral TFP index that shifts the production function of sector j over time.[10] For convenience, I have suppressed the time subscript. Moreover, capacity utilization and adjustment costs are ignored. It then follows that

(6.2) $d \ln X_j = d \ln Z_j + \epsilon_{Cj} \, d \ln KC_j + \epsilon_{Ej} \, d \ln KE_j + \epsilon_{Sj} \, d \ln KS_j$
$+ \epsilon_{Lj} \, d \ln LAB_j + \epsilon_{Rj} \, d \ln RD_j,$

where ϵ represents the output elasticity of each input and $d \ln Z_j$ is the rate of Hicks-neutral TFP growth. If we now impose the assumption of competitive input markets and constant returns to scale, so that

$$\alpha_{Cj} + \alpha_{Ej} + \alpha_{Sj} + \alpha_{Lj} = 1,$$

it follows that an input's factor share (α_j) will equal its output elasticity. Let us now employ the standard measure of TFP growth π_j for sector j:

(6.3) $\ln X_j = \ln Z_j + \alpha_{Cj} \ln KC_j + \alpha_{Ej} \ln KE_j + \alpha_{Sj} \ln KS_j + \alpha_{Lj} \ln LAB_j/dt$
$+ \epsilon_{Rj} \ln RD_j.$

Let us now define labor productivity LP for sector j as

(6.4) $$LP_j \equiv X_j/LAB_j.$$

If we again impose the assumption of competitive input markets and constant returns to scale, it follows that

(6.5) $\ln LP_j = \ln Z_j + \alpha_{Cj} \ln kc_j + \alpha_{Ej} \ln ke_j + \alpha_{Sj} \ln ks_j + \alpha_{Rj} \ln RD_j,$

where lowercase symbols indicate the amount of input per worker.

I next include the change in average worker skills in the production function. There are two possible approaches. Let the effective or quality-adjusted labor input in sector j be given by $Q_j = LAB_j \, S_j$, where S measures average worker skills in sector j. Then equation 6.1 can be rewritten as

(6.6) $X_j = Z_j \, f_j^*(KC_j, KE_j, KS_j, Q_j, RD_j).$

Again assuming competitive input markets and constant returns to scale (to the traditional factors of production) and still using equation 6.5 to define labor productivity growth, we obtain

(6.7) $\ln LP_j = \ln Z_j + \alpha_{Cj} \ln kc_j + \alpha_{Ej} \ln ke_j + \alpha_{Sj} \ln ks_j + \alpha_{Lj} \ln S_j$
$+ \epsilon_{Rj} \ln RD_j.$

In this formulation, labor productivity should be proportional to average worker quality.

The second approach derives from the standard human capital earnings function. From Mincer (1974),

(6.8) $\text{Ln } w = a_0 + a_1 S,$

where w is the wage, S is the worker's level of schooling (or skills), a_0 and a_1 are constants, and a_1 is the rate of return to schooling. By definition, the wage share in sector j is $\alpha_{Lj} = w_j \text{ LAB}_j/X_j$. Under the assumptions of competitive input markets and constant returns to scale, $\alpha_{Lj} = \epsilon_{Lj}$, a constant. Therefore, $X_j/\text{LAB}_j = w_j/\epsilon_{Lj}$. In this case, effective labor input Q is given by the equation $\text{Ln } Q = S + \ln \text{LAB}$. It follows from equation 6.5 that

(6.9) $\ln \text{LP}_j = \ln Z_j + \alpha_{Cj} \ln kc_j + \alpha_{Ej} \ln ke_j + \alpha_{Sj} \ln ks_j + \alpha_{Lj} S_j$
$$+ \epsilon_{Rj} \ln \text{RD}_j.$$

In this case, the *logarithm* of labor productivity is proportional to the average worker quality.

Finally, under the assumptions of competitive input markets and constant returns to scale, $w_j = \alpha_{Lj} X_j/\text{LAB}_j$, where w_j is the average wage in sector j. As a result, from equations 6.7 and 6.9, there are two alternative wage equations:

(6.7′) $\ln w_j = \ln(\alpha_{Lj}) + \ln Z_j + \alpha_{Cj} \ln kc_j + \alpha_{Ej} \ln ke_j + \alpha_{Sj} \ln ks_j$
$$+ \alpha_{Lj} \ln S_j + \epsilon_{Rj} \ln \text{RD}_j$$

(6.9′) $\ln w_j = \ln(\alpha_{Lj}) + \ln Z_j + \alpha_{Cj} \ln kc_j + \alpha_{Ej} \ln ke_j + \alpha_{Sj} \ln ks_j + \alpha_{Lj} S_j$
$$+ \alpha_{Rj} \ln \text{RD}_j.$$

Unfortunately, there is not much more mileage that we can obtain from these neoclassical wage equations in order to obtain a prediction for the *inequality* of labor earnings since wage inequality measures the dispersion of wages *among individual workers,* and data are not available on differences in capital or R&D spending among individual employees. However, we can obtain a prediction for the effect of the variance of Q among individual workers since we do have data on this. In fact, there are two alternative predictions. From equation 6.7′ we would expect that Var(ln w) varies directly with Var(ln S), where the variance of the logarithm of earnings is a standard index of earnings inequality. From equation 6.9′ it follows that Var(ln w) varies directly with Var(S). In the case of schooling as a measure of worker quality, it follows from equation 6.8 that Var(ln w) varies directly with a_1^2 Var(S). In other words, according to the human capital model, the variance of the logarithm of earnings changes proportionally with the product of the variance of schooling and the rate of return to schooling.

A.2 Time-Series Regression Analysis

I next turn to multivariate regression for the 1947–2000 period. The general estimating equation is given by

(6.10) $\text{GINIFAM}_t = \beta_0 + \beta_1\ \text{TFPGRT}_t + \beta_2\ \text{RDGDP}_t$

$+ \beta_3\ \text{EQPXOCAPEPGRT}_t + \beta_4\ \text{OCAPEPGRT}_t$

$+ \beta_5\ \text{EXPGDP}_t + \beta_6\ \text{IMPGDP}_t + \beta_7\ \text{UNION}_t$

$+ \beta_8\ \text{MINWAGE}_t + \beta_9\ \text{SERVTOT}_t + \beta_{10}\ \text{VARSCHOOL}_t$

$\times\ \text{SCHOOLRETSQ}_t + u_t,$

where GINIFAM_t is the Gini coefficient for family income in year t, TFPGRT_t is TFP growth in year t, RDGDP_t is the ratio of R&D expenditures to GDP in year t, EQPXOCAPEPGRT_t is the growth in the total net stock of equipment and machinery less OCA per worker (PEP) in year t, OCAPEPGRT_t is the growth of the net stock of OCA per worker in year t, EXPGDP_t is the ratio of exports to GDP in year t, IMPGDP_t is the ratio of imports to GDP in year t, UNION_t is the unionization rate in year t, MINWAGE_t is the minimum wage (in constant dollars) in year t, SERVTOT_t is the ratio of service to total employment in year t, VARSCHOOL_t is the variance of schooling in year t, SCHOOLRETSQ_t is the square of the rate of return to schooling in year t, and u_t is a stochastic error term.[11]

Several modifications to equations 6.7′ and 6.9′ have been made. First, I have included RDGDP, the ratio of R&D expenditures to GDP, instead of the rate of growth of the stock of R&D capital since the former is directly measurable.[12] Second, I have included machinery and equipment (excluding OCA) but omitted structures since the machinery, equipment, and structures series are highly collinear. Moreover, as alternatives to OCAPEPGRT and EQPXOCAPEPGRT, I have also used INVOCAPEP and INVEQPXOCAPEP, investment in OCA and non-OCA equipment per worker. Third, I have added both export and import intensity. Several researchers have argued that export or import competition may increase the wage gap between highly paid and low-paid workers. Fourth, I have added UNION, the unionization rate. Since unions typically negotiate contracts involving relatively tight wage structures, the argument here is that wage dispersion should be negatively associated with the degree of unionization.

Fifth, I have included MINWAGE, the minimum wage in constant dollars. If an increase in the minimum wage raises the wages of the lowest-paid workers (without affecting those of highly paid workers), then wage dispersion should be negatively associated with the minimum wage (in constant dollars). Sixth, I have also included SERVTOT, service employment as a share of total employment. As I suggested earlier, since services generally have greater earnings inequality than goods-producing industries, earnings dispersion should rise with the share of service employment, and wage growth should be negatively associated with the change in the share of service workers.[13] I have also included control variables for the unemployment rate, the share of property income in total income, and the number of female-headed households as a share of total households.

With regard to lagged versus contemporaneous effects, technological change likely affects wage dispersion with a lag since it may take time for the job structure or the pay structure to react to changes in the technology in use. A similar argument may apply to changes in international competition. As a result, I have entered TFPGRT, RDGDP, EQPXOCAGRT, OCAGRT, IN-VOCAPEP, INVEQPXOCAPEP, EXPGDP, and IMPGDP with a one-year lag.[14] On the other hand, it is likely that the minimum wage level, the distribution of employment between services and goods producers, the variance of schooling, and the return to schooling, as well as the unemployment rate, the property income share, and the share of female-headed households are likely to affect current income immediately. As a result, these variables are entered contemporaneously. The effect of the unionization rate is a bit ambiguous since it may affect income concurrently or with a lag, so I have tried both forms. The best fit is provided by the contemporaneous union rate.

Appendix table 6.1 shows the results. With regard to the technology and investment variables, the most consistently significant one is OCA investment per worker lagged one period. The coefficient of this variable is positive and significant at the 1 percent level in six of the eight cases shown and at the 5 percent level in the other two.[15] This variable provides a better fit than OCA growth per worker, whose coefficient is positive in all cases, significant at the 10 percent level in four cases, and not significant in the other four. The coefficient of non-OCA equipment investment per worker is negative but not significant (specification 2).[16]

Both the annual rate of TFP growth (specification 4) and the annual rate of labor productivity growth (results not shown) have positive coefficients but are also not significant. Industry R&D (as a share of GDP) and the number of full-time equivalent scientists and engineers engaged in R&D per employee have positive coefficients but are not significant (results not shown).

Among the trade variables, the best fit is provided by exports as a percentage of GDP, which has a negative coefficient that is not significant (specification 5). The other trade variables, including imports as a share of GDP and the sum of exports and imports as a share of GDP, all have negative coefficients but are not significant.

With regard to the institutional and structural variables, the most significant is the unionization rate, which has the predicted negative sign and is significant at the 1 or 5 percent level in seven of the eight cases and at the 10 percent level in the remaining case. The minimum wage in constant dollars also has the predicted negative sign; however, its coefficient is not significant in the first six specifications but is significant at the 1 percent level in the last two. The reason for the latter result is the shorter time period used in the regression: 1956–2000 instead of 1947–2000.[17]

Among the control variables, the most consistent one is the civilian unemployment rate. It is included in the specification to control for the cyclical effects of the economy on inequality (inequality normally rises during a recession and declines during a recovery). The coefficient has the predicted

Appendix 6.1. Time-Series Regressions of Family Income Inequality on Technological, Structural, and Institutional Variables, 1947–2000

Independent Variables	Specification							
	(1)	(2)	(3)	(4)	(5)	(6)	(7)	(8)
Constant	0.422 **	0.445 **	0.435 **	0.425 **	0.460 **	0.439 **	0.459 **	0.448 **
	(14.70)	(12.03)	(15.51)	(14.42)	(12.73)	(13.45)	(19.14)	(18.03)
Unemployment rate	0.214 *	0.211 *	0.203 *	0.244 **	0.233 **	.208 *	0.152	0.155 #
	(2.55)	(2.49)	(2.35)	(2.59)	(2.68)	(2.39)	(1.49)	(1.69)
Unionization rate	−0.290 *	−0.354 **	−0.302 **	−0.271 *	−0.374 **	−0.260 *	−0.315 **	−0.326 **
	(2.33)	(2.57)	(2.68)	(2.26)	(2.83)	(2.04)	(3.49)	(2.52)
OCA investment per worker (1 period lag)	0.023 *	0.027 **	0.027 **	0.026 **	0.027 **	0.024 *	0.032 **	0.031 **
	(2.35)	(2.64)	(2.79)	(2.73)	(2.78)	(2.35)	(4.03)	(3.89)
Non-OCA equipment investment per worker (1 period lag)	−0.056							
	(0.97)							
Minimum wage (1995 dollars)			−0.236	−0.225	−0.186	−0.194	−0.841 **	−0.832 **
			(1.32)	(1.24)	(1.03)	(1.07)	(3.15)	(3.03)
TFP growth (3-year running average)				0.122				
				(1.18)				
Ratio of exports to GDP in current $ (1 period lag)					−0.189			
					(1.29)			
Variance of schooling						−0.141		
						(0.44)		

(continued)

Appendix 6.1. (*continued*)

Independent Variables	Specification							
	(1)	(2)	(3)	(4)	(5)	(6)	(7)	(8)
Variance of schooling times rate of return to schooling squared							0.064 (1.27)	0.083 (1.41)
R^2	0.93	0.93	0.93	0.93	0.93	0.93	0.95	0.95
Adjusted R^2	0.92	0.93	0.93	0.92	0.93	0.92	0.94	0.95
Standard error	0.0063	0.0062	0.0061	0.0062	0.0062	0.0063	0.0060	0.0060
Durbin-Watson	1.94	1.96	2.04	2.11	2.06	2.06	1.93	1.95
Sample size	54	54	54	54	54	54	45	45
Period	1947–2000	1947–2000	1947–2000	1947–2000	1947–2000	1947–2000	1956–2000	1956–2000
Est. tech.	AR(1)	AR(1)	AR(1)	AR(1)	AR(1)	AR(1)	AR(1)	IV, AR(1)

Note: The dependent variable is the Gini coefficient for family income inequality (GINIFAM). The absolute value of the t-statistic is in parentheses below the coefficient. See the appendix for data sources and methods.

Key:

AR(1): Autoregressive process, first-order: $u_t = e_t + r_1 u_{t-1}$, where u_t is the error term of the original equation and e_t is a stochastic term assumed to be identically and independently distributed.

IV: Instrumental variables. The instruments are as follows: (1) unemployment rate, (2) investment in OCA per PEP, (3) variance of schooling, (4) minimum wage in 1995 dollars, and (5) ratio of exports to GDP.

Significance levels: # significant at the 10% level; * significant at the 5% level; ** significant at the 1% level.

positive sign and is significant at the 1 or 5 percent level in six of the eight cases and at the 10 percent level in a seventh.

With the exception of the unionization rate and the unemployment rate, the other structural and control variables are not statistically significant. A positive coefficient is expected for the ratio of employment in service sectors to total employment because earnings inequality in service sectors is, in the main, greater than earnings inequality in goods industries. The coefficient is positive but not significant. A positive coefficient is also expected for the ratio of white-collar to total employment since mean earnings and the dispersion of earnings are greater among white-collar than blue-collar workers. The coefficient of this variable is likewise positive but not significant. The coefficient of the number of part-time workers as a percentage of total employment is also not significant, with a value essentially equal to zero. The coefficients of both the number of female-headed families as a percentage of total families and personal property income as a share of total personal income have the predicted positive sign, but neither is significant.

The results for OCA investment per worker, the unionization rate, and the unemployment rate are robust over a wide range of alternative specifications. Only a few of the regression equations are shown in appendix table 6.1.

The variance of schooling is added in specification 6. Its coefficient is (perversely) negative but not statistically significant. The negative coefficient is extremely robust over a wide range of alternative specifications. In specification 7, the theoretically preferred variable, the product of the variance of schooling and the rate of return to schooling squared, is included. The coefficient of this variance has the predicted positive sign but is not significant.

Because much of the theoretical work on rising earnings inequality (such as the skill-biased technological change hypothesis) posits that the same forces that have caused earnings inequality to increase have also caused the return to schooling to rise, it is likely that the rate of return to schooling is an endogenous variable. Therefore, specification 8 uses an instrumental variable (IV) estimation procedure, with the minimum wage in constant dollars and the ratio of exports to GDP as instruments in place of the rate of return variable.[18] The results are virtually identical to those of specification 7, though now the coefficient of variance of schooling, multiplied by the rate of return to schooling squared, has a slightly higher coefficient value and t-statistic.[19]

The goodness of fit for the eight equations shown in appendix table 6.1 is extraordinarily high: R^2 statistics ranging from 0.93 to 0.95 and adjusted R^2 statistics ranging from 0.92 to 0.94. The Durbin-Watson statistic is in the acceptable range—very close to 2.0.[20] It is also of note that the regression results for the various variables used in the analysis remain quite robust among alternative specifications, including the use of lagged values for both the investment, technology, and trade variables.

To gauge the quantitative significance of this set of variables in accounting for changes in inequality over time, I next perform a growth-accounting exercise (results not shown). I divide the sample into two periods: 1947–1968, when inequality declined, and 1968–1997, when inequality increased. The contribution of each factor is determined as the product of its regression coefficient and the change in the value of the variable over the period. Three different specifications are used.

Between 1947 and 1968, the Gini coefficient declined from 37.6 to 34.8 (2.8 points). By far the largest positive contribution to the decrease in inequality is made by the increase in the minimum wage, from $2.73 to $7.01 (in 1995 dollars) per hour. The increased minimum wage accounts for some 30 percent of the decrease in inequality. None of the other variables prove to be very important. However, some 90 percent of the decline remains unexplained by the variables used in the regressions.[21]

The regression results do a much better job of accounting for the rise in inequality between 1968 and 2000, when the Gini coefficient increased from 34.8 to 43.0 (8.2 points). In this case, the increase in OCA investment per worker makes the largest contribution, accounting for 44–52 percent of the increased inequality. The second largest contributor is the sharp drop in the unionization rate from 23.0 to 13.4 percent. This decline explains 30–42 percent of the increase in the Gini coefficient. The decline in the hourly minimum wage (in 2000 dollars), from $7.31 to $5.15, makes a small contribution in the first two growth-accounting exercises but accounts for 22 percent of the decline in the third exercise (section C). The unemployment rate plays a small role because it increased very modestly between 1968 and 2000, from 3.6 to 4.0 percent. The 3-year running average of TFP growth also changed very little between 1968 and 2000, from 0.91 to 0.84 percent per year. The increase in export intensity, from 5.0 to 11.8 percent of GDP, offset the increase in inequality by 1.22 points (15 percent). The human capital variable, the variance of schooling times the rate of return to schooling squared, plays almost no role in explaining the rise in inequality. Though the rate of return to schooling increased during this period, the variance of schooling declined, and the value of this variable also fell, from 0.238 to 0.166. For these years, only 10–20 percent of the rise in inequality is left unaccounted for (the "unexplained residual").

A.3   Pooled Cross-Industry Regression Analysis on Skill Inequality

I next investigate changes in skill inequality over time at the industry level.[22] The dependent variable in these regressions is the change in the coefficient of variation of substantive complexity (SC) over the 10-year period. The statistical technique is based on pooled cross-section time-series regressions on industries and for the decades that correspond with the decennial census data. The period of analysis is 1970–2000.[23] The sample consists of 44 industries in the two time periods, 1970–1980 and 1980–1990, and 32 industries in the 1990–2000 period.[24] The error terms are assumed to be independently distributed but may not be identically distributed; I use the White procedure for a heteroschedasticity-consistent covariance matrix in the estimation (see White 1980). The estimating model is

$$(6.11) \quad \text{DELCVSC}_{jt} = \beta_0 + \beta_1 \text{ TFPGRT}_{jt} + \beta_2 \text{ RDSALES}_{jt}$$
$$+ \beta_3 \text{ EQPXOCAPEPGRT}_{jt} + \beta_4 \text{ OCAPEPGRT}_{jt}$$
$$+ \beta_5 \text{ DELEXPGDO}_{jt} + \beta_6 \text{ DELIMPGDO}_{jt}$$
$$+ \beta_7 \text{ DELUNION}_{jt} + u_{jt},$$

where DELCVSC_{jt} is the period change in the coefficient of variation of substantive complexity (SC) in industry j over period t, TFPGRT_{jt} is the annual average TFP growth in industry j over period t, RDSALES_{jt} is the average ratio of R&D expenditures to net sales in industry j over period t, $\text{EQPXINVOCAPEP}_{jt}$ is the investment in total equipment less OCA per worker (PEP) in industry j over period t, INVOCAPEPGRT_{jt} is the investment in OCA per worker in industry j over period t, DELEXPGDO_{jt} is the period change in the ratio of exports to gross output in industry j over period t, DELIMPGDP_{jt} is the period change in the ratio of imports to GDP in industry j over period t, DELUNION_{jt} is the period change in the unionization rate in industry j over period t, and u_{jt} is a stochastic error term.[25]

Generally speaking, factors that affect industry earnings inequality should be similar to those that affect industry skill inequality. However, two modifications to equation 6.7' have been made. First, I have used *change* in inequality as the dependent variable. Industry skill inequality reflects both the size of the sector and the number and degree of heterogeneity of detailed industries included in the aggregated sector. As a result, the industry classification scheme will affect the rank order of industries in terms of measured inequality. On the other hand, the change in skill inequality over time should not be directly affected by the classification scheme, which is the justification for using inequality change as the dependent variable. Second, I correspondingly use the period change in export and import intensity, as well as that of the unionization rate, as independent variables instead of their average value over the period.

Results are shown in appendix table 6.2. The most significant variable is investment in OCA per worker, which has a positive coefficient significant at the 1 percent level. The coefficient of investment in equipment less OCA per employee is positive but not significant. The change in the rate of unionization over the period has the predicted negative effect on the change in skill inequality, and its coefficient is significant at the 5 percent level in two of the three cases shown here and significant at the 10 percent level in the other.

The change in imports as a share of total sales is found to have a positive effect on earnings inequality changes, but its coefficient is not significant. However, the coefficient of the change in the export share is negative and

Appendix 6.2.   Regressions of the Change in the Coefficient of Variation of Substantive Complexity (SC) Using Pooled Industry Data, 1970–2000

Independent Variables	(1)	(2)	(3)
Constant	−0.058 **	−0.058 **	−0.059 **
	(6.06)	(6.04)	(6.24)
Investment in equipment less OCA	0.062	0.055	0.069
(in 1,000s, 2000 dollars) per worker	(0.65)	(0.57)	(0.73)
Investment in OCA	0.049 **	0.049 **	0.042 *
(in 1,000s, 2000 dollars) per worker	(2.70)	(2.69)	(2.30)
Change in the	−0.165 *	−0.150 #	−0.130 #
unionization rate	(2.14)	(1.85)	(1.64)
Change in the ratio	0.058	0.057	0.066
of imports to sales	(1.02)	(1.03)	(1.17)
Change in the ratio	−0.455 #	−0.459 #	−0.721 *
of exports to sales	(1.78)	(1.79)	(2.45)
Period TFP growth		0.136	
		(0.69)	
Ratio of R&D expeditures			0.482 #
to sales			(1.80)
R^2	0.16	0.17	0.19
Adjusted R^2	0.13	0.12	0.14
Standard error	0.0623	0.0624	0.0617
Sample size	120	120	120

Note: The sample consists of pooled cross-section, time-series data with observations on each of the 44 industries in 1970–1980 and 1980–1990 (sector 45, public administration, is excluded because of a lack of appropriate capital stock data) and 32 industries in 1990–2000. Dummy variables are included for time periods 1970–1980 and 1980–1990 (results not shown). The coefficients are estimated using the White procedure for a heteroschedasticity-consistent covariance matrix. The absolute value of the t-statistic is in parentheses below the coefficient. See the appendix for data sources and methods.

Significance levels: # significant at the 10% level; * significant at the 5% level; ** significant at the 1% level.

significant at the 5 percent level in one of the three cases and significant at the 10 percent level in the other two.

The coefficients of TFP growth, as well as labor productivity growth (results not shown), are positive but not significant. However, the coefficients of R&D expenditures as a share of sales and the number of scientists and engineers engaged in R&D per employee (results not shown) are positive and significant at the 5 percent level.

A dummy variable discriminating between service and goods industries is also introduced. Its coefficient is negative, indicating that, once having controlled for other factors, skill inequality growth tends to be lower (but not significant) in services than among goods producers (results not shown).

Notes

1. A related argument is that immigration may also have increased the relative pool of low-skilled workers in the last twenty years or so, likewise putting downward pressure on their relative wages. There is some evidence that locations that have numerous immigrants are characterized by larger wage differentials between less schooled and more schooled workers than those with fewer immigrants. See Borjas, Freeman, and Katz (1992) for a discussion of this issue and evidence that changing immigration patterns might have contributed to the secular rise in earnings inequality.
2. I am, of course, primarily interested in the inequality of labor earnings in this analysis. Unfortunately, the consistent time-series for these series are rather short, beginning only in 1967 at the earliest. Moreover, none of them covers both the slightly downward drift in inequality between the late 1940s and the late 1960s and the sharp increase in the 1980s and 1990s. Analysis (not shown here) indicates that most of the labor earnings series tend to correlate highly with the family income inequality series (a correlation coefficient of 0.91 for the variance of the logarithm of labor earnings from 1967 to 2001 derived from the CPS annual demographic files); I use the latter as a proxy for inequality in personal labor earnings.

   Moreover, in the regression analysis in the appendix to this chapter, I control for three factors that may account for much (if not most) of the deviation between income and earnings inequality. The first is the unemployment rate, which controls, in part, for the fact that some families receive zero labor income. Not surprisingly, its movement is cyclical over time, whereas family income inequality has trended rather continuously upward since the late 1960s. As a result, the correlation of the unemployment rate with family income inequality is rather low (only 0.27). The second control variable is the number of female-headed families as a percentage of total families. It is included since this group has historically had the lowest level of family income of any family type, and a large part of its income has taken the form of government transfers. Its share has trended almost continuously upward from 1959 to 2003, from 10 percent to 19 percent. As result, it is strongly correlated with family income inequality—a correlation coefficient of 0.78.

   The third variable in this group is personal property income, defined as the sum of rent, dividends, interest, and one-half of proprietors' income, as a share of total personal income. It is included since it constitutes part of the difference between family income and labor earnings (the other major part is government transfer income). Its time path is somewhat similar to that of family income inequality. This variable shows a slightly downward trend from 1947 to 1972 (from 21 to 18 percent), followed by an upward trajectory to 24 percent in 2003. As a result, its correlation coefficient with family income inequality is very high (0.84).

3. TFP growth is defined as

$$\text{TFPGRTH}_t = dY_t/Y_t - \alpha dL_t/L_t - (1 - \alpha)dK_t/K_t,$$

where Y_t is GDP (in 2000 dollars) at time t, L_t is the total labor input, K_t is the capital input, and α is the average wage share over the period. The labor input is measured by persons engaged in production (PEP), and the capital input by the fixed nonresidential net capital stock (in 2000 dollars). See the appendix for details. A second index of TFP growth was also used, with full-time equivalent employees (FTEE) as the measure of labor input. Since the data are for discrete time periods, the Tornqvist-Divisia measure, based on average period shares, is used in the actual estimation.

4. Indeed, OCACM (the sum of communications equipment and OCA) per PEP has an even higher correlation coefficient with family income inequality, 0.84.

5. The source for 1956 to 1979 is Mattila (1984), which is based on the rate of return to four years of college relative to four years of high school for male workers. I extended the series to 2000 on the basis of CPS data on the ratio of annual earnings between male college graduates and male high school graduates (figure 1.8). The rate of return was estimated using the standard internal rate of return to schooling formula under the assumption that the ratio in earnings between college and high school graduates remains constant over the life cycle and that college graduates begin work four years later, on average, than high school graduates.

6. The correlation between the square of the rate of return to college and the Gini coefficient for family income is 0.66.

7. With the adoption of the North American Industrial Classification System (NAICS) in the United States in 1997, a major change occurred in the occupational classifications used between the 1990 and 2000 decennial censuses. As a result, it was not possible to update this analysis to 2000.

8. The effect of employment shifts on overall skill inequality is also a function of the correlation between the average skill level of an industry and its employment growth. Since the more skill-intensive industries grew faster during this period, this effect by itself led to greater skill inequality. However, since employment also shifted toward industries with lower skill inequality, the net effect of the employment shifts was to lower overall skill inequality.

9. Because the underlying Census of Population public use samples were not available for all six census years, it is not possible to compute earnings inequality at the industry level.

10. This is a modified form of the production function used by Stiroh (2002).

11. I do not have annual time-series data on the variance of skills, so this variable could not be included here.

12. The two forms are equivalent. The proof is that RDGDP $= dR/X$. From equations 2 and 4 it follows that

$$\pi = \epsilon_R(dR/R) = \epsilon_R(dR/X)(X/R) = (\epsilon_R X/R)(dR/X).$$

Therefore,

$$\beta_2 = (\epsilon_R X/R) = (dX/X)(X/R)/(dR/R) = dX/dR.$$

13. Another variable that was tried but did not prove significant is the change in the share of women in the labor force. The argument is that because of women's increasing participation in the labor force and because of the historically lower wages they receive, their increased number in the labor force may lead to an increase in the overall variance of earnings. However, this variable did not prove significant.
14. Longer lags were also tried, but the 1-year delay seems to provide the best fit.
15. Also significant at the 1 or 5 percent level are computer investment per PEP and investment in OCACM per PEP.
16. A similar result holds for the growth of non-OCA equipment per worker.
17. Similar results hold for the ratio of the minimum wage to average hourly earnings of the workforce (results not shown).
18. Both variables are highly correlated with the rate of return to schooling.
19. I use GINIFAM as the dependent variable in specifications 7 and 8 for comparability with the results for specifications 1–6. An alternative form follows from equation 6.8 that

$$\ln[\text{Var}(\ln E)] = 2\ln(b_1) + \ln[\text{Var}(S)].$$

As a result, an alternative specification is a regression of the logarithm of family income inequality on both the logarithm of the rate of return to schooling and the logarithm of the variance of schooling. This form was also estimated with IV. In this case, the coefficient of the logarithm of the rate of return to schooling is positive, and the coefficient of the logarithm of the variance of schooling is negative, but neither one is significant. The coefficient of the unemployment rate remains positive and significant at the 10 percent level.
20. Another test that was performed is the Augmented Dickey-Fuller (ADF) unit root test for nonstationarity in the dependent variable. The regression includes one lagged value of the dependent variable. The results are as follows:

| | | MacKinnon | |
Variables Included	ADF t-Statistic	Critical Value (1%)	Reject Unit Root?
No constant; no time trend	−5.003	−2.611	Yes
A constant; no time trend	−5.169	−3.571	Yes
A constant; a time trend	−6.263	−4.158	Yes

Similar results are found using multiple lagged terms of the dependent variable.
21. The results for specification 8 (section C) cover only the 1956–1968 period, when the Gini coefficient was virtually unchanged. As a result, the growth-accounting results are not especially meaningful.

22. Data on earnings inequality at the industry level are not available.
23. Data on unionization rates are not available before the mid-1960s, so it is not possible to compute the change in the unionization rate, one of the principal variables in the analysis, for the 1960s.
24. The 1950s cannot be included in the regression analysis because the R&D series begins fully only in 1958. The government sector is excluded because of a lack of data on OCA investment. Moreover, because of a major change in industrial classification in 1997 with the adoption of the NAICS in the United States, the 1990–2000 sample consists of only 32 industries (excluding the government sector).
25. I do not have industry-level data on the variance of schooling, so this variable could not be included here.

7

Skills and Changing Comparative Advantage

7.1 Introduction

This chapter considers the relationship between the changing skill base of
the U.S. labor force and the country's shifting comparative advantage in the
international arena. Standard trade theory predicts that a country will export
those products that intensively use the resources it has in abundance and
import products that are intensive in resources that it lacks. It was generally believed, for example, that the United States exported capital-intensive
goods and imported labor-intensive ones, but empirical work shows that U.S.
exports tend to be human-capital intensive and its imports capital intensive
(the so-called Leontief paradox).

In this chapter I investigate the skill composition of exports and imports.
Does the United States tend to export products that utilize highly skilled
labor and import those that utilize low-skilled labor? How have these trade
patterns changed over time? Do they reflect the changing skill composition
of the U.S. labor force, which has shifted in favor of cognitive and interactive
skills and away from motor skills? With the growth of the information economy (assuming that we are in the forefront of the world in that dimension),
is the comparative advantage of the United States shifting in that direction
as well?

A related issue concerns the R&D intensity of U.S. trade. During the 1960s
and 1970s the major export strength of the United States lay in industries
whose research was heavily subsidized by the U.S. government (particularly
the Department of Defense), including aircraft, armaments, mainframe computers, and medical equipment (see Dollar and Wolff 1993). Is the United
States still exporting R&D—intensive products?

The data analysis is based on U.S. input-output data from 1947 to 1996[1] and on U.S. census of population data on employment by occupation and industry, education, and skills for decennial census years 1950, 1960, 1970, 1980, 1990, and 2000. I present statistics on the skill and educational content of U.S. exports and imports from 1950 to 2000. Calculations are also provided of the share of information workers "embodied" in trade in the same period. I provide statistics on the total capital, equipment, computer, and R&D content of U.S. trade flows from 1947 to 1996, as well as on the relative labor costs and productivity performance of U.S. exports and imports. On the basis of input-output data, it is possible to compute both the direct and indirect content of trade.

I find that the comparative advantage of the United States in international trade has been in industries high in cognitive and interactive skills and low in motor skills, and the skill gap between exports and imports has widened over time. U.S. exports also have a high content in terms of knowledge workers and a low content in terms of goods workers relative to imports, and the gap has grown over time as well. The results also show that imports are more capital and equipment intensive than exports, but in this case the difference has diminished over time. Moreover, by 1987 exports were more intensive in office, computing, and accounting equipment (OCA) than imports. In contrast, while in 1958 the R&D intensity of U.S. exports was much greater than that of imports, by 1996 the R&D intensity of imports was slightly greater than that of exports. I also find that labor productivity rose faster in export than import industries, and the unit labor cost of export industries relative to import industries declined almost steadily over time.

Section 7.2 of this chapter reviews the literature on the skill composition of trade. Section 7.3 presents descriptive statistics on the composition of U.S. trade from 1947 to 1996. The factor content of trade is analyzed in section 7.4 and section 7.5 presents concluding remarks. The accounting framework used in the analysis is developed in the appendix of this chapter.

7.2 Review of Literature

With regard to trade patterns, two distinct approaches can be used to explain the reasons different countries specialize in different industries. The first is the Heckscher-Ohlin model with factor-price equalization (see Heckscher [1919] 1949 and Ohlin 1933). The key assumption in the model is that all countries face the same technology but differ in the relative abundance of factors of production, from which it can be shown that factor prices will be equalized across countries. The main implication of this model is that trade specialization is dictated by relative factor abundance. In particular, a country will export products that intensively use those resources it has in relative abundance and import products that intensively use the resources it lacks.

This prediction has been subject to a long series of studies comparing the resource content of exports with that of the domestic substitutes for imported products in a single country. This is legitimate since, by the assumptions of the Heckscher-Ohlin model, the technology a country uses to produce products it imports is the same as that used in other countries to produce these products. Moreover, the factor prices faced in the countries are the same, making the relative costs identical.

The most widely known tests of the effects of relative factor endowments on trade patterns were conducted by Leontief (1956, 1964), using input-output data for the United States. The main finding is that, despite the fact that the United States was then the most capital-intensive country in the world, it exported goods that were relatively labor intensive and imported goods that were relatively capital intensive. This phenomenon became known as the Leontief paradox. Many explanations were offered for the Leontief paradox, including (1) R&D differences among countries, (2) skill differentials among countries, (3) differences in educational attainment and other human capital attributes, and (4) the relative abundance of land and other natural resources (see Caves 1960 for more discussion).

In a later study, Bowen, Leamer, and Sveikauskas (1987) computed the amount of each of twelve factors of production embodied in the net exports of 27 countries in 1967 on the basis of the U.S. input-output matrix of total input requirements for that year. These factor contents were then compared to the relative factor abundance of the 27 countries. Using regression tests, they found no correspondence between the two (in contradiction to the Heckscher-Ohlin model).

Trefler (1993, 1995) used another technique to investigate the Leontief paradox. Like Bowen, Leamer, and Sveikauskas (1987), he first computed both the labor and capital requirements of the net exports of a set of countries on the basis of the technology matrix of a single country (the United States). He then compared the labor and capital requirements with the national endowments of both labor and capital to determine whether the Leontief paradox held. It did in general. He then relaxed the assumption of factor-price equalization and showed that cross-country differences in factor prices could account for the fact that more capital-abundant countries had net exports that were labor intensive, and conversely.

The second approach for analyzing trade patterns among countries derives from Ricardian trade theory, which emphasizes intercountry differences in technology and factor prices. The modern variant of the Ricardian approach is the technology gap model, whose central premise is that technology gaps and differences in innovativeness between countries will be a major source of trade flows (see, for example, Posner 1961 or Fagerberg 1988). While the Heckscher-Ohlin model is essentially a static model, the technology gap model emphasizes technical change as the key source of (changing) comparative advantage.

Empirical analysis of this model relies on cross-national data to compare trade patterns and technology indicators. Dosi, Pavitt, and Soete (1990), using data for 40 manufacturing industries over the 1963–1977 period, found that patenting activity was a significant determinant of export share among OECD countries, with the exception of several resource-based industries and several in which patents are not a reliable indicator of innovative activity. Other variables that generally proved significant were labor productivity and capital intensity.

Amable and Verspagen (1995) have also reported that patents proved to be a significant determinant of export share in a majority of 18 manufacturing industries for five countries from 1970 to 1991. Wage costs were significant in a third of the sectors, while investment played a role in only a few sectors. Verspagen and Wakelin (1997) have also discovered a major effect of R&D intensity on net exports among a sample of nine OECD countries from 1970 to 1988 for 11 of 22 manufacturing industries.

Other trade economists emphasize the role of relative unit labor costs in international competitiveness. Fagerberg (1988) found that a country's relative unit labor costs were statistically significant as a determinant of a country's trade balance but that the effect was much weaker than that from technological variables. Dosi, Pavitt, and Soete (1990) have also reported a much stronger effect of labor productivity than unit labor costs on exports of total manufacturing.

Wolff (1995), using data for the five major OECD countries from 1970 to 1987 and controlling for country size, has found that aggregate export performance was significantly related to relative productivity growth, the growth in capital intensity, R&D intensity, and capital vintage. Wolff (1997b) used Balassa's (1965) revealed comparative advantage (RCA) index, which measures the ratio of a country's share of a given export commodity in total world exports of that commodity to a country's share of manufacturing exports in total world manufacturing exports, as an indicator of trade specialization. A similar index, the revealed product advantage (RPA), was used for total production (output) shares by industry. On the basis of data for 13 manufacturing industries in 14 OECD countries from 1970 to 1992, the results show that total factor productivity (TFP) growth was a powerful predictor of the change in RPA. It was also significantly related to the change in RCA for the 1982–1992 period but, in general, not for the 1970–1982 period. On the other hand, the change in relative labor costs was generally negatively related to the change in RCA and in RPA for the 1970–1982 period but was not significant for the 1982–1992 period.

In a follow-up study, Wolff (1999b) has found that improvement in relative labor productivity was a powerful predictor of the change in RPA among 33 manufacturing industries in 14 OECD countries from 1970 to 1993. The rate of capital formation also played an important role in the determination of RPA among low-tech industries but was less significant for medium-tech industries and not significant for high-tech ones. The results also show that relatively higher unit labor costs usually reduced competitiveness and hence RPA among low-tech industries.

A few studies have examined the skill content of trade. In one of the earliest, Keesing (1965) used U.S. data for five occupational groups and 15 industries to classify workers into skilled and unskilled categories. Comparisons of the skill content of exports were made among nine OECD countries in 1957. Keesing found that, relative to other countries, U.S. exports were the most skill intensive, followed by those of West Germany, Sweden, and the United Kingdom. Japan ranked last in this group. Engelbrecht (1996) looked at the skill content of German exports and imports in 1976, 1980, and 1984. Using detailed occupational data, he concluded that comparative advantage resulted more from specialization in particular skill types than from the overall human capital endowment of a country. German exports, for example, were strongly endowed with labor from skilled manual occupations (such as metal workers, tool makers, and mechanics) and engineers.

Lee and Schluter (1999) also looked at the skill content of U.S. trade over the period 1972–1992. They constructed a dichotomous variable for skilled and unskilled workers on the basis of nine major occupational groups and found that the ratio of highly skilled to low-skilled workers was greater for exports than imports, but the difference in the ratios remained relatively unchanged over this period.

7.3 The Composition of U.S. Trade

Table 7.1 shows the percentage composition of exports. In 1996, the most important U.S. export was nonelectrical industrial machinery, which made up 12.6 percent of all exports. This category includes OCA. In 1996, OCA by itself constituted 5.1 percent of all exports. The second most important export was electrical and electronic equipment, accounting for 9.3 percent, followed by shipping and other transportation services (8.2 percent), motor vehicles and parts (6.9 percent), chemicals and chemical products (5.6 percent), other transportation equipment such as aircraft (5.4 percent), and wholesale and retail trade (4.8 and 4.6 percent, respectively). Altogether, industrial machinery, electrical and electronic and transportation equipment, and chemicals made up almost 40 percent of all exports.

Some very striking changes have occurred in export composition over the half century. In 1947, the most important U.S. export (excluding transportation services) was processed food products, at 10.9 percent, followed by agriculture, forestry, and fishing (9.5 percent); nonelectrical industrial machinery (9.2 percent); primary metal products such as steel (9.0 percent); motor vehicles and parts (5.7 percent); and textile mill products such as fabrics (5.5 percent). Since 1947, agriculture and food exports have steadily declined in relative importance, from 20.3 percent to 6.5 percent in 1996, as did exports of primary metal products, from 9.0 to 1.9 percent.

Table 7.1. Percentage Composition of U.S. Exports, with Industries Ranked by 1996 Exports

Industry	1947	1958	1967	1977	1987	1996
Industrial machinery except electrical	9.2	12.7	14.3	12.8	10.9	12.6
Electric and electronic equipment	3.2	4.5	5.4	6.5	7.4	9.3
Shipping and other transport services	13.0	12.0	10.6	6.7	8.8	8.2
Motor vehicles and equipment	5.7	4.8	5.5	7.9	7.6	6.9
Chemicals and allied products	3.8	5.3	6.0	5.3	5.9	5.6
Other transportation equipment	2.4	4.5	5.5	5.8	7.4	5.4
Retail trade	2.9	3.7	3.6	4.4	4.4	4.8
Wholesale trade	2.9	3.7	3.6	4.4	4.2	4.6
Real estate	0.3	1.3	1.6	2.6	3.4	4.6
Instruments and related products	1.1	1.4	2.4	2.4	4.0	4.1
Agriculture, forestry, and fishing	9.5	9.8	9.0	9.2	4.5	3.7
Food and related products	10.9	6.7	5.2	5.1	3.8	3.5
Rubber and plastic products	1.6	2.9	2.7	2.2	2.6	3.0
Fabricated metal products	2.2	2.9	3.6	4.0	3.4	2.4
Insurance	0.2	0.1	0.1	0.2	2.4	2.1
Banking, credit, and investment companies	0.2	0.1	0.1	0.2	2.4	2.1
Primary metal products	9.0	5.0	4.4	2.6	1.7	1.9
Paper and allied products	1.7	1.6	2.0	1.8	2.1	1.8
Petroleum and coal products	3.1	3.4	2.1	2.3	2.1	1.5
Business and repair services, except auto	0.2	0.7	0.6	1.0	0.7	1.1
Professional services and nonprofits	0.2	0.6	0.6	1.0	0.7	1.1
Apparel and other textile products	1.8	0.8	0.7	0.7	0.5	1.1
Lumber and wood products	1.0	0.6	1.0	1.4	1.2	0.9
Tobacco products	1.3	2.3	1.6	1.2	0.8	0.9
Amusement and recreation services	0.7	1.3	0.9	0.3	0.4	0.8
Textile mill products	5.5	1.3	0.9	1.2	0.8	0.8
Printing and publishing	0.4	0.5	0.7	1.0	0.7	0.7
Miscellaneous manufactures	1.0	0.6	0.9	0.9	0.9	0.7
Stone, clay, and glass products	1.0	0.9	0.9	0.8	0.6	0.6
Telephone and telegraph	0.2	0.3	0.4	0.7	1.1	0.6
Oil and gas extraction	1.2	0.2	0.3	0.2	0.5	0.6
Coal mining	2.1	1.7	0.8	1.5	0.8	0.3
Correlation with 1996 export composition	0.64	0.83	0.89	0.91	0.97	1.00

Note: Exports are in current dollars. Industries are classified according to a 45-sector aggregation. Only industries that account for 1 percent or more of exports in any year are listed.

206

Textile mill products plummeted from 5.5 to 0.8 percent. Both industrial machinery and motor vehicles remained high over the half century, actually increasing their share. The biggest gains were made by electrical and electronic equipment, from 3.2 to 9.3 percent.

As table 7.2 shows, the three leading imports in 1996 were motor vehicles and parts (14.2 percent), nonelectrical industrial machinery (14.1 percent), and electric and electronic equipment (13.2 percent). Together, this group composed 41.5 percent of all imports. It is also of note that these three

Table 7.2. Percentage Composition of U.S. Imports, with Industries Ranked by 1996 Imports

Industry	1947	1958	1967	1977	1987	1996
Motor vehicles and equipment	0.2	6.0	3.3	12.2	18.9	14.2
Industrial machinery except electrical	1.2	2.9	7.6	5.2	10.9	14.1
Electric and electronic equipment	0.1	1.3	6.7	7.6	11.5	13.2
Oil and gas extraction	5.1	11.4	6.0	23.8	7.2	8.4
Apparel and other textile products	0.4	0.4	0.3	4.1	6.5	6.7
Chemicals and allied products	3.1	3.7	4.3	3.6	4.9	5.8
Primary metal products	10.3	12.8	20.5	8.1	4.5	4.3
Instruments and related products	1.8	1.8	2.0	2.0	4.0	3.9
Miscellaneous manufactures	2.2	2.4	3.2	2.5	3.8	3.5
Food and related products	29.0	12.4	7.5	5.5	4.5	3.4
Rubber and plastic products	0.4	0.7	1.9	2.1	2.9	3.2
Agriculture, forestry, and fishing	15.4	8.4	5.7	1.9	1.7	2.6
Fabricated metal products	0.3	1.7	3.1	2.0	2.8	2.5
Other transportation equipment	0.3	1.2	1.8	1.5	2.4	2.1
Leather and leather products	0.5	0.5	0.5	1.8	2.3	2.0
Paper and allied products	14.5	9.6	7.2	2.6	2.5	2.0
Petroleum and coal products	2.7	6.2	5.5	7.6	3.3	1.8
Lumber and wood products	4.5	4.9	4.6	2.4	1.6	1.6
Transportation	0.3	0.1	0.6	0.2	0.6	1.3
Stone, clay, and glass products	0.9	1.6	1.6	1.2	1.6	1.3
Furniture and fixtures	0.0	0.0	0.2	0.5	1.3	1.2
Textile mill products	3.4	5.5	4.8	1.1	1.2	0.9
Banking, credit, and investment companies	1.1	0.2	0.2	0.2	0.4	0.3
Insurance	1.0	0.2	0.2	0.2	0.4	0.3
Mining of nonmetallic minerals	2.9	1.9	1.1	0.4	0.2	0.2
Tobacco products	2.9	0.3	0.1	0.2	0.2	0.1
Metal mining	7.1	7.0	4.9	1.3	0.3	0.0
Correlation with 1996 import composition:	0.13	0.38	0.49	0.70	0.96	1.00

Note: Imports are in current dollars. Industries are classified according to a 45-sector aggregation. Only industries that account for 1 percent or more of imports in any year are listed.

industries were among the top four industries in terms of exports. In a somewhat distant fourth place in terms of imports were oil and natural gas (8.4 percent), followed by apparel and other textiles (6.7 percent) and chemicals and chemical products (5.8 percent).

There have been more dramatic changes in import composition than in exports from 1947 to 1996. In 1947 the leading import sector was, by far, processed foods and food products, accounting for 29.0 percent of all imports. This was followed by agricultural, forestry, and fishing products (15.4 percent), paper and paper products (14.5 percent), primary metal products such as steel (10.3 percent), and metal mining, including iron and copper (7.1 percent). Agriculture, food products, and primary metal products were also among the four leading exports in 1947.

Between 1947 and 1996, processed foods and food products declined steadily from 29.0 to 3.4 percent of all imports, agriculture from 15.4 to 2.6 percent, paper and paper products from 14.5 to 2.0 percent, and metal mining from 7.1 percent to virtually zero. The share of primary metal products in total imports, after doubling from 10.3 to 20.5 percent between 1947 and 1967, tailed off to 4.3 percent in 1996. In contrast, the import share of non-electrical industrial machinery rose steadily between 1947 and 1996, from 1.2 to 14.1 percent, as did that of electrical and electronic equipment, from almost zero to 13.2 percent, and apparel, from 0.4 to 6.7 percent. Imports of motor vehicles and parts were volatile, first increasing from virtually zero in 1947 to 6.0 percent in 1958, dropping to 3.3 percent in 1967, expanding to 18.9 percent by 1987 (a reflection of the surge in Japanese car imports), and then diminishing to 14.2 percent in 1996. The other notable change is that oil imports swelled from 5.1 percent of all imports in 1947 to 23.8 percent in 1977, reflecting the steep oil price increases of the mid-1970s, and then abated to 8.4 percent in 1996.

Overall, import composition changed much more than export composition. The correlation between 1947 and 1996 import shares is a meager 0.13. The correlation rises to only 0.28 between 1958 and 1996 import shares, then to 0.49 between 1967 and 1996 shares, 0.70 between 1977 and 1996 shares, and finally to 0.96 between 1987 and 1996 shares. In contrast, the correlation between 1947 and 1996 export shares is a fairly high 0.64, and the correlation between 1958 and 1996 export shares already reaches 0.83. In sum, while the composition of U.S. exports has remained fairly constant since the late 1950s, import composition has stabilized only since the late 1980s.

7.4 The Factor Content of U.S. Exports and Imports

I next turn to the skill content of U.S. exports and imports. The analysis is based on the total (direct plus indirect) labor requirements of exports and of the domestic substitutes for imports (see the appendix to chapter 7 for the accounting framework).[2] As in previous studies, the subsequent analysis of comparative advantage is based on a comparison of the factors of production needed to produce exports with those needed to produce the domestic equivalent of imports. The technique receives theoretical justification in the Heckscher-Ohlin model by the assumption that technology is the same among countries that trade with one another. Another limitation of this kind of analysis is that a large part of trade is intra-industry. With the available data, we cannot distinguish between low-end and high-end imports or exports, and it is necessary to assume that the factor content of exports from an industry is the same as that of the domestic substitutes for the imports.[3]

Both the export and import vectors include retail and wholesale trade margins and transportation margins.[4] The former represents the value added of domestic wholesale and retail activities involved in the sales of the exports, and the latter represents the shipping costs borne by U.S.-based shippers. Since retail, wholesale, and shipping inputs accompany any set of exports and imports, they are not really indicative of comparative advantage. It makes sense to exclude these margins when analyzing comparative advantage, which I do in the tables that follow. Calculations were also performed for total exports and imports and for exports and imports, excluding only retail and wholesale trade margins, but are not shown here. The pattern of results is, by and large, very similar to those shown in the text tables.

7.4.1 Skill Composition

Table 7.3 shows the results for the total skill content of U.S. trade. The main result is that the comparative advantage in U.S. international trade has been in industries intensive in both cognitive and interactive skills. Moreover, the comparative advantage in high cognitive and interactive skill industries has been rising.

In 1950, the average substantive complexity (SC) content of exports was 3.44, compared to an average SC score of 3.39 for imports—a difference of 0.05 (section A of table 7.3). By 2000, the average SC level of exports grew by 32 percent to 4.53 and that of imports by 25 percent to 4.25, so that the gap increased sixfold to 0.30.

Another interesting comparison is that between the cognitive skill content of exports and imports and the average cognitive skill content of all output. At first blush, the results are surprising: The average SC content of both exports and imports is lower than that of the total economy. However, the reason is that the highest SC scores are found in services such as finance, insurance, real estate, business services, and the government, which are to a large extent nontradeables.

Results for interactive skills (IS) (section B) are quite similar to those for cognitive skills. The interactive skill content of total exports is greater than that of total imports, and the gap has widened over time, in this case from a difference of 0.00 in 1950 to 0.14 in 2000. Here, too, both exports and imports have a lower IS content than the whole economy because the industries with

Table 7.3.   Average Skill Content of U.S. Exports and Imports, 1950–1990

Skill Type	1950	1960	1970	1980	1990	2000	% Change 1950–2000
A. Substantive Complexity (SC)							
Exports	3.44	3.59	3.76	3.92	4.15	4.53	31.6
Imports	3.39	3.42	3.59	3.73	3.84	4.25	25.3
Difference	0.05	0.16	0.18	0.19	0.30	0.28	
Total economy	3.75	3.81	4.07	4.23	4.38	4.61	23.0
B. Interactive Skills (IS)							
Exports	1.45	1.55	1.63	1.74	1.94	2.09	44.3
Imports	1.45	1.46	1.51	1.61	1.74	1.95	34.3
Difference	0.00	0.09	0.12	0.13	0.20	0.14	
Total economy	2.19	2.21	2.27	2.31	2.37	2.43	10.7
C. Motor Skills (MS)							
Exports	5.37	5.37	5.39	5.38	5.25	5.11	−4.8
Imports	5.28	5.34	5.43	5.42	5.32	5.22	−1.1
Difference	0.09	0.04	−0.03	−0.04	−0.08	−0.11	
Total economy	5.11	5.13	5.17	5.10	5.01	4.86	−4.9
D. Mean Educational Attainment							
Exports	9.26	10.14	11.00	12.14	12.82	13.27	43.4
Imports	9.00	9.97	10.91	12.00	12.57	13.11	45.7
Difference	0.26	0.17	0.10	0.13	0.25	0.16	
Total economy	9.40	10.30	11.50	12.50	13.00	13.41	42.6

Note: Exports and imports exclude wholesale and retail trade and transportation margins. The average direct plus indirect skill content of exports and imports is given by $S\lambda°E/\lambda E$ and $S\lambda°M/\lambda M$, respectively, where a superscript zero (°) indicates a diagonal matrix with the indicated vector on the diagonal.

an especially high IS content are finance, insurance, real estate, business services, and the government, which primarily serve the domestic market.

The results for motor skills (MS) are just the opposite of those for SC and IS. In 1950, exports were more motor skill intensive than imports. However, by 1970 the average motor skill content of imports was higher, and by 2000 the gap had enlarged to −0.11. In this case, the motor skill content of both exports and imports is greater than that of the total economy because of the high concentration of blue-collar workers in goods-producing industries, which are more heavily involved in international trade than services.

The results for actual educational attainment are a bit of a surprise. They show that workers in export industries have a higher mean schooling level than those employed in import industries, but the gap was actually lower in 2000 than in 1950.

Table 7.4 shows a decomposition of the change in the average skill levels of exports and imports in a "trade" and an "industry" effect. The trade effect shows what happens to the average skill content of exports and imports as a result of the change in the composition of exports and imports over the period if technology remains constant during that time. The industry effect shows how much the average skill content of exports and imports varies as a result of the change in technology (both industry skill levels and interindustry and labor coefficients) if the composition of exports and imports remains constant during that time.

Between 1950 and 2000, exports shifted toward industries with relatively high SC levels, such as industrial machinery, electrical equipment, and

Table 7.4. Decomposition of the Change in Skill Levels into Trade and Industry Effects, 1950–2000

	Decomposition			Percentage Decomposition		
Skill Type	Trade Effect	Industry Effect	Total Change	Trade Effect	Industry Effect	Total Change
A. Substantive Complexity (SC)						
Exports	0.23	0.85	1.09	22	78	100
Imports	−0.03	0.88	0.86	−3	103	100
Difference	0.15	0.08	0.23	66	34	100
B. Interactive Skills (IS)						
Exports	0.07	0.57	0.64	11	89	100
Imports	−0.18	0.67	0.50	−36	136	100
Difference	0.11	0.03	0.14	77	23	100
C. Motor Skills (MS)						
Exports	0.11	−0.37	−0.26	−44	144	100
Imports	0.20	−0.14	−0.06	349	−249	100
Difference	−0.13	−0.07	−0.20	64	36	100
D. Mean Educational Attainment						
Exports	−0.08	4.10	4.01	−2	102	100
Imports	−0.27	4.38	4.11	−7	107	100
Difference	1.65	−1.75	−0.10	−1706	1806	100

Note: Exports and imports exclude wholesale and retail trade and transportation margins. The change in the average skill level generated by exports is given by

$$[(S^1\lambda^{01}e^2/\lambda^1e^2 - S^1\lambda^{01}e^1/\lambda^1e^1) + (S^2\lambda^{02}e^2/\lambda^2e^2 - S^2\lambda^{02}e^1/\lambda^2e^1)]/2 +$$

$$[(S^2\lambda^{02}e^1/\lambda^2e^1 - S^1\lambda^{01}e^1/\lambda^1e^1) + (S^2\lambda^{02}e^2/\lambda^2e^2 - S^1\lambda^{01}e^2/\lambda^1e^2)]/2,$$

where a superscript 1 indicates period 1 and a superscript 2 indicates period 2. The first bracketed term (the "trade effect") shows the average effect of changes in export composition (from e^1 to e^2) on average skills, and the second bracketed term (the "technology effect") shows the average effect of changes in both industry labor coefficients and industry skill levels on the overall skill level. A similar decomposition can be used for the change in the average skill levels of imports. Average period weights are used to provide an exact decomposition.

chemicals. This shift would have raised the average SC content of exports by 0.23 (see section A). Both changes in total labor coefficients and changes in average SC levels within industry would have raised the average SC score of exports by another 0.85 points, for a total change of 1.09 in SC over the period. At the same time, imports shifted slightly away from higher cognitive skill industries, while changes in technology and other industry effects advanced the average SC level by 0.88, about the same as for exports. As a result, of the 0.23 increase in the difference of average SC levels between exports and imports over the four decades, 66 percent was due to changes in export and import composition, and the other 32 percent was due to differences in changes of technical and occupational coefficients between export industries and their suppliers on the one hand and importers and their suppliers on the other hand.

Between 1950 and 2000, exports moved slightly in favor of industries with higher IS levels while imports shifted in favor of lower IS industries. The industry effect was somewhat stronger for exports than imports, so that more than three-fourths of the widening gap in IS levels between exports and imports was due to the trade effect.

Average motor skills in export industries declined by 0.26 between 1950 and 2000, while in import industries they fell by a more moderate 0.06. Interestingly, both imports and exports shifted in favor of higher motor skill industries, but the shift was much more marked among imports (particularly in the 1950–1970 period). Coefficient changes had a relatively small effect on motor skills in the 1950–1970 period but a strong negative effect in the later two decades, causing a greater reduction in motor skills among exporters than among import industries. As a result, 64 percent of the 0.20 point decline in the difference in average motor skills between exports and imports over the five decades was due to a stronger shift of imports to high motor skill industries, and the other 36 percent was due to the greater decline in motor skills among exporters and their suppliers than among import industries and their suppliers.

The pattern for mean educational attainment is quite different. From 1950 to 2000, both exports and imports shifted away from industries with higher schooling levels, but the effect was greater for imports. The industry effect was strong for both export and import industries, reflecting primarily the rising levels of educational achievement among workers in all sectors, but again slightly stronger for imports. Though the trade and industry effects offset each other, the mean education of workers in import industries (and their suppliers) grew slightly more than that of workers in export industries (and their suppliers) over the five decades.

7.4.2 Information Workers

Workers are divided into four groups: knowledge, data, service, and goods workers. Information workers are the sum of knowledge and data workers.

The overall results show that exports are more intensive in their use of information workers than imports and less intensive in their employment of goods-producing workers, and the difference has widened over time.

The basic data are again from the U.S. decennial censuses of 1950, 1960, 1970, 1980, 1990, and 2000. In the classification schema, professional and technical workers are generally classified as knowledge or data workers, depending on whether they are producers or users of knowledge. Management personnel are taken to perform both data and knowledge tasks since they produce new information for administrative decisions and also use and transmit this information. Clerical workers are classed as data workers for obvious reasons. I classify as goods-processing workers all labor that transforms or operates on materials or physical objects. These include craft workers, operatives (including transportation workers who move physical goods), and unskilled labor. The remaining group is made up of service workers, who primarily perform personal services (see chapter 5 and appendix table A.4 for more details on the classification scheme).

Results are based on the total employment by occupation generated by exports and imports (table 7.5). In 1950, exports were slightly more intensive

Table 7.5.   Employment of Information and Goods Workers as a Percentage of Total Employment Generated by Exports and Imports: Direct plus Indirect Labor Input, 1950–2000

Class of Worker	1950	1960	1970	1980	1990	2000	Percentage Point Change 1950–1990
A. Knowledge Workers							
Exports	5.2	6.5	9.0	10.7	13.9	21.4	16.2
Imports	4.4	5.7	8.2	9.8	11.5	19.2	14.8
Difference	0.8	0.7	0.8	0.9	2.4	2.2	1.4
Total economy	7.5	8.0	9.6	11.0	12.9	15.2	7.7
B. Data Workers							
Exports	18.9	21.0	25.7	30.4	32.4	30.1	11.2
Imports	16.5	19.3	24.7	28.8	28.5	26.3	9.8
Difference	2.4	1.6	1.0	1.6	3.9	3.7	1.3
Total economy	29.2	34.2	39.6	41.5	41.9	43.6	14.4
C. Goods Workers							
Exports	71.4	65.4	57.8	50.6	44.9	44.5	−26.9
Imports	75.4	69.4	61.2	54.9	53.3	51.7	−23.7
Difference	−4.0	−4.0	−3.4	−4.3	−8.4	−7.2	−3.2
Total economy	51.7	43.5	36.0	31.4	29.0	24.3	−27.4

Note: Exports and imports exclude wholesale and retail trade and transportation margins. The total (direct plus indirect) employment by occupation generated by exports and imports is given by $n(I - A)^{-1}E$ and $n(I - A)^{-1}M$, respectively.

than imports in their use of knowledge workers. The employment of knowledge workers generated by exports was 5.2 percent of the total employment generated by exports in 1950, compared to 4.4 percent for imports. The share of knowledge workers employed in the production of exports rose from 5.2 to 21.4 percent between 1950 and 2000—a gain of 16.2 percentage points. In contrast, the share of knowledge workers producing import substitutes expanded from 4.4 to 19.2 percent—a somewhat lower increase of 19.2 percentage points. As a result, the gap between the share of knowledge workers employed in export versus import production widened from 0.8 to 2.2 percentage points over the five decades. Moreover, the knowledge worker intensity of exports was below the economy-wide average from 1950 to 1980. However, by 1990 it exceeded the overall figure, and by 2000 it was well above the overall average.

The pattern is quite similar for data workers. Exports are more intensive than imports in their use of data workers. While data workers, as a share of the total workers producing exports, climbed from 19 to 30 percent between 1950 and 2000, the share producing import substitutes rose from 17 to 26 percent (see section B). As a result, the difference between exports and imports in the data worker share grew from 2.4 to 3.7 percentage points. Altogether, the gap between exports and imports in the share of information workers swelled from 3.2 to 6.0 percentage points over the five decades.

While exports are intensive in their use of information workers, imports are relatively intensive in goods-producing workers, as section C shows. It is first of note that both exports and import substitutes absorb a much higher share of goods workers than the overall economy—a reflection of the heavy bias of international trade toward manufactures. In 1950, goods-producing workers constituted 75.4 percent of the employment generated by the production of import substitutes, compared to 71.4 percent for export producers—a difference of 4.0 percent. As for the whole economy, the proportion of goods workers generated by both exports and imports declined over time. For exports, the share fell from 71.4 to 44.5 percent, a drop of 26.9 percentage points; for imports, the share fell less, by 23.7 percentage points, from 75.4 to 51.7 percent. As a result, the difference between imports and exports in the share of goods workers almost doubled between 1950 and 2000, from 4.0 to 7.2 percentage points. The evidence clearly shows that U.S. exports are becoming relatively more intensive in their use of information workers over time while imports are becoming relatively more intensive in their use of blue-collar workers.

The decompositions shown in table 7.6 identify some of the reasons for the changes in the relative share of information and goods workers in export and import industries. Between 1950 and 2000, both exports and imports shifted toward industries with a higher share of knowledge and data workers and a lower share of goods workers. The trade effect for knowledge workers was about the same for exports and imports, but, for both data and goods workers, the trade effect was stronger for imports than for exports. The industry

Table 7.6.   Decomposition of the Change in Percentage Share of Information and
Goods Workers in Total Employment into Trade and Industry Effects, 1950–2000

	Decomposition			Percentage Decomposition		
Skill Type	Trade Effect	Industry Effect	Total Change	Trade Effect	Industry Effect	Total Change
A. Knowledge Workers						
Exports	3.6	12.6	16.2	22	78	100
Imports	3.8	10.9	14.8	26	74	100
Difference	0.1	1.3	1.4	5	95	100
B. Data Workers						
Exports	3.1	8.0	11.2	28	72	100
Imports	3.9	5.9	9.8	40	60	100
Difference	−0.9	2.2	1.3	−65	165	100
C. Goods Workers						
Exports	−6.2	−20.7	−26.9	23	77	100
Imports	−7.5	−16.2	−23.7	32	68	100
Difference	0.7	−3.9	−3.2	−22	122	100

Note: Exports and imports exclude wholesale and retail trade and transportation margins. The change in the share of employment of a given class of worker generated by exports is given by

$$[(b^1\lambda^{01}e^2/\lambda^1e^2 - b^1\lambda^{01}e^1/\lambda^1e^1) + (b^2\lambda^{02}e^2/\lambda^2e^2 - b^2\lambda^{02}e^1/\lambda^2e^1)]/2+$$
$$[(b^2\lambda^{02}e^1/\lambda^2e^1 - b^1\lambda^{01}e^1/\lambda^1e^1) + (b^2\lambda^{02}e^2/\lambda^2e^2 - b^1\lambda^{01}e^2/\lambda^1e^2)]/2,$$

where b is a row vector showing employment of a given class of worker (such as knowledge workers) as a share of industry employment. The first bracketed term is the trade effect, and the second bracketed term is the industry effect.

effects for both exports and imports were positive for knowledge and data workers and negative for goods workers, but here the effects were considerably greater among export industries. Moreover, the industry effects dominated the trade effects for both exports and imports. As a result, of the 1.4 percentage point difference in the change of the share of knowledge workers generated by exports and imports, 95 percent was attributable to the faster growth of knowledge intensity among exports industries and their suppliers than among import industries and their suppliers.

Likewise, more than 100 percent of the 1.3 percentage point increase in the gap in the share of data workers was due to the higher growth of data worker intensity among exporters than importers, while imports shifted more toward data-intensive industries than exports. Similarly, more than 100 percent of the 3.2 percentage point decline in the difference in the share of goods workers between exports and imports was ascribable to the slower contraction of goods-worker intensity among import industries than among export industries, while the shift in import composition led to a larger decline in the share of goods workers than did the shift in export composition.

Table 7.7.   Capital and R&D Intensity of U.S. Exports and Imports:
Direct plus Indirect Capital, Labor, and R&D Input, 1947–1996

Type of Capital	1947	1958	1967	1977	1987	1996	Ratio of 1996 to 1947
A. Ratio of Total Net Capital (1,000s of 1992 dollars) to Employment							
Exports	29.4	51.0	63.5	87.2	93.7	103.8	3.53
Imports	34.6	71.0	81.7	129.2	102.1	114.1	3.29
Ratio	0.85	0.72	0.78	0.67	0.92	0.91	
Total economy	54.7	65.8	76.9	83.5	87.7	95.6	1.75
B. Ratio of Net Equipment (1,000s of 1992 dollars) to Employment							
Exports	9.4	17.5	23.1	34.7	38.9	46.2	4.91
Imports	10.5	20.3	26.4	39.0	40.7	47.5	4.51
Ratio	0.89	0.86	0.87	0.89	0.96	0.97	
Total economy	14.7	16.5	19.9	22.2	25.2	29.5	2.01
C. Ratio of OCA (100s of 1992 dollars) to Employment[a]							
Exports	0.5	0.9	0.9	1.7	10.8	40.5	78.26
Imports	0.9	1.1	0.8	1.7	9.0	34.6	37.98
Ratio	0.57	0.87	1.01	1.01	1.20	1.17	
Total economy	0.9	1.2	1.1	1.6	9.2	33.9	39.64
D. Ratio of R&D Expenditures to Net Sales (Percent)[b]							
Exports	—	1.77	1.91	1.51	2.61	2.15	1.21
Imports	—	0.89	1.18	1.37	2.55	2.17	2.44
Difference		0.88	0.73	0.14	0.07	−0.03	
Total manufacturing	—	2.70	2.92	2.27	3.40	3.03	1.12

Note: Exports and imports exclude wholesale and retail trade and transportation margins. The total employment and capital generated by exports is given by λE and γE, respectively. The total employment and capital generated by imports is given by λM and γM, respectively.

a. The government sector is not included.

b. R&D data are available only for manufacturing. The total (direct plus indirect) R&D intensity of exports and imports is given by $R(I-A)^{-1}E/1(I-A)^{-1}E$ and $R(I-A)^{-1}M/1(I-A)^{-1}M$, respectively. The ratios are 1996 to 1958.

7.4.3 Capital Intensity of Exports and Imports

Section A of table 7.7 shows the capital intensity of exports and imports. The results show a pronounced and continuous rise in the capital intensity of exports from 1947 to 1996. In contrast, the capital intensity of imports rose steeply between 1947 and 1977 and then slipped from 1977 to 1997. The reason is the tremendous increase, in the 1970s, of oil imports, which is a very capital-intensive industry (see table 7.2). Another finding is that the capital intensity of both exports and imports was below the overall capital-labor ratio of the economy in 1947 but equal to or greater than overall capital intensity in 1996. Imports, in fact, exceeded the overall capital-labor ratio by 1958 and remained above average through 1996, while exports exceeded it beginning in 1977. This indicates a shifting of both exports and imports toward more capital-intensive industries (primarily durable manufacturing).

The results show that, in fact, imports have been more capital intensive than exports (the Leontief paradox). However, what is more telling is that the capital intensity of exports relative to imports, after falling between 1947 and 1977 from a ratio of 0.85 to 0.67, climbed to 0.91 in 1996. The capital intensity of exports rose by a factor of 3.5 between 1947 and 1996, compared to a 3.3-fold increase for imports. These results indicate a gradual shifting of the comparative advantage of the United States back toward capital-intensive goods since 1977.

Section B shows the results for total net stocks of equipment per worker. Again, we find a continuous rise in the equipment intensity of both exports and imports between 1947 and 1996. In 1947, both exports and imports were less equipment intensive than the overall economy, but by 1958 imports and by 1967 exports had exceeded the economy-wide ratio of equipment to employment. The results also show the equipment intensity of exports rising faster than that of imports from 1947 to 1996—a ratio of 4.9 compared to 4.5. As a result, the equipment intensity of exports relative to imports grew from a ratio of 0.89 in 1947 to 0.97 in 1996, with most of the gain occurring after 1977. Here, too, the comparative advantage of the United States is clearly shifting back toward industries with a high equipment-to-worker ratio.

The results are even more dramatic for OCA per worker (see section C). The OCA intensity of exports has grown twice as fast as that of imports between 1947 and 1996. Moreover, while imports were more intensive in OCA than exports in 1947, the situation reversed in 1967, and by 1996 the OCA intensity of exports relative to imports reached 1.17. The comparative advantage of the United States now lies in industries that intensively use office and computing equipment.

The decompositions in table 7.8 highlight some of the reasons for this re-markable turnaround in the capital intensity of exports relative to imports. As section A shows, the ratio of total net capital per worker generated by exports increased by $74,400 (in 1992 dollars) between 1947 and 1977. Of this, $83,900 (or 113 percent) was accounted for by the rising capital intensity of export industries. Changes in export composition favored labor-intensive industries, but the effect was small. Changes in technical coefficients in import industries had an even stronger effect on the increase in the capital-to-labor ratio generated by imports in this period, accounting for $122,400 (or 154 percent) of the total gain of $79,500. However, imports shifted away from capital-intensive industries (mainly agriculture and primary metal products) toward low capital-intensive ones (primarily industrial machinery, electrical equipment, and motor vehicles), accounting for a $42,900 decline in the capital-to-labor ratio of import industries. As a result, the growth in the capital intensity of exports relative to imports was entirely due to changes in

Table 7.8. Decomposition of the Change in Capital and R&D Intensity into Trade
and Industry Effects, 1947–1996

	Decomposition			Percentage Decomposition		
Skill Type	Trade Effect	Industry Effect	Total Change	Trade Effect	Industry Effect	Total Change
A. Ratio of Total Net Capital (1,000s of 1992 dollars) to Employment						
Exports	−9.5	83.9	74.4	−13	113	100
Imports	−42.9	122.4	79.5	−54	154	100
Ratio	0.12	−0.06	0.06	207	−107	100
B. Ratio of Net Equipment (1,000s of 1992 dollars) to Employment						
Exports	−6.3	43.1	36.8	−17	117	100
Imports	−16.8	53.8	37.0	−45	145	100
Ratio	0.18	−0.10	0.08	228	−128	100
C. Ratio of OCA (100s of 1992 dollars) to Employment						
Exports	5.6	34.4	40.0	14	86	100
Imports	17.1	16.6	33.7	51	49	100
Ratio	−1.81	2.41	0.60	−301	401	100
D. Ratio of R&D Expenditures to Net Sales (Percentage Points)[a]						
Exports	0.50	−0.12	0.38	132	−32	100
Imports	1.26	0.02	1.28	98	2	100
Ratio	−0.77	−0.14	−0.91	85	15	100

Note: Exports and imports exclude wholesale and retail trade and transportation margins. The
change in the capital-labor ratio generated by exports is given by

$$[(\gamma^1 e^2/\lambda^1 e^2 - \gamma^1 e^1/\lambda^1 e^1) + (\gamma^2 e^2/\lambda^2 e^2 - \gamma^2 e^1/\lambda^2 e^1)]/2+$$
$$[(\gamma^2 e^1/\lambda^2 e^1 - \gamma^1 e^1/\lambda^1 e^1) + (\gamma^2 e^2/\lambda^2 e^2 - \gamma^1 e^2/\lambda^1 e^2)]/2.$$

The first bracketed term is the trade effect, and the second bracketed term is the industry effect.
The change in R&D expenditures as a share of net sales generated by exports is given by

$$[(\rho^1 e^2/q^1 e^2 - \rho^1 e^1/q^1 e^1) + (\rho^2 e^2/q^2 e^2 - \rho^2 e^1/q^2 e^1)]/2+$$
$$[(\rho^2 e^1/q^2 e^1 - \rho^1 e^1/q^1 e^1) + (\rho^2 e^2/q^2 e^2 - \rho^1 e^2/q^1 e^2)]/2.$$

a. R&D data are available only for manufacturing. The decomposition covers 1958–1996 only.

export and import composition (mainly the latter), which was partially offset by technological changes in the export and import industries and their
suppliers.

Results are even stronger for the equipment per worker (section B). In
this case, the ratio of the equipment intensity of exports relative to imports
rose from 0.89 in 1947 to 0.97 in 1996. The change in the equipment-to-
employment ratio generated by exports of $36,800 was due to the rising
capital intensity of export industries, which was offset in part by shifts in
export composition toward low equipment-intensive industries. Similarly,
the rising equipment intensity of imports, amounting to $37,000, was due to

both the rising capital intensity of import industries and the negative effects of changing import composition. As with total capital intensity, the growth of the ratio in equipment intensity between exports and imports during this period emanated entirely from the trade effect (mainly changes in import composition), which was counterbalanced, in part, by the industry effect.

The pattern is different for OCA per worker. The ratio of OCA intensity of exports relative to imports increased from 0.57 in 1947 to 1.17 in 1996. The evidence here indicates that the composition of exports shifted toward industries that were intensive in their use of computers and office machinery, accounting for 14 percent of the total growth of OCA per worker of $4,000 from 1947 to 1996. The other 86 percent was due to the rising investment in OCA per worker in export industries and their suppliers. Imports likewise shifted toward computer-intensive industries, particularly after 1977. Over the full 1947–1996 period, 51 percent of the overall gain of $3,370 in OCA per worker among import industries was attributable to changes in import composition, and the other 49 percent to increases in OCA intensity in import industries and their suppliers. Over the half century, imports shifted more strongly than exports toward computer-intensive industries, while computer intensity rose much faster in export industries than in import industries. As a result, the rise in the ratio of OCA intensity in exports relative to imports during this period was entirely due to the faster growth of OCA per worker in export industries than in import industries, while shifts in export and import composition had a negative effect on this ratio.

7.4.4 R&D Intensity of Exports and Imports

Section D of table 7.7 shows both R&D expenditures generated by exports and imports as a percentage of net sales. The results are surprising. The R&D intensity of U.S. exports in 1958 was almost twice as great as that of imports. The R&D intensity of both exports and imports increased between 1958 and 1987 and then fell off somewhat in 1996. However, from 1958 to 1996, R&D intensity rose much faster for imports than for exports—a factor of 2.4 versus 1.2. As a result, by 1996 the R&D intensity of imports was slightly greater than that of exports. Interestingly, neither exports nor imports were as R&D intensive as overall manufacturing.

The decomposition shown in section D of table 7.8 indicates some of the reasons behind the falling R&D intensity of export industries relative to import industries. The effect of the changing composition of exports and imports explains almost the entirety of the decline in the R&D intensity of exports relative to imports. Between 1958 and 1996, both exports and imports shifted toward more R&D–intensive industries, but the effect of the shift was more than twice as great for imports. Export growth was particularly strong in electrical and electronic equipment and scientific instruments, while imports gained share in motor vehicles, electrical and electronic equipment, chemicals, scientific instruments, and especially industrial machinery.

Moreover, overall R&D expenditures in manufacturing, after declining from 2.70 percent of net sales in 1958 to 2.27 percent in 1977, increased to 3.03 percent in 1996. On net, the change in R&D coefficients (the industry effect) was essentially washed out between the two periods. The fact that the trade effect was much stronger for imports than exports accounts for 85 percent of the elimination of the gap in R&D intensity between exports and imports.

7.4.5 Labor Costs and Labor Productivity of Exports and Imports

The final part of the analysis considers the average labor costs of both exports and imports. According to Ricardian trade theory, a country will export those products whose cost is relatively low and import those products whose cost is relatively high. Though the relevant comparison is with other trading countries, one might still expect that a country will export the products of those industries that pay relatively low wages and import the products of industries with high wages.

The results are a bit surprising (table 7.9). Export industries and their suppliers were paying 9 percent more than import industries and their suppliers in 1947 but 2 percent less by 1977 (section A). Between 1977 and 1996, the situation reversed, and average wages among exporters rose relative to import industries. By 1996, export industries were paying 4 percent more than import industries. Moreover, both export and import industries paid wages lower than the economy-wide average wage in 1947 but higher than average in 1996. Section B shows another measure of labor costs: employee compensation plus half of proprietors' income per person engaged in production (PEP). Results are almost identical. By this measure, exporters paid 8 percent higher wages than import industries in 1947 and 5 percent higher wages in 1996.

Between 1947 and 1996, labor productivity grew faster in export than in import industries: 2.2 versus 2.0 percent per year (section C). In 1947, output per FTEE was 6 percent higher in import industries than in export industries, but in 1996 it was 5 percent higher for exporters. Labor productivity also grew faster among both exports and imports than in the total economy over the 49-year stretch because of the heavy concentration of manufactured goods in trade.

Changes in unit labor cost reflect both changes in worker compensation and labor productivity. In 1947 export industries had higher unit labor costs than import industries (section D), a reflection of their higher wages. However, in this case, we see an almost continuous decline in the unit labor costs of export industries relative to import industries between 1947 and 1996. The reason is the higher productivity growth of export industries relative to import industries, not the declining relative wages of export industries. By 1996, unit labor costs of exports were slightly below those of import industries.

Table 7.9.   Labor Costs of U.S. Exports and Imports: Direct plus Indirect Labor Input, 1947–1996

Labor Cost Component	1947	1958	1967	1977	1987	1996	Ratio of 1996 to 1947
A. Employee Compensation per FTEE (1,000s of 1992 dollars)							
Exports	15.6	21.4	27.8	35.5	38.4	39.4	2.53
Imports	14.3	20.8	27.9	36.2	37.9	37.8	2.65
Ratio	1.09	1.03	1.00	0.98	1.01	1.04	
Total economy	15.8	21.5	27.0	32.6	34.7	34.8	2.20
B. Employee Compensation plus Half Proprietors' Income per PEP (1,000s of 1992 dollars)							
Exports	15.8	21.5	27.6	35.4	37.9	39.2	2.48
Imports	14.7	20.8	27.7	36.3	37.4	37.2	2.53
Ratio	1.08	1.03	1.00	0.98	1.01	1.05	
Total economy	15.0	20.4	26.3	31.7	33.1	33.7	2.25
C. Output (GDP) per FTEE (1,000s of 1992 dollars)							
Exports	24.1	31.8	41.7	48.1	59.4	70.7	2.94
Imports	25.6	33.2	42.1	51.9	55.6	67.2	2.62
Ratio	0.94	0.96	0.99	0.93	1.07	1.05	
Total economy	30.1	38.1	46.3	53.1	57.5	61.1	2.03
D. Unit Labor Cost							
Exports	0.65	0.67	0.67	0.74	0.65	0.56	0.86
Imports	0.56	0.63	0.66	0.70	0.68	0.56	1.01
Difference	0.09	0.05	0.00	0.04	−0.04	−0.01	
Total economy	0.53	0.56	0.58	0.61	0.60	0.57	1.08

Note: Exports and imports exclude wholesale and retail trade and transportation margins.

Key:
  FTEE: Full-time equivalent employees
  PEP: Persons engaged in production

Average wages generated directly and indirectly by exports is given by $w(I - A)^{-1}E/\lambda E$.

Average wages generated directly and indirectly by imports is given by $w(I - A)^{-1}M/\lambda M$.

The average unit labor cost generated directly and indirectly by exports is given by $w(I - A)^{-1}E/qE$.

The average unit labor cost generated directly and indirectly by imports is given by $w(I-A)^{-1}M/qM$.

7.5 Conclusions

The composition of both exports and imports changed considerably during the postwar period. In 1947, the most important U.S. exports in rank order (excluding wholesale and retail trade and transportation services) were food products, agricultural products, industrial machinery, primary metal products, motor vehicles, and textiles. Of this group, only industrial machinery could be considered high tech, and only motor vehicles medium tech. By 1996, industrial machinery exports ranked first, followed by electrical and electronic equipment, motor vehicles, chemicals, and other transportation equipment such as aircraft. These are all high-tech or medium-tech industries.

In 1947 the leading import was, by far, processed foods and food products, followed by agricultural products, paper and paper products, primary metal products, and metal mining—all low-tech industries. In 1996, the three leading imports were motor vehicles, industrial machinery, and electric and electronic equipment, all medium or high tech. So, while U.S. exports gradually shifted away from low-tech industries and toward medium- and high-tech ones, the shift was even more pronounced for U.S. imports.

The principal finding is that the comparative advantage of the United States lies in cognitive and interactive skill-intensive products, and the comparative advantage in cognitive and interactive skills increased between 1950 and 1990. The finding of a higher skill content of exports than imports is consistent with the results of Lee and Schluter (1999), although they did not find that the gap widened over time. With the exception of 1950, imports have been more motor skill intensive than exports, and that difference also widened over this period. Workers employed in export industries have had a higher mean schooling level than those in import industries, but the gap actually lessened over the half century. The widening gap in cognitive, interactive, and motor skills between exports and imports was due primarily to changes in the composition of exports and imports. Changing trade composition also favored exports over imports in terms of mean schooling, but this effect was more than offset by the industry effect, which favored imports. The fact that the cognitive skill content widened between exports and imports while their schooling content lessened is traceable to the shift of imports toward industries whose cognitive skill and schooling levels were in balance.

The results also show that exports are more intensive than imports in their use of knowledge and data workers and less intensive in their employment of goods-producing workers, and these differences have widened over time. The dominant factor in these trends is the greater absorption of information workers and the greater displacement of goods workers among export producers than import industries, rather than shifts in the composition of trade.

The results here provide new confirmation that imports are more capital intensive than exports. However, in this case, the capital intensity of exports relative to imports has been climbing since 1977. The results also show that, while imports are more equipment intensive than exports, the equipment intensity of exports rose faster than that of imports during these years. The OCA intensity of exports has also grown much faster than that of imports, and by 1987 exports were more OCA intensive than imports. These results thus indicate a gradual shifting of the comparative advantage of the United States back toward capital-intensive goods since 1977, particularly toward industries with a high equipment and OCA intensity.

All of the growth in the total capital and equipment intensity of exports relative to imports from 1947 to 1996 was due to changes in export and import composition (mainly the latter) and was partially offset by a greater rise in capital intensity among import industries. In contrast, the increase in the OCA intensity of exports relative to imports over this period was due entirely to the faster growth of OCA per worker in export industries than in import industries, while shifts in export and import composition had a negative effect on the ratio.

While the R&D intensity of U.S. exports was almost twice as great as that of imports in 1958, it was slightly higher in import industries in 1996. Almost the entirety of the growth in R&D intensity in imports relative to exports is explained by changes in trade composition—particularly, growing imports of motor vehicles, industrial machinery, electrical equipment, chemicals, and scientific instruments during these years.

There is no indication that average wages or employee compensation grew faster in import than in export industries, as might be expected by the Ricardian theory of comparative advantage. However, labor productivity rose faster in export than in import industries between 1947 and 1996. As a result, the unit labor cost of export industries declined almost steadily relative to import industries during this period, as Ricardian theory would predict.

In sum, we find that the United States exports brain power (cognitive and interactive skills) and imports muscle power (motor skills). It also substitutes information for blue-collar workers. Moreover, the gap in skill and information content between exports and imports has gradually been widening. These results suggest that the occupational structure of the U.S. workforce has been shifting into high cognitive skill jobs and away from motor skill intensive blue-collar jobs faster than that of other advanced industrial countries.

U.S. exports reflect a higher level of schooling than do U.S. imports, but in this case the gap has not changed over time. The likely reason is that other OECD countries have experienced a rapid catch-up in educational attainment. Evidence of this is provided in Wolff (2000). Moreover, as chapter 2 points out, a growth in educational achievement does not necessarily correlate with an increase in cognitive skills in the actual workplace.

The gradual loss of comparative advantage in R&D–intensive products also reflects a catch-up in R&D by other OECD countries. According to the National Science Board (1998), Japan's R&D intensity (the ratio of R&D expenditures to GDP) has grown steadily since 1980, and by 1995 Japan's R&D intensity was 2.78 percent, compared to 2.52 percent in the United States, 2.28 percent in Germany, 2.34 percent in France, and 2.05 percent in the United Kingdom.

Although the United States no longer has the edge in R&D and may lose it in education, it has taken the lead in another aspect of high-tech production —computer intensity—and is gradually reclaiming its advantage in total capital and equipment intensity. This is likely a reflection of the gradual erosion in the human capital advantage of the United States vis-à-vis other OECD countries. The trends also suggest that the Leontief paradox may be over-turned in the near future. However, this may create a new paradox since the United States is no longer the most capital-abundant country in the world (according to the OECD International Sectoral Database, in 1995 the United States ranked behind Germany, the Netherlands, and Belgium in overall cap-ital intensity).

The results on productivity and labor costs are consistent with my earlier studies (Dollar and Wolff 1993; Wolff 1995b, 1997b, 1999), which found on the basis of cross-national evidence that changes in industry net exports were positively related to industry productivity growth and negatively related to changes in unit labor cost. They also support the technology gap model of trade. On the other hand, these results, together with the findings on cap-ital and R&D intensity, are hard to reconcile with the standard (and static) Heckscher-Ohlin model.

Appendix

Accounting Framework and Skill Measures

The input-output model is as follows, and all vectors and matrices are 45-order and in constant (1992) dollars unless otherwise indicated (see the data appendix for sources and methods):

X = column vector of gross output by sector
E = column vector of exports by sector
M = column vector of imports by sector[5]
D = column vector of domestic consumption by sector (household consumption, investment, and government expenditures)
$Y = D + E - M$ = column vector showing the final output by sector
A = square matrix of interindustry input-output coefficients

Then,

(7.1) $$X = AX + Y.$$

Also, let

e = column vector of export coefficients, where $e_i = E_i / \Sigma E_i$
m = column vector of import coefficients, where $m_i = M_i / \Sigma I_i$
L = row vector of labor coefficients, showing employment per unit of output
K = row vector of capital coefficients, showing total capital per unit of output
R = row vector showing R&D expenditures as a percentage of net sales by industry
S = row vector showing average skill scores of workers by industry
w = row vector showing average employee compensation in 1992 dol-lars by industry

$N = 267$ by 45 employment matrix, where N_{ij} shows the total employment of occupation i in industry j

$n = 267$ by 45 employment coefficient matrix, showing employment by occupation per unit of output, where $n_{ij} = N_{ij}/X_j$

$B = 267$-order column vector of total employment by occupation, where $B_i = \Sigma_j N_{ij}$

$I =$ identity matrix

$1 =$ row or column vector of ones

Then,

(7.2) $$B = nX = n(I - A)^{-1}Y.$$

Also, define

$\lambda = L(I-A)^{-1}$, which shows the direct plus indirect labor requirements per unit of output

$\gamma = K(I - A)^{-1}$, which shows the direct plus indirect capital requirements per unit of output

$\rho = R(I-A)^{-1}$, which shows the direct plus indirect R&D requirements per unit of output

$q = 1(I-A)^{-1}$, which shows the direct plus indirect output by industry in constant (1992) dollars generated per constant dollar of final output

Notes

1. As of May 2005, the U.S. benchmark input-output table for 2002 has still not been released by the Bureau of Economic Analysis, so the results could not be updated beyond this point.
2. An alternative calculation is based on the direct labor requirements of each industry. The vectors nE and nM give the direct labor requirements by occupation to produce the exports and the same array of domestic goods that correspond to the imports of a given year, respectively. Results are quite similar, though differences in factor content between exports and imports, as expected, are somewhat larger.
3. A further limitation, as noted in footnote 1, is that noncompetitive imports cannot be included in the analysis since, by definition, such imports do not have domestic substitutes. However, this is a relatively small share of total imports—only 12 percent in 1996.
4. Technically, the wholesale and retail margins also include the value added of the "rest of the world" sector. In the case of imports, these margins appear as negative entries since imports generally generate domestic value added in U.S. retailing, wholesaling, and transport industries.
5. Technically, there are two types of imports recorded within the U.S. input-output framework. The first, called "competitive" or "comparable" imports, are those for which there are direct domestic substitutes, such as Japanese cars. These are recorded in the row in which there are domestic substitutes and are summed in the import column in final demand. It is

not possible to identify the destination of these imports by industry or final user. The second, called "noncompetitive," "transferred," or "noncomparable" imports, are those for which there are no direct domestic substitutes, such as rubber. These are recorded in a separate row in the interindustry matrix by sector of destination. The calculations of skill or capital embodied in imports are performed only for competitive imports.

8

Conclusions and Policy Recommendations

1.1 Introduction

In this final chapter of the book, I summarize the research contained in the preceding seven chapters and consider some of its policy implications. Current policy discussions in Washington have emphasized better education of the labor force and improved training because these are seen as key remedies for three major problems that ail the economy: (1) They will lead to higher skills and high-paying jobs and thus increase the real wage; (2) they will lead to a more equitable distribution of skills in the labor force and thus reduce inequality; and (3) they will help promote productivity growth in the economy and thus indirectly boost labor earnings. The results contained in this volume cast doubt on each of these presumed remedies. Indeed, it does not appear that this course is a panacea for any of these major problems.

This chapter first presents a recap of the major findings of the preceding chapters. Policy prescriptions are then offered in the concluding part.

8.2 Summary of Principal Findings

8.2.1 Education, Skills, and Wages

Chapters 1 and 2 document that one of the great success stories of the postwar era is the tremendous growth in schooling achievement by the U.S. population. Median years of schooling among all adults (age 25 and over) grew from 9.0 years in 1947 to 13.6 in 2003, with most of the gain occurring before 1973. Mean years of schooling among employed workers increased from 9.4 in 1948 to 13.7 in 2000, with 40 percent of the change after 1973. The percentage of adults who completed high school grew from 33 percent in 1947 to 85 percent in 2003, with about half the gain occurring before 1973 and half afterward. The percentage of college graduates in the adult population surged from 5 percent in 1947 to 28 percent in 2003, with almost two-thirds of the progress made after 1973.

Results from chapter 2 also indicate that, with the exception of motor skills, worker skill levels continued to increase after 1970. Moreover, rates of skill growth were about the same after 1970 as before. Cognitive skills (substantive complexity) grew at an annual rate of 0.42 percent from 1950 to 1970 and by 0.42 percent from 1970 to 2000; interactive skills by 0.18 percent before 1970 and 0.22 percent after; and the composite skill index by 0.35 percent before and 0.30 percent after.

Results from chapter 6 indicate that, according to the substantive complexity measure SC, the composite skill score CP, and educational attainment, a pronounced rightward shift of the distribution of skills occurred during the postwar period, with a big decline of the least skilled jobs and a correspondingly large increase of the most skilled jobs. The share of total employment in the bottom skill quintile based on SC scores declined from 27 to 16 percent, while the employment share of the top quintile increased from 10 to 29 percent over the 1950–2000 period. The fraction of adults with fewer than four years of high school fell from 66 percent in 1950 to 15 percent in 2000, and the proportion with four years or more of college increased from 6 to 26 percent.

Human capital theory argues that rising schooling and skills will cause, or at least be associated with, rising wages. However, according to all of the measures of employee compensation, the growth in average wages reached a near standstill by 1973. The Bureau of Labor Statistics series on real hourly wages shows a 75 percent increase between 1947 and 1973 and an 8 percent decline from 1973 to 2000. According to the National Income and Product Accounts, employee compensation per full-time equivalent worker grew by 95 percent from 1947 and 1973 and by only 11 percent from 1973 to 2000. Again, according to the same data source, employee compensation plus half of proprietors' income showed a gain of 103 percent from 1947 to 1973 and also an 11 percent gain from 1973 to 2000.

These four sets of results constitute the basis of one of the main paradoxes the book explores—namely, that while educational achievement and worker skill levels have continued to increase since the early 1970s, earnings adjusted for inflation have generally stagnated. Moreover, annual time-series regressions of earnings growth on the change in educational attainment, after controlling for a host of other factors such as unionization and international trade, fail to produce a significant (or even a positive) coefficient on the change in average schooling levels (see chapter 3). Pooled cross-industry regressions establish a small but positive effect of changes in average educational achievement among workers within an industry on the change in average industry earnings, but the coefficient is again not statistically significant. Likewise, both time-series and cross-industry regressions, after controlling for the same set of factors, show no significant effect of skill changes on earnings growth. Finally, in the growth-accounting analysis, neither the positive change in schooling nor the growth of skills played a substantial role in explaining the slowdown of wage growth after 1970.

While both worker skills and educational attainment rose from 1950 to 2000, the latter far outpaced the former. Cognitive skills grew at an annual rate of 0.4 percent over this period, interactive skills by 0.2 percent, and the composite skills index by 0.3 percent. In contrast, median years of schooling of adults increased by 0.8 percent per year, mean years of schooling of employed workers by 0.7 percent per year, the share of adults with a high school degree by 1.8 percent per year, and the share of adults with a college degree by 2.9 percent per year. Moreover, when we look at the timing of these increases by decade, we find that skill growth peaked in the 1960s in all dimensions, while gains in educational achievement generally peaked in the 1970s.

These results form the basis of another paradox explored in the book—namely, that educational attainment has risen faster than skill requirements in the last three decades. Moreover, these findings emphasize the lack of correspondence between the growth in the demand for cognitive skills (as roughly reflected in the direct skill measures) and the supply of such skills, as reflected in the educational achievement of the population. Indeed, they suggest that, since the 1960s, the U.S. educational system has been producing more educated workers than the workplace can absorb.

Chapter 5 also documents the rapid growth of information workers in the U.S. economy. Information workers as a group grew from 37 percent of total employment in 1950 to 59 percent in 2000. Most of the growth in information employment did not take place among highly skilled, highly paid professionals and managers (knowledge workers) but rather among moderately skilled, relatively low-paid clerical and sales workers (data workers). Moreover, the time patterns are quite different for knowledge-producing and data workers, with the increase in the share of the former accelerating from 0.5 percentage points during the 1950s to 2.3 percentage points in the 1990s and that of the latter slowing down from 5.0 to 1.7 percentage points.

8.2.2 Productivity and Wages

Another anomaly arises when we compare gains in average earnings with labor productivity growth in the economy. According to conventional economic theory (with a standard constant returns to scale production function and under the assumption of competitive input markets), real wages should rise at the same rate as average labor productivity. From 1947 to 1973, U.S. labor productivity grew by 2.4 percent per year, and real employee compensation per full-time equivalent employee increased by 2.6 percent. After 1973, productivity slowed, but wages slowed even more. From 1973 to 1979, the former averaged 0.5 percent per year, while wages actually declined in real terms. From 1979 to 2003, productivity recovered to 1.2 percent per year, but wages recovered to only 0.6 percent per year (chapters 1 and 3).

8.2.3 Productivity and Skills

While wages have not risen commensurately with skills, neither has productivity either at the industry level or in the aggregate. The lack of correspondence between productivity growth and skill change constitutes the third of the four paradoxes the book explores.

What is the connection between skills and productivity? Human capital theory predicts that rising skills will lead to increasing productivity. Yet, between the 1970s and 1980s, when skill growth fell, productivity growth picked up. Likewise, while educational attainment grew faster in the 1970s and 1980s, overall productivity growth was higher in the 1950s and 1960s. Moreover, at the industry level, the sectors with the highest skills—namely services—have had the lowest productivity growth.

Cross-industry regressions provide no evidence that the increase of worker skills or educational attainment is significantly associated with gains in industry productivity. There is also no clear connection between high levels of skill within an industry and high rates of productivity growth. Indeed, paradoxically, the evidence points to just the opposite—namely, that high-skill industries (such as finance, insurance, business services, medical services, education, and the government) have historically had low productivity growth. Productivity growth has been much higher in low-skill industries (mainly in agriculture, mining, manufacturing, and transportation), where automation can displace labor due to the substitutability of fixed capital for low-skill labor.

There are several possible reasons for these findings. First, the causal relation between productivity and schooling may be the reverse of what is normally assumed. In particular, as per capita income rises within a country, schooling opportunities increase, and more and more students may seek a college education. Second, the skills acquired in formal education, particularly at the university level, may not be relevant to the workplace. Rather, higher education may perform a screening function, and a university degree may serve employers mainly as a signal of potential productive ability. As enrollment rates rise, screening or educational credentials may increase in importance, and a higher proportion of university graduates may become overeducated relative to the actual skills required in the workplace.

A third possibility is that university education may be associated with rent-seeking activities rather than productive ones. This may be true for many professional workers, such as lawyers, accountants, advertising personnel, and brokers. A fourth possible explanation is the increasing absorption of university graduates by "cost disease" sectors characterized by low productivity growth, such as health, teaching, law, and business. These are essentially labor activities and, as such, are not subject to the types of automation and mechanization that occur in manufacturing and other goods-producing industries.

8.2.4 Inequality and Skill Differences

Chapter 6 documents three striking trends. First, the dispersion (variance) of schooling within the adult population has declined dramatically since the early 1970s. Second, among employed workers, the dispersion of skill levels, as measured by both substantive complexity and the composite skill index, has also diminished since 1970. Third, a pronounced rightward shift also occurred in the distribution of schooling, cognitive skills, and the composite skill index, with a very large decline in low-skill jobs and a corresponding increase in high-skill positions. Yet, despite these three trends, family income inequality and labor earnings inequality have risen sharply in the United States since the early 1970s. These results constitute the fourth paradox investigated in the book.

Results of time-series regressions of income inequality on the variance of schooling, as well as on other factors such as the unemployment rate and the unionization rate, are quite perverse, with the dispersion of schooling found to be *negatively* though not significantly associated with income inequality (information on the variance of schooling among workers is not available at the industry level). However, the rate of return to schooling multiplied by the variance of schooling is found to be positively though, again, not significantly, related to the level of income inequality. In the growth-accounting analysis, changes in neither the variance of schooling nor the rate of return to schooling multiplied by the variance of schooling contributed to the rise in inequality after 1970. Indeed, because both declined slightly in value after 1970, their contribution is actually slightly negative.

8.2.5 But Aren't the Returns to Education Rising?

Both chapter 6 in this book and a myriad of previous studies have documented rising returns to education over the last quarter century. The ratio in annual earnings between male college graduates and male high school graduates climbed from 1.50 in 1975 to 1.88 in 2003. For females, the ratio rose from 1.45 in 1975 to 1.74 in 2003. Moreover, according to my estimates, the rate of return to a college education jumped from 11.9 percent in 1975 to 16.9 percent in 2000. Moreover, the cross-occupation regressions of occupational earnings on occupational skill also show positive and significant coefficients on cognitive skills, motor skills, and, in later years, interactive skills.

Yet, despite the pervasive evidence of a rising return to schooling, rising educational achievement has not translated into increasing average wages at the aggregate level. Both annual time-series regressions and cross-industry regressions fail to establish any significant connection between gains in earnings and changes in either skill levels or educational attainment.

The seeming paradox is resolved when we differentiate between *relative* pay among workers at different schooling levels and absolute changes in wages. The rising positive association we observe in the cross-section simply says that college graduates get paid more than high school graduates, and this differential has widened over time. However, the differential can grow either because college graduates are being paid more in absolute terms over time and/or because high school graduates are being paid less. As chapter 3 points out, the evidence indicates that, while real earnings of college graduates haven risen moderately since the early 1970s, those of high school graduates have remained flat, and those of other educational groups have declined. This divergence in earnings accounts for the rising returns to education in the last two decades.

The confusion results because, in human capital theory, rising educational attainment is associated with gains in worker productivity and hence increases in real earnings. Rising returns to education in conjunction with the relative growth in the number of more educated workers (particularly college graduates) must imply gains in average real pay. However, in the screening model alluded to earlier, stagnating or even falling real wages are consistent with a rise in educational achievement together with increasing returns to schooling since there is no direct productivity link between educational attainment and worker productivity. As a result, rising returns to education have helped obfuscate stagnating or falling average real wages.

These results are not inconsistent with those of Krueger (1993) and Autor, Katz, and Krueger (1998), who have found an earnings premium of 15 percent or more for users of computers relative to workers who do not use computers. However, the apparent mechanism is not that computer users have seen their real earnings grow substantially but rather that nonusers have seen their real earnings drop. Indeed, the further diffusion of computers to new segments of the labor force is not likely to raise *average earnings;* rather, according to the econometric results, it will likely lower average pay.

8.2.6 What about the Much-Vaunted "New Economy"?

As I note in chapter 1, many people have pinned their hopes for a revival of earnings growth (and perhaps a decline in earnings inequality) on the IT revolution. However, I do not find any special magic associated with computerization and information technology in general. In fact, just the contrary. Regression results from the pooled-industry analysis indicate that computerization has been *deskilling*, with a negative and significant relationship between OCA investment per worker and the growth of both cognitive and interactive skills (chapter 2). However, computer investment has a positive and significant association with the growth in knowledge workers and a correspondingly negative and significant association with the increase in data workers (chapter 5). Although knowledge workers are high skill and data workers medium skill, the negative effect on data workers outweighs the positive effect on knowledge workers, leading to a net reduction in skill levels. Results from pooled cross-industry regressions show a strong positive association between computerization and the dispersion of cognitive skills (chapter 6). There is also no evidence that OCA enhanced productivity (at least more than normal equipment investment), though it did have a pronounced effect on employment restructuring (chapter 4). Taken altogether, these results suggest that the IT revolution has led to a hollowing out of the middle of the skill distribution by eliminating medium-skill jobs.

OCA investment has a decidedly *negative* and significant association with the growth of average earnings on the basis of both the time-series regressions and the pooled cross-industry analysis (chapter 3). Results of the time-series regressions show that OCA investment is positively associated with greater earnings inequality, particularly in the 1980s and 1990s (chapter 6). In the growth-accounting analysis, computerization is found to be the principal source of rising earnings inequality since 1970 (at least among the factors considered in the analysis)—accounting for about half of its increase.

I have also found that so-called high-tech industries, as defined by R&D intensity or OCA investment, are not necessarily high-skill or high-wage sectors (chapter 3). In fact, industry wage differentials depend on many other factors besides technology.

8.2.7 The Role of International Trade

Expanding international trade has some association with changes in both labor earnings and earnings inequality. Export intensity is negatively and significantly related to the growth of labor earnings in the time-series analysis and does not turn up significant in the pooled cross-industry regressions (chapter 3). On the other hand, the growth in import intensity does not appear to have a significant effect on the level of earnings (chapter 3). In the growth-accounting exercises, neither the growth of imports nor the growth of exports plays much of a role in accounting for the stagnation of earnings after 1973.

Changes in both import intensity and export intensity appear to be unrelated to the increase of earnings inequality in the time-series regressions (chapter 6). In the growth-accounting analysis, rising imports play only a very small role in accounting for the rise of earnings inequality after 1973, and exports play virtually no role. On the other hand, rising exports are associated with a reduction in the variance of cognitive skills, though the change in import intensity is not statistically significant.

Rising export intensity has a significant role in accounting for the growth of interactive skills and the decline in motor skills and has a positive but not significant association with gains in cognitive skills (chapter 2). The change in import intensity is once again not statistically significant. A significant positive association is also found between increases in export intensity and the rise in the share of knowledge workers in total employment and a positive but statistically insignificant association with the change in the share of data workers in employment. Once again, import intensity does not appear as a significant determinant. These findings are roughly consistent with those reported in chapter 7, in which the comparative advantage of the United States is found to lie in high cognitive skill and interactive skill industries. Between 1950 and 2000 the skill gap between exports and imports in these two dimensions widened. Conversely, exports have become less intensive in their use of motor skills, and the motor skill gap between exports and imports decreased sharply over the half century. Exports have also been more intensive than imports in their use of information workers and less intensive in their employment of goods-producing workers, and the difference has widened dramatically over time.

8.2.8 Institutional Factors

Unionization is often cited as a factor that helps maintain high earnings and reduce earnings inequality. There is strong evidence from time-series regressions that the decline in unionization played a significant role in explaining rising wage inequality in the United States (chapter 6). Evidence also shows that the reduction in union membership contributed to the stagnation of average pay after 1973 (chapter 3). The unionization variable is positive and significant in the time-series analysis and positive but not significant in the pooled cross-industry analysis. However, unionization per se does not appear to be related to industry productivity growth (chapter 4) or to the change in skill levels (chapter 2).

The decline in the minimum wage also contributed to the stagnation of average earnings since the early 1970s (chapter 3). Moreover, there is evidence (though mixed) that the decline in the minimum wage partially accounts for rising earnings inequality over the same period (chapter 6).

8.2.9 Shifts in Product Demand

Another factor that might affect the demand for skills and, by implication, earnings is the change in product demand. If, for example, consumer demand shifts toward products that require less skilled labor to produce, then economy-wide skill requirements will fall. This process can be analyzed by decomposing the change in overall skill levels into two proximate causes: changes in product composition and changes in technology at the industry level. On this basis, it was found that, between 1950 and 2000, a bit more than half of the growth in cognitive skills among workers was due to changes in technology at the industry level and somewhat less than half resulted from shifts of employment toward more skill-intensive industries.

Employment generally shifted out of higher-wage goods-producing in-dustries and toward lower-paying services in the postwar period, creating a downward bias on average earnings. During the 1950s and 1960s, this downward drag was offset by a sharp decline in the employment share in very low-paying agriculture. As a result, during this time the net effect of employment shifts was minimal, and changes of earnings at the industry level accounted for nearly all of the growth in overall mean earnings. How-ever, after 1970, further declines in agricultural employment were small, and the employment shift effect became relatively important, offsetting in-creases in pay at the industry level by 62 percent between 1970 and 2000. Over the full half century, the total increase in average earnings was due to increases in pay at the industry level, and the industry shift effect played almost no role.

Both changes in technology at the industry level and shifts in employ-ment among industries could play a role in accounting for the decline in overall skill inequality. The results of chapter 6 show that the decline is pre-dominantly due to changes in technology at the industry level rather than to the shift of employment toward those industries with low skill inequality (primarily, services) and away from high skill inequality industries (mainly goods producers).

With regard to the growth of information employment, one possibility is that it is attributable to an increase in the economy's demand for products with a high information content. A second possibility is that technology has favored information jobs over blue-collar ones and caused a substitution of information workers for goods and service workers within the structure of production of industries. A third possibility is that differential rates of pro-ductivity movements among the industries of the economy (the "unbalanced growth" effect) would cause the employment of one type of worker to grow relative to another.

Chapter 5 demonstrates that about 40 percent of the growth in the share of knowledge workers in total employment and two-thirds of the increase in the share of data workers from 1950 to 2000 are attributable to the un-balanced growth effect. However, this effect diminished between the 1950s and 1980s and then rebounded in the 1990s, a reflection first of the general overall slowdown in productivity growth and then its recovery. On the pro-duction side of the economy, almost 60 percent of the growth in the share of knowledge workers and about a third of the growth in the share of data workers are accounted for by the substitution of these workers for other types of workers. The substitution effect increased in importance in the case of knowledge workers but diminished for data workers, except for a resurgence in the 1990s. In contrast, demand shifts toward heavily information-using products contributed virtually nothing to the growth of information employ-ment. In other words, the relative growth in information workers has come through changes in production technology, not through the substitution of information-intensive products for others among final consumers.

8.2.10 Overall Assessment

Unfortunately, the book is mainly negative in its conclusions. First, education, even skill enhancement, does not lead to higher wages (chapter 3). This remains true even after controlling for a host of other characteristics that may affect earnings. Second, there is no evidence that rising levels of schooling or skill are associated with increased productivity (chapter 4). This conclusion likewise holds after controlling for other pertinent characteristics. Third, the pronounced decline in the dispersion of educational attainment and the more moderate declines in the variance of worker skills did not culminate in a reduced level of earnings inequality (chapter 6). Fourth, computerization has not led to a spurt in earnings growth—just the opposite, in fact. Moreover, it is a principal culprit in the rise in earnings inequality in the last three decades.

8.2.11 One Final Piece of the Puzzle?

The story would not be complete without some consideration of what has happened to profits and property income in the last half century. While most of the discussion of rising inequality has focused on the labor market and increasing wage disparities, an equally salient shift has been the rise in the share of profits in national income in the last quarter century or so.

As we saw in chapter 1 (figure 1.12), the net profit share in national income fell by 7.2 percentage points between its peak value of 32.0 percent in 1950 and its low point of 24.8 percent in 1970. It then generally drifted upward, rising by 4.6 percentage points between 1970 and 2003, reaching 29.4 percent in 2003.

The rising share of profits in national income is, not surprisingly, connected to the stagnation of the real wage. In general, when the real wage rises at the same rate as overall productivity, the wage and profit shares remain fixed over time. During the "golden age" (1947–1973) of capitalism in the United States, wages actually kept up with productivity. During this period, U.S. labor productivity grew by 2.4 percent per year, and wages (employee compensation per full-time equivalent employee), adjusted for inflation, increased by 2.6 percent per year.

After 1973, productivity slowed, but wages slowed even more. From 1973 to 1979, productivity averaged 0.5 percent per year, while wages actually declined in real terms. Between 1979 and 2003, productivity growth recovered to 1.2 percent per year, but wage growth picked up to only 0.6 percent per year. Labor's share of total income fell from 72.9 to 70.6 percent.

The excess went to increased profitability. The net profit rate declined by 7.5 percentage points between 1947 and its low point of 13.1 percent in 1982. It then climbed by 7.4 percentage points to 20.5 percent in 2003, well above its low point in 1982 and close to its overall peak of 22.7 percent in 1948. Also, since 1982, the corporate profit rate (corporate profits as a percentage of corporate capital) more than doubled, from 4.6 to 9.9 percent. The results clearly show that the stagnation of earnings in the United States since the early 1970s has translated into rising profits in the economy

The rise in corporate profitability has, in turn, helped fuel the record boom in the stock market (the simple correlation between the S&P 500 index and the profit rate is 0.45). The mass media has created the impression that stock ownership has spread far and wide among the U.S. population. It is true that the share of households owning stock either outright or indirectly through mutual funds, trusts, or various pension accounts has risen from 24 percent in 1983 to 52 percent in 2001, the last date for which statistics are available. Despite the overall gains in stock ownership, only 40 percent had total stock holdings worth $5,000 or more, and only 35 percent owned $10,000 or more of stock. Moreover, more than three-quarters of all stocks were owned by households earning $75,000 or more (about the top quarter of households) (see Wolff 2000 for details).

Rising profitability in the U.S. economy has led to a growing share of property income, defined as the sum of rent, dividends, interest, and one-half of proprietors' income, in total personal income. Its time path is similar to family income inequality. This variable shows a slightly downward trend from 1947 to 1972 (from 21 to 18 percent), followed by an upward trajectory to a peak of 24 percent in 1989 and then a decline to 21 percent in 2003. Its correlation coefficient with family income inequality is very high: 0.84.

What effect has rising property income had on the distribution of income? Though stock ownership has spread in the United States, particularly over the last decade, stocks still remain highly concentrated in the hands of the rich, and many families who do own stock hold only relatively small amounts. As a result, the increasing proportion of property income in total income is another factor that has led to a growth in overall income inequality.[1]

8.3 Policy Remedies

What kinds of policies can best reverse the stagnation of real wages and rising inequality in the United States? One can divide policy solutions into three general strategies. The first is to prepare people for the labor market and then rely on market solutions. The second is to engage in direct government intervention. A third and broader approach is to redress the balance of power between labor and capital that has shifted in favor of the latter in the last two decades.

Before contrasting these three approaches, it is useful to consider that the remedy for a problem does not have to be the reverse of the cause. For example, the causes of homelessness are manifold, including poverty, rising housing and rental prices, and family breakup. However, the solution is relatively simple—provide more subsidized housing and expand the housing stock. Likewise, whatever the cause of the common cold is, one can treat it by drinking a lot of liquids, taking two aspirins, and getting plenty of rest.

8.3.1 Education Policy

Current policy discussions in this country emphasize the need for better education of the labor force and the importance of the school-to-work transition. The underlying theme is that more education, more training, apprenticeship programs, and, in general, more skills will lead to a more productive labor force and hence higher wages, and a more equal distribution of income will presumably ensue from a more equal distribution of human capital. A more recent policy objective is to promote computer literacy with the same objectives in mind. This represents the market-solution approach. The government helps provide the skills; then the market rewards these skills.

This kind of approach is emphasized by Murnane and Levy (1996a), who argue that what students need now in the workplace are the "new basic skills." These include the "hard" skills, such as math, problem solving, and reading (at levels beyond those normally achieved by the typical high school graduate), as well as "soft" skills, such as interpersonal and communications skills and the ability to use computers. Examples are presented that demonstrate that modern firms pay particular attention to recruiting workers with these skills and encouraging employees to develop such abilities.

There is now abundant evidence that workers benefit in the job market when they receive additional training and education. However, it is much less clear that, in the aggregate, average earnings will rise or that economic inequality will decline if the government enhances opportunities for U.S. citizens to improve their job skills. In fact, one of the key findings of my book is the growing separation between pay on the one hand and skills and education on the other hand. It is not clear how much effect closing the skills (or education) gap will have on closing the wage gap. Indeed, we have already been quite successful at reducing educational inequality (and, to a lesser extent, skills disparities). Moreover, it is not clear that upgrading educational levels or skills will be of much benefit in raising earnings.

Indeed, the notion that upskilling the workforce as the path to high-wage jobs must be called seriously into question. It is not likely that we are going to educate ourselves into a "high road" path. Education does not translate directly into skills, and skills (and education) do not translate directly into higher wages. We must divorce wages policy from skill policy.

These findings do not imply that we should abandon our educational and training programs entirely but rather that we should refocus them on the changing needs of the workplace. In particular, with regard to primary and secondary school education, the declining role of education as a factor in economic growth may reflect the declining quality of schools. A major overhaul of schools may be required to improve academic quality and upgrade basic academic skills. (For example, actual classroom hours spent on academic subjects is 50–70 percent greater per academic year in European and Japanese schools.) We might want to consider targeting training to the actual needs of employers through a German-style apprenticeship program.

While the findings of the book do not lend much support for education as an ingredient in raising wages, reducing earnings inequality, or even promoting economic growth, it is still the case that education serves other functions besides being either a conduit to the job market or an investment. Here are some examples: First, education leads to a more knowledgeable citizenry for a democratic society (this was the original rationale for public education in the United States). Second, greater schooling and skills lead to more satisfying work opportunities. Third, in a technologically advanced society such as the United States, education has become necessary for making rational consumption decisions. Fourth, schooling is essential if citizens are to deal effectively with a complex governmental bureaucracy such as that of the United States. Even if the economic rationale for investment in education has waned, these other factors have given greater urgency for a well-educated populace.

8.3.2 Government Intervention

The research contained in this book suggests that state intervention may be necessary for raising the fortunes of the working poor and middle class. Despite what the causes are, government interventions can *reverse* rising inequality. Indeed, we may need to expand government transfers and provide tax relief for low-wage workers in order to reduce inequality and increase posttax real wages. We must also shore up the worker "safety net" that has frayed over the last three decades.

Here are some possible measures:

Restore the Minimum Wage   The minimum wage in 2003 was down 34 percent in real terms from its peak level in 1968. My results indicate that the declining minimum wage was a factor in the stagnation of average earnings since the early 1970s. David Lee (1999) shows that the downward drift of wages for the bottom quartile of wage earners since the early 1970s is closely tied to movements in the minimum wage. Raising the minimum wage will help increase the earnings of low-wage workers.

The traditional objection to raising the minimum wage is that it will increase unemployment. However, in 1968, when the minimum wage was $7.81 in 2003 dollars, the unemployment rate was only 3.6 percent. Moreover, work by Card and Krueger (1995) has shown that raising the minimum wage need not result in a reduction in the number of low-paid workers. Indeed, in their study of fast-food workers in New Jersey, Card and Krueger found just the opposite. Their explanation is that a higher wage gives firms an incentive to train workers and upgrade their skills. Though this work has not been without criticism, it seems clear that the negative employment effects of a higher minimum wage are rather minor (if they exist at all).

How about a Living Wage?   A more ambitious aim would be to create a living wage for all workers. Even restoring the minimum wage to its 1968 peak would yield annual labor earnings of only $15,620 in 2003 (assuming 2,000 hours of work during the year). This would not have proved sufficient to raise a family of four above the poverty line in 2003 (the poverty threshold was $18,809).

The first living wage law was enacted in Baltimore in 1994. In the year 2000, 41 municipalities had some form of living wage ordinance that covered city contractors and private businesses that receive government subsidies or tax breaks or that lease public land. These laws set a wage floor of about $10 per hour for workers employed in these businesses. At this wage level, the full-time annual earnings of a single worker in the family would enable a family of four to cross the poverty line. In many municipalities, the living wage ordinance also requires the business to provide health insurance coverage to all of its workers. Efforts to pass a living wage provision are now going on in about 75 additional localities.

The coverage of these laws is extremely limited at present. In 2000, only about 46,000 workers were covered by these provisions (in comparison to some 28 million workers who earn $8 or less an hour). However, the extension of living wage laws to broader and broader segments of the workforce might be viewed as an ultimate goal of minimum wage legislation. Moreover, many living wage campaigns are attempting to raise the minimum wage to $12 per hour, which is close to what the federal minimum wage would be today if it were indexed not only to the CPI but also to the growth of worker productivity since 1968.[2]

Extend the Earned Income Tax Credit (EITC)   The EITC provides supplemental pay to low-wage workers in the form of a tax credit on their federal income tax return. This credit is refundable, so, if the family owes no income taxes or taxes lower than the credit, the Internal Revenue Service sends the family a check for the net amount of the tax credit. According to calculations by Seidman (2001) for fiscal year 1999, the EITC cost the federal government $30.6 billion. In contrast, federal, state, and local government expenditures on Temporary Assistance to Needy Families (TANF) amounted to only $23.7 billion. In 1999, almost 19 million people received some amount of earned income tax credit.

The EITC was first added to the personal income tax code in 1975 in order to offset increased Social Security taxes in that year. Since that time, the credit has been expanded substantially. Three different schedules are in effect now: (1) a very small credit for single-person households and couples without children, (2) a larger credit for families with one child, and (3) a still larger credit for families with two or more children. For a family with two children, the tax credit is figured as follows: For each dollar of earned (labor) income up to $9,720, the family receives a credit of 40 cents, for a maximum benefit of $3,888. The credit remains at this level up to $12,690 of earned income and is then phased out by 21 cents on each additional dollar earned up to $31,152. After this point, the credit disappears. A person working 2,000 hours a year at the minimum wage would thus not earn enough to lift a family of four above the poverty threshold, but this pay plus the EITC would be more than sufficient.

The fact that the EITC is tied to work has insulated the program from political attack from conservatives and even allowed it to expand over the last decade, while other social welfare spending has been cut back. An expansion of this credit will further raise the posttax income of low-income families and should be pursued, particularly since it has broad bipartisan support.

However, this provision has a number of problems. First, in many ways it gives firms an easy way out of directly increasing the wages of low-paid workers. Instead of sharing productivity gains directly with labor in the form of enhanced wages, this approach allows companies to rely on general government revenue to provide the wage increases that should be coming from enhanced profits. In this sense, the EITC winds up subsidizing employers, who might otherwise have to increase wages in the absence of this program.

Second, it would be more effective in the long run to increase the pretax wages of low-end workers directly, rather than relying on a tax subsidy. There are limits on how much taxpayers in general would be willing to subsidize low-wage work. Moreover, much of the subsidy comes from other workers, rather than from companies, so the EITC represents to a large extent a transfer of income from one group of workers to another.

Third, unlike raising the minimum wage, the EITC does not provide the same incentive to employers to upgrade the skills of their low-paid workers (if we find the Card and Krueger results plausible). Indeed, the usual story about the connection between wages and skill reverses cause and effect. If we keep wages low, firms will have little incentive to train workers and upgrade their skills. If we raise the minimum wage, firms will invest in workers in order to raise their productivity (marginal product) to the level of the higher wage.[3]

Extend the Unemployment Insurance (UI) Coverage Period to 52 Weeks and Increase UI Benefits   Currently, the UI system provides benefits to unemployed workers for a maximum of 26 weeks.[4] According to calculations from Baumol and Wolff (1999), only 35 percent of unemployed persons received benefits in 1997, down from 64 percent in 1961. This change was due to the increasing duration of unemployment over time and the consequent exhaustion of benefits. Moreover, in 1997, the average weekly UI benefit paid out was $193, almost exactly the same in real terms as in 1965, and the replacement rate (the weekly benefit divided by the weekly wage) was 33.5 percent in 1997, down from 36.6 percent in 1980.

One rationale for the establishment of the UI system is that it would provide unemployed workers with breathing room so that they do not have to settle for the first job they are offered but might instead search for a job that better matches their skills (and presumably pays higher wages). Extending the UI coverage period and raising the weekly benefit check will afford workers with additional time and greater income support to improve their choice of jobs.

Make Health Insurance Portable (or, Better, Provide Universal Health Coverage)   One strong motivation for remaining at a job is to hold on to health insurance. This reduces mobility and, ceteris paribus, results in poorer matches between worker skills and jobs and, on net, reduces wages. Providing for portable health insurance would remove this obstacle to increasing job mobility and providing workers with an opportunity to find a better job. A similar argument would favor portable pensions.

Of course, it would be preferable to make health insurance a required benefit in all jobs. This would make the portability of health insurance unnecessary. Indeed, the provision of universal health insurance, as is found in almost all other advanced industrial countries, will serve this purpose even better.

Make Social Security Taxes Less Regressive   Almost all of the discussion of "double taxation" has focused on the fact that corporate profits are taxed as part of the corporate income tax, and then dividends are taxed in personal income. However, wages are also subject to double taxation—first as personal income and second as part of the payroll tax.

Moreover, because of the existence of a maximum taxable wage base and the fact that higher-income families receive a smaller proportion of their total income from labor earnings, Social Security taxes are regressive.[5] In addition, according to estimates of Mitrusi and Poterba (2000), nearly two-thirds of U.S. families pay more in Social Security taxes than in income taxes.

We can make Social Security taxes more progressive. Lower-wage workers should be subject to a smaller tax rate (currently at 7.65 percent) than higher-wage workers. Moreover, the earnings cap should be lifted entirely (it is currently indexed to the CPI). This, by the way, would have the added effect of making lower-wage workers cheaper relative to high-wage workers (over the wage cap) because employers must match their workers' Social Security contributions. If the payroll tax on low-wage workers were reduced and that on high-wage workers increased, then the relative demand for low-wage workers would rise.

Make Personal Income Taxes More Progressive   As I discuss in chapter 1 (see figure 1.4), tax cuts over the postwar period have generally favored the rich more than the poor. Since 1946, the top marginal tax rate has fallen by 60 percent, the marginal rate at $135,000 (in 1995 dollars) by 47 percent, the marginal rate at $67,000 by 31 percent, and the rate at $33,000 by 39 percent. Tax policy in the last five decades has also benefited capital over labor. This has manifested itself in three ways: (1) the increased burden of payroll taxes (up from 12 percent of total federal revenue in 1955 to 35 percent in 2000); (2) the tax preference given to long-term capital gains and dividends in the personal income tax code; and (3) the gradual reduction in corporate income taxes (from 27 percent of total federal receipts in 1955 to 10 percent in 2000).[6]

It is true that the addition of the EITC to the tax code has added a modest increase to the progressivity of the personal tax code. However, overall, the progressivity of the personal income tax has faded in the last two decades. Moreover, comparisons between the United States and other advanced industrial countries (including Canada), which face similar labor market conditions, indicate that the tax systems of these countries are more progressive and more effective in reducing posttax income inequality (see Wolff 1997c, chapter 16, for more discussion of these issues).

8.3.3 Reempowering Labor

The evidence presented in chapter 3 indicates that the decline in unionization played the most important role in explaining the stagnation of average pay after 1973 (accounting for some 30 percent of the slowdown in earnings growth). Chapter 6 also offers strong evidence that the decline in unionization played a significant role in explaining rising wage inequality (accounting for about a third of the increase in inequality). Chapter 3 also shows that the slowdown in both productivity growth and capital investment had significant effects on movements in wages over time. However, these results have to be interpreted cautiously since, if unions were stronger, then technology and investment would not have had as great an impact on wages. In other words, the devolution of institutional forces in the United States has given market forces greater latitude to operate on wages.

The cross-national evidence points to the importance of unionization in explaining inequality differences. DiNardo and Lemieux (1997), for example, compared the rise of wage inequality in Canada and the United States and estimated that two-thirds of the faster rise of inequality in the latter from 1981 to 1988 was due to a more severe decline in the rate of unionization. Blau and Kahn (1996), using a large sample of OECD countries, have attributed more than half of the intercountry differences in wage inequality among men to differences in unionization patterns. Since these other advanced industrial countries (particularly Canada) were subject to the same market forces as the United States, it seems clear that unions act as a countervailing force to rising inequality.

Chapters 3 and 6 document the erosion of unions in the United States, down from 23 percent of the labor force in 1973 to 13 percent in 2003. However, even this change probably understates the true loss of power among organized labor. One seminal event is Ronald Reagan's dismissal of union air controllers during their 1982 strike, which marked the beginning of a sea change in the government's attitude toward labor. Indeed, it is perhaps not merely coincidental that the wage share began to decline and profitability to increase right around 1982.

The fortunes of labor have indeed waned over the last two decades, and capital has become ascendant. Indeed, the returns to work in general have atrophied, while the returns to capital have climbed. This shift in class power has fueled the stock market boom and contributed to the rising inequality of income in this country.

The country needs unions to once again act as a countervailing force on the economic scene. Labor has been getting squeezed in the United States over the last three decades. Computerization and expanded international trade, particularly growing imports of manufactures from low-wage countries, have reinforced the power of capital over labor by continually shaking up the job structure and making it difficult for unions to maintain their constituency. Another factor is that capital is more mobile than labor internationally, and direct foreign investment has expanded enormously in the last two decades. Therefore, it is easier for companies to seek out low-wage labor in other countries than it is for labor is to seek out high-wage employment in the United States.

Reform Labor Laws   How can we shift power back to unions? A rejuvenated labor movement in the private sector would be the most helpful mechanism (there are some indications that union membership is finally beginning to pick up after years of decline). Steps should be taken to help promote unionization in the workplace. This can start with the reform of existing labor law. Other work has documented the way in which existing labor law is biased against the establishment of new unions. Indeed, the certification process is notoriously difficult. Unions now need to be well funded, with deep pockets, to survive the opposition from management in order to get approved. New labor laws can make this process much easier.

Unions Must Reinvent Themselves   Unions also have an image problem today. They are variously perceived as Luddites, who resist technical change; as a powerful monopsonist that engages in featherbedding; as lobbying groups with their own vested interests; and as a privileged elite in the labor movement, who advance the interests of their members only.

The union movement must also help reestablish itself as an important player on the national scene. Unions were set up for the industrial age of mass production, before the advent of information technology. With the advent of the "new economy" and the globalization of international trade and capital flows, unions have lost their traditional stronghold among industrial blue-collar workers. Though they have made some progress among low-skilled service workers and in the public sector, they have not been able to make inroads among other white-collar workers, especially in the service industries. Unions must develop new strategies to penetrate these areas. Moreover, unions must reestablish their credentials on the national scene by promoting the interests of all workers, regardless of union status.

Restrain the Fed   More fundamentally, in order to get labor back on track, it is perhaps necessary to shift the norms of wage setting. Currently the norm appears to be that wages should keep up with inflation—that is, real wage growth should effectively be zero. Indeed, Alan Greenspan has referred to the "traumatized worker" effect—namely, that during the late 1990s and 2000, workers were unable to bargain up wages despite historically low unemployment rates because the institutional basis of their bargaining strength had eroded. The result is a far cry from the 1950s and 1960s, when the norm was that real wages should grow at the same rate as labor productivity.

The federal government has also played a role in this transformation. It used to act as referee between labor and capital. Since the early 1980s, however, it has come to favor capital over labor. In particular, the Department of the Treasury, which has historically represented the interests of Wall Street, has become the dominant player in the executive branch. The other major culprit is the Federal Reserve Board, which has raised interest rates and used moral suasion over the last two decades to clamp down on the economy once wages began to rise.

With U.S. labor productivity now running at 3–4 percent per year, according to the latest Bureau of Labor Statistics numbers, perhaps it is time to think about boosting wages. The Federal Reserve Board should curtail its exuberance in cracking down on wages whenever "wage inflation" appears. If the Fed starts to send out a positive message that it is okay if wages grow with productivity, this may eventually help to reestablish the wage norms of the early postwar period.

Notes

1. As chapter 6 reports, the coefficient of the share of property income in total personal income is not significant in the time-series regressions. However, it is likely that part of the reason for this result is the CPS data used in the analysis "topcodes" income at $100,000, so that the Gini coefficients compiled by the CPS understate the true level of inequality. Indeed, the Internal Revenue Service's "Statistics of Income" bulletin reveals a much higher level of income inequality during the 1990s than is reported in the CPS data.
2. See Moberg (2000) for more discussion of living wage ordinances.
3. See Bernstein (2000) for more discussion of the earned income tax credit.
4. This is often extended to 39 weeks during a general recession.
5. This applies only to the Old Age, Survivors, and Disability Insurance (OASDI) program. The Medicare portion is not subject to a maximum.
6. The data sources for this section are Wolff (1997c), chapter 16, updated with figures from the *Statistical Abstract of the United States, 2001*.

Data Appendix

A.1 Overview

The creation of industry skill measures from the *Dictionary of Occupational Titles (DOT)* data required that the occupation skill scores be weighted by the occupational employment mix of the industry. An occupation-by-industry matrix was therefore necessary for each of the census years covered in the study—1950, 1960, 1970, 1980, 1990, and 2000. This required an occupation and industry classification scheme that would enable the census occupation-by-industry data to be made compatible for these years. The source of the skill scores was the *DOT* (1977), which is based on data collected over the 1966–1974 period. These *DOT* occupations were mapped to census classifications by Roos and Treiman (in Miller et al. 1980). On the basis of a more aggregated classification, the Roos and Treiman scores were applied to the hours matrices to obtain skill unit matrices. Each of the columns (industries) was then summed and divided by total hours to get the average industry skill. The change in average industry skill levels between 1950 and 2000 therefore reflects only changes in the occupational mix of hours worked for each industry.

As this summary suggests, the development of these skill measures entailed the following steps, which I next describe in more detail: (1) determining the industry and occupation classifications to be used, (2) making the census occupation-by-industry data consistent over time in the classification scheme, (3) transforming the census employment matrices to an hours basis, and (4) imputing a skill level to each occupation/industry cell and deriving the industry average skill level.

A.2 Industry and Occupation Classifications

The objective is to define occupational classifications as precisely as possible in order to best capture changes in the occupational mix of industries. Although I wanted to keep the size of the matrices manageable, the original constraint was to choose a level of occupational detail that would enable me to reclassify the 1960 and 1980 census data to the 1970 definitions. The 1970 classifications were used for two reasons. First, the *DOT* skill measures were already available for these categories. Second, the comparability tables were available from the Employment Division of the Census Bureau, which allowed alignment of both the 1960 and the 1980 census occupation and industry classification schemes with that of 1970.

In addition, it was necessary to ensure consistency between the census industry classification and the input-output industry definitions used by the Bureau of Economic Analysis (BEA) and the industry classification scheme of the Bureau of Labor Statistics (BLS). This last concern stemmed from the need to use the BEA interindustry data and the BLS consistent series of industry output and hours worked for productivity analysis. Based on these considerations, a classification scheme of 267 occupations and 64 industries was used, as shown in appendix tables A.1 and A.2.

A.3 Consistency of the Employment Matrices

The most difficult and time-consuming part of the process of generating the skill unit matrices was the remaking of the 1960 and 1980 census matrices so that they were compatible with the 1970 employment matrix of 267 occupations and 64 industries. The Census Bureau has developed comparability tables between the 1960 and 1970 classification schemes (U.S. Department of Commerce 1972) and between the 1970 and 1980 classifications (U.S. Department of Commerce 1986). These tables are necessary because substantial changes in occupation and industry classifications have been introduced with each new census. For example, the 297 occupations in the occupation-by-industry matrix of the 1960 census were expanded to 441 in the 1970 matrix. In addition, "in some cases, a portion of a category was shifted to another to make each more homogeneous" (U.S. Department of Commerce 1972, 1).

The 1960–1970 comparability tables show the percentage and number of 1960 workers in each 1960 occupation that would be included in each 1970 occupational category. For example, on the basis of the 1970 definition of accountants, there were 495,886 accountants in 1960. Most of them (95.7 percent) were in the 1960 accountants category. The rest (4.3 percent) were defined in 1960 as statisticians and agents nec (not elsewhere classified) or clerical and kindred workers nec.

Data Appendix Table A.1.   Classification of Industries, 64-Sector Aggregation

Sector Number	Sector Name	1970 Census Code	45-Sector Scheme
1	Agriculture, forestry, and fishing	017–029	1
2	Metal mining	47	2
3	Coal mining	48	3
4	Oil and gas extraction	49	4
5	Nonmetallic minerals, except fuels	57–58	5
6	Construction	067–078	6
7	Meat and dairy	268, 269	7
8	Grain mill products	279	7
9	Beverage industries	289	7
10	Canning, bakery, confectionery, and other	278, 287, 288, 297, 298	7
11	Tobacco products	299	8
12	Textile mill products	307–318, 327	9
13	Apparel and other textile products	319	10
14	Logging and lumber	107	11
15	Wood products, except furniture	108, 109	11
16	Furniture and fixtures	118	12
17	Paper and allied products	328–337	13
18	Printing and publishing	338, 339	14
19	Chemicals and allied products	347–349, 358, 367–369	15
20	Drugs and medicines	357	15
21	Paints, varnishes, related products	359	15
22	Petroleum and coal products	377, 378	16
23	Rubber, miscellaneous plastic products	379, 387	17
24	Leather and leather products	388–397	18
25	Glass and glass products	119	19
26	Cement, concrete, gypsum, plaster products	127	19
27	Structural clay and pottery products	128, 137	19
28	Misc. nonmetallic mineral, stone products	138	19
29	Steel and iron industries	139, 147	20
30	Nonferrous metals	148, 149	20
31	Cutlery, hand tools, and other hardware	157	21
32	Fabricated metal, including ordnance	158–169, 258	21
33	Farm machinery and equipment	178	22
34	Computers and office equipment	188, 189	22
35	Machinery nec, except electrical	177, 179, 187, 197, 198	22
36	Electrical machinery, equipment, supplies	199–209	23
37	Motor vehicles and equipment	219	24

248

Data Appendix Table A.1.   (*continued*)

Sector Number	Sector Name	1970 Census Code	45-Sector Scheme
38	Aircraft and parts	227	25
39	Ship and boat building and repair	228	25
40	Other transportation equipment	229, 237, 238	25
41	Professional and photo equip. and watches	239–257	26
42	Miscellaneous manufacturing	259, 398	27
43	Transportation	407–429	28
44	Telephone and telegraph	448, 449	29
45	Radio and television broadcasting	447	30
46	Electric, gas, and sanitary services	467–479	31
47	Wholesale trade	507–599	32
48	Retail trade	607–699	33
49	Banking; credit and investment companies	707–709	34
50	Insurance	717	35
51	Real estate	718	36
52	Hotels, motels, and lodging places	777, 778	37
53	Barber and beauty shops	787, 788	38
54	Advertising	727	39
55	Auto services and repair	749, 757	40
56	Amusement and recreation services	807–817	41
57	Medical services	828–837, 839–848	42
58	Hospitals	838	42
59	Educational services	857–868	43
60	Legal, engineering, architectural, accounting, other professional services	849, 888–897	44
61	Museums, religious organizations, and nonprofit membership organizations	869–887	44
62	Business, repair, and personal services, nec	728–748, 758–767, 769, 779, 789–799	38, 39
63	Postal service	907	45
64	Public administration	917, 927, 937	45

Note: "Nec" stands for "not elsewhere classified."

While this information allowed me to get the right count of workers using the 1970 definition, the objective was to create a new row for accountants in the 1960 occupation-by-industry matrix so that the new total for accountants could be distributed across industries. Because all of the accountants in the 1960 table were already included under the 1970 classification scheme, the problem in this case was limited to distributing the remaining 4.3 percent

Data Appendix Table A.2.   Classification of Occupations into 267 Categories

Occupation Number	Occupation Name	1970 Census Code
1	Accountants	1
2	Architects	2
3	Computer programmers	3
4	Computer systems analysts	4
5	Computer specialists, nec	5
6	Aero- and aeronautical engineers	6
7	Chemical engineers	10
8	Civil engineers	11
9	Electrical and electronic engineers	12
10	Industrial engineers	13
11	Mechanical engineers	14
12	Metal, material, mining, and petrochemical engineers	15, 020, 021
13	Sales engineers	22
14	Engineers, nec	23
15	Farm management advisers, foresters, conservationists, and home mgmt. advisers	024–026
16	Judges	30
17	Lawyers	31
18	Librarians, archivists, and curators	32, 033
19	Actuaries, statisticians, and operation research analysts	34, 036, 055
20	Mathematicians	35
21	Agricultural scientists	42
22	Biological scientists	44
23	Chemists	45
24	Geologists, physicists, and astronomers	51, 053
25	Life and physical scientists, nec	43, 052, 054
26	Personnel and labor relations workers	56
27	Chiropractors	61
28	Dentists	62
29	Optometrists	63
30	Pharmacists	64
31	Physicians, medical and osteopathic	65
32	Veterinarians	72
33	Podiatrists and health practitioners, nec	71, 073
34	Dietitians	74
35	Registered nurses	75
36	Therapists	76
37	Health technologists and technicians	080–085, 426
38	Clergy	86
39	Religious workers, nec	90
40	Social scientists	091–096
41	Social workers	100
42	Recreation workers	101

Data Appendix Table A.2. *(continued)*

Occupation Number	Occupation Name	1970 Census Code
43	Teachers, college and university	102–140
44	Adult education teachers	141
45	Elementary and secondary teachers	142, 144
46	Preschool and kindergarten teachers	143
47	Teachers, except college and university, nec	145
48	Agricultural, biological, and chemical technicians	150, 151
49	Draftspersons	152
50	Electrical engineering technicians	153
51	Engineering and science technicians, nec	154–162
52	Airplane pilots	163
53	Air traffic controllers	164
54	Flight engineers	170
55	Tool programmers, numerical control	172
56	Technicians, nec, including radio operators	171, 173
57	Vocational and educational counselors	174
58	Designers	183
59	Editors and reporters	184
60	Writers, artists, and entertainers, nec	175–182, 185–194
61	Research workers, not specified	195
62	Bank officers and financial managers	201, 202
63	Buyers and shippers: farm, wholesale, retail	203, 205
64	Credit wokers	210
65	Funeral directors and embalmers	211, 165
66	Health administrators	212
67	Construction inspectors, public admin.	213
68	Inspectors, except construction, pub. admin.	215
69	Managers and superintendents, buildings	216
70	Office managers, nec	220
71	Ship officers, pilots, and pursers	221
72	Administrators, public admin., nec	222
73	Officials of lodges, societies, and unions	223
74	Postmasters and mail superintendents	224
75	Purchasing agents and buyers, nec	225
76	Railroad conductors	226
77	Restaurant, cafeteria, and bar managers	230
78	Sales managers and department heads, retail	231
79	Sales managers, except retail trade	233
80	School admin., college, elementary, secondary	235, 240
81	Managers and administrators, nec	245
82	Advertising agents and salespeople	260
83	Auctioneers, demonstrators, hucksters	261–264

(continued)

Data Appendix Table A.2.　(*continued*)

Occupation Number	Occupation Name	1970 Census Code
84	Insurance agents, brokers, and underwriters	265
85	Newspaper sellers	266
86	Real estate agents and brokers	270
87	Stock and bond salespeople	271
88	Sales representatives, manufacturing and wholesale	281, 282
89	Sales clerks, retail; salespeople	283, 284, 285
90	Bank tellers	301
91	Bookkeepers	305
92	Cashiers	310
93	Collectors, bills and accounts	313
94	Dispatchers and starters, vehicles	315
95	File clerks	325
96	Insurance adjusters and examiners	326
97	Library attendants and assistants	330
98	Mail carriers, post office	331
99	Messengers and office workers	333
100	Miscellaneous clerical workers	303, 311, 312, 314, 320–323, 332, 334, 362, 383, 392–395
101	Office machine operators	341–355
102	Payroll and timekeeping clerks	360
103	Postal clerks	361
104	Real estate appraisers	363
105	Receptionists	364
106	Secretaries	370–372
107	Shipping and receiving clerks	374
108	Statistical clerks	375
109	Stenographers	376
110	Stock clerks and storekeepers	381
111	Teacher aides, except school monitors	382
112	Telegraph operators	384
113	Telephone operators	385
114	Ticket station and express agents	390
115	Typists	391
116	Bakers	402
117	Blacksmiths	403
118	Boilermakers	404
119	Brick, stonemasons, and tile setters	410, 411, 560
120	Bulldozer, excavating, grading operators	412, 436
121	Cabinetmakers	413
122	Carpenters and apprentices	415, 416
123	Cement and concrete finishers	421
124	Compositors, typesetters, and apprentices	422, 423
125	Crane, derrick, hoist operators	424

Data Appendix Table A.2. (*continued*)

Occupation Number	Occupation Name	1970 Census Code
126	Decorators and window dressers	425
127	Electricians and apprentices	430, 431
128	Electric power line workers and cable workers	433
129	Electro- and stereotypers and engravers	434, 435
130	Forepersons, nec	441
131	Forge and hammer operators	442
132	Painters	443, 510–512, 543
133	Glaziers	445
134	Heat treaters, annealers, and temperers	446
135	Inspectors nec, scalers, and graders	450, 452
136	Jewelers and watchmakers	453
137	Job and die setters, metal	454
138	Locomotive engineers and fire fighters	455, 456
139	Machinists and apprentices	461, 462
140	Air conditioning, heating and refrigeration repairpersons	470
141	Aircraft mechanics	471
142	Machinery mechanics and repairpersons, nec	472–481
143	Household appliance mechanics	482
144	Loom fixers	483
145	Office machine mechanics and repairpersons	484
146	Radio and television repairpersons	485
147	Railroad and car shop mechanics	486
148	Miscellaneous mechanics and repairpersons	491–495
149	Millers of grain, flour, and feed	501
150	Millwrights	502
151	Metal molders and apprentices	503, 504
152	Motion picture projectionists	505
153	Opticians, lens grinders and polishers	506
154	Pattern and model makers, except paper	514
155	Photoengravers and lithographers	515
156	Plasterers and apprentices	520, 521
157	Plumbers, pipe fitters, and apprentices	522, 523
158	Power station operators	525
159	Press operators, plate printers, and apprentices	530, 531
160	Rollers and finishers, metal	533
161	Roofers and slaters	534
162	Sheetmetal workers and tinsmiths	535, 536
163	Shipfitters	540

(*continued*)

Data Appendix Table A.2. *(continued)*

Occupation Number	Occupation Name	1970 Census Code
164	Shoe repairpersons	542
165	Stationary engineers	545
166	Structural metal craftspersons	550
167	Tailors	551
168	Phone installers, repairpersons, and line workers	552–554
169	Tool and die makers and apprentices	561, 562
170	Upholsterers	563
171	Craftspersons and related workers, nec	401, 405, 420, 440, 444, 516, 546, 571–575
172	Asbestos and insulation workers	601
173	Assemblers	602
174	Blasters and powder workers	603
175	Bottling and canning operatives	604
176	Chain, rod, and ax operators: surveying	605
177	Checkers, examiners, and inspectors: manufacturing	610
178	Clothing ironers and pressers	611
179	Cutting operatives, nec	612
180	Dressmakers and seamstresses, except factory	613
181	Drillers: earth	614
182	Drywall installers and lathers	615
183	Dyers	620
184	Filers, polishers, sanders, and buffers	621, 651
185	Furnace operators, smelt workers and pourers	622
186	Garage workers and gas station attendants	623
187	Graders and sorters: manufacturing	624
188	Produce graders and packers, nec	625
189	Heaters: metal	626
190	Laundry and dry cleaning operatives, nec	630
191	Meat cutters and butchers	631, 633
192	Packers and wrappers, except produce	634, 643
193	Metal platers	635
194	Mine operatives, nec	640
195	Mixing operatives	641
196	Oilers and greasers, except automotive	642
197	Painters: manufactured articles	644
198	Photographic process workers	645
199	Drill press operatives	650
200	Lathe and milling machine operatives	652
201	Precision machine operatives, nec	653
202	Punch and stamping press operatives	656

Data Appendix Table A.2. *(continued)*

Occupation Number	Occupation Name	1970 Census Code
203	Riveters and fasteners	660
204	Sailors and deckhands	661
205	Sawyers	662
206	Sewers and stitchers	663
207	Shoemaking machine operatives	664
208	Solderers	665
209	Stationary fire fighters	666
210	Carding, lapping, and combing operatives	670
211	Knitters, loopers, and toppers	671
212	Spinners, twisters, and winders	672
213	Weavers	673
214	Textile operatives, nec	674
215	Welders and flame cutters	680
216	Winding operatives, nec	681
217	Machine operatives, misc. specified	636, 690
218	Miscellaneous operatives	692–695
219	Transportation operatives	701–705
220	Forklift and tow motor operatives	706
221	Motor operators: mine, factory, logging camp, etc.	710
222	Parking attendants	711
223	Railroad brakepersons	712
224	Railroad switchpersons	713
225	Taxicab drivers and chauffeurs	714
226	Truck drivers	715
227	Animal caretakers, except farm	740
228	Construction laborers	750, 751
229	Fishers and oyster workers	752
230	Freight and materials handlers	753
231	Garbage collectors	754
232	Gardeners and groundskeepers, except farm	755
233	Longshore operators and stevedores	760
234	Lumbermen, raftsmen, and woodchoppers	761
235	Stock handlers	762
236	Teamsters	763
237	Vehicle washers and equipment cleaners	764
238	Warehouse operators, nec	770
239	Miscellaneous laborers	780
240	Not specified laborers	785
241	Farmers and farm managers	801, 802
242	Farm forepersons and farm labor	821–824
243	Cleaning service workers	901–903
244	Food service workers except private household	910, 911, 913, 914, 916

(continued)

Data Appendix Table A.2.   (*continued*)

Occupation Number	Occupation Name	1970 Census Code
245	Cooks except private household	912
246	Waiters	915
247	Health aides, including dental assistants and trainees	921–923
248	Nursing aides, orderlies, and attendants	925
249	Practical nurses including lay midwives	924, 926
250	Flight attendants	931
251	Attendants: recreation and amusement	932
252	Attendants: personal service, nec	933, 934
253	Barbers	935
254	Boarding and lodging housekeepers	940
255	Bootblacks	941
256	Child care workers except private household	942
257	Elevator operators	943
258	Hairdressers and cosmetologists	944, 945
259	Housekeepers except private household	950
260	School monitors and ushers (recreation)	952, 953
261	Welfare service aides	954
262	Crossing guards and bridge tenders	960
263	Fire fighters and fire protection workers	961
264	Guards, watchmen, marshals, and constables	962, 963
265	Police officers and detectives	964
266	Sheriffs and bailiffs	965
267	Private household workers	980–984

Note: "Nec" stands for "not elsewhere classified."

among the industries. For this particular occupation, the remaining employment was distributed proportional to the distribution of workers classified in 1960 as accountants (the other 95.7 percent). Thus, the industry row was simply scaled up by a factor of 1.045.

Moreover, about three-quarters of the residual group that would have been redefined as accountants in 1970 had been listed as clerical workers in 1960. These workers amounted to only about 1.2 percent of the 1960 clerical and kindred workers occupational category. The remainder (98.8 percent) were allocated to other occupations according to the comparability table, with 37.7 percent of this 1960 occupation making up 100 percent of the 1970 occupation labeled "not specified clerical workers."

For some large 1970 occupations (for example, assemblers, filers and polishers, laborers nec, and secretaries), the 1960–1970 comparability tables provided the industry distribution for 1960. For example, in the case of assemblers, the 1970 definition included all of those defined as assemblers in 1960 (686,752 workers) as well as 97,060 operatives and kindred workers nec and 2,463 laborers nec in the 1960 scheme. The comparability table allocated these 97,060 operatives to 27 different industries, while the laborers were all allocated to the sawmills and planing mills industry. The new 1960 assemblers row, based on the 1970 definition, was derived by adding the original 1960 assemblers row to the operatives and laborers employment figures allocated to the appropriate industries. Similar procedures were carried out for each of the 267 occupations and 64 industries.

Based on a sample of 125,000 records from the 1970 census, the 1970–1980 comparability tables provided the percentage of each 1980 occupation or industry that had been defined as a 1970 occupation or industry. These percentages were used to transform the 1980 census occupation-by-industry matrix to 1970 occupations and industries. If accountants are again used as an example, this required summing 3.9 percent of financial managers, 97.5 percent of accountants and auditors, 24.92 percent of other financial officers, 10.87 percent of inspectors and compliance officers, and 2.05 percent of bookkeepers and accounting and auditing clerks to obtain the equivalent 1970 category of accountants.

No industry-specific allocations of these 1980 occupations to their corresponding 1970 classifications were available. As a result, to create a 1980 occupation-by-industry matrix with 1970 definitions, I added together the indicated proportions of these five 1980 occupations across all industries. This procedure implicitly assumed that the portion of each of these occupations that would be classified as accountants in 1970 was distributed across industries in the same proportions as the segment that would not be classified as accountants in 1970. Thus, for example, the 25 percent of other financial officers in 1980 who would have been defined as accountants in the 1970 classification scheme were distributed across industries in the same proportions as were all other financial officers.

The 1990 occupation and industry classification schemes used by the U.S. Census Bureau were very close to those used in the 1980 census. It was necessary to aggregate only a limited number of occupation and industry categories in the 1990 census data to obtain the same classification scheme as used in the 1980 data. The 1950 occupation and industry classifications were roughly similar to those for 1960. No comparability tables with 1960 were available from the U.S. Census Bureau, so the alignment was done separately by occupation and industry.

The 2000 occupation and industry classifications represent another major change in the classification system. Part of the reason is that, since 1997, the U.S. statistical agencies have adopted the North American Industrial Classification System (NAICS), which resulted in a major change in industry categories. The occupational classification system was also considerably revamped. Fortunately, the U.S. Census Bureau also provides concordance tables between the 1990 and 2000 occupation and industry classification schemes (http://www.census.govmain/www/cen2000.html).

A.4 The Hours Matrices

From 1970 census data on average weekly hours and average weeks worked per year, it was possible to estimate average annual hours of work for each occupation in 1970. The industry cells of each occupation row were then multiplied by that occupation's average annual hours to obtain total hours worked in each occupation-by-industry cell. This required the rather strong assumption that hours worked for each occupation do not vary across industries.

The hours matrices for 1950, 1980, 1990, and 2000 were created in similar fashion. However, for 1950 and 1960 I was unable to obtain information on weeks worked per year by occupation and therefore used the 1970 figures.

For each *DOT* skill measure, each element of the hours matrix was multiplied by the corresponding skill matrix for that year. A matrix was required because the *DOT* occupational skill scores often varied by industry. These matrices were also different for each of the six years used in the study (1950, 1960, 1970, 1980, 1990, and 2000) because the skill scores were available at a more detailed occupational level (591) than were my employment matrices (267). As a result, a weighted average was often necessary to create skill scores at the 267-occupation level. Since the weights consisted of occupational employment figures at the 591-occupation level, which differed in each of the census years, skill scores for each element of the occupation-by-industry matrix also differed among the four years (see Howell and Wolff 1991a for details).

A.5 List of Variables Used in the Statistical Analysis: Sources and Methods

A.5.1 Skill Measures

These measures are as follows: (a) substantive complexity (SC), (b) interactive skills (IS), (c) motor skills (MS), and (d) composite skill index (CP). The annual time-series for the skill measures is derived from decennial skill scores and interpolated scores for intervening years based on annual data on employment by occupation for 12–15 major occupations. Sources for the occupational data are as follows: (a) U.S. Department of Commerce, Census Bureau, *Historical Statistics of the U.S.: Colonial Times to 1970*, bicentennial ed., part 2 (Washington, D.C.: GPO), 1978; (b) U.S. Department of Labor, Bureau of Labor Statistics, *Handbook of Labor Statistics 1978*, Bulletin 2 (Washington, D.C.: GPO), 1979; (c) U.S. Department of Labor, Bureau of Labor Statistics, *Handbook of Labor Statistics 1989*, Bulletin 23 (Washington, D.C.: GPO), 1990; (d) U.S. Department of Commerce, Census Bureau, *Statistical Abstract of the United States, 1997*, 117th ed. (Washington, D.C.: GPO), 1997; (e) U.S. Department of Labor, *Report of the American Workplace* (Washington, D.C.: GPO), 1994; and (f) Eva E. Jacobs, ed., *Handbook of U.S. Labor Statistics*, 2d ed. (Lanham, Md.: Bernan Press), 1998.

A.5.2 Educational Attainment

Included under educational attainment are (a) median years of schooling, adult population; (b) percentage of adults with four or more years of high school; and (c) percentage of adults with four or more years of college. Source: U.S. Census Bureau, *Current Population Reports,* http://www.census.gov/hhes/income/histinc/. "Adults" refers to people who are at least 25 years of age in the noninstitutional population (excluding members of the armed forces living in barracks). Also considered are the mean years of schooling of employed workers. Source: U.S. Bureau of Labor Statistics, *Labor Composition and U.S. Productivity Growth, 1948–90,* Bulletin 2426 (Washington, D.C.: GPO), 1993. Figures are for the private business sector. Mean schooling is calculated by weighting educational attainment of workers by hours of work. The figures are updated to 2000 on the basis of worksheet data graciously provided by Larry Rosenblum of the Bureau of Labor Statistics.

A.5.3 Employee Compensation and Employment Data

1. BLS mean hourly and weekly earnings: Figures are from the Bureau of Labor Statistics and refer to the wages and salaries of production and nonsupervisory workers in the total private sector. Source: U.S. Council of Economic Advisers, *Economic Report of the President, 2005, 1999,* and *1981* (Washington, D.C.: GPO), 2005, 1999, and 1981, respectively.
2. BLS employment cost index (ECI): Figures are from the BLS employment cost index for private industry, including both wages and salaries and employers' costs for employees' benefits, as of December of that year. The index controls for the influence of employment shifts among occupations and industries. Sources: U.S. Department of Labor, *Report on the American Workforce, 1995* (Washington, D.C.: GPO), 1995; and the U.S. Council of Economic Advisers, *Economic Report of the President, 2005* (Washington, D.C.: GPO), 2005.
3. NIPA employee compensation: Figures are from the National Income and Product Accounts (NIPA), http://www.bea.gov/bea/dn2/home/annual_industry.htm. No adjustment is made for hours worked. Employee compensation includes wages, salaries, and benefits. Proprietors' income is net income of self-employed people, including partners in businesses and owners of unincorporated businesses.
4. NIPA employment data: Figures are from NIPA, http://www.bea.gov/bea/dn2/home/annual_industry.htm. The number of full-time equivalent employees (FTEEs) equals the number of employees on full-time schedules plus the number of employees on part-time schedules converted to a full-time basis. The number of FTEEs in each industry is the product of the total number of employees and the ratio of average weekly hours per employee for all employees to average weekly hours per employee on full-time schedules. Persons engaged in production (PEP) equals the number of full-time

and part-time employees plus the number of self-employed people. Unpaid family workers are not included.
5. CPS earnings data: Figures are from the Current Population Survey, available on the Internet. The overall median is computed as a weighted average of male and female median earnings, with employment shares as weights. The data refer to people who are at least 15 years old with earnings beginning in March 1980, and people who are at least 14 years old as of March of the following year for previous years. Prior to 1989 earnings are for civilian workers only.

A.5.4 Output, Investment, and Capital Stock Data

1. Investment data refer to nonresidential fixed investment in constant (2000) dollars and GDP to GDP in constant (2000) dollars. Source: U.S. Bureau of Economic Analysis, NIPA, http://www.bea.gov/bea/dn2/home/annual_industry.htm.
2. Capital stock figures are based on chain-type quantity indexes for net stock of fixed capital in constant (2000) dollars, year-end estimates. Equipment and structures, including IT equipment, are for the private (nongovernment) sector only. Information processing and related equipment includes (a) computers and peripheral equipment, (b) other office and accounting machinery, (c) communication equipment, (d) instruments, and (e) photocopy and related equipment. Source: U.S. Bureau of Economic Analysis, CD-ROM NCN-0229, "Fixed Reproducible Tangible Wealth of the United States, 1925–1997," and http://www.bea.gov/bea/dn2/home/annual_industry.htm. For technical details, see Katz and Herman (1997).
3. Investment flows by both industry and type of equipment or structures are for the private (nongovernment) sector only. Source: U.S. Bureau of Economic Analysis, CD-ROM NCN-0229, "Fixed Reproducible Tangible Wealth of the United States, 1925–1997," and http://www.bea.gov/bea/dn2/home/annual_industry.htm.
4. Average age of capital by type of equipment or structures is for the private (nongovernment) sector only. Source: U.S. Bureau of Economic Analysis, CD-ROM NCN-0229, "Fixed Reproducible Tangible Wealth of the United States, 1925–1997," and http://www.bea.gov/bea/dn2/home/annual_industry.htm.

A.5.5 Research and Development Data

1. R&D expenditures performed by industry include company, federal, and other sources of funds. Company-financed R&D performed outside the company is excluded. "Private" refers to privately funded R&D performed in company facilities, including all sources except federally financed R&D. "Basic" refers to basic research performed in company facilities; "applied" refers to applied research performed in company facilities; and "development" refers to development R&D performed in company facilities. The series run from 1953 to

2003. The series on industry-level data covers the period from 1957 to 2003. Sources: National Science Foundation, *Research and Development in Industry* (Arlington: National Science Foundation), various years, and http://www.nsf.gov/sbe/srs/nsf01305/htmstart.htm.

2. Full-time equivalent scientists and engineers engaged in R&D per FTEE. Series at both the aggregate and industry level run from 1957 to 2003. Sources: National Science Foundation, *Research and Development in Industry* (Arlington: National Science Foundation), various years, and http://www.nsf.gov/sbe/srs/nsf01305/htmstart.htm.

A.5.6 TFP Growth (TFPGRTH)

The formula for the average annual growth in total factor productivity is

$$\text{TFPGRTH}_t = dY_t/Y_t - \alpha dL_t/L_t - (1 - \alpha)dK_t/K_t,$$

where Y_t is GDP at time t, L_t is the total labor input, K_t is the capital input, and α is the average wage share over the period. The labor input is measured by PEP, and the capital input by the fixed, nonresidential net capital stock (in 2000 dollars). The wage share is measured as the ratio of employee compensation to GDP, both in current dollars, averaged over the relevant time period (for example, 1947–2003 for aggregate TFP). The sources for the data are given earlier. A second index of TFP growth was also used, with FTEE as the measure of labor input. Since the data are for discrete time periods, the Tornqvist-Divisia measure, based on average period shares, is used in the actual estimation.

A.5.7 Imports and Exports

Source for the aggregate data: U.S. Bureau of Economic Analysis, National Income and Product Accounts, http://www.bea.gov/bea/dn/home/gdp.htm. Sources for the industry-level data are U.S. input-output data for 1947, 1958, 1963, 1967, 1972, 1977, 1982, 1987, 1992, and 1996, provided on computer tape or diskette by the Bureau of Economic Analysis, and, for 2000, provided directly by the BEA as part of its annual input-output series. Source: http://www.bea.gov/bea/dn2/i-o_annual.htm. The data are interpolated for 1950, 1960, 1970, 1980, and 1990.

A.5.8 Service Sector Employment

Sectors include wholesale and retail trade; finance, insurance, real estate; personal and business services; and government. The employment concept is PEP. Source: U.S. Bureau of Economic Analysis, National Income and Product Accounts, http://www.bea.gov/bea/dn2/home/annual_industry.htm.

A.5.9 Unionization

Percentage of labor force covered by unions. Estimates for 1950–1983 are the annual average number of dues-paying members reported by labor unions. Estimates for 1983–2003 are annual averages from the Current Population Survey. Data exclude professional and public employee associations. Sources: (a) U.S. Department of Labor, Bureau of Labor Statistics, *Handbook of Labor Statistics 1978,* Bulletin 2 (Washington, D.C.: GPO), 1979; (c) U.S. Department of Labor, Bureau of Labor Statistics, *Handbook of Labor Statistics 1989,* Bulletin 23 (Washington, D.C.: GPO), 1990; and (d) Eva E. Jacobs, ed., *Handbook of U.S. Labor Statistics,* 2d ed. (Lanham, Md.: Bernan Press), 1998. Sources for the industry-level data include (in addition to those cited earlier) Kokkelenberg and Sockell (1985); Hirsch and Macpherson (1993), accompanying data files; Bureau of Labor Statistics, Office of Employment Projections, Output and Employment database; and the Bureau of Labor Statistics, http://www.bls.gov/news.release/union2.t03.htm.

A.5.10 Minimum Wage

Source: U.S. Census Bureau, *Statistical Abstract of the United States: 2003,* 123rd ed. (Washington, D.C.: GPO), 2003.

A.5.11 Input-Output Data

The basic data are 85-sector U.S. input-output tables for 1947, 1958, 1963, 1967, 1972, 1977, 1982, 1987, 1992, 1997, and 2000 (see appendix table A.3). The 1947, 1958, and 1963 tables are available only in single-table format.[1] The 1967, 1972, 1977, 1982, 1987, 1992, 1997, and 2000 data are available in separate make-and-use tables. The 2000 input-output table is provided directly by the BEA as part of its annual input-output series. Source: http://www.bea.gov/bea/dn2/i-o_annual.htm.

For details on the construction of the input-output tables, see the following: for 1963, U.S. Interindustry Economics Division (1969); for 1967, U.S. Interindustry Economics Division (1974); for 1972, Ritz (1979) and Ritz, Roberts, and Young (1979); for 1977, U.S. Interindustry Economics Division (1984); for 1982, U.S. Interindustry Economics Division (1991); for 1987, Lawson and Teske (1994); and for 1992, Lawson (1997).

Five sectors—R&D, business travel, office supplies, scrap and used goods, and inventory valuation adjustment—appeared in some years but not in others (the earlier years for the first three sectors and the later years for the last two sectors). In order to make the accounting framework consistent over the four years of analysis, I eliminated these sectors from both gross and final output. I did this by distributing the inputs used by these sectors proportional to either the endogenous sectors that purchased the output of these five sectors or to final output.[2]

Data Appendix Table A.3.   Concordance among the Various Industrial Classification Schemes Used in This Book

45-Sector Classification		1970 Census Codes[a]	BEA 85-Order Codes[b]	1987 SIC Codes	64-Order Scheme	10-Order Scheme
Number	Name					
1	Agriculture, forestry, and fishing	017–029	1–4	01–09	1	1
2	Metal mining	47	5–6	10	2	2
3	Coal mining	48	7	11, 12	3	2
4	Oil and gas extraction	49	8	13	4	2
5	Mining of nonmetallic minerals, except fuels	57, 058	9–10	14	5	2
6	Construction	067–078	11, 12	15–17	6	3
7	Food and related products	268–298	14	20	7–10	4
8	Tobacco products	299	15	21	11	4
9	Textile mill products	307–309, 317–318	16–17	22	12	4
10	Apparel and other textile products	329, 327	18–19	23	13	4
11	Lumber and wood products	108, 109	20–21	24	14–15	4
12	Furniture and fixtures	118	22–23	25	16	4
13	Paper and allied products	328–337	24–25	26	17	4
14	Printing and publishing	338, 339	26	27	18	4
15	Chemicals and allied products	347–349, 357–359	27–30	28	19–21	4
16	Petroleum and coal products	377, 378	31	29	22	4
17	Rubber and miscellaneous plastic products	379, 387	32	30	23	4
18	Leather and leather products	388–397	33–34	31	24	4
19	Stone, clay, and glass products	119, 127–128,	35–36	32	25–28	5
20	Primary metal products	139, 147–149	37–38	33	29–30	5

(continued)

Data Appendix Table A.3. (continued)

45-Sector Classification		1970 Census Codes[a]	BEA 85-Order Codes[b]	1987 SIC Codes	64-Order Scheme	10-Order Scheme
Number	Name					
21	Fabricated metal products, including ordnance	157–159, 167–169, 258	13, 39–42	34	31–32	5
22	Industrial machinery and equipment, except electrical	177–179, 187–189, 197–198	43–52	35	33–35	5
23	Electric and electronic equipment	199, 207–209	53–58	36	36	5
24	Motor vehicles and equipment	219	59	371	37	5
25	Other transportation equipment	227–229, 237–238	60–61	37	38–40	5
26	Instruments and related products	239, 247–249	62–63	38	41	5
27	Miscellaneous manufactures	259	64	39	42	4
28	Transportation	407–429	65	40–42, 44–47	43	6
29	Telephone and telegraph	448–449	66	481, 482, 489	44	6
30	Radio and TV broadcasting	447	67	483, 484	45	6
31	Electric, gas, and sanitary services	467–79	68	49	46	6
32	Wholesale trade	507–599	69A	50–51	47	7
33	Retail trade	600–699	69B, 74	52–59	48	7
34	Banking; credit and investment companies	707–709	70A	60–62, 67	49	8
35	Insurance	717	70B	63–64	50	8
36	Real estate	718	71B	65–66	51	8
37	Hotels, motels, and lodging places	777, 778	72A	70	52	9
38	Personal services	769, 779–799	72 (part)	72	53, 62[c]	9
39	Business and repair services except auto	727–748, 758–767	73C, 72 (part)	73, 76	54, 62[c]	9

40	Auto services and repair	749, 757	75	75	55	9
41	Amusement and recreation services	807–817	76	78–79	56	9
42	Health services, including hospitals	828–848	77A	80	57–58	9
43	Educational services	857–868	77B (part)	82	59	9
44	Legal and other professional services and nonprofit organizations	849, 869–897	73A, 73B, 77B (part)	81, 83, 84, 86, 87, 89	60–61	9
45	Public administration	907–947	78, 79, 84	43[d]	63–64	10

Notes:

a. 1970 Census of Population industry classification scheme

b. Bureau of Economic Analysis 85-sector industrial classification system for input-output data (1987 version)

c. Business and Personal Services nec (census codes 728–48, 758–67, 779, 789–799 and 64-sector code 62) split proportionately between two sectors

d. U.S. postal service only

Employment and capital stock by input-output industry, as well as output in current and constant dollars, were all obtained from BLS worksheets for the period 1958–2000. The worksheet data on output and employment update the BLS *Time Series Data for Input-Output Industries* (Washington, D.C.: GPO), 1979; and the BLS *Historical Output and Employment Data Series* (on diskette). The worksheet data on capital stock update the *Economics Capital Stock Database* (on diskette) of the U.S. Bureau of Industry, obtained in January of 1983.

These data were used to construct labor coefficients, capital coefficients, and sectoral price deflators. In addition, the deflator for transferred imports was calculated from the NIPA import deflator, that for the "rest of the world" industry was calculated as the average of the NIPA import and export deflator, and the deflator for the inventory valuation adjustment was computed from the NIPA change in the business inventory deflator. Source: U.S. Bureau of Economic Analysis, National Income and Product Accounts, http://www.bea.gov/bea/dn2/home/annual_industry.htm.

The 85 industries are divided into two groups, goods and services. The goods industries include agriculture (1–4), mining (5–10), construction (11–12), manufacturing (13–64), transportation (65), communications (66–67), and utilities (68).[3] Services include trade (69), finance, insurance, and real estate (70–71), government services (78, 79, 82), and all other services (72–77, 84). I include communications, transportation, and utilities in the goods sector because, for the purposes here, they have relatively easily measured output and are more like the other goods industries than services.

The 1950, 1960, 1970, 1980, and 1990 input-output tables are estimated from the benchmark U.S. input-output tables. The 1950 table is interpolated from those for 1947 and 1958; the 1960 table is interpolated from those for 1958 and 1963; the 1970 table is interpolated from those for 1967 and 1972; the 1980 table is interpolated from those for 1977 and 1982; and the 1990 table is interpolated from those for 1987 and 1992. The 2000 input-output table is directly provided by the BEA. The 85-sector tables are then aggregated to 45 industries, according to the aggregation scheme in appendix table A.3.

A.5.12 Inequality Data

The source for the Gini coefficient for family income is the U.S. Census Bureau, Current Population Survey, March supplement, http://www.census.gov/ftp/pub/hhes/www/incpov.htm1.

A.5.13 Miscellaneous Data

1. Property income and personal income: U.S. Bureau of Economic Analysis, National Income and Product Accounts, http://www.bea.gov/bea/dn/nipaweb/index.asp.
2. Number of female householders and total number of families: U.S. Census Bureau, Current Population Survey, March supplement, http://www.census.gov/ftp/pub/hhes/www/incpov.htm1.

Data Appendix Table A.4.　Occupational Skill Scores and Classification into
Knowledge, Data, Service, and Goods Workers

Occupation Number	Occupation Name	Skill Score			Information Group Category
		SC	IS	MS	
1	Accountants	6.9	2.25	2.9	Knowledge
2	Architects	9.5	2.5	6.9	Knowledge
3	Computer programmers	7.4	2.5	4.3	Knowledge
4	Computer systems analysts	7.6	2.5	3.4	Knowledge
5	Computer specialists, nec	7.5	5.38	3.3	Knowledge
6	Aero- and aeronautical engineers	8.7	2.75	6.4	Knowledge
7	Chemical engineers	9	2.5	6.7	Knowledge
8	Civil engineers	8.2	2.5	7.5	Knowledge
9	Electrical and electronic engineers	7.7	2.5	7.2	Knowledge
10	Industrial engineers	8.3	2.75	4.9	Knowledge
11	Mechanical engineers	7.5	2.62	6.6	Knowledge
12	Metal, material, mining, and petrochemical engineers	9.02	2.5	6.18	Knowledge
13	Sales engineers	6.7	3.38	4.2	Data
14	Engineers, nec	8.2	2.5	6.4	Knowledge
15	Farm management advisers, foresters, conservationists, and home mgmt. advisers	5.5	3.24	5.09	Knowledge
16	Judges	9.6	10	0	Knowledge
17	Lawyers	0	9.5	2.2	Knowledge
18	Librarians, archivists, and curators	5.85	4.68	2.79	Knowledge
19	Actuaries, statisticians, and operation research analysts	7.44	2.34	3.35	Knowledge
20	Mathematicians	9.5	2.5	3.2	Knowledge
21	Agricultural scientists	6.75	3.5	5.9	Knowledge
22	Biological scientists	8.6	2.3	7.6	Knowledge
23	Chemists	9.2	2.5	7.5	Knowledge
24	Geologists, physicists, and astronomers	9.5	2.75	7.05	Knowledge
25	Life and physical scientists, nec	9.15	2.5	5.49	Knowledge
26	Personnel and labor relations workers	6.8	5.13	2.5	Data/Serv
27	Chiropractors	6.6	10	9.4	Data/Serv
28	Dentists	8.8	9.63	7.9	Data/Serv
29	Optometrists	7.2	10	7.8	Data/Serv
30	Pharmacists	7.6	2.5	7.8	Data
31	Physicians, medical and osteopathic	8.9	9.38	9.9	Data/Serv

(*continued*)

Data Appendix Table A.4. *(continued)*

Occupation Number	Occupation Name	Skill Score			Information Group Category
		SC	IS	MS	
32	Veterinarians	8	7.25	9.7	Data/Serv
33	Podiatrists, and health practitioners, nec	6.55	9.94	8.8	Data/Serv
34	Dietitians	6.4	6.38	4	Data/Serv
35	Registered nurses	6.1	1.88	6.6	Data/Serv
36	Therapists	6.3	6.38	6.6	Data/Serv
37	Health technologists and technicians	5.47	1.91	7.35	Data
38	Clergy	9.3	10	2.2	Data/Serv
39	Religious workers, nec	7.5	8.13	2.6	Data/Serv
40	Social scientists	7.59	4.43	3.38	Knowledge
41	Social workers	6.7	8.25	2.3	Data/Serv
42	Recreation workers	6.8	6.38	3.2	Data
43	Teachers, college and university	8.09	7.26	2.82	Knowledge
44	Adult education teachers	6.6	7.38	3.4	Data
45	Elementary and secondary teachers	6.28	7.5	3.35	Data
46	Preschool and kindergarten teachers	5	5.63	4.4	Data
47	Teachers, except college and university, nec	7.2	7.25	6.3	Data
48	Agricultural, biological, and chemical technicians	5.29	1.92	6.89	Data
49	Draftspersons	6.5	1	8.3	Data
50	Electrical engineering technicians	6.2	2.13	8.3	Data
51	Engineering and science technicians, nec	5.75	2.25	6.8	Data
52	Airplane pilots	6.7	2.62	7.3	Data/Serv
53	Air traffic controllers	6	2.38	5.8	Data
54	Flight engineers	6.6	2.5	7.1	Data
55	Tool programmers, numerical control	6.2	2.5	3.7	Data
56	Technicians, nec, including radio operators	4.8	2.43	5.59	Data
57	Vocational and educational counselors	7.5	8.75	3	Data/Serv
58	Designers	7.4	2.25	7.7	Knowledge
59	Editors and reporters	7.7	4.38	3.7	Knowledge
60	Writers, artists, and entertainers, nec	7.13	3.68	6.53	Knowledge
61	Research worker, not specified	7	4.88	4.5	Knowledge

Occupation Number	Occupation Name	Skill Score			Information Group Category
		SC	IS	MS	
62	Bank officers and financial managers	7.47	6.53	2.62	Know/Data
63	Buyers and shippers: farm, wholesale, retail	6.32	4.06	3.4	Data
64	Credit workers	7.1	2.75	2.3	Data
65	Funeral directors and embalmers	6	2.31	4.55	Data/Serv
66	Health administrators	7	6.88	3.4	Know/Data
67	Construction inspectors, public admin.	6.7	2.5	3.9	Data
68	Inspectors, except construction, pub. admin	5	2.12	4.42	Data
69	Managers and superintendents, buildings	5.4	3.38	3.8	Data/Serv
70	Office managers, nec	6.3	2.75	2.4	Data
71	Ship officers, pilots, and pursers	5.6	5.13	6.4	Know/Data
72	Administrators, public admin., nec	6.32	4.3	3	Know/Data
73	Officials of lodges, societies, and unions	6.8	4.5	2.5	Know/Data
74	Postmasters and mail superintendents	5.9	3.13	2.2	Know/Data
75	Purchasing agents and buyers, nec	6.3	4.13	2.9	Data
76	Railroad conductors	5.2	2.62	4.2	Data
77	Restaurant, cafeteria and bar managers	5.7	2.62	3.6	Data/Serv
78	Sales managers and department heads, retail	6.2	4.25	2.7	Know/Data
79	Sales managers, except retail trade	7.1	3.38	2.3	Know/Data
80	School admin., college, elementary, secondary	7.2	7.83	2.5	Know/Data
81	Managers and administrators, nec	6.06	3.91	3.18	Know/Data
82	Advertising agents and salespeople	5.8	3.87	2.8	Data
83	Auctioneers, demonstrators, hucksters	3.77	3.6	4.13	Data
84	Insurance agents, brokers, and underwriters	6.4	3.5	3.4	Data

(*continued*)

Data Appendix Table A.4.   (*continued*)

Occupation Number	Occupation Name	Skill Score			Information Group Category
		SC	IS	MS	
85	Newspaper sellers	0.7	3.63	2.3	Data
86	Real estate agents and brokers	5.3	3.75	3.3	Data
87	Stock and bond salespeople	7	3.63	2.6	Data
88	Sales representatives, manufacturing and wholesale	4.6	3.63	3.05	Data
89	Sales clerks, retail; salespeople	3.9	2.8	4.3	Data
90	Bank tellers	5.6	2.5	8.2	Data
91	Bookkeepers	4.4	0.25	6.1	Data
92	Cashiers	3.2	2.5	7.3	Data
93	Collectors, bills and accounts	4.1	3.13	2.3	Data
94	Dispatchers and starters, vehicles	4.1	2.88	3.1	Data
95	File clerks	2.9	2	4.6	Data
96	Insurance adjusters and examiners	6	6.5	2.3	Data
97	Library attendants and assistants	3.5	2.25	4.2	Data
98	Mail carriers, post office	3.2	2.5	5.3	Data
99	Messengers and office workers	1.2	1.88	2.9	Data
100	Miscellaneous clerical workers	3.41	2.2	4.63	Data
101	Office machine operators	3.02	1.1	6.07	Data
102	Payroll and timekeeping clerks	3.9	0.88	6.8	Data
103	Postal clerks	3.1	2.13	4.8	Data
104	Real estate appraisers	4.1	2.5	2.2	Data
105	Receptionists	3.8	2.5	2.8	Data
106	Secretaries	5.5	2.5	8.3	Data
107	Shipping and receiving clerks	3	0.5	3.9	Data
108	Statistical clerks	3.6	1.25	5	Data
109	Stenographers	3.1	2.5	7.1	Data
110	Stock clerks and storekeepers	2.9	0.75	3.7	Data
111	Teacher aides, except school monitors	4.5	4.13	2.9	Data
112	Telegraph operators	3.6	2	6.8	Data
113	Telephone operators	2.9	2.75	5.7	Data
114	Ticket station and express agents	4.4	2.88	3.6	Data

Data Appendix Table A.4. (*continued*)

Occupation Number	Occupation Name	Skill Score			Information Group Category
		SC	IS	MS	
115	Typists	2.6	1.75	6.7	Data
116	Bakers	4	0.37	6.5	Goods
117	Blacksmiths	3.7	0	7.8	Goods
118	Boilermakers	4.9	2.13	6.3	Goods
119	Brick, stonemasons, and tile setters	4.29	0.27	6.64	Goods
120	Bulldozer, excavating, grading operators	2.94	0.34	5.87	Goods
121	Cabinetmakers	4.4	0	6.9	Goods
122	Carpenters and apprentices	4.7	0.25	7	Goods
123	Cement and concrete finishers	3.1	2.13	5.9	Goods
124	Compositors, typesetters, and apprentices	4.5	0.63	7.3	Goods
125	Crane, derrick, hoist operators	2.2	1.75	5.5	Goods
126	Decorators and window dressers	6	1.5	8.7	Goods
127	Electricians and apprentices	6	2.25	7	Goods
128	Electric power line and cable workers	4.6	2	7.3	Goods
129	Electro- and stereotypers and engravers	4.32	0.45	7.39	Goods
130	Forepersons, nec	5.63	5.23	4.75	Data
131	Forge and hammer operators	2.8	2.13	6.2	Goods
132	Painters	4.3	0.22	8.17	Goods
133	Glaziers	3.4	0.12	6	Goods
134	Heat treaters, annealers, and temperers	2.9	0.75	5.8	Goods
135	Inspectors nec, scalers, and graders	4.19	1.58	4.35	Goods
136	Jewelers and watchmakers	5.1	0	7.3	Goods
137	Job and die setters, metal	4.4	1.13	6.8	Goods
138	Locomotive engineers and fire fighters	3.5	2.38	6.2	Goods
139	Machinists and apprentices	4.8	0.25	8.2	Goods
140	Air conditioning, heating and refrigeration repairpersons	4.9	1.75	6.5	Goods
141	Aircraft mechanics	5.1	0.5	7.1	Goods
142	Machinery mechanics and repairpersons, nec	4.58	1.44	7.37	Goods

(*continued*)

Occupation Number	Occupation Name	Skill Score			Information Group Category
		SC	IS	MS	
143	Household appliance mechanics	3.9	1.5	6.1	Goods
144	Loom fixers	4	2.5	7.3	Goods
145	Office machine mechanics and repairpersons	5.6	1.25	6.6	Goods
146	Radio and television repairpersons	4.6	0.37	7.8	Goods
147	Railroad and car shop mechanics	4.4	0.12	6	Goods
148	Miscellaneous mechanics and repairpersons	4.42	0.57	6.94	Goods
149	Millers of grain, flour, and feed	2.4	0.88	4.6	Goods
150	Millwrights	5.5	0	7.2	Goods
151	Metal molders and apprentices	3.3	0.88	6.1	Goods
152	Motion picture projectionists	4.3	2.25	7.4	Goods
153	Opticians, lens grinders and polishers	4.5	0.5	7.2	Goods
154	Pattern and model makers, except paper	4.7	0	7.1	Goods
155	Photoengravers and lithographers	4.7	0.5	7.2	Goods
156	Plasterers and apprentices	4.3	2.38	7	Goods
157	Plumbers, pipe fitters, and apprentices	4.8	0.25	7.1	Goods
158	Power station operators	3.8	1.75	5.3	Goods
159	Press operators, plate printers, and apprentices	3.79	1.5	7	Goods
160	Rollers and finishers, metal	1.9	0.5	5	Goods
161	Roofers and slaters	3.1	0	6.5	Goods
162	Sheetmetal workers and tinsmiths	4.9	0.19	7	Goods
163	Shipfitters	4.8	0	6.7	Goods
164	Shoe repairers	3.8	2	7.2	Goods
165	Stationary engineers	4.2	0.75	5.7	Goods
166	Structural metal craftspersons	3.8	2	6.3	Goods
167	Tailors	3.7	1.37	7.4	Goods
168	Phone installers, repairpersons, and line workers	4.55	0.85	7.32	Goods
169	Tool and die makers and apprentices	5	0.12	8	Goods

Data Appendix Table A.4. (*continued*)

Occupation Number	Occupation Name	Skill Score			Information Group Category
		SC	IS	MS	
170	Upholsterers	3.6	0	7.6	Goods
171	Craftspersons and kindred workers, nec	3.1	0.79	6.63	Goods
172	Asbestos and insulation workers	1.9	1.62	5.7	Goods
173	Assemblers	1.8	0.12	5.6	Goods
174	Blasters and powder workers	5	2.5	7.1	Goods
175	Bottling and canning operatives	1	0	5.8	Goods
176	Chain, rod, and ax operators: surveying	1.9	2.13	4	Goods
177	Checkers, examiners, and inspectors: manufacturing	2.6	0.5	5.8	Goods
178	Clothing ironers and pressers	0.5	0	5	Goods
179	Cutting operatives, nec	1.9	0.25	5.3	Goods
180	Dressmakers and seamstresses, except factory	3.4	1.62	7.6	Goods
181	Drillers: earth	2.7	1	5.4	Goods
182	Drywall installers and lathers	2.8	1.13	6.5	Goods
183	Dyers	1.9	0.25	4.9	Goods
184	Filers, polishers, sanders, and buffers	2.23	0.12	5.52	Goods
185	Furnace and smelt operators and pourers	1.6	1.37	5.4	Goods
186	Garage workers and gas station attendants	2.3	2.25	3.2	Goods
187	Graders and sorters: manufacturing	1.1	0	4.7	Goods
188	Produce graders and packers, nec	1	0.12	5.4	Goods
189	Heaters: metal	3.6	2.5	6.6	Goods
190	Laundry and dry cleaning operatives, nec	1.2	0.25	3.9	Goods
191	Meat cutters and butchers	2	0.28	6.5	Goods
192	Packers and wrappers, except produce	1.2	0	5.25	Goods
193	Metal platers	3.4	0.25	6.2	Goods
194	Mine operatives, nec	2.37	0.33	5.16	Goods
195	Mixing operatives	1.9	0.25	4.4	Goods
196	Oilers and greasers, except automotive	0.8	0.25	4.7	Goods

(*continued*)

Data Appendix Table A.4. *(continued)*

Occupation Number	Occupation Name	Skill Score			Information Group Category
		SC	IS	MS	
197	Painters: manufactured articles	2.6	0.12	6.7	Goods
198	Photographic process workers	3.2	0.63	6.8	Goods
199	Drill press operatives	1.9	0.12	6.1	Goods
200	Lathe and milling machine operatives	2.1	0	6	Goods
201	Precision machine operatives, nec	2.9	0.12	5.8	Goods
202	Punch and stamping press operatives	2.9	0.5	5.4	Goods
203	Riveters and fasteners	1.8	0	5.1	Goods
204	Sailors and deckhands	1.6	0.88	5.3	Goods
205	Sawyers	2.2	0.12	5.1	Goods
206	Sewers and stitchers	1.7	0.25	7.2	Goods
207	Shoemaking machine operatives	1.2	0.25	5	Goods
208	Solderers	1.9	0	5.9	Goods
209	Stationary fire fighters	2.8	1	5.7	Goods
210	Carding, lapping, and combing operatives	1.5	0.25	5.8	Goods
211	Knitters, loopers, and toppers	1.2	1.37	5.8	Goods
212	Spinners, twisters, and winders	1.2	0.25	5.8	Goods
213	Weavers	2.5	0.12	6.7	Goods
214	Textile operatives, nec	1.7	0.5	5.5	Goods
215	Welders and flame cutters	3.4	0.25	6.6	Goods
216	Winding operatives, nec	2.3	0.12	5.6	Goods
217	Machine operatives, misc. specified	2.06	0.49	5.15	Goods
218	Miscellaneous operatives	2	0.5	5.2	Goods
219	Transportation operatives	2.3	2.4	4.95	Goods
220	Forklift and tow motor operatives	1.2	0.25	5.4	Goods
221	Motor operators: mine, factory, logging camp, etc.	2.4	1.37	5.9	Goods
222	Parking attendants	1.4	1.25	3.6	Goods
223	Railroad brake operators	2.2	2.5	5.2	Goods
224	Railroad switch operators	1.2	2.25	5	Goods
225	Taxicab drivers and chauffeurs	2.1	2.25	6	Goods
226	Truck drivers	2.2	1.25	5.9	Goods

Data Appendix Table A.4. (*continued*)

Occupation Number	Occupation Name	Skill Score			Information Group Category
		SC	IS	MS	
227	Animal caretakers, except farm	1.4	1.37	5.8	Goods
228	Construction laborers	1.3	1.62	5	Goods
229	Fishers and oyster workers	1.7	0.37	4.5	Goods
230	Freight and materials handlers	1.4	0.37	3.5	Goods
231	Garbage collectors	0.3	0.5	3.6	Service
232	Gardeners and groundskeepers, except farm	1.2	0.37	3.7	Service
233	Longshoremen and stevedores	1.4	1.13	4	Goods
234	Lumbermen, raftsmen, and woodchoppers	1.7	0.12	5	Goods
235	Stock handlers	1.7	0.5	3.9	Goods
236	Teamsters	1.8	0	5.7	Goods
237	Vehicle washers and equipment cleaners	1.1	0.37	3.6	Goods
238	Warehouse workers, nec	1.1	0.12	3.6	Goods
239	Miscellaneous laborers	1.3	0.37	3.96	Goods
240	Not specified laborers	1.3	0.37	3.9	Goods
241	Farmers and farm managers	5.2	2.44	5	Goods
242	Farm forepersons and farm labor	1.3	0.63	5.2	Goods
243	Cleaning service workers	1.64	0.83	4.32	Service
244	Food service workers, except private household	1.22	0.79	3.73	Service
245	Cooks except private household	3.9	2.13	5.5	Service
246	Waiters	2.1	1.37	3.3	Service
247	Health aides (including dental assistants and trainees)	4.34	1.65	5.22	Service
248	Nursing aides, orderlies, and attendants	1.1	1.37	5.6	Service
249	Practical nurses including lay midwives	3.5	1.31	6	Service
250	Flight attendants	3.8	2.38	3.7	Service
251	Attendants: recreation and amusement	2.7	2.62	4.1	Service
252	Attendants: personal service, nec	1.7	1.75	3.5	Service
253	Barbers	4.6	1.37	7.7	Service

(*continued*)

Data Appendix Table A.4.   (*continued*)

Occupation Number	Occupation Name	Skill Score			Information Group Category
		SC	IS	MS	
254	Boarding and lodging housekeepers	5.2	5.75	3.3	Service
255	Bootblacks	0	1.25	3.6	Service
256	Child care workers except private household	1	1.5	3	Service
257	Elevator operators	1.7	2.25	4.1	Service
258	Hairdressers and cosmetologists	5.2	1.37	9.1	Service
259	Housekeepers except private household	3.7	3.63	3.5	Service
260	School monitors and ushers (recreation)	2.7	2.99	3.88	Service
261	Welfare service aides	5.2	4.88	3.1	Service
262	Crossing guards and bridge tenders	1.6	2.25	3.1	Service
263	Fire fighters and fire protection workers	4.2	2.88	6.7	Service
264	Guards, watchmen, marshals, and constables	2.79	2.5	3.5	Service
265	Police officers and detectives	4.1	2.88	5.3	Service
266	Sheriffs and bailiffs	3.5	2.5	5.3	Service
267	Private household workers	0.9	1.28	3.89	Service

Key:
  Nec: "not elsewhere classified"
  SC: substantive complexity score
  IS: interactive skill score
  MS: motor skill score
  Knowledge: knowledge worker
  Data: data worker
  Service: service worker
  Goods: goods worker
  Know/Data: knowledge/data worker
  Data/Serv: data/service worker

A.6 List of Symbols Used in the Book

Chapter 2

N = the occupation-by-industry employment matrix, where N_{ij} shows the total employment of occupation i in industry j

H = row vector showing total employment by industry, where $H_j = \Sigma_i N_{ij}$

h = row vector showing the distribution of employment among industries, where $h_j = H_j / \Sigma H_j$

S = row vector showing the average skill level by industry

s = hS' = a scalar showing the overall average skill level of employed workers

Chapter 3

$\bar{e} = \Sigma\, u_j w_j$ = overall average earnings of employees

f = generic symbol for a mathematical function

KC = 45-order row vector showing the stock of OCA equipment in each sector

KO = 45-order row vector showing the stock of total capital less OCA in each sector

LAB = 45-order row vector showing total employment in each sector

LP_j = standard measure of labor productivity growth for sector j

Q = 45-order row vector showing quality-adjusted labor input by industry

RD = 45-order row vector showing the stock of R&D capital by industry

u_j = share of workers in industry j

w_{OCC} = 267-order column vector showing average wages in 1992 dollars by occupation

w_j = average earnings in industry j

X = 45-order column vector of gross output in constant (1992) dollars by sector

Z = 45-order row vector (Z_j is a Hicks-neutral TFP index that shifts the production function of sector j over time)

ϵ = output elasticity of an input

π_j = standard measure of TFP growth for sector j

Chapter 4

A = the square matrix of interindustry input-output coefficients, where A_{ij} indicates the amount of input i (in 1992 dollars) required per unit of output j (in 1992 dollars)

c = an employment distribution matrix, showing the percentage distribution of employment by occupation within each sector, where $c_{ij} = N_{ij}/H_j$

f = generic symbol for a mathematical function

g = 45-order square matrix of capital coefficients, where g_{ij} indicates the amount of capital of type i (in 1992 dollars) required per unit of output j (in 1992 dollars)

INT = 45-order row vector showing total intermediate inputs in each sector

KC = 45-order row vector showing the stock of OCA equipment in each sector

KO = 45-order row vector showing the stock of total capital less OCA in each sector

LAB = 45-order row vector showing total employment in each sector

LP_j = the standard measure of labor productivity growth for sector j

p = 45-order row vector of prices, where p_j is the price of output j

Q = 45-order row vector showing quality-adjusted labor input by industry

RD = 45-order row vector showing the stock of R&D capital by industry

w_{OCC} = 267-order column vector showing average wages in 1992 dollars by occupation

X = 45-order column vector of gross output in constant (1992) dollars by sector

Z = 45-order row vector (Z_j is a Hicks-neutral TFP index that shifts the production function of sector j over time)

ϵ = the output elasticity of an input

π_j = the standard measure of TFP growth for sector j

Chapter 5

A = the square matrix of interindustry input-output coefficients, where A_{ij} indicates the amount of input i (in 1992 dollars) required per unit of output j (in 1992 dollars)

B = a column vector of total employment by occupation, where $B_i = \Sigma_j N_{ij}$

c = an employment distribution matrix, showing the percentage distribution of employment by occupation within each sector, where $c_{ij} = N_{ij}/H_j$

H = row vector showing total employment by industry, where $H_j = \Sigma_i N_{ij}$

L = a row vector of labor coefficients showing total employment per unit of output, where $L_j = H_j/X_j$

N = the employment matrix, where N_{ij} shows the total employment of occupation i in industry j

n = 267 by 45 employment coefficient matrix, showing employment by occupation per unit of output, where $n_{ij} = N_{ij}/X_j$

X = column vector showing the total output (gross domestic output, or GDO) by sector

Y = column vector showing the final output by sector

y = a column vector showing the percentage distribution of total final output by sector, where $y_i = Y_i/\Sigma Y_i$

Chapter 6

f = generic symbol for a mathematical function

KC = 45-order row vector showing the stock of OCA equipment in each sector

KE = 45-order row vector showing the stock of equipment capital less OCA in each sector

KS = 45-order row vector showing the stock of plant and other structures in each sector

LAB = 45-order row vector showing total employment in each sector

LP_j = the standard measure of labor productivity growth for sector j

Q = 45-order row vector showing quality-adjusted labor input by industry

RD = 45-order row vector showing the stock of R&D capital by industry

X = 45-order column vector of gross output in constant (1992) dollars by sector

Z = 45-order row vector (Z_j is a Hicks-neutral TFP index that shifts the production function of sector j over time)

ϵ = the output elasticity of an input

π_j = the standard measure of TFP growth for sector j

Chapter 7

A = 45-order square matrix of technical interindustry input-output coefficients, where A_{ij} indicates the amount of input i (in 1992 dollars) required per unit of output j (in 1992 dollars)

B = 267-order column vector of total employment by occupation, where $B_i = \Sigma_j N_{ij}$

b = 45-order row vector showing the employment of a given class of workers (such as knowledge workers) as a share of total industry employment

D = 45-order column vector of domestic consumption in constant (1992) dollars by sector (household consumption, investment, and government expenditures)

E = 45-order column vector of exports in constant (1992) dollars by sector

e = 45-order column vector of export coefficients, where $e_i = E_i/\Sigma E_i$

1 = row or column vector of ones

I = identity matrix

K = 45-order row vector of capital coefficients, showing total capital per unit of output

L = 45-order row vector of labor coefficients, showing employment per unit of output, where $L_j = H_j/X_j$

$M = $ 45-order column vector of imports in constant (1992) dollars by sector

$m = $ 45-order column vector of import coefficients, where $m_i = M_i/\Sigma M_i$

$N = $ 267 by 45 employment matrix, where N_{ij} shows the total employment of occupation i in industry j and where $H_j = \Sigma_i N_{ij}$

$n = $ 267 by 45 employment coefficient matrix, showing employment by occupation per unit of output, where $n_{ij} = N_{ij}/X_j$

$q = 1(I - A)^{-1} = $ 45-order row vector showing the direct plus indirect output by industry in constant (1992) dollars generated per constant dollar of final output

$R = $ 45-order row vector showing R&D expenditures as a percentage of net sales by industry

$S = $ 45-order row vector showing average skill scores of workers by industry

$w = $ 45-order row vector showing average employee compensation in 1992 dollars by industry

$X = $ 45-order column vector of gross output in constant (1992) dollars by sector

$Y = D+E-M = $ 45-order column vector in constant (1992) dollars showing the final output by sector

$\gamma = K(I - A)^{-1} = $ 45-order row vector showing the direct plus indirect capital requirements per unit of output

$\lambda = L(I - A)^{-1} = $ 45-order row vector showing the direct plus indirect labor requirements per unit of output

$\rho = R(I - A)^{-1} = $ 45-order row vector showing the direct plus indirect R&D requirements per unit of output

Notes

1. The single-table format relies on the so-called BEA transfer method. See Kop Jansen and ten Raa (1990) for a discussion of this method and its associated methodological difficulties.
2. The allocation of the scrap sector was handled differently in the make-use framework of the 1967, 1977, and 1987 tables. See ten Raa and Wolff (1991) for details.
3. Sector numbers refer to the standard BEA 85-sector classification scheme. See, for example, U.S. Interindustry Economics Division (1984) for details.

References

Acs, Gregory, and Sheldon Danziger (1993), "Educational Attainment, Industrial Structure, and Male Earnings through the 1980s," *Journal of Human Resources,* Vol. 28, No. 3, Summer, pp. 618–648.

Adams, James D. (1997), "Technology, Trade, and Wages," NBER Working Paper No. 5940, February.

——— (1999), "The Structure of Firm R&D, the Factor Intensity of Production, and Skill Bias," *Review of Economics and Statistics,* Vol. 81, No. 3, August, pp. 499–510.

Adler, Paul (1986), "New Technologies, New Skills," *California Management Review,* Vol. 29, No. 1, Fall, pp. 9–28.

Allen, Steven G. (2001), "Technology and the Wage Structure," *Journal of Labor Economics,* Vol 19, No. 2, April, pp. 440–483.

Amable, Bruno, and Bart Verspagen (1995), "The Role of Technology in Market Share Dynamics," *Applied Economics,* Vol. 27, pp. 197–204.

Arrow, Kenneth (1962), "The Economic Implications of Learning by Doing," *Review of Economic Studies,* Vol. 29, No. 2, June, pp. 155–173.

——— (1973), "Higher Education as a Filter," *Journal of Public Economics,* Vol. 2, No. 3, pp. 193–216.

Atkinson, Anthony B., Lee Rainwater, and Timothy Smeeding (1995), *Income Distribution in Advanced Economies: The Evidence from the Luxembourg Income Study (LIS)* (Paris: OECD).

Autor, David, Lawrence F. Katz, and Alan B. Krueger (1998), "Computing Inequality: How Computers Changed the Labor Market," *Quarterly Journal of Economics,* Vol. 113, No. 4, November, pp. 1169–1214.

Autor, David, Frank Levy, and Richard J. Murnane (2003), "The Skill Content of Recent Technological Change: An Empirical Exploration," *Quarterly Journal of Economics,* Vol. 118, No. 4, November, pp. 1279–1334.

Bailey, Martin, and Robert Gordon (1988), "The Productivity Slowdown, Measurement Issues, and the Explosion in Computer Power," *Brookings Papers on Economic Activity,* Vol. 2, pp. 347–432.

Balassa, Béla (1965), "Trade Liberalization and 'Revealed' Comparative Advantage," *Manchester School,* Vol. 33, May, pp. 99–123.

Bartel, Ann P. (1998), "Formal Employee Training Programs and Their Impact on Labor Productivity: Evidence from a Human Resource Survey," NBER Working Paper No. 3026.

———, and Frank R. Lichtenberg (1987), "The Comparative Advantage of Educated Workers in Implementing New Technology," *Review of Economics and Statistics,* Vol. 69, February, pp. 1–11.

Bartel, Ann P., and Nachum Sicherman (1999), "Technological Change and Wages: An Interindustry Analysis," *Journal of Political Economy,* Vol. 107, No. 2, April, pp. 285–325.

Baumol, William J. (1967), "Macroeconomics of Unbalanced Growth: The Anatomy of Urban Crisis," *American Economic Review,* Vol. 57, June, pp. 415–426.

———, Sue Anne Batey Blackman, and Edward N. Wolff (1989), *Productivity and American Leadership: The Long View* (Cambridge: MIT Press).

Baumol, William J., and Edward N. Wolff (1999), "Technical Progress and Sharply Lengthened Time between Jobs," mimeo, October.

Becker, Gary S. (1964), *Human Capital: A Theoretical and Empirical Analysis* (New York: Columbia University Press and National Bureau of Economic Research).

——— (1975), *Human Capital: A Theoretical and Empirical Analysis,* 2d ed. (New York: Columbia University Press and National Bureau of Economic Research).

Bell, Daniel (1973), *The Coming of Post-industrial Society* (New York: Basic Books).

Beniger, James R. (1986), *The Control Revolution: Technological and Economic Origins of the Information Society* (Cambridge: Harvard University Press).

Berman, Eli, John Bound, and Zvi Griliches (1994), "Changes in the Demand for Skilled Labor within U.S. Manufacturing: Evidence from the Annual Survey of Manufactures," *Quarterly Journal of Economics,* Vol. 109, pp. 367–398.

Berman, Eli, John Bound, and Stephen Machin (1998), "Implications of Skill-Biased Technological Change: International Evidence," *Quarterly Journal of Economics,* Vol. 113, No. 4, November, pp. 1245–1279.

Bernard, Andrew B., and J. Bradford Jensen (1997), "Exporters, Skill Upgrading, and the Wage Gap," *Journal of International Economics,* Vol. 42, pp. 3–31.

——— (1999), "Exporting and Productivity," NBER Working Paper No. 7135, May.

——— (2000), "Understanding Increasing and Decreasing Wage Inequality," in Robert C. Feenstra, ed., *The Impact of International Trade on Wages* (Chicago: University of Chicago Press), pp. 227–268.

Berndt, Ernst R., and Catherine J. Morrison (1995), "High-Tech Capital For-

mation and Economic Performance in U.S. Manufacturing Industries,"
Journal of Econometrics, Vol. 69, pp. 9–43.

————, Ernst R., Chatherine J. Morrison, and Larry S. Rosenblum (1992),
"High-Tech Capital Formation and Labor Composition in U.S. Manufacturing Industries," NBER Working Paper No. 4010.

Bernstein, Jared (2000), "Two Cheers for the EITC," *American Prospect,* Vol.
11, No. 15, June 19–July 3, pp. 64–67.

Betts, Julian R. (1997), "The Skill Bias of Technological Change in Canadian
Manufacturing Industries," *Review of Economics and Statistics,* Vol. 79,
No. 1, February, pp. 146–150.

Bhagwati, Jagdish, and Vivek Dehejia (1993), "Freer Trade and Wages of the
Unskilled: Is Marx Striking Again?" Paper presented at the Conference
on the Influence of Trade on U.S. Wages, American Enterprise Institute,
Washington, D.C., September.

Bhagwati, Jagdish, and Marvin Kosters (1994), *Trade and Wages: Leveling
Wages Down?* (Washington, D.C.: AEI Press).

Bishop, John (1991), "Achievement, Test Scores, and Relative Wages," in
Marvin Kosters, ed., *Workers and Their Wages* (Washington, D.C.: AEI
Press), pp. 146–190.

Blackburn, McKinley (1990), "What Can Explain the Increase in Earnings
Inequality among Males?" *Industrial Relations,* Vol. 29, No. 3, Fall, pp.
441–456.

————, David Bloom, and Richard B. Freeman (1990), "The Declining Position of Less-Skilled American Males," in Gary Burtless, ed., *A Future of
Lousy Jobs?* (Washington, D.C.: Brookings Institution), pp. 31–67.

Blackburn, McKinley, and David Neumark (1993), "Omitted-Ability Bias and
the Increase in the Return to Schooling," *Journal of Labor Economics,* Vol.
11, No. 3, pp. 521–544.

Blanchflower, David G., Andrew J. Oswald, and Peter Sanfey (1996), "Wages,
Profits, and Rent-Sharing," *Quarterly Journal of Economics,* Vol. 111, No.
1, February, pp. 227–251.

Blau, Francine D., and Lawrence M. Kahn (1996), "International Differences
in Male Wage Inequality: Institutions versus Market Forces," *Journal of
Political Economy,* Vol. 104, No. 4, August, pp. 791–836.

Bluestone, Barry (1990), "The Impact of Schooling and Industrial Restructuring on Recent Trends in Wage Inequality in the United States," *American
Economic Review Papers and Proceedings,* Vol. 80, No. 2, May, pp. 303–
307.

————, and Bennett Harrison (1988a), "The Growth of Low-Wage Employment, 1963–86," *American Economic Review Papers and Proceedings,*
Vol. 78. No. 2, May, pp. 124–128.

———— (1988b), *The Great U-Turn: Corporate Restructuring and the Polar-
ization of America* (New York: Basic Books).

Borjas, George J., Richard B. Freeman, and Lawrence F. Katz (1992), "On the
Labor Market Effects of Immigration and Trade," in George J. Borjas and
Richard B. Freeman, eds., *Immigration and the Workforce: Economic Con-
sequences for the United States and Source Areas* (Chicago: University of
Chicago Press).

Borjas, George J., and Valerie A. Ramey (1994), "The Relationship between

Wage Inequality and International Trade," in Jeffrey H. Bergstrand, Thomas F. Cosimano, John W. Houck, and Richard G. Sheehan, eds., *The Changing Distribution of Income in an Open U.S. Economy* (Amsterdam: North-Holland), pp. 217–241.

——— (1995), "Foreign Competition, Market Power, and Wage Inequality: Theory and Evidence," *Quarterly Journal of Economics,* Vol. 110, pp. 1075–1110.

Bound, John, and George E. Johnson (1992), "Changes in the Structure of Wages in the 1980s: An Evaluation of Alternative Explanations," *American Economic Review,* Vol. 82, pp. 371–392.

Bowen, Harry P., Edward E. Leamer, and Leo Sveikauskas (1987), "Multi-country, Multifactor Tests of the Factor Abundance Theory," *American Economic Review,* Vol. 77, No. 5, December, pp. 791–809.

Braverman, Harry (1974), *Labor and Monopoly Capital* (New York: Monthly Review Press).

Bresnahan, Timothy (1999), "Computerization and Wage Dispersion: An Analytical Reinterpretation," *Economic Journal,* Vol. 109, No. 456, June, pp. F390–F415.

———, Eric Brynjolfsson, and Lorin Hitt (2002), "Information Technology, Workplace Organization, and the Demand for Skilled Labor: Firm-Level Evidence," *Quarterly Journal of Economics,* Vol. 117, February, pp. 339–376.

Brynjolfsson, Eric, and Lorin Hitt (1996), "Computers and Productivity Growth: Firm-Level Evidence," mimeo, MIT Sloan School, July.

——— (1998), "Information Technology and Organizational Design: Evidence from Micro Data," mimeo, MIT Sloan School, January.

Burtless, Gary (1995), "International Trade and the Rise in Earnings Inequality," *Journal of Economic Literature,* Vol. 33, June, pp. 800–816.

Cappelli, Peter (1993), "Are skill Requirements Rising? Evidence from Production and Clerical Jobs," *Industrial and Labor Relations Review,* Vol. 46, No. 3, April, pp. 515–530.

Card, David (1992), "The Effect of Unions on the Structure of Wages: A Longitudinal Analysis," *Econometrica,* Vol. 64, pp. 957–979.

———, and Alan B. Krueger (1995), *Myth and Measurement: The New Economics of the Minimum Wage* (Princeton: Princeton University Press).

Caves, Richard E. (1960), *Trade and Economic Structure: Models and Methods* (Cambridge: Harvard University Press).

Cawley, John, James Heckman, and Edward Vytlacil (1997), "Cognitive Ability and the Rising Return to Education," mimeo.

Chakraborty, Arreya, and Mark Kazarosian (1999), "Product Differentiation and the Use of Information Technology: Evidence from the Trucking Industry," NBER Working Paper No. 7222, July.

Council of Economic Advisers (1981), *Economic Report of the President* (Washington, D.C.: GPO).

——— (1999), *Economic Report of the President, 1999* (Washington, D.C.: GPO).

——— (2005), *Economic Report of the President, 2005* (Washington, D.C.: GPO).

Danziger, Sheldon, and Peter Gottschalk (1995), *America Unequal* (New York: Russell Sage Foundation).

David, Paul A. (1991), "Computer and Dynamo: The Modern Productivity Paradox in a Not-Too-Distant Mirror," in *Technology and Productivity: The Challenge for Economic Policy* (Paris: OECD), pp. 315–348.

Davis, Steven J. (1992), "Cross-Country Patterns of Change in Relative Wages," *NBER Macroeconomics Annual* (Cambridge: MIT Press), pp. 239–292.

———, and John Haltiwanger (1991), "Wage Dispersion between and within U.S. Manufacturing Plants, 1963–1986," *Brookings Papers on Economic Activity: Microeconomics*, pp. 115–180.

Deardorff, Alan V. (1982), "The General Validity of the Heckscher-Ohlin Theorem," *American Economic Review*, Vol. 72, pp. 683–694.

Denison, Edward F. (1962), *The Sources of Economic Growth in the United States and the Alternatives Before Us*, CED Supplementary Paper No. 13 (New York, NY: Committee for Economic Development).

——— (1979), *Accounting for Slower Economic Growth: The United States in the 1970s* (Washington, D.C.: Brookings Institution).

——— (1983), "The Interruption of Productivity Growth in the United States," *Economic Journal*, Vol. 93, pp. 56–77.

Denny, Michael, and Melvyn Fuss (1983), "The Effects of Factor Prices and Technological Change on the Occupational Demand for Labor: Evidence from Canadian Telecommunications," *Journal of Human Resources*, Vol. 17, No. 2, pp. 161–176.

Dickens, William T., and Lawrence F. Katz (1987), "Interindustry Wage Differences and Industry Characteristics," in Kevin Lang and Jonathan Leonard, eds., *Unemployment and the Structure of Labor Markets* (Oxford: Basil Blackwell), pp. 48–89.

DiNardo, John E., Nicole M. Fortin, and Thomas Lemieux (1996), "Labor Market Institutions and the Distribution of Wages, 1973–1992: A Semi-Parametric Approach," *Econometrica*, Vol. 64, No. 5, September, pp. 1001–1044.

DiNardo, John E., and Thomas Lemieux (1997), "Diverging Male Wage Inequality in the United States and Canada, 1981–1988: Do Institutions Explain the Difference?" *Industrial and labor Relations Review*, Vol. 50, No. 4, July, pp. 629–651.

DiNardo, John E., and Jorn-Steffen Pischke (1997), "The Returns to Computer Use Revisited: Have Pencils Changed the Wage Structure Too?" *Quarterly Journal of Economics*, Vol. 112, No. 1, pp. 291–303.

Doeringer, Peter (1991), *Turbulence in the American Workplace* (New York: Oxford University Press).

———, and Michael J. Piore (1971), *Internal Labor Markets and Manpower Analysis* (Lexington, Mass.: D. C. Heath).

Dollar, David, and Edward N. Wolff (1993), *Competitiveness, Convergence, and International Specialization* (Cambridge: MIT Press).

Doms, Mark, Timothy Dunne, and Kenneth B. Troske (1997), "Workers, Wages, and Technology," *Quarterly Journal of Economics*, Vol. 107, No. 1, pp. 253–290.

Dosi, Giovanni, Keith Pavitt, and Luc Soete (1990), *The Economics of Technical Change and International Trade* (London: Harvester Wheatsheaf).

Dunlop, John (1957), "Wage Contours," in George W. Taylor and Frank C. Pierson, eds., *New Concepts of Wage Determination* (New York: McGraw-Hill).

Dunne, Timothy, Lucia Foster, John Haltiwanger, and Kenneth Troske (2004), "Wage and Productivity Dispersion in U.S. Manufacturing: The Role of Computer Investment," *Journal of Labor Economics,* Vol. 22, No. 2, pp. 347–429.

Dunne, Timothy, and John A. Schmitz Jr. (1992), "Wages, Employer Size, Wage Premia, and Employment Structure: Their Relationship to Advanced-Technology Usage in U.S. Manufacturing Establishments," U.S. Department of Commerce, Center for Economic Studies Discussion Paper CES 92–16, December.

Eakin, Kelly (1994), "Union Algebra: Unionization, Productivity, and Labor Intensity Restrictions," *Journal of Productivity Analysis,* Vol. 5, pp. 81–98.

Engelbrecht, Hans-Jürgen (1996), "The Composition of the Human Capital Stock and the Factor Content of Trade: Evidence from West(ern) Germany," *Economic System Research,* Vol. 8, No. 3, pp. 271–297.

Fagerberg, Jan E. (1988), "International Competitiveness," *Economic Journal,* Vol. 98, June, pp. 355–374.

Falk, Martin, and Karja Seim (1999), "The Impact of Information Technology on High-skilled Labour in Services: Evidence from Firm Level Panel Data," Mannheim, Germany, ZEW Discussion Paper No. 99–58

Feenstra, Robert C., and Gordon H. Hanson (1995), "Foreign Investment, Outsourcing, and Relative Wages," NBER Working Paper No. 5121, May.

——— (1997), "Productivity Measurement and the Impact of Trade and Technology on Wages: Estimates for the U.S., 1972–1990," NBER Working Paper No. 6052, June.

——— (1999), "The Impact of Outsourcing and High-technology Capital on Wages: Estimates for the United States, 1979–1990," *Quarterly Journal of Economics,* Vol. 114, No. 3, August, pp. 907–940.

Ferguson, William D. (1996), "Explaining the Rising Wage-productivity Gap of the 1980s: Effects of Declining Employment and Unionization," *Review of Radical Political Economics,* Vol. 28, No. 2, pp. 77–115.

Fortin, Nicole M., and Thomas Lemieux (1997), "Institutional Changes and Rising Wage Inequality: Is There a Linkage?" *Journal of Economic Perspectives,* Vol. 11, Spring, pp. 75–96.

Frank, Robert, and Philip Cook (1995), *The Winner-take-all Society* (New York: Free Press).

Franke, R. H. (1989), "Technological Revolutions and Productivity Decline: The Case of U.S. Banks," in T. Forester, ed., *Computers in the Human Context: Information Technology, Productivity, and People* (Cambridge: MIT Press).

Freeman, Christopher (1987), "Information Technology and the Change in the Techno-Economic Paradigm," in Christopher Freeman and Luc Soete, eds., *Technical Change and Full Employment* (Oxford: Basil Blackwell).

Freeman, Richard B. (1976), *The Over-educated American* (New York: Academic Press).

——— (1993), "How Much Has De-Unionization Contributed to the Rise in Male Earnings Inequality?" in Sheldon Danziger and Peter Gottschalk, eds., *Uneven Tides: Rising Inequality in America* (New York: Russell Sage Foundation), pp. 133–163.

——— (1995), "Are Your Wages Set in Beijing?" *Journal of Economic Perspectives,* Vol. 9, No. 3, pp. 15–32.

———, and Lawrence F. Katz (1991), "Industrial Wage and Employment Determination in an Open Economy," in John W. Abowd and Richard B. Freeman, eds., *Immigration, Trade, and Labor Markets* (Chicago: NBER), pp. 235–259.

Freeman, Richard B., and James L. Medoff (1984), *What Do Unions Do?* (New York: Basic Books).

Gaston, Noel, and Daniel Treffler (1994), "Protection, Trade, and Wages: Evidence from U.S. Manufacturing," *Industrial and Labor Relations Review,* Vol. 47, No. 4, July, pp. 574–593.

Gera, Sundera, Wulung Gu, and Frank Lee (1999), "Information Technology and Productivity Growth: An Empirical Analysis for Canada and the United States," *Canadian Journal of Economics,* Vol. 32, No. 2, April, pp. 384–407.

Gill, Indermit S. (1989), "Technological Change, Education, and Obsolescence of Human Capital: Some Evidence for the U.S." Mimeo, November.

Gittleman, Maury (1992), "Changes in the Rate of Return to Education in the U.S., 1973–1987," Ph.D. diss., New York University.

——— (1994), "Earnings in the 1980s: An Occupational Perspective," *Monthly Labor Review,* July, pp. 16–27.

Glynn, Andrew (1997), "Low Pay and Employment Performance," Oxford University Working Paper.

Goldin, Claudia, and Lawrence F. Katz (1998), "The Origins of Technology-Skill Complementarity," *Quarterly Journal of Economics,* Vol. 113, August, pp. 693–732.

Gordon, David M. (1996), *Fat and Mean: The Corporate Squeeze of Working Americans and the Myth of Managerial "Downsizing"* (New York: Free Press).

Griliches, Zvi (1969), "Capital-Skill Complementarity," *Review of Economics and Statistics,* Vol. 51, November, pp. 465–468.

——— (1970), "Notes on the Role of Education in Production Functions and Growth Accounting," in W. Lee Hansen, ed., *Education, Income, and Human Capital,* Vol. 35: *Studies in Income and Wealth* (New York: National Bureau of Economic Research and Columbia University Press), pp. 71–115.

——— (1979), "Issues in Assessing the Contribution of Research and Development to Productivity Growth," *Bell Journal of Economics,* Vol. 10, No. 1, Spring, pp. 92–116.

——— (1980), "R&D and the Productivity Slowdown," *American Economic Review,* Vol. 70, No. 2, May, pp. 343–347.

——— (1992), "The Search for R&D Spillovers," *Scandinavian Journal of Economics,* Vol. 94, pp. 29–47.

——— (1996), "Education, Human Capital, and Growth: A Personal Perspective," NBER Working Paper No. 5426, January.

Grogger, Jeff, and Eric Eide (1996), "Changes in College Skills and the Rise in the College Wage Premium," *Journal of Human Resources,* Vol. 30, No. 2, pp. 280–301.

Groshen, Erica (1991a), "Source of Intra-Industry Wage Dispersion: How Much Do Employers Matter?" *Quarterly Journal of Economics,* Vol. 106, No. 3, February, pp. 869–884.

——— (1991b), "Rising Inequality in a Salary Survey: Another Piece of the Puzzle," Federal Reserve Bank of Cleveland Working Paper No. 9121.

———, and David I. Levine (1998), "The Rise and Decline (?) of U.S. Internal Labor Markets," Federal Reserve Bank of New York Research Paper No. 9819.

Grubb, W. Norton, and Robert H. Wilson (1989), "Sources of Increased Inequality in Wages and Salaries, 1960–1980," *Monthly Labor Review,* April, pp. 3–13.

Handel, Michael (1988), "Computers and the Wage Structure," mimeo, Harvard University, January.

Head, Simon (2003), *The New Ruthless Economy: Work and Power in the Digital Age* (New York: Oxford University Press).

Heckscher, Eli. (1919), "The Effect of Foreign Trade on the Distribution of Income." Reprinted in 1949 in H. S. Ellis and L. A. Metzler, eds., *Readings in the Theory of International Trade* (Homewood, Ill.: Richard D. Irwin), pp. 272–300.

Hernstein, Richard, and Charles Murray (1994), *The Bell Curve* (New York: Basic Books).

Hirsch, Barry T. (1991), *Labor Unions and the Economic Performance of Firms* (Kalamazoo, Mich.: W.E. Upjohn Institute).

———, and Albert N. Link (1984), "Unions, Productivity, and Productivity Growth," *Journal of Labor Research,* Vol. 5, No. 1, Winter, pp. 29–37.

Hirsch, Barry T., and David A. Macpherson (1993), "Union Membership and Coverage Files from the Current Population Surveys: Note," *Industrial and Labor Relations Review,* Vol. 46, No. 3, April 1993, pp. 574–578.

Hirschhorn, Larry (1986), *Beyond Mechanization* (Cambridge: MIT Press).

Horowitz, M., and I. Hernstadt (1966), "Changes in Skill Requirements of Occupations in Selected Industries," in National Commission on Technology, Automation, and Economic Progress, *The Employment Impact of Technological Change,* Appendix, Volume 2 to *Technology and American Economy* (Washington D.C.: GPO), pp. 223–287.

Horrigon, Michael W., and Ronald Mincy (1993), "The Minimum Wage and Earnings and Income Inequality," in Sheldon Danziger and Peter Gottschalk, eds., *Uneven Tides: Rising Inequality in America* (New York: Russell Sage Foundation).

Howell, David R. (1997), "Institutional Failure and the American Worker: The Collapse of Low-Skill Wages," *Public Policy Brief,* Jerome Levy Economics Institute.

———, and Edward N. Wolff (1991a). "Trends in the Growth and Distribution of Skills in the U.S. Workplace, 1960–1985." *Industrial and Labor Relations Review,* Vol. 44, No. 3, April, pp. 486–502.

——— (1991b). "Skills, Bargaining Power, and Rising Interindustry Wage Inequality since 1970," *Review of Radical Political Economics,* Vol. 23, Nos. 1&2, Spring & Summer, pp. 30–37.

————— (1992), "Technical Change and the Demand for Skills by U.S. Industries," *Cambridge Journal of Economics,* Vol. 16, pp. 127–146.

Hubbard, Thomas N. (2001), "Information, Decisions, and Productivity: On-board Computers and Capacity Utilization in Trucking," mimeo, March 26.

Jacobs, Eva E., ed. (1998), *Handbook of U.S. Labor Statistics,* Second Edition (Lanham, Md.: Bernan Press).

Jaffe, Adam B. (1986), "Technology Opportunity and Spillovers of R&D: Evidence from Firms' Patents, Profits, and Market Value," *American Economic Review,* Vol. 76, pp. 984–1001.

Jencks, Christopher (1972), *Inequality: A Reassessment of the Effect of Family and Schooling in America* (New York: Basic Books).

————— (1979), *Who Gets Ahead?* (New York: Basic Books).

—————, and Meredith Phillips (1998), "America's Next Achievement Test," *American Prospect,* September–October, No. 40, pp. 44–53.

Johnson, George E., and Frank P. Stafford (1993), "International Competition and Real Wages," *American Economic Review Papers and Proceedings,* Vol. 83, No. 2, May, pp. 127–130.

Jorgenson, Dale W., and Barbara M. Fraumeni (1993), "Education and Productivity Growth in a Market Economy," *Atlantic Economic Journal,* Vol. 21, No. 2, pp. 1–25.

Jorgenson, Dale W., Gollop, Frank M., and Fraumeni, Barbara (1987), *Productivity and U.S. Economic Growth* (Cambridge: Harvard University Press).

Jorgenson, Dale W., and Kevin J. Stiroh (1999), "Information Technology and Growth," *American Economic Review,* Vol. 89, No. 2, May, pp. 109–115.

————— (2000), "Raising the Speed Limit: U.S. Economic Growth in the Information Age," *Brooking Papers on Economic Activity,* No. 1, pp. 125–211.

Juhn, Chinhui (1999), "Wage Inequality and Demand for Skill: Evidence from Five Decades," *Industrial and Labor Relations Review,* Vol. 52, No. 3, April, pp. 424–443.

—————, Kevin M. Murphy, and Brooks Pierce (1993), "Wage Inequality and the Returns to Skill," *Journal of Political Economy,* Vol. 101, pp. 410–442.

Karoly, Lynn A. (1992), "Changes in the Distribution of Individual Earnings in the United States from 1967 to 1986," *Review of Economics and Statistics,* Vol. 74, No. 1, February, pp. 107–115.

—————, and Jacob Alex Klerman (1994), "Using Regional Data to Reexamine the Contribution of Demographic and Sectoral Changes to Increasing U.S. Wage Inequality," in Jeffrey H. Bergstrand, Thomas F. Cosimano, John W. Houck, and Richard G. Sheehan, eds., *The Changing Distribution of Income in an Open U.S. Economy* (Amsterdam: North-Holland), pp. 183–216.

Katz, Arnold J., and Shelby W. Herman (1997), "Improved Estimates of Fixed Reproducible Tangible Wealth, 1929–1995," *Survey of Current Business,* Vol. 77, May, pp. 69–92.

Katz, Lawrence F., Gary W. Loveman, and David G. Blanchflower (1993), "A Comparison of Changes in the Structure of Wages in Four OECD Countries," NBER Working Paper No. 4297, March.

Katz, Lawrence F., and Kevin M. Murphy (1992), "Changes in Relative Wages, 1963–1987: Supply and Demand Factors," *Quarterly Journal of Economics,* Vol. 107, No. 1, pp. 35–78.

Keefe, Jeffrey H. (1991), "Numerically Controlled Machine Tools and Worker Skills," *Industrial and Labor Relations Review,* Vol. 44, No. 3, April, pp. 503–519.

Keesing, Donald B. (1965), "Labor Skills and International Trade: Evaluating Many Trade Flows with a Single Measuring Device," *Review of Economics and Statistics,* Vol. 47, No. 3, August, pp. 287–294.

Kokkelenberg, Edward C., and Donna R. Sockell (1985), "Union Membership in the United States, 1973–1981," *Industrial and Labor Relations Review,* Vol. 38, No. 4, July, pp. 497–543.

Kop Jansen, Pieter, and Thijs ten Raa (1990), "The Choice of Model in the Construction of Input-Output Matrices," *International Economic Review,* Vol. 31, No. 1, pp. 213–227.

Kravis, Irving B. (1956), "'Availability' and Other Influences on the Commodity Composition of Trade," *Journal of Political Economy,* Vol. 64, pp. 143–155.

Krueger, Alan B. (1993), "How Computers Have Changed the Wage Structure: Evidence from Microdata," *Quarterly Journal of Economics,* Vol. 108, February, pp. 33–60.

——, and Lawrence H. Summers (1987), "Reflections on the Inter-Industry Wage Structure," in K. Lang and J. Leonard, eds., *Unemployment and the Structure of Labor Markets* (Oxford: Basil Blackwell), pp. 17–47.

—— (1988), "Efficiency Wages and the Inter-industry Wage Structure," *Econometrica,* Vol. 56, March, pp. 259–294.

Krugman, Paul A. (1995), "Technology, Trade, and Factor Prices," NBER Working Paper No. 5355, November.

——, and Robert Z. Lawrence (1994), "Trade, Jobs, and Wages," *Scientific American,* April, pp. 44–49.

Lawrence, Robert Z., and Matthew J. Slaughter (1993), "Trade and U.S. Wages: Great Sucking Sound or Small Hiccup?" *Brookings Papers on Economic Activity: Microeconomics,* No. 2, pp. 161–210.

Lawson, Anne M. (1997), "Benchmark Input-output Accounts for the U.S. Economy, 1992," *Survey of Current Business,* Vol. 77, No. 11, November, pp. 36–83.

Lawson, Anne M., and Teske, D. A. (1994), "Benchmark Input-Output Accounts for the U.S. Economy, 1987," *Survey of Current Business,* Vol. 74, April, pp. 73–115.

Leamer, Edward E. (1984), *Sources of International Comparative Advantage* (Cambridge: MIT Press).

—— (1992), "Wage Effects of a U.S.-Mexican Free Trade Agreement," NBER Working Paper No. 3991.

—— (1996), "Wage Inequality from International Competition and Technological Change: Theory and Country Experience," *American Economic Review Papers and Proceedings,* Vol. 86, No. 2, May, pp. 309–314.

Lee, B., and W. Shu (1997), "Where Has Information Technology Productivity Been Buried?" *Proceedings of the Fourth International Decision Sciences Institute Meeting,* Sydney, Australia, July.

Lee, Chinkook, and Gerald Schluter (1999), "Effect of Trade on the Demand for Skilled and Unskilled Workers," *Economic System Research,* Vol. 11, No. 1, pp. 49–65.

Lee, David S. (1999), "Wage Inequality in the United States during the 1980s: Rising Dispersion or Falling Minimum Wage?" *Quarterly Journal of Economics,* Vol. 114, August, pp. 977–1023.

Lehr, William, and Frank Lichtenberg (1998), "Computer Use and Productivity Growth in U.S. Federal Government Agencies, 1987–1992," *Journal of Industrial Economics,* Vol. 44, No. 2, June, pp. 257–279.

———— (1999), "Information Technology and Its Impact on Productivity: Firm-Level Evidence from Government and Private Data Sources, 1977–1993," *Canadian Journal of Economics,* Vol. 32, No. 2, April, pp. 335–362.

Leontief, Wassily (1953), "Domestic Production and Foreign Trade: The Capital Position Re-examined," *Proceedings of the American Philosophical Society,* Vol. 97, pp. 332–349.

———— (1956), "Factor Proportions and the Structure of American Trade: Further Theoretical and Empirical Analysis," *Review of Economics and Statistics,* Vol. 38, No. 4, November, pp. 386–407.

———— (1964), "International Comparisons of Factor Cost and Factor Use," *American Economic Review,* Vol. 54, pp. 335–345.

———— (1982), "The Distribution of Work and Income," *Scientific American,* Vol. 247, No. 3, pp. 188–204.

———— (1983), "Technological Advance, Economic Growth, and the Distribution of Income," *Population and Development Review,* Vol. 9, No. 3, pp. 403–410.

Lerman, Robert I. (1997), "Is Earnings Inequality Really Increasing?" Mimeo, Urban Institute, Washington, D.C.

Leslie, Derek (1985), "Real Wage Growth, Technical Change, and Competition in the Labor Market," *Review of Economics and Statistics,* Vol. 67, No. 4, November, pp. 640–647.

Levy, Frank, and Richard Murnane (1992), "U.S. Earnings Levels and Earnings Inequality: A Review of Recent Trends and Proposed Explanations," *Journal of Economic Literature,* Vol. 30, No. 3, September, pp. 1333–1381.

———— (1996a), *Teaching the New Basic Skills* (New York: Free Press).

———— (1996b), "With What Skills Are Computers a Complement?" *American Economic Review Papers and Proceedings,* Vol. 86, No. 2, May, pp. 258–262.

Levy, Frank, and Richard Murnane, John B. Willett (1995), "The Growing Importance of Cognitive Skills in Wage Determination," *Review of Economics and Statistics,* Vol. 77, No. 2, May, pp. 251–266.

Lichtenberg, Frank R. (1995), "The Output Contribution of Computer Equipment and Personnel: A Firm-level Analysis," *Economics of Innovation and New Technology,* Vol. 3, No. 4, pp. 201–217.

Link, Albert N. (1981), "Basic Research and Productivity Increase in Manufacturing: Some Additional Evidence," *American Economic Review,* Vol. 71, December, pp. 1111–1112.

Loveman, G. W. (1988), "An Assessment of the Productivity Impact of Information Technologies," in *Management in the 1990s* (Cambridge: MIT Press).

Lynch, Lisa M., and Sandra E. Black (1998), "Beyond the Incidence of Employer-Provided Training," *Industrial and Labor Relations Review,* Vol. 52, No. 1, October, pp. 64–81.

Machlup, Fritz (1962), *The Production and Distribution of Knowledge in the United States* (Princeton: Princeton University Press).

Maddison, Angus (1982), *Phases of Capitalist Development* (Oxford: Oxford University Press).

——— (1987), "Growth and Slowdown in Advanced Capitalist Economies: Techniques of Quantitative Assessment," *Journal of Economic Literature,* Vol. 25, pp. 649–706.

——— (1991), *Dynamic Forces in Capitalist Development* (Oxford: Oxford University Press).

Mairesse, Jacques, and Pierre Mohnen (1990), "Recherche-développpment et productivité: un sorvol de la littérature économétrique," *Economie et Statistique,* Vol. 237–238, pp. 99–108.

Mansfield, Edwin (1965), "Rates of Return from Industrial Research and Development," *American Economic Review,* Vol. 55, No. 2, May, pp. 310–322.

——— (1980), "Basic Research and Productivity Increase in Manufacturing," *American Economic Review,* Vol. 70, No. 5, December, pp. 863–873.

Masters, Stanley H. (1969), "An Interindustry Analysis of Wages and Plant Size," *Review of Economics and Statistics,* Vol. 51, No. 3, August, pp. 341–345.

Mattila, J. Peter (1984), "Determinants of Male School Enrollments: A Time-Series Analysis," *Review of Economics and Statistics,* Vol. 64, No. 2, May, pp. 242–251.

Milkman, Ruth, and Cydney Pullman (1991), "Technological Change in an Auto Assembly Plant: The Impact on Workers' Tasks and Skills," *Work and Occupations,* Vol. 18, No. 2, May, pp. 123–147.

Miller, Ann R., Donald J. Treiman, Pamela S. Cain, and Patricia A. Roos (1980), *Work, Jobs and Occupations: A Critical Review of the Dictionary of Occupational Titles* (Washington, D.C.: National Academy Press).

Mincer, Jacob (1974), *Schooling, Experience, and Earnings* (New York: NBER).

——— (1991), "Human Capital, Technology, and the Wage Structure: What Do the Time Series Show?" NBER Working Paper No. 3581, January.

Mincer, Jacob, and Yoshio Higuchi (1988), "Wage Structures and Labor Turnover in the United States and Japan," *Journal of the Japanese and International Economics,* Vol. 2, pp. 97–113.

Mishel, Lawrence, Jared Bernstein, and John Schmitt (1997), "Did Technology Have Any Effect on the Growth of Wage Inequality in the 1980s and 1990s?" Report, Economic Policy Institute, Washington, D.C., December.

Mitrusi, Andrew, and James Poterba (2000), "The Changing Importance of Income and Payroll Taxes on U.S. Families," mimeo, October.

Moberg, David (2000), "Martha Jernegons's New Shoes," *American Prospect,* Vol. 11, No. 15, June 19–July 3, pp. 50–53.

Mohnen, Pierre (1992), *The Relationship between R&D and Productivity Growth in Canada and Other Major Industrialized Countries* (Ottawa: Canada Communications Group).

Murphy, Kevin, Andre Schleifer, and Robert W. Vishny (1991), "Allocation of Talent: Implications for Growth," *Quarterly Journal of Economics,* Vol. 106, pp. 503–530.

Murphy, Kevin M., and Finis Welch (1991), "The Role of International Trade in Wage Differentials," in Marvin Kosters, ed., *Workers and Their Wages* (Washington, D.C.: AEI Press), pp. 39–69.

——— (1993a), "Industrial Change and the Rising Importance of Skill," in Sheldon Danziger and Peter Gottschalk, eds., *Uneven Tides: Rising Inequality in America* (New York: Russell Sage Foundation), pp. 101–132.

——— (1993b), "Occupational Change and the Demand for Skill, 1940–1990," *American Economic Review Papers and Proceedings,* Vol. 83, No. 2, May, pp. 122–126.

National Science Board (1998), *Science and Engineering Indicators* (Arlington, Va.: National Science Foundation), NSB 98–1.

National Science Foundation, *Research and Development in Industry* (Washington, D.C.: GPO), various years.

Nelson, Richard R. (1964), "Aggregate Production Functions and Medium-Range Growth Projections," *American Economic Review,* Vol. 54, September, pp. 575–605.

———, and Edmund S. Phelps (1966), "Investment in Humans, Technological Diffusion, and Economic Growth," *American Economic Review,* Vol. 61, No. 2, pp. 69–75.

Neumark, David, Mark Schweitzer, and William Wascher (2004), "Minimum Wage Effects throughout the Wage Distribution," *Journal of Human Resources,* Vol. 39, No. 2, pp. 425–450.

Noble, David F. (1984) *Forces of Production* (New York: Oxford University Press).

Ohlin, Bertil (1933), *Interregional and International Trade* (Cambridge: Harvard University Press.

Oliner, Stephen, and Daniel Sichel (1994), "Computers and Output Growth Revisited: How Big Is the Puzzle?" *Brookings Papers on Economic Activity,* Vol. 2, pp. 273–334.

——— (2000), "The Resurgence of Growth in the Late 1990s: Is Information Technology the Story?" *Journal of Economic Perspectives,* Vol. 14, Fall, pp. 3–22.

Osterman, Paul (1986), "The Impact of Computers on the Employment of Clerks and Managers," *Industrial and Labor Relations Review,* Vol. 39, pp. 163–189.

——— (1994), "How Common Is Workplace Transformation and Who Adopts It?" *Industrial and Labor Relations Review,* 47, No. 2, January, pp. 173–187.

——— (1995), "Skill, Training, and Work Organization in American Establishments," *Industrial Relations,* Vol. 34, No. 2, April, pp. 125–146.

Parsons, Daniel J., Calvin C. Gotlieb, and Michael Denny (1993), "Productivity and Computers in Canadian Banking," *Journal of Productivity Analysis,* Vol. 4, June, pp. 91–110.

Porat, Marc U. (1977), *The Information Economy: Definition and Measurement,* Office of Telecommunications Special Publication 77–12, U.S. Department of Commerce (Washington, D.C.: GPO), May.

Posner, M. (1961), "International Trade and Technical Change," *Oxford Economic Papers,* Vol. 13, No. 3, October, pp. 323–341.

ten Raa, Thijs, and Edward N. Wolff (1991), "Secondary Products and the Measurement of Productivity Growth," *Regional Science and Urban Economics,* Vol. 21, No. 4, December, pp. 581–615.

Reich, Michael (1998), "Are U.S. Corporations Top-Heavy? Managerial Ratios in Advanced Capitalist Countries," *Review of Radical Political Economics,* Vol. 30, No. 30, September, pp. 33–45.

Reich, Robert (1991), *The Work of Nations: Preparing Ourselves for Twenty-first Century Capitalism* (New York: Knopf).

Ricardo, David (1821), *On the Principles of Political Economy and Taxation,* 3d ed., in Piero Sraffa, ed. (1951), *The Works and Correspondences of David Ricardo,* Vol. 1 (Cambridge: Cambridge University Press).

Richardson, D. J. (1995), "Income Inequality and Trade: How to Think, What to Conclude?" *Journal of Economic Perspectives,* Vol. 9, pp. 33–55.

Ritz, Philip M. (1979), "The Input-Output Structure of the U.S. Economy, 1972," *Survey of Current Business,* Vol. 59, No. 2, February, pp. 34–72.

————, Eugene P. Roberts, and Paula C. Young (1979), "Dollar Value Tables of the 1972 Input-Output Study," *Survey of Current Business,* Vol. 59, No. 4, April, pp. 51–72.

Rubin, Michael Rogers, and Mary Taylor Huber (1986), *The Knowledge Industry in the United States, 1960–1980* (Princeton: Princeton University Press).

Rumberger, Russell W. (1981), "The Changing Skill Requirements of Jobs in the U.S. Economy," *Industrial and Labor Relations Review,* Vol. 34, No. 4, July, pp. 578–591.

Sachs, Jeffrey D., and Howard J. Shatz (1994), "Trade and Jobs in U.S. Manufacturing," *Brookings Papers on Economic Activity: Microeconomics,* No. 1, pp. 1–84.

Samuelson, Paul A. (1948), "International Trade and the Equalization of Factor Price," *Economic Journal,* Vol. 58, pp. 163–184.

Schultz, Theodore W. (1960), "Capital Formation by Education," *Journal of Political Economy,* Vol. 68, No. 6, pp. 571–583.

———— (1961), "Investment in Human Capital," *American Economic Review,* Vol. 51, No. 1, pp. 1–17.

———— (1971), *Investment in Human Capital: The Role of Education and of Research* (New York: Free Press).

Seidman, Laurence S. (2001), "Assets and the Tax Code," in Thomas M. Shapiro and Edward N. Wolff, eds., *Assets for the Poor: The Benefits of Spreading Asset Ownership* (New York: Russell Sage Foundation), pp. 324–356.

Shaiken, Harley (1984), *Work Transformed: Automation and Labor in the Computer Age* (New York: Holt, Rinehart, and Winston).

Siegel, Donald (1997), "The Impact of Computers on Manufacturing Productivity Growth: A Multiple-Indicators, Multiple-Causes Approach," *Review of Economics and Statistics,* Vol. 79, February, pp. 68–78.

————, and Zvi Griliches (1992), "Purchased Services, Outsourcing, Computers, and Productivity in Manufacturing," in Zvi Griliches, ed., *Output Measurement in the Service Sector* (Chicago: University of Chicago Press).

Slichter, Sumner (1950), "Notes on the Structure of Wages," *Review of Economics and Statistics,* Vol. 22, February, pp. 80–89.

Spence, Michael (1973), "Job Market Signaling," *Quarterly Journal of Economics,* Vol. 87, No. 3, pp. 355–374.

Spenner, Kenneth I. (1983),"Deciphering Prometheus: Temporal Changes in Work Content," *American Sociological Review,* Vol. 48, December, pp. 824–837.

——— (1988) "Technological Change, Skill Requirements, and Education: The Case for Uncertainty," in Richard M. Cyert and David C. Mowery, eds., *The Impact of Technological Change on Employment and Economic Growth* (Cambridge, Mass.: Ballinger), pp. 131–184.

Steindel, Charles (1992), "Manufacturing Productivity and High-Tech Investment," *Federal Reserve Bank of New York Quarterly Review,* Vol. 17, December, pp. 39–47.

Stiroh, Kevin J. (1998), "Computers, Productivity, and Input Substitution," *Economic Inquiry,* Vol. 36, No. 2, April, pp. 175–191.

——— (2002), "Are ICT Spillovers Driving the New Economy?" *Review of Income and Wealth,* Vol. 48, No. 1, March, pp. 33–58.

Trefler, Daniel (1993), "International Factor Price Differences: Leontief Was Right!" *Journal of Political Economy,* Vol. 101, pp. 961–987.

——— (1995), "The Case of Missing Trade and Other Mysteries," *American Economic Review,* Vol. 85, pp. 1029–1046.

U.S. Bureau of the Census (1978), *Historical Statistics of the U.S.: Colonial Times to 1970,* Bicentennial Edition, Part 2 (Washington, D.C.: GPO).

——— (1997), *Statistical Abstract of the United States,* 113th ed. (Washington, D.C.: GPO).

——— (1999), *Statistical Abstract of the United States,* 115th ed. (Washington, D.C.: GPO).

——— (2003), *Statistical Abstract of the United States,* 119th ed. (Washington, D.C.: GPO).

U.S. Bureau of Labor Statistics (1979a), *Handbook of Labor Statistics 1978,* Bulletin 2000 (Washington, D.C.: GPO).

——— (1979b), *Time Series Data for Input-Output Industries,* Bulletin 2018 (Washington, D.C.: GPO).

——— (1990), *Handbook of Labor Statistics 1989,* Bulletin 2340 (Washington, D.C.: GPO).

——— (1993), *Labor Composition and U.S. Productivity Growth, 1948–1990,* Bulletin 2426, December (Washington, D.C.: GPO).

U.S. Council of Economic Advisers (various years), *Economic Report of the President* (Washington, D.C.: GPO).

U.S. Department of Education, National Center for Educational Statistics (1996), *Digest of Education Statistics,* NCES 96–133 (Washington, D.C.: GPO).

U.S. Department of Labor (1977), *Dictionary of Occupational Titles,* 4th ed. (Washington, D.C.: GPO).

——— (1994), *Report of the American Workplace* (Washington, D.C.: GPO).

U.S. House of Representatives, Committee on Ways and Means (1994), *Overview of Entitlement Programs: 1994 Green Book* (Washington, D.C.: GPO), July 15.

U.S. Interindustry Economics Division (1969), "The Input-Output Structure of the U.S. Economy: 1963," *Survey of Current Business*, Vol. 49, No. 11, November.

——— (1974), "The Input-Output Structure of the U.S. Economy: 1967," *Survey of Current Business*, Vol. 54, No. 2, February, pp. 24–56.

——— (1984), "The Input-Output Structure of the U.S. Economy: 1977," *Survey of Current Business*, Vol. 64, No. 5, May, pp. 42–84.

——— (1991), "Benchmark Input-Output Accounts for the U.S. Economy, 1982," *Survey of Current Business*, Vol. 71, No. 7, July, pp. 30–71.

Vanek, J. (1968), "The Factor Proportions Theory: The *N*-factor Case," *Kyklos*, Vol. 21, No. 4, pp. 749–756.

Vernon, R. (1966), "International Investment and International Trade in the Product Cycle," *Quarterly Journal of Economics*, Vol. 80, pp. 190–207.

——— (1979), "The Product-cycle Hypothesis in a New International Environment," *Oxford Bulletin of Economics and Statistics*, Vol. 41, pp. 255–267.

Verspagen, Bart, and K. Wakelin (1997), "Trade and Technology from a Schumperterian Perspective," *International Review of Applied Economics*, Vol. 11, No. 2, May, pp. 181–194.

Welch, Finis R. (1970), "Education in Production," *Journal of Political Economy*, Vol. 78, January–February, pp. 35–59.

White, H. (1980), "A Heteroskedasticity-consistent Covariance Matrix Estimator and a Direct Test for Heteroskedasticity," *Econometrica*, Vol. 48, May, pp. 817–838.

Wolff, Edward N. (1991), "Productivity Growth, Capital Intensity, and Skill Levels in the U.S. Insurance Industry, 1948–1986," *Geneva Papers on Risk and Insurance*, Vol. 16, No. 59, April, pp. 173–190.

——— (1995), "Technological Change, Capital Accumulation, and Changing Trade Patterns over the Long Term," *Structural Change and Economic Dynamics*, Vol. 6, No. 1, March, pp. 43–70.

——— (1996a), "Technology and the Demand for Skills," *OECD Science, Technology, and Industry Review*, Vol. 18, pp. 96–123.

——— (1996b), *Top Heavy: A Study of Increasing Inequality of Wealth in America*, updated and expanded ed. (New York: New Press).

——— (1997a), "Spillovers, Linkages, and Technical Change," *Economic Systems Research*, Vol. 9, No. 1, March, pp. 9–23.

——— (1997b), "Productivity Growth and Shifting Comparative Advantage on the Industry Level," in Jan Fagerberg, Par Hansson, Lars Lundberg, and Arne Melchior, eds., *Technology and International Trade* (Cheltenham, UK: Edward Elgar), pp. 1–19.

——— (1997c), *Economics of Poverty, Inequality, and Discrimination* (Cincinnati: South-Western College Publishing).

——— (1999a) "The Productivity Paradox: Evidence from Indirect Indicators of Service Sector Productivity Growth," *Canadian Journal of Economics*, Vol. 32, No. 2, April, pp. 281–308.

——— (1999b), "Specialization and Productivity Performance In Low-, Medium-, and High-Tech Manufacturing Industries," in Alan Heston and Robert E. Lipsey, eds., *International and Interarea Comparisons of Income, Output, and Prices*, Vol. 61: *Studies of Income and Wealth* (Chicago: University of Chicago Press for the NBER), pp. 419–452.

———— (2000), "Why Stocks Won't Save the Middle Class," in Jeff Madrick, ed., *Unconventional Wisdom: Alternative Perspectives on the New Economy* (New York: Century Foundation Press), pp. 107–132.

———— (2001), "Human Capital Investment and Economic Growth: Exploring the Cross-Country Evidence," *Structural Change and Economic Dynamics,* Vol. 11, No. 4, December, pp. 433–472.

———— (2002), "Computerization and Structural Change" *Review of Income and Wealth,* Vol. 48, No. 2, March, pp. 59–75.

————, and Maury Gittleman (1993), "The Role of Education in Productivity Convergence: Does Higher Education Matter?" in Eddy Szirmai, Bart van Ark, and Dirk Pilat, eds., *Explaining Economic Growth: Essays in Honour of Angus Maddison* (New York : North-Holland), pp. 147–167.

Wood, Adrian (1991), "How Much Does Trade with the South Affect Workers in the North?" *World Bank Research Observer,* Vol. 6, pp. 19–36.

———— (1994), *North-South Trade, Employment, and Inequality: Changing Fortunes in a Skill-Driven World* (New York: Oxford University Press).

———— (1998), "Globalization and the Rise in Labour Market Inequalities," *Economic Journal,* Vol. 108, pp. 1463–1482.

————, and Edward Anderson (1998), "Does the Heckscher-Ohlin Theory Explain Why the Demand for Unskilled Labour in the North First Accelerated, Then Decelerated?" Institute for Development Studies, University of Sussex, mimeo.

Wozniak, Gregory D. (1987), "Human Capital, Information, and the Early Adoption of New Technology," *Journal of Human Resources,* Vol. 21, No. 1, Winter, pp. 101–112.

Zuboff, Shoshanna (1988). *In the Age of the Smart Machine: The Future of Work and Power* (New York: Basic Books).

Index